MASTERING
LONG EXPOSURE

THE DEFINITIVE GUIDE FOR PHOTOGRAPHERS

ANTONY ZACHARIAS

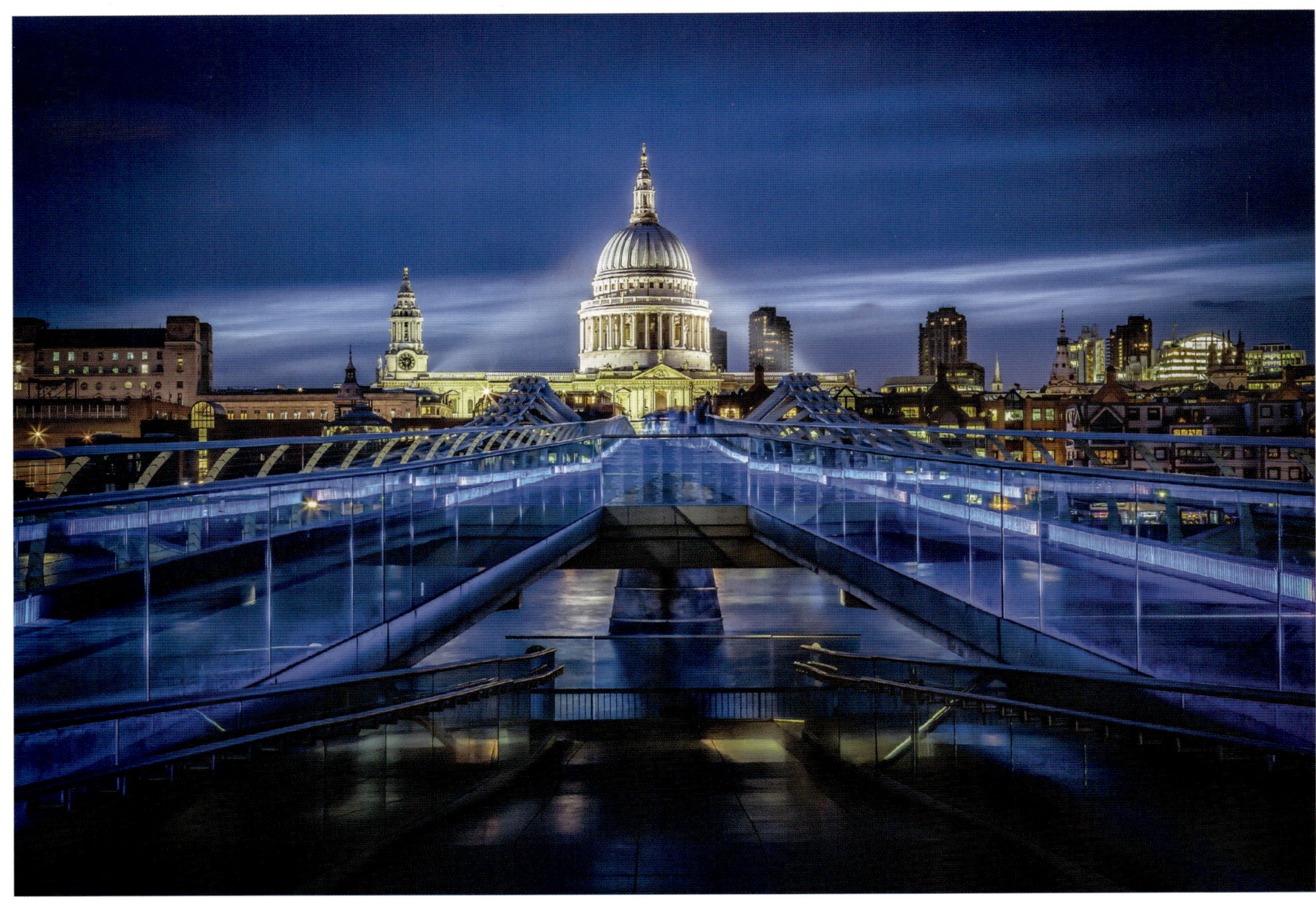

Above: There were numerous pedestrians walking around when this shot was taken, but the slow shutter speed meant their movement was not recorded. In this instance a long exposure has effectively "cleaned up" the scene.

Focal length: 50mm

Aperture: f/16

Shutter speed: 28 sec.

ISO: 100

MASTERING
LONG EXPOSURE

THE DEFINITIVE GUIDE FOR PHOTOGRAPHERS

ANTONY ZACHARIAS

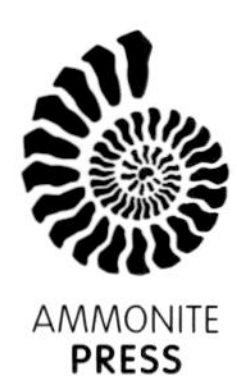

AMMONITE
PRESS

First published 2018 by
Ammonite Press
an imprint of Guild of Master Craftsman Publications Ltd.
Castle Place, 166 High Street, Lewes, East Sussex, BN7 1XU, United Kingdom

Reprinted 2022

Text and images © Antony Zacharias with the exception of the following:
p54–55 © Sylvia Wright; p108–109 © Janne Parviainen;
p138–139 © Chris Keeney; p150–151 © Jens Ludwig.

ISBN 978-1-78145-321-6

All rights reserved.

The rights of Antony Zacharias to be identified as the author of this work have
been asserted in accordance with the Copyright, Designs, and Patents Act 1988,
Sections 77 and 78.

No part of this publication may be reproduced, stored in a retrieval system,
or transmitted in any form or by any means without the prior permission
of the publishers and copyright owner.

While every effort has been made to obtain permission from the copyright
holders for all material used in this book, the publishers will be pleased to hear
from anyone who has not been appropriately acknowledged, and to make the
correction in future reprints.

The publishers and author can accept no legal responsibility for any
consequences arising from the application of information, advice,
or instructions given in this publication.

British Library Cataloging in Publication Data: A catalog record of this
book is available from the British Library.

Publisher: Jason Hook
Designer: Robin Shields
Editor: Chris Gatcum

Typeface: Helvetica Neue
Color reproduction by GMC Reprographics
Printed in China

Contents

Introduction

Photography is primarily about capturing a moment in time. In many genres of photography this moment is fleeting and perhaps lasts for mere fractions of a second, but there are times when it can be more desirable—or necessary—to record a longer period of time, ranging from full seconds to minutes, or even hours.

Compressing time into a single image is the very essence of long exposure photography. Unlike some other photographic fields, no two images will ever be the same, as each period of time that passes will provide a unique set of conditions that will not be repeated. The movement that is captured during the exposures will continue, irrespective of whether the shutter is open or not: clouds will continue to move through the sky, water will flow through rivers and tidal oceans, and the movement of people, and flora in the wind, will continue to make unrepeatable patterns. All of these elements will create a unique image that cannot be duplicated.

As a photographer, there is also an undeniable pleasure in slowing down the photographic process. You need to think ahead and visualize the intended image and predict how the scene might unfold as the exposure elapses. The nature of creative long exposures is that it is not necessarily about capturing the scene immediately in front of the camera, but conveying what a period of time does to a particular composition.

Some of this movement can be anticipated; you can find out where in the sky the sun will set, or the Milky Way will rise, for example, and this is an integral part of creating a visually compelling base composition. However, other elements in a scene will be harder to predict, and it is frequently these lesser-considered components that can make or break an image. Some require extra thought when setting up a composition, but at other times you just need a bit of luck for the elements to align.

This book will explore numerous techniques that can be used to produce a wide variety of long exposure imagery. Some will naturally require longer exposure times to record sufficient light, while others demand additional equipment, such as filters and tripods to make your photographs possible. In either case, the ability to capture long passages of time in a single frame can produce spectacular and inimitable images that are visually distinctive and highly personal compared to the repeatability of many other photographic genres.

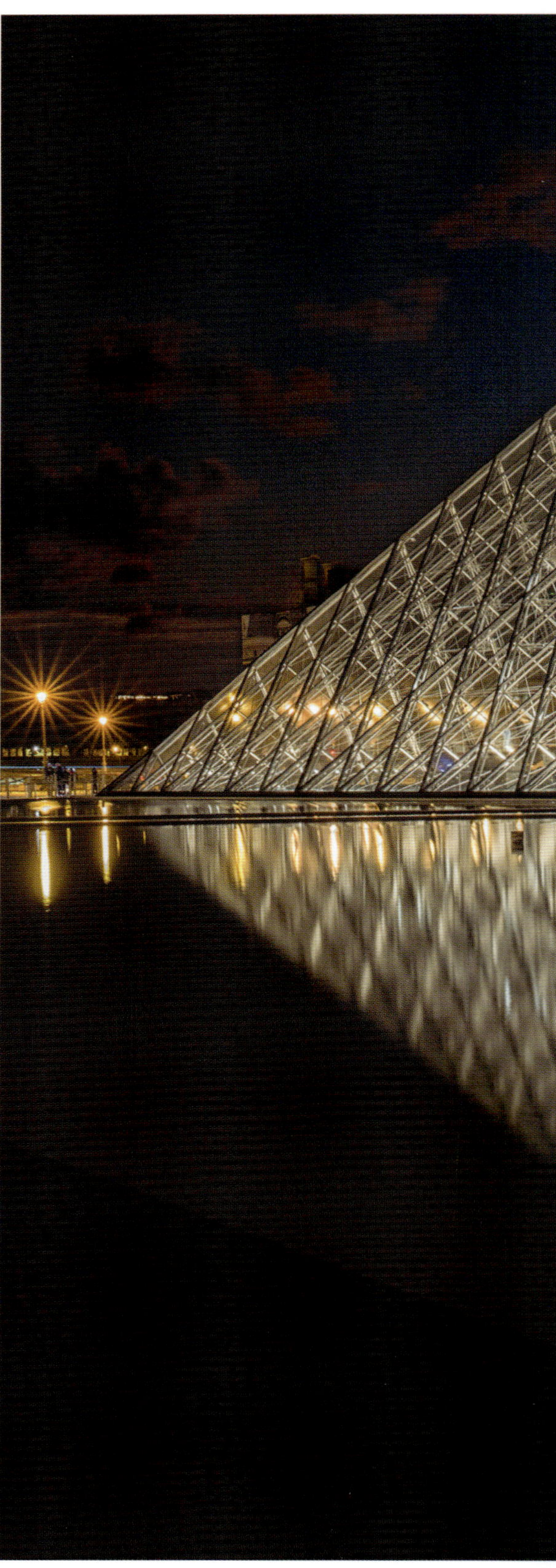

Right: When there is not much wind it is possible to capture spectacular reflections that can be used compositionally in the final image.

Focal length: 28mm

Aperture: f/16

Shutter speed: 6 sec.

ISO: 200

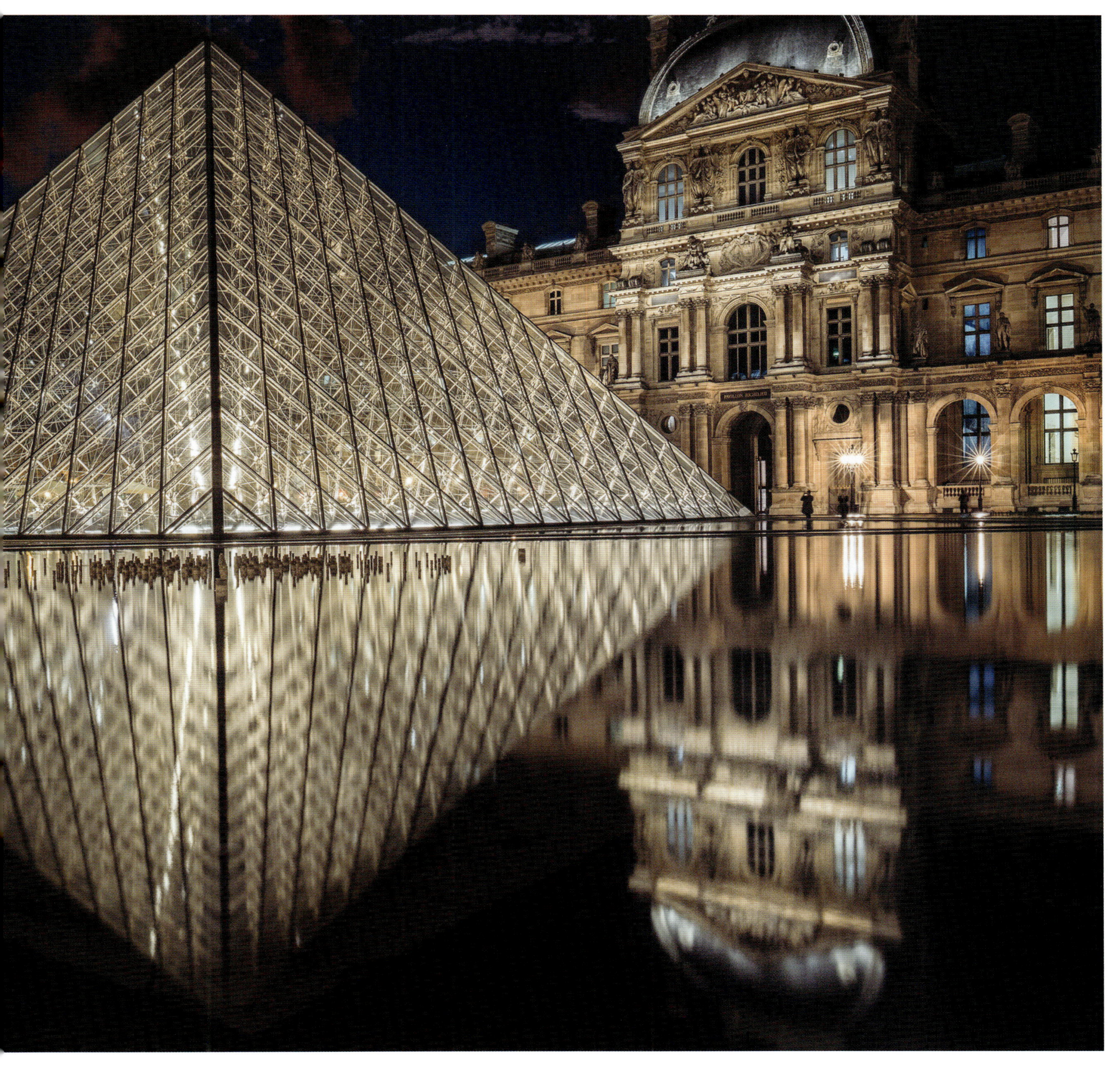

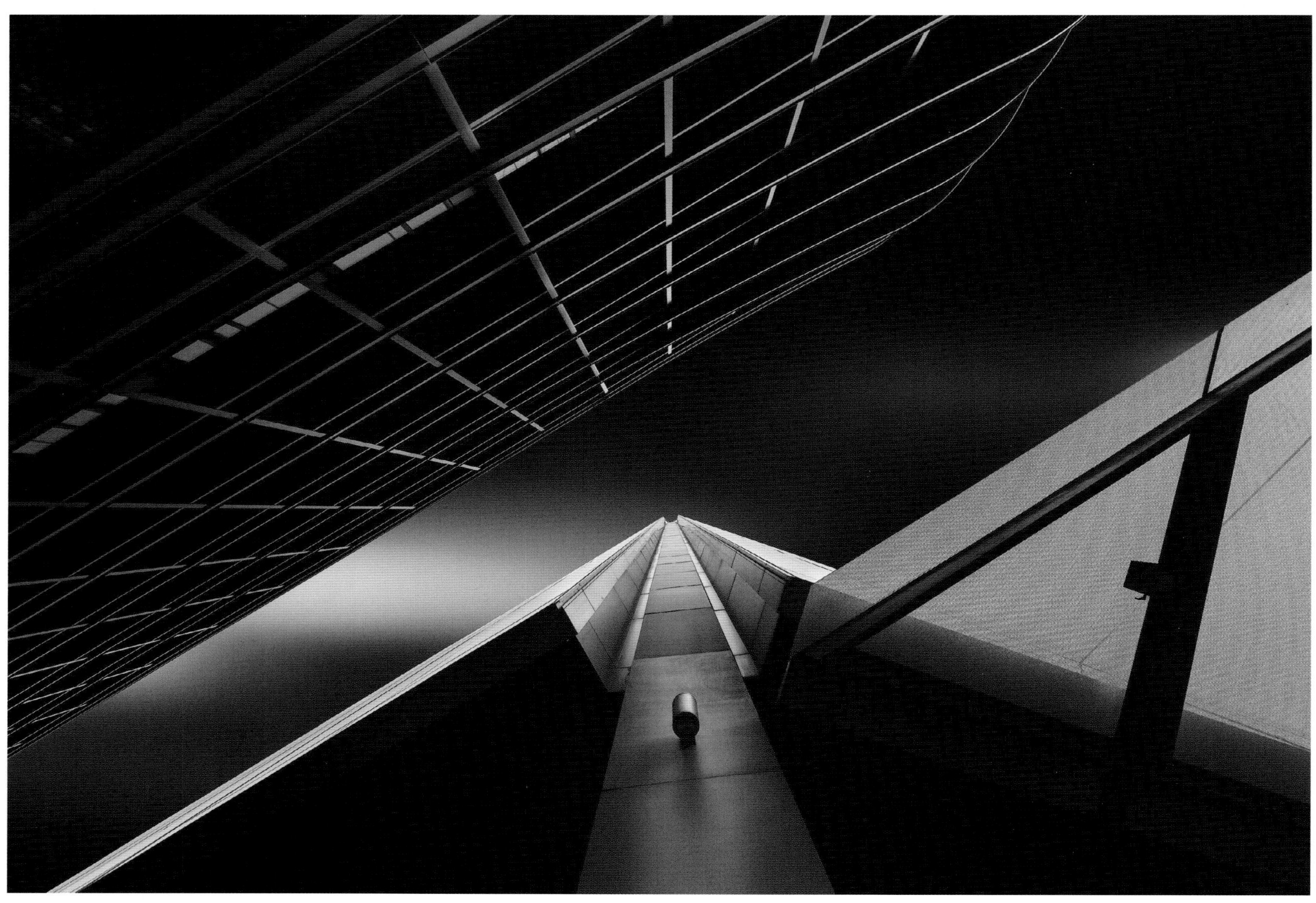

Above: Neutral density filters lengthen exposure times in daylight and can compress many minutes into a single photograph. Architecture and black-and-white processing work very well together to break down any distractions and create unique images based on shape and form.

Focal length: 16mm

Aperture: f/16

Shutter speed: 127 sec.

ISO: 100

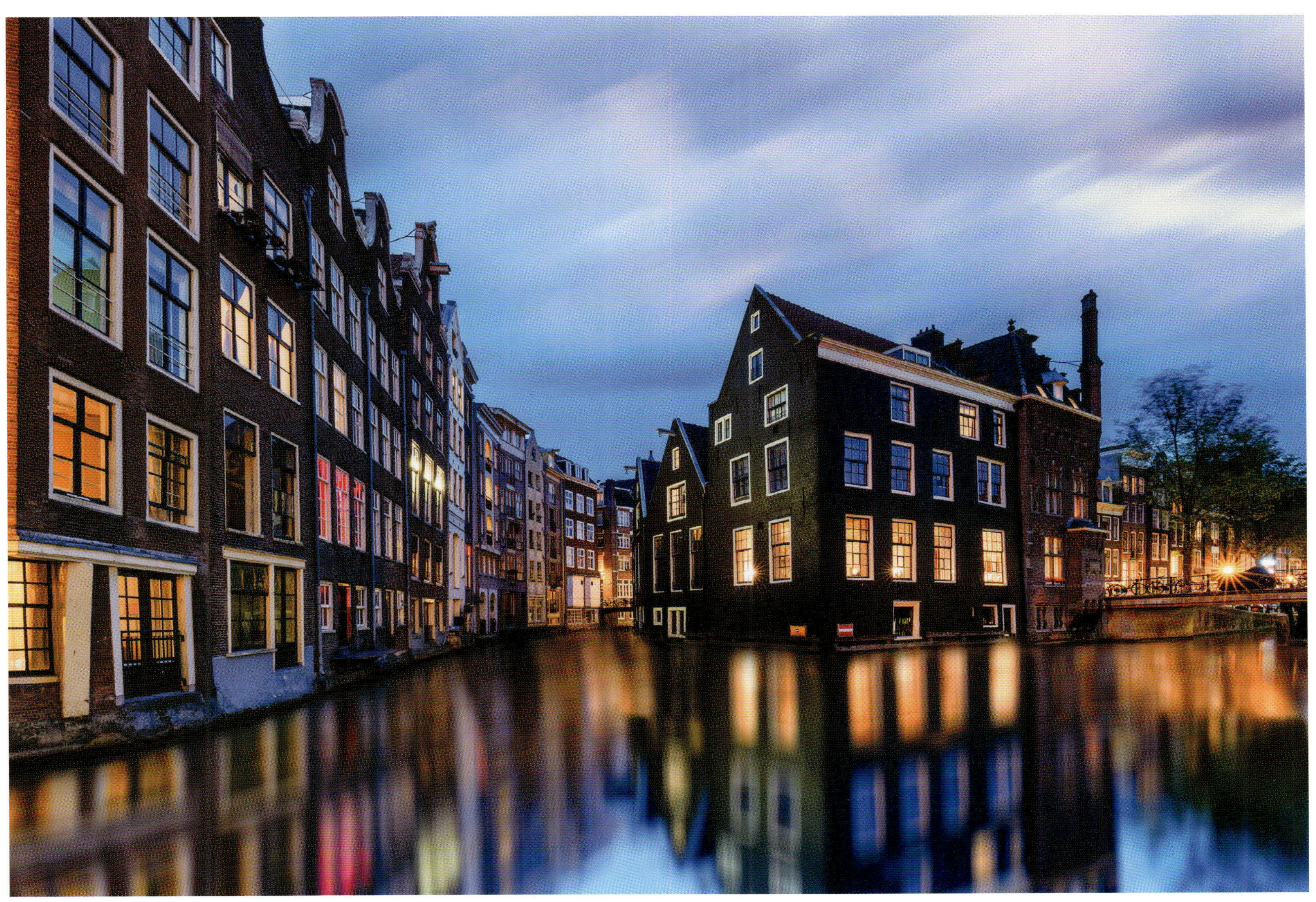

Above: As the sun dips below the horizon and the city lights up, you get a mix of artificial color and deep blue tones in the sky. This is known as the "blue hour," and can result in compelling images.

Focal length: 16mm

Aperture: f/11

Shutter speed: 49 sec.

ISO: 100

Chapter 1
Equipment

Long exposure photography can be more demanding on the camera you use than many other genres. Extended exposure times create a number of issues that can all too easily affect the quality of the final image: problems such as noise, focusing difficulties, and challenges in obtaining the correct exposure all need to be addressed. This style of photography is also more reliant on other key pieces of equipment, such as remote releases, tripods, "fast" lenses, and filters. However, with a mixture of the right equipment, practice, and knowledge, the rewards can be spectacular. When everything comes together, the extra effort is definitely worthwhile!

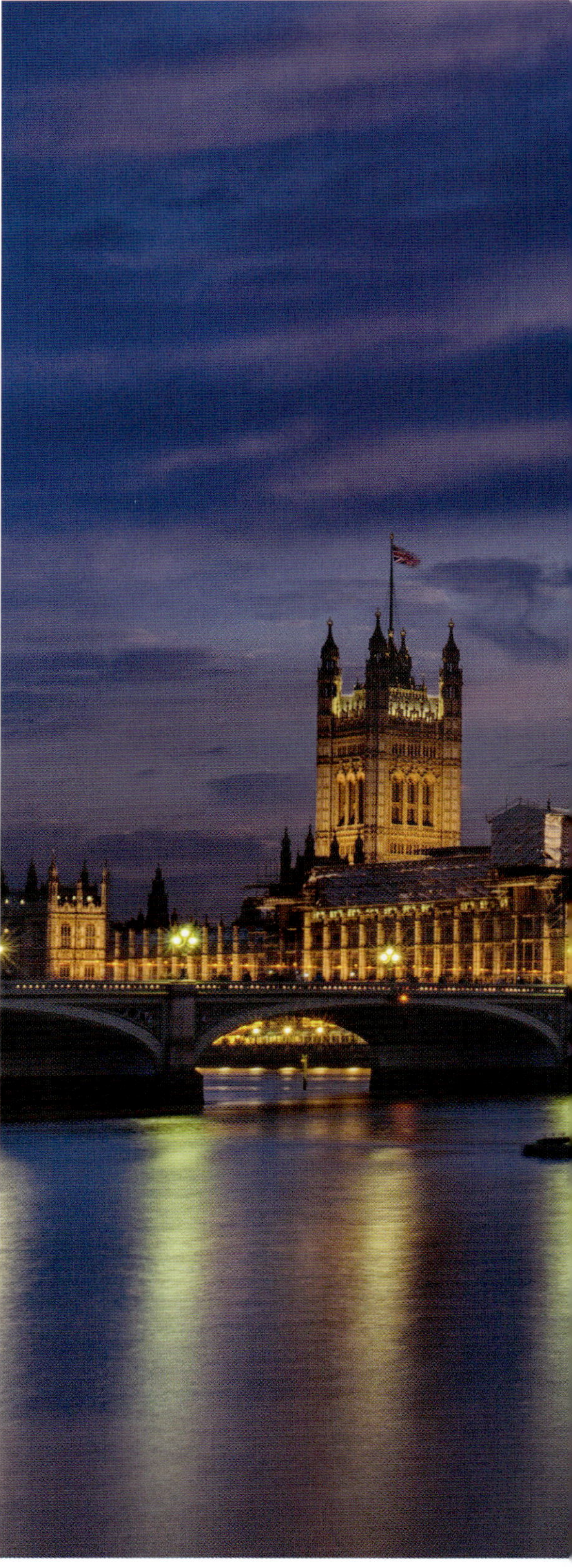

Right: Long exposure photography can be a demanding genre. This low-light scene required a slow shutter speed and therefore a stable camera to capture the image.

Focal length: 32mm
Aperture: f/18
Shutter speed: 30 sec.
ISO: 100

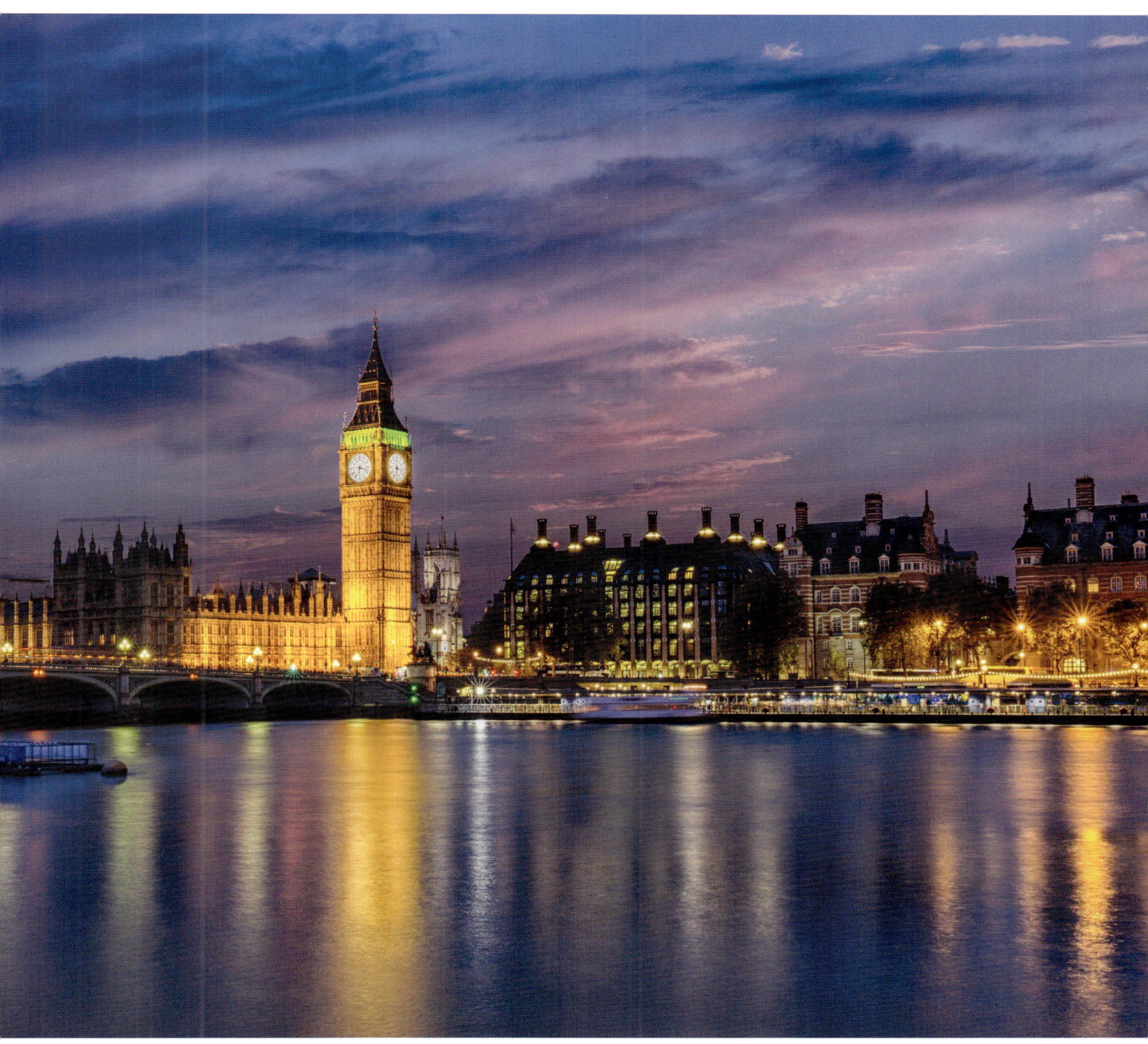

Camera Requirements

There are many cameras available, ranging from smartphones and point-and-shoot compacts to DSLR and mirrorless models. While they all have their place for certain types of photography, smartphones and point-and-shoot compacts are *not* ideal for long exposures. It is vital that the camera has a few key features, including full manual control and "Bulb" mode. While switching the camera to manual can be daunting to many, the freedom to select a specific aperture and shutter speed is essential in challenging conditions.

Sensor Size

The sensor inside the camera is an important component when it comes to long exposure photography. There are currently three standard sensor sizes used in DSLR and mirrorless cameras, as shown in the grid below.

SENSOR SIZE	SIZE IN MM (W X H)
1/2.5"	5.76 x 4.29
1/2.3"	6.17 x 4.55
1/1.8"	7.18 x 5.32
2/3"	8.8 x 6.6
1"	13.2 x 8.8
Four Thirds & Micro Four Thirds	17.3 x 13
Canon APS-C	22.3 x 14.9
Other APS-C	23.6 x 15.6
APS-H	27.9 x 18.6
35mm/full-frame	36 x 24
Medium format	44 x 33

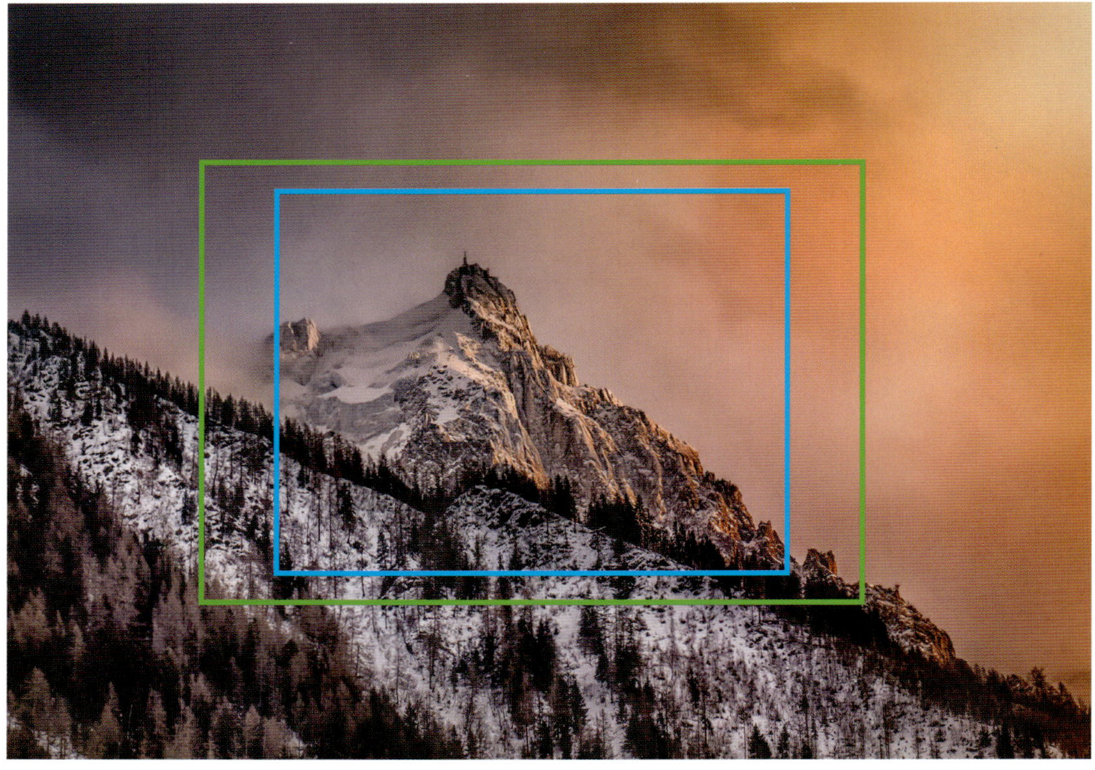

Above: This image was taken with a full-frame camera, which has a sensor measuring 36 x 24mm. The green box indicates how much smaller a cropped, APS-C sensor is, while the blue box represents the relative size of the sensor inside a Micro Four Thirds camera.

Focal length: 37mm

Aperture: f/16

Shutter speed: 25 sec.

ISO: 100

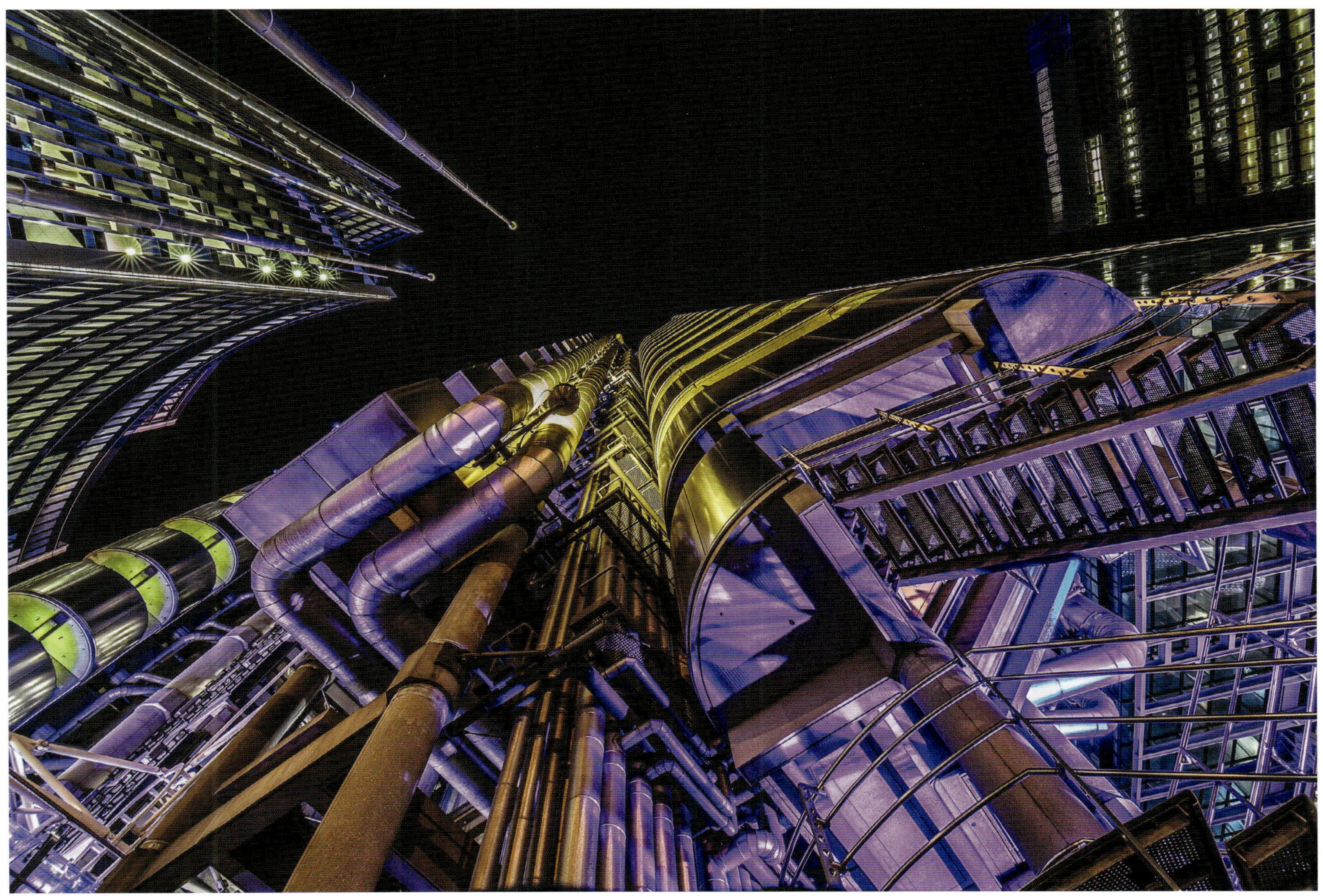

Full frame

A full-frame sensor is the same size as a 35mm film frame (36 x 24mm) and is considered to deliver the best image quality compared to crop sensors (APS-C) and Micro Four Thirds cameras. Full-frame sensors are more expensive, but have a bigger surface area, which allows them to have larger light-receiving photosites (see page 15). They also generate less noise at higher ISO settings.

Above: A full-frame sensor can record plenty of information and has outstanding capabilities when it comes to capturing "clean" detail in low-light situations.

Focal length: 14mm

Aperture: f/18

Shutter speed: 30 sec.

ISO: 200

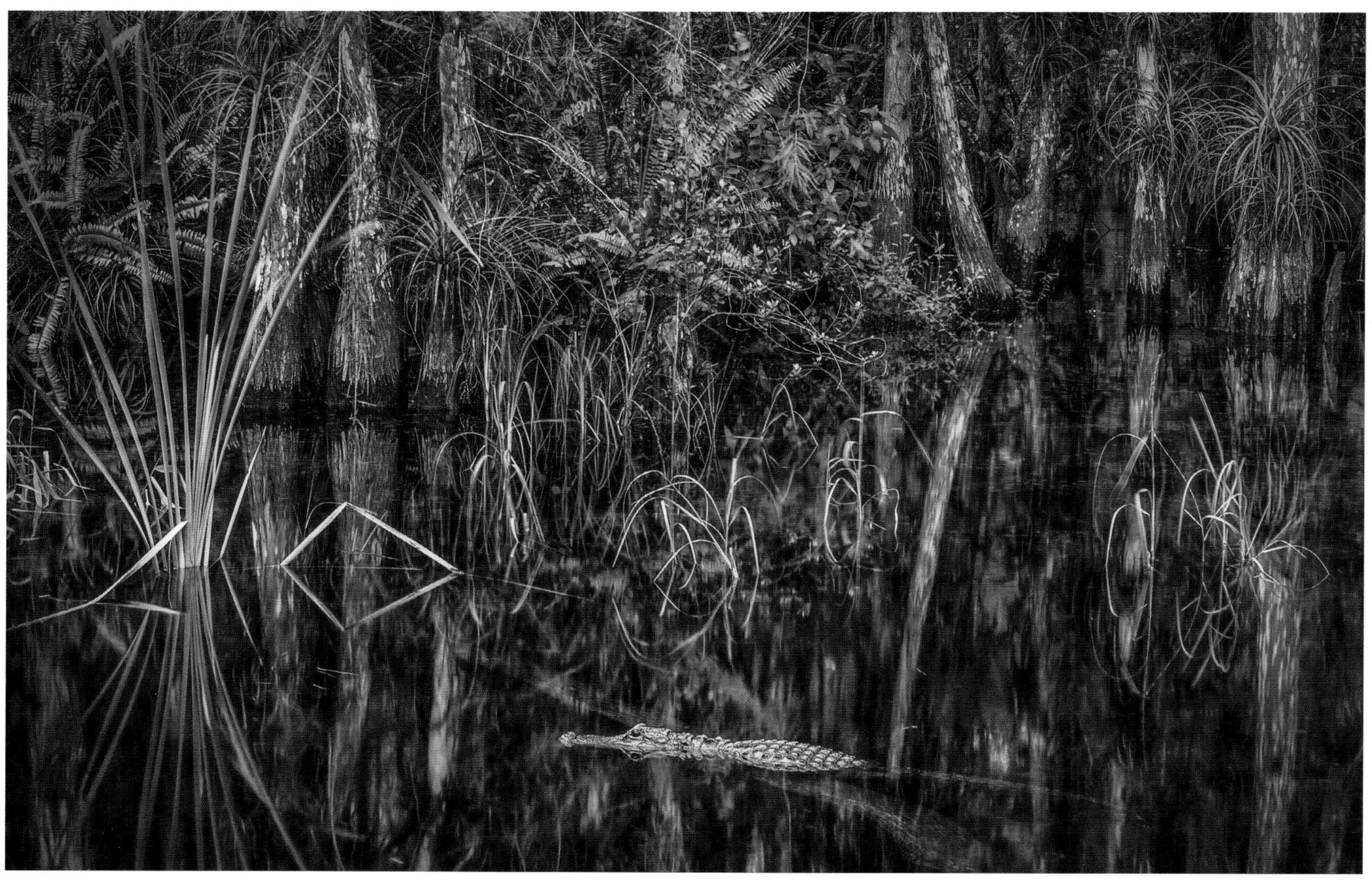

APS-C

An APS-C or "cropped format" sensor is usually
in the region of 30% smaller than a full-frame
sensor. Compared to a full-frame sensor, an APS-
C-sized sensor effectively crops the image and
reduces the field of view of the lens. Consequently
a cropped sensor increases the focal length of
a lens by around 1.5x or 1.6x depending on the
make and model of the camera. The simple way
to calculate the effective focal length of a lens is
to multiply the lens' *actual* focal length by the crop
factor. For example, a 100mm lens on a camera
with a 1.6x crop factor will have an effective focal
length of 160mm (100 x 1.6).

Above: Using a camera with a crop sensor effectively
extends a lens' focal length. This helped me capture
this scene in the Florida Everglades from the safety
of the shoreline.

Focal length: 120mm

Aperture: f/16

Shutter speed: 1.5 sec.

ISO: 100

Micro Four Thirds

The Micro Four Thirds camera standard uses
17.3 x 13mm sized sensors that are virtually half
the size of a full-frame sensor. This increases the
focal length by a factor of 2x, so a 100mm lens
on a Micro Four Thirds camera will actually behave
more like a 200mm lens. However, as the sensor
has a smaller surface area, the light-receiving
photodiodes will also be smaller and/or the
camera's resolution will be lower. This can affect
low-light performance and noise levels.

Megapixels

The resolution of a camera's sensor is measured in megapixels, which is simply the number of pixels that the sensor can generate: the more pixels there are, the larger the resulting image will be. However, there is a common mistaken belief that a higher number of pixels will provide better overall image quality. This is not necessarily true.

While APS-C and Micro Four Thirds sensors can have megapixel counts comparable to full-frame cameras, the photosites on the small-format sensors will need to be smaller and closer together. Photosites are the tiny elements that "catch" light:

each photosite generates one pixel in the final image. It follows that the bigger the photosites are, the better a camera's low-light performance will be, as more light can be captured.

Consequently, a reduction in the number of photosites/pixels can actually *improve* image quality, as the photosites can be made physically larger. It is a compromise, though, as reducing the pixel count makes the resulting images smaller. Consequently, camera and sensor manufacturers have to walk a fine line between high resolution and optimum image quality.

MEDIUM FORMAT

Medium-format cameras have sensor sizes in the region of 44 x 33mm (or larger), which results in a surface area almost twice as large as a full-frame sensor. This enables them to have a lot of large photosites, allowing them to deliver high resolution *and* high quality. However, this typically comes with a high financial cost.

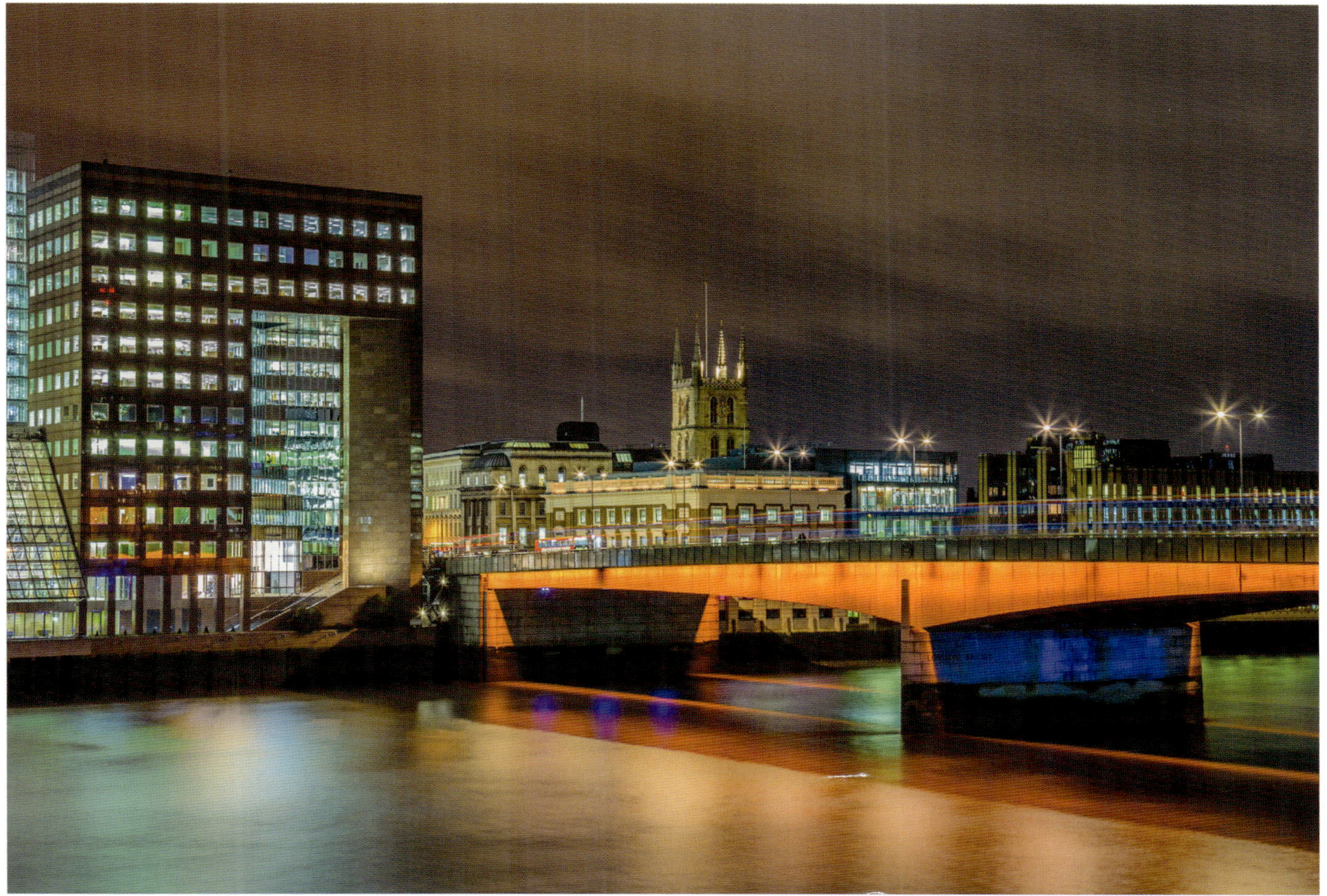

Left: The photosites on a camera's sensor catch the light coming through the lens, which is then turned into image information in the form of pixels. For low-light photography the simple rule is that bigger sensors are better, as they enable a higher number of large photosites. This image was shot using a high-resolution, full-frame DSLR camera.

Focal length: 60mm

Aperture: f/16

Shutter speed: 25 sec.

ISO: 100

Lenses

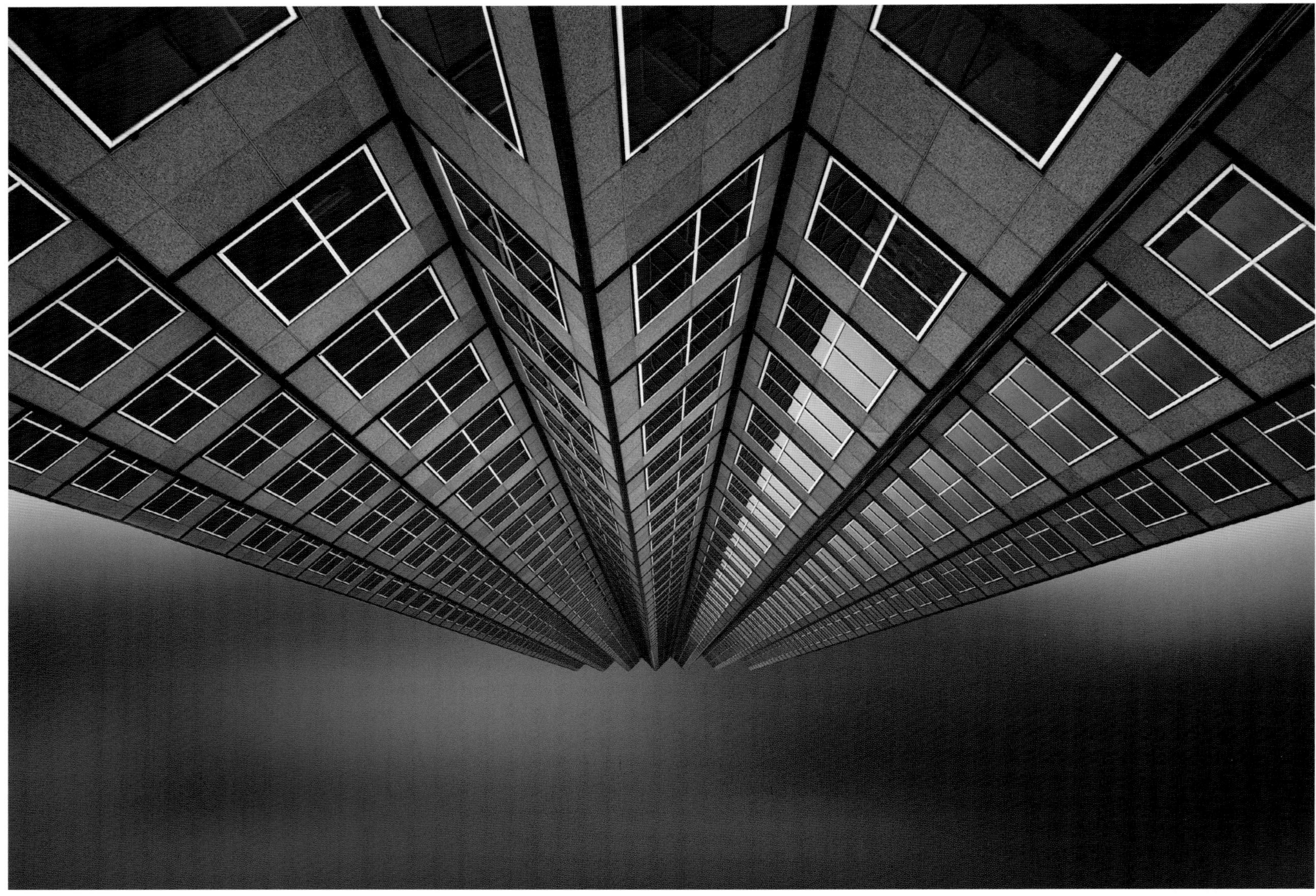

DSLR and mirrorless cameras let you change lenses. This flexibility in choosing the focal length and aperture range of the lenses you use allows more control over how the final image will look, so one of the first decisions that should be taken, before any camera settings are considered, is what lens should be used.

The first consideration is focal length. Do you need a wide angle of view from a short focal length lens, or would a longer, telephoto focal length be preferred? This generally comes down to how much of the scene you want to include in the final image and your shooting position, but don't forget to take the crop factor of your sensor into account.

Above: Although it's a wideangle lens, a 24mm focal length was not quite wide enough to capture the whole of the building in this scene, so the composition had to be altered slightly.

Focal length: 24mm

Aperture: f/11

Shutter speed: 42 sec.

ISO: 100

Aperture

The aperture in a lens controls how much light is able to pass through to the camera's sensor. A wider aperture will allow more light to enter the camera, which can be advantageous in low-light environments. The trade-off, however, is the effect on depth of field, which may be a concern when you want the entire scene to remain in focus.

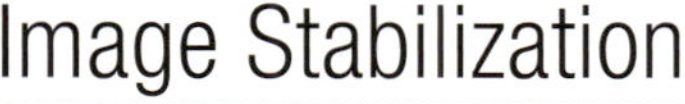

Tip

Lenses with large maximum apertures are known as "fast" lenses. These lenses are more expensive and weigh more, as they have larger glass elements inside them. They also require larger filters due to a wider diameter front element.

Image Stabilization

Many lenses come with a form of image stabilization, which is known by a variety of names, depending on the manufacturer. This can help to minimize camera shake when you are shooting handheld using slower shutter speeds, but it is important to turn it off when the camera is on a tripod, as the stabilization function can "trick" the camera into introducing vibrations, even though it is fixed and still.

Prime & Zoom

A "prime" lens has a fixed focal length and will often have a "fast" maximum aperture. These lenses can deliver outstanding image quality and have fantastic light-gathering abilities, making them an ideal choice for long exposure photography. However, the downside is that a large number of lenses may be required to cover a range of focal lengths.

The main advantage of a zoom lens is simple: it allows a wide range of focal lengths to be covered by a single lens. This has framing and compositional advantages over a prime lens, as no physical movement is required, so you're more likely to get the precise shot you're after.

With the exception of "fast" (and expensive) professional zooms, most zoom lenses have variable apertures, which means that the maximum aperture changes throughout the range of focal lengths. This can be important if your exposure calculations have been made based on certain settings, as changing the composition by zooming in or out may change the required exposure.

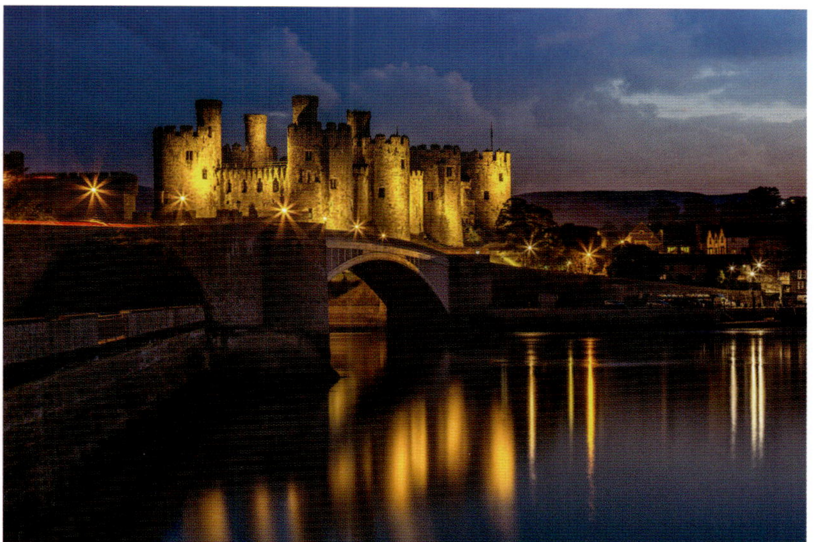

Left: Using a reasonably wide aperture setting of f/5.6 allowed more light to pass through to the sensor, but it still provided sufficient depth of field to keep the whole of the image in sharp focus.

Focal length: 67mm

Aperture: f/5.6

Shutter speed: 45 sec.

ISO: 100

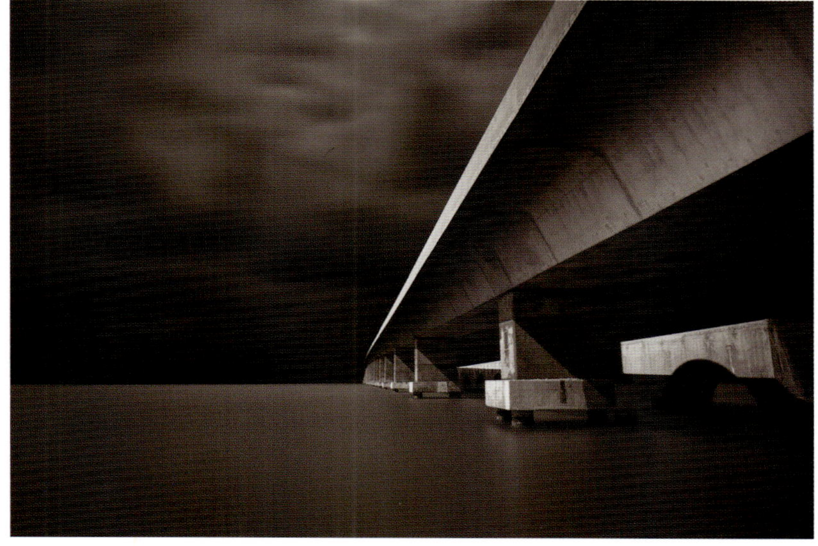

Left: Some lenses have sensors that automatically turn image stabilization off when it thinks the camera is tripod mounted. However, it is better to get into the habit of turning image stabilization off yourself, especially if you have some lenses without "auto deactivation."

Focal length: 23mm

Aperture: f/16

Shutter speed: 51 sec.

ISO: 100

Shutter Release

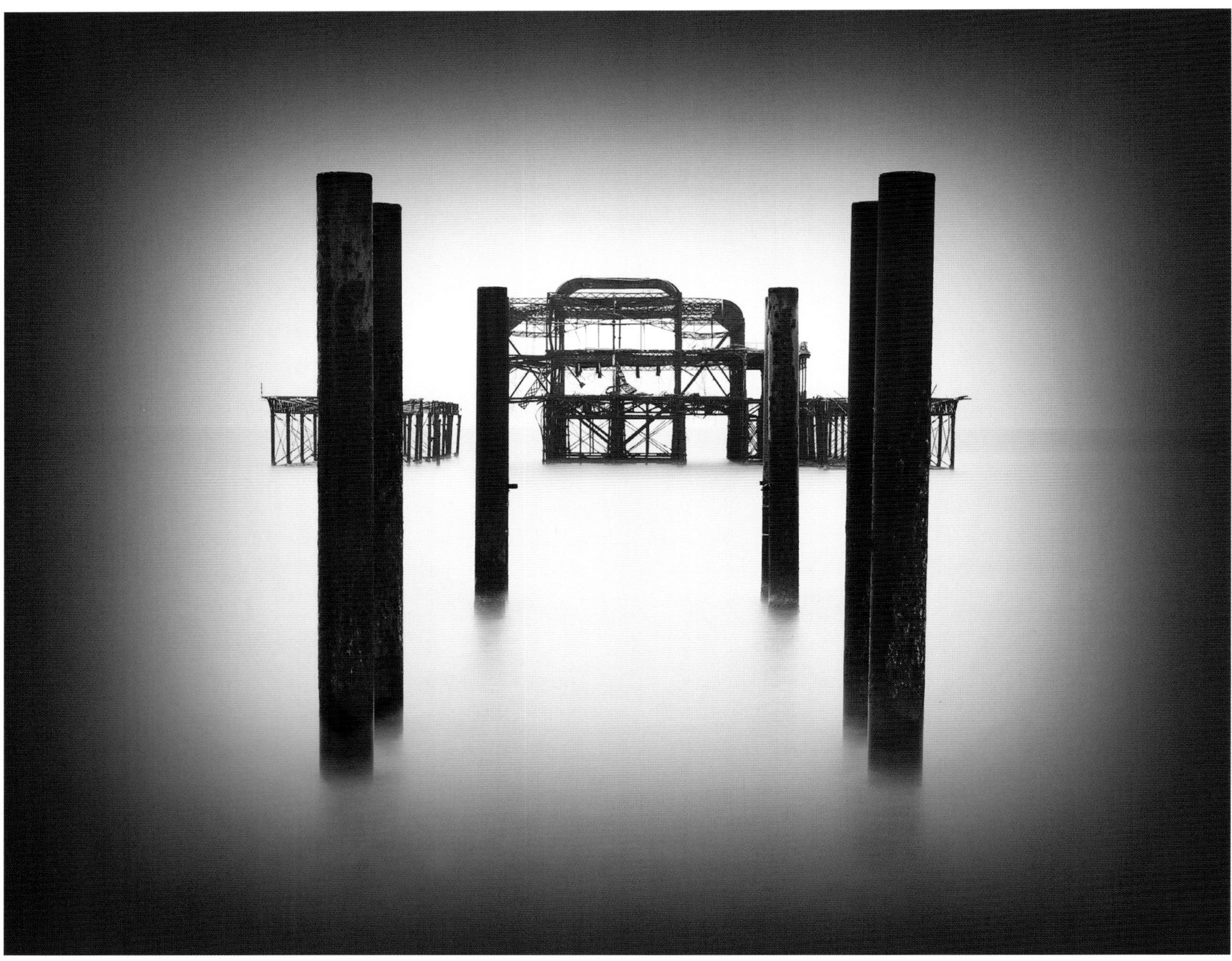

In addition to a camera and lens (or lenses), a key piece of equipment for long exposure photography is a shutter release or remote, which allows the camera to be triggered without you physically touching it. This will ensure that no unnecessary movement affects the overall image quality, as even the slightest vibrations can cause an image to be blurred. This is especially important when you are using the camera's Bulb mode (see page 52), as a shutter release will let you hold the shutter open manually for seconds, minutes, or hours.

The simplest type of shutter release connects to the camera by a cable and has a button that can be locked into position to keep the shutter open. More advanced versions add additional features, such as timers (intervalometers), so the camera can be programmed to take a set of images at specific times. Although this is the most reliable type of shutter release, the main disadvantage is that it is attached to the camera, so you have to remain close to the camera to trigger the shutter.

A wireless remote release achieves the same result, but is not joined to the camera by a cable. These can be useful to trigger the camera from a distance—and guarantee you won't accidentally jar the camera—but they usually require line-of-sight to the camera itself. The main downside is that if the batteries in a wireless remote stop working, you lose the whole remote trigger. This could be a problem if you find yourself working in a remote location with no spare batteries to hand.

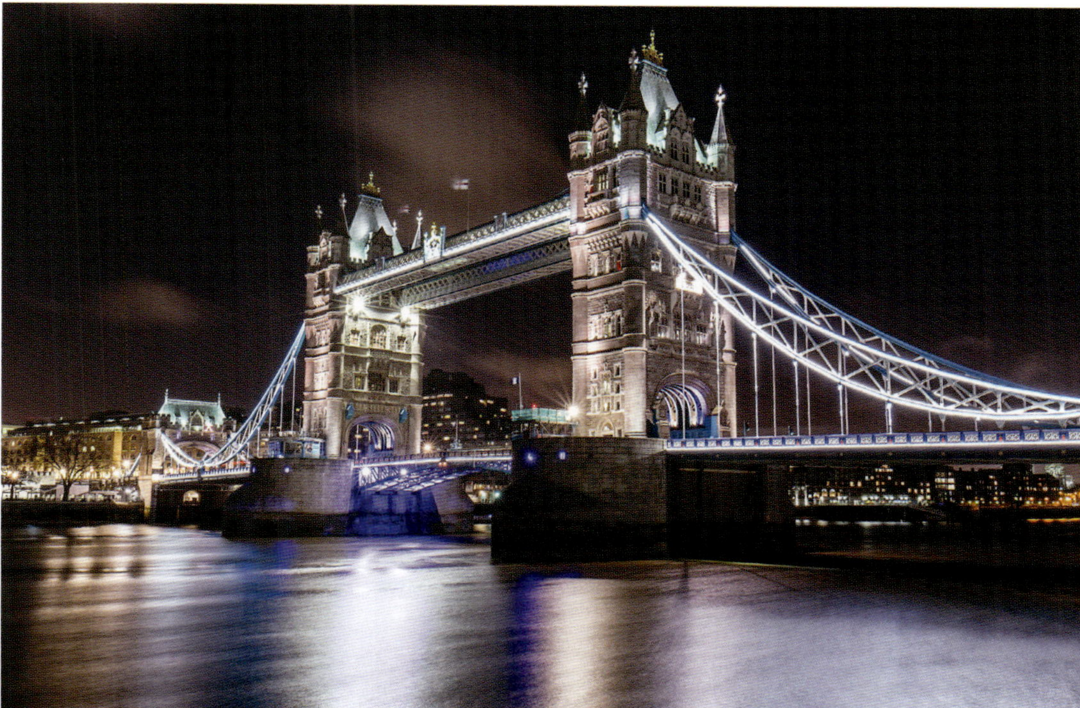

Above: For this image of Tower Bridge in London I had forgotten my remote release, so I used the camera's self-timer mode to release the shutter. The shot is completely unaffected by camera shake.

Focal length: 31mm

Aperture: f/16

Shutter speed: 15 sec.

ISO: 200

Tips

- If you forget your shutter release or your wireless remote stops working, use the camera's self-timer mode. This will introduce a delay (typically 10 seconds) between you physically pressing the camera's shutter-release button and the shutter firing. This delay is usually enough to ensure that any vibrations have died down before the exposure starts.

- Mirror lock-up is a feature found on most DSLR cameras. It allows you to lock the camera's mirror in its "up" position prior to making an exposure. When activated, the first press of the shutter release flips the mirror up, and a second press opens the shutter. Breaking the mechanical process into two distinct stages means that any potential vibration caused by the mirror flipping up can be allowed to abate before the exposure starts.

Tripods

Camera movement is one of the leading causes of unintentional blurring, resulting in unusable images. Thankfully it is also one of the easiest issues to eliminate. When long exposure times are used, it is vital that the camera remains as still as possible, and no matter how "good" you think you are at handholding a camera, a solid camera support is essential.

The most common—and most stable—option is a tripod. Advances in lightweight materials and rigidity offer photographers a multitude of styles, across a range of price brackets. Most tripods come in two separate parts: the "legs" and the "head." This lets you choose from a wider range of combinations (from different manufacturers if you want) to suit your individual needs.

Generally speaking, a strong, lightweight tripod is the ideal choice, so carrying it to a location is easy and not something you try to avoid. A carbon-fiber model gives the best strength-to-weight performance, but is going to be quite a bit more expensive than a heavier aluminum tripod of comparable size.

Naturally, windy conditions mean that a sturdy tripod is required, but additional stability will inevitably mean an increase in weight. Many tripod legs provide a hook beneath the central column, so your camera bag can be attached to provide for more weight and stability if required; this is worth looking out for.

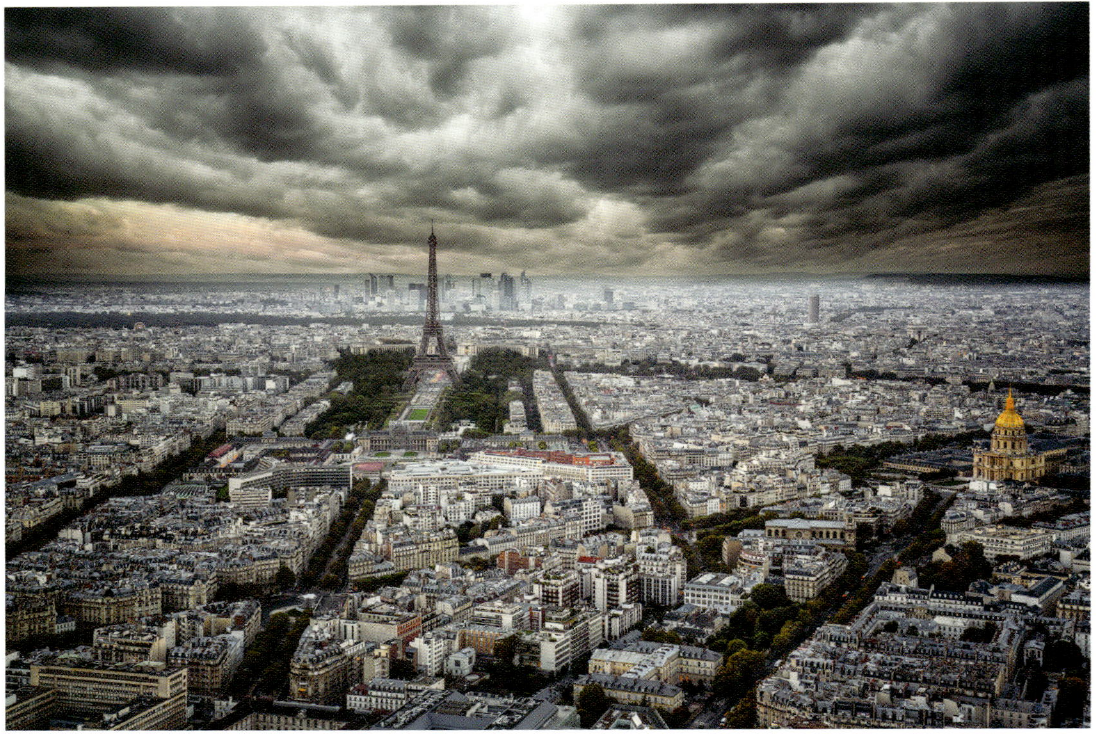

Above: This viewpoint in Paris was elevated and exposed to strong gusts of wind, so despite a relatively short shutter speed it was vital that the camera was on a tripod to ensure complete sharpness. Even with a tripod I still timed the exposure to coincide with momentary drops in wind speed.

Focal length: 47mm

Aperture: f/16

Shutter speed: 3 sec.

ISO: 100

Tips

- Ensure that any tripod you buy can easily bear the weight of your camera body and longest/heaviest lens. It is better to buy a tripod with a slightly heavier weight rating, rather than one that's at the limit of your kit.

- The maximum height of a tripod is very important. Although most tripods have an extendable center column, this is extremely unstable, so it should generally be used as a last resort.

- Tripods with a high number of leg extensions will fold down smaller, making them more portable, but they will also be less stable.

- The minimum height of a tripod is important, as it will extend your shooting options.

Right: Remember to look after your tripod. When taking images at a beach, salt water and sand need to be rinsed off the tripod legs as soon as possible.

Focal length: 47mm

Aperture: f/22

Shutter speed: 5 sec.

ISO: 100

Tripod Heads

The tripod head is what the camera attaches to and there are various head styles, each with its own benefits. As it allows you to fine tune your composition, it is important to choose a head that is easy to use and control.

The most common tripod head is a ball head, which uses a ball-and-socket design to position the camera. This type of head is fast to use, as you can tilt and turn the camera in multiple directions at once before locking it off with a single control. It is important to ensure that the locking mechanism is strong enough to deal with the camera and lens combination, otherwise your camera may not stay fixed in position.

An alternative is a three-way pan head, which has separate controls for three different axis of movement. This allows the camera to be moved more precisely, as each control can be locked independently, but it is usually slower to use. Three-way heads tend to be heavier than standard ball-head designs, especially if you opt for a geared three-way head.

Tips

- A quick-release plate attaches to the bottom of the camera and allows it to be quickly attached to and removed from the tripod head.

- An L-bracket is a plate that allows the camera to be mounted horizontally or vertically. This can prevent the tripod from becoming unstable with the camera placed in certain positions, and also makes it quick and easy to switch from a horizontal to an upright composition.

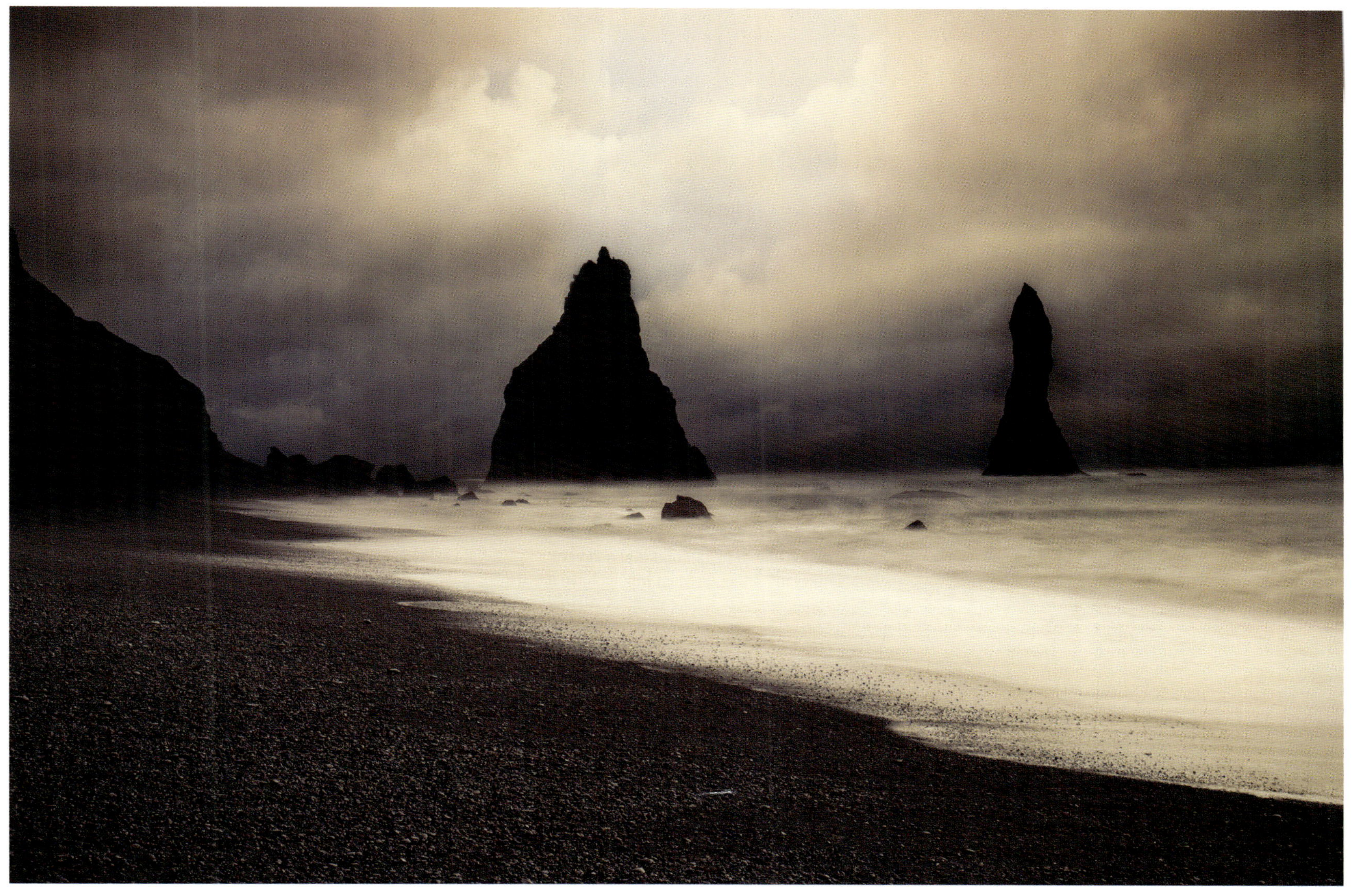

Additional Accessories

There are countless photographic accessories available, although some are more useful than others. An essential item is a camera bag. It is important to have something that is comfortable to carry, as camera gear can be heavy. Adequate protection is also paramount.

For anyone walking with their camera, a good backpack can help distribute the weight and it will usually allow you to store more non-photographic gear alongside your camera equipment. It is a good idea to look for a bag that has a waterproof cover so you can protect your kit if you get caught out in a downpour.

However, rather than choose a large bag to carry every last piece of equipment that you own, try to anticipate what kind of subjects you will be shooting and pack accordingly. Personally, I use a large camera bag to store all of my kit, but will select what I need and transfer those items into a smaller day-pack for individual outings. It is easy to feel the need to take all your camera gear with you, but it is exceptionally rare that you will use everything you own and carrying all of this weight can soon become tiring.

ESSENTIAL EXTRAS

- **Memory cards** It is vital that you carry adequate memory cards with you. Do not buy budget or off-brand cards as you do not want to risk them becoming corrupt or failing and losing your images. If your camera supports dual cards then it is a good idea to save images simultaneously to both cards. Try to purchase cards with a fast write speed, so images can be recorded quickly from the camera. Although manufacturers are always increasing card capacities, it is better to use a greater number of smaller cards so you don't lose as many images if a card fails.

- **Spare batteries** Have spare batteries with you at all times. Longer exposure times can use up batteries very quickly (as will relying on Live View shooting). Make sure you recharge the batteries immediately after every shoot so they are ready for the next outing.

- **Lens cloth** Dust, rain, water, fingerprints, and so on can all affect your final image. Keeping your lenses and filters clean can remove the need for unnecessary postproduction.

- **Headlamp/flashlight** Night shooting will usually mean there is minimal available light. A small flashlight can prove invaluable when it comes to locating items in your camera bag, light painting, and generally finding your way in the dark.

- **Spanners for tripod** Always carry the small hex keys that may be needed to tighten your tripod head and quick-release plate. If they come loose—which can sometimes happen—you don't want to be stuck without a usable tripod, especially if you've traveled a significant distance to your location.

- **Waterproof cover** Fast-moving clouds can make excellent subjects for long exposure photography, but it can be difficult to predict when a downpour may occur. A low-cost camera rain cover will allow you to continue shooting if the weather turns. They are extremely small and light, and easily carried on location.

- **Silica crystals** Taking camera gear from cold to hot locations, such as an air-conditioned car into a humid landscape can easily lead to the build up of condensation. Keep a few sachets of silica crystals in your camera bag to absorb any excess moisture.

- **Apps** There are numerous apps for smartphones and tablets to assist photographers in their endeavors. Weather apps can provide useful information including tide times and sunrise/sunset information, while apps that determine the moonrise or Milky Way rise and setting locations will prove invaluable if you're preparing to shoot the stars.

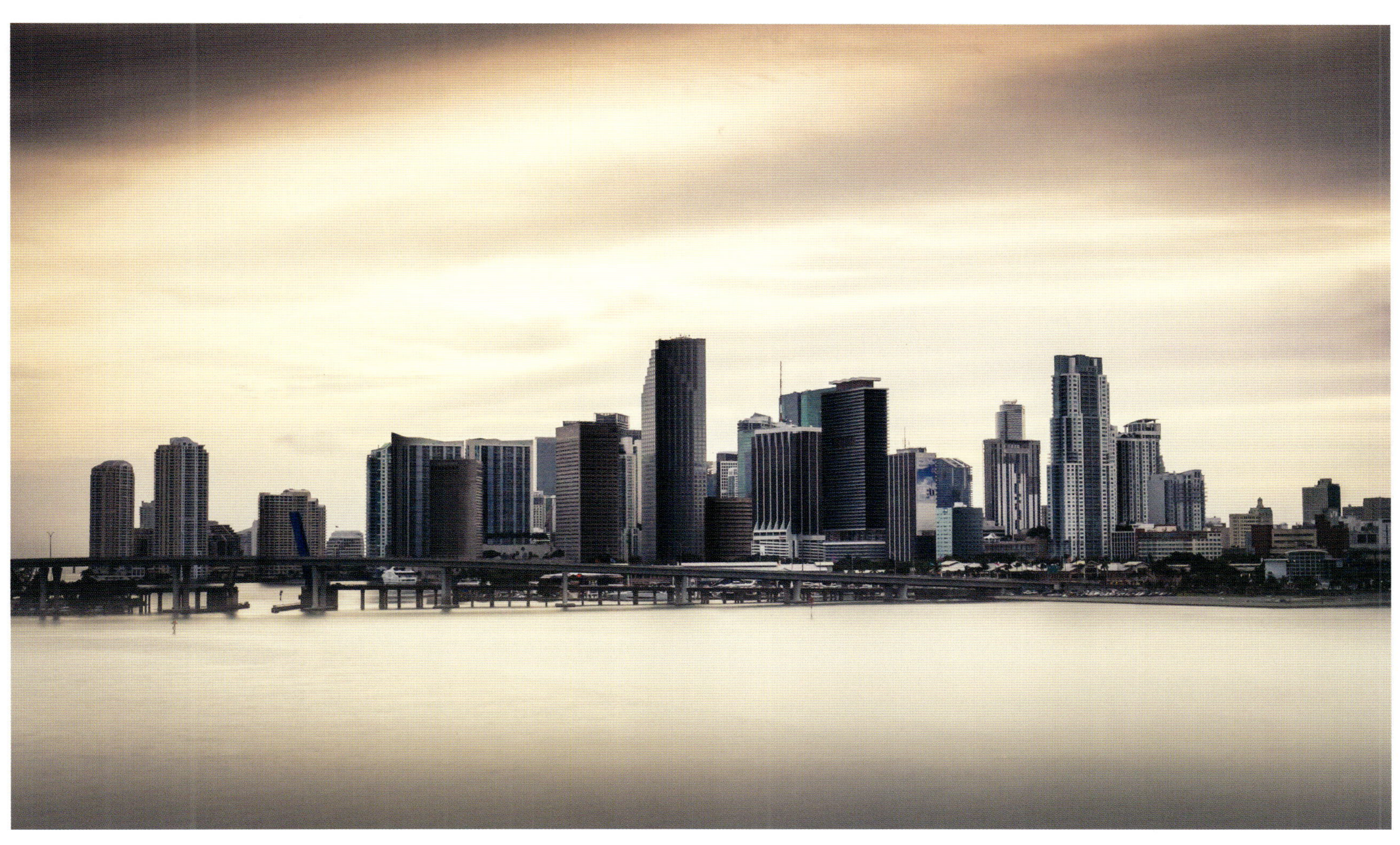

Above: For this image of the Miami skyline I stepped out of a cool car into the warm location. The change in humidity led to an immediate build up of condensation on the lens. Silica crystals absorb excess moisture in these situations, helping you to avoid the problem.

Focal length: 60mm

Aperture: f/7.1

Shutter speed: 67 sec.

ISO: 100

Chapter 2
Technical Considerations

Long exposure photography is a genre that encompasses a wide range of scenarios, from extreme low light to extended shutter times created by filtering bright sunlight. In many cases you will encounter difficulties with focusing, gauging the exposure, depth of field, noise, and blur, all of which can wreak havoc if they are not considered prior to shooting. Therefore, a good understanding of basic camera control is needed if you want to ensure the best results: the technical capabilities of your camera, lenses, and other equipment can only carry you so far.

This chapter sets out the fundamental skills needed for this broad area of photography. These key concepts of photographic control are vital in ensuring that all scenarios can be dealt with correctly and will guarantee that your images not only match your intended vision, but are also realized at the highest possible standard.

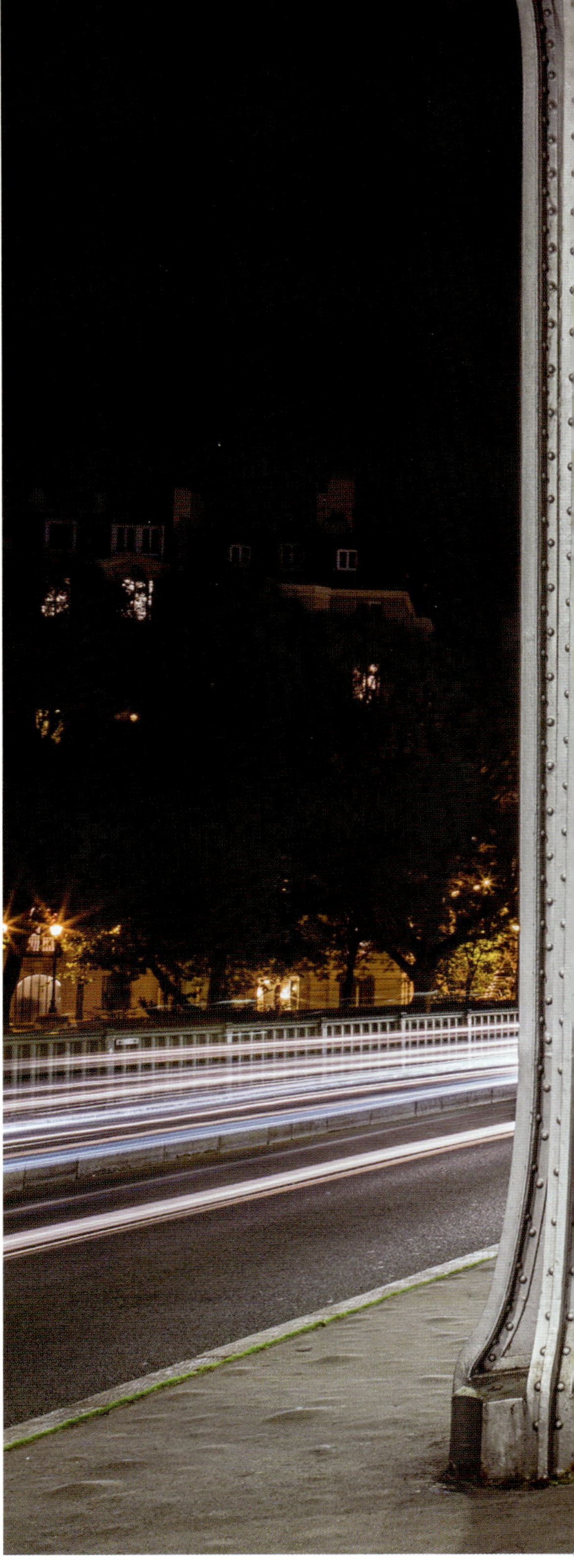

Right: The long exposure time used for this image in Paris allowed me to capture the car light trails, which add an extra dimension to the photograph.

Focal length: 32mm

Aperture: f/20

Shutter speed: 15 sec.

ISO: 200

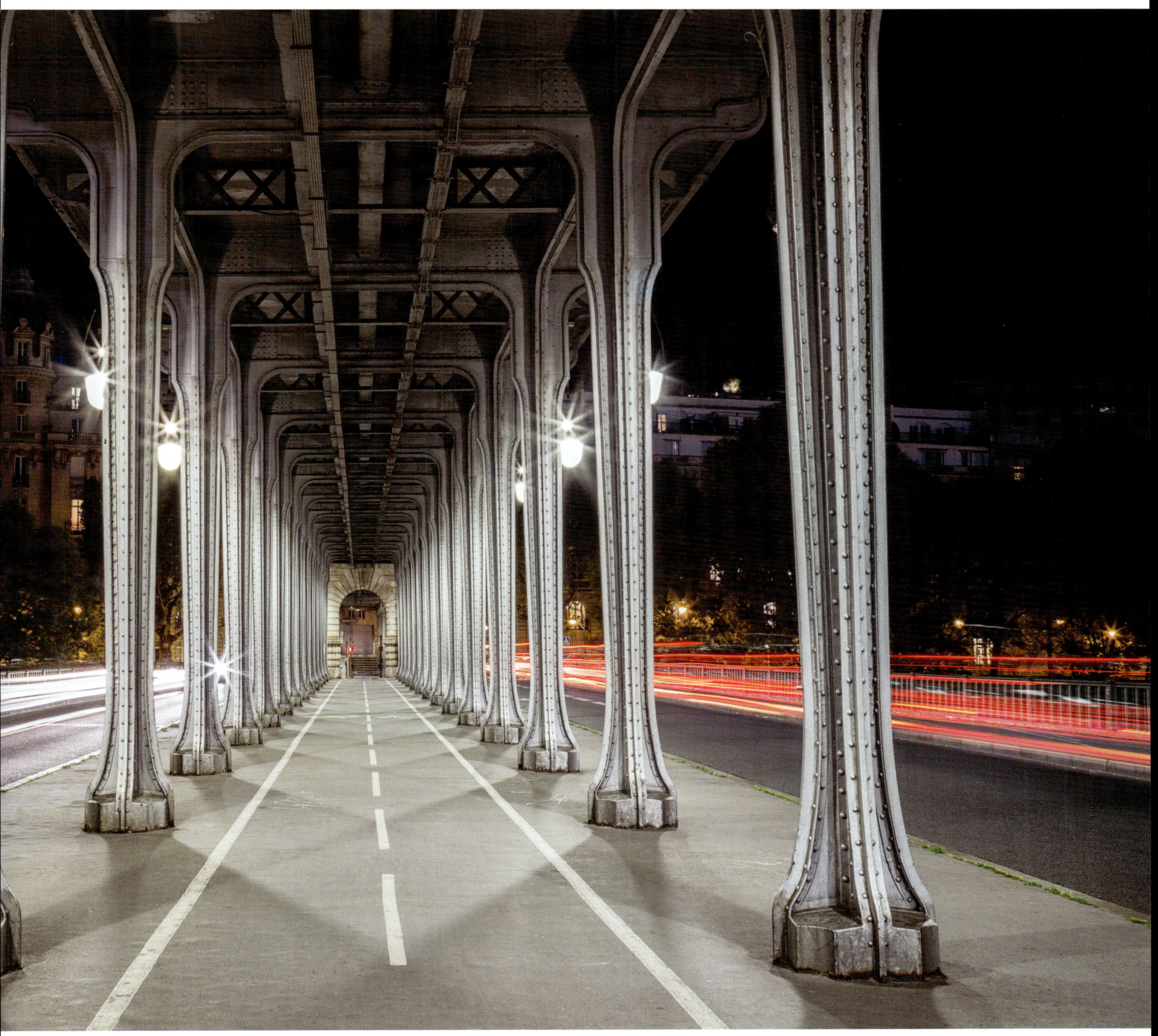

Aperture

The aperture in the lens is essentially a hole of variable size that controls the amount of light that can enter the camera. The size of the aperture is expressed as an f/stop, which is a fraction; technically, an f/stop is the focal length of the lens divided by the diameter of the entrance pupil (the lens opening). Therefore a larger aperture = a smaller f/stop = more light reaching the sensor.

The presumption here might be that long exposure photography requires more light and therefore a larger aperture should always be used. This is not necessarily the case, though, as aperture affects depth of field, which is the area in an image in front of and behind the point of focus that appears acceptably sharp. Put simply, a larger aperture provides less depth of field, so images have a much smaller range of sharp focus. Conversely, a smaller aperture (bigger f/stop number) results in a larger depth of field, so more of a scene will appear "sharp."

The choice of aperture also has an effect on the exposure time. As smaller apertures allow less light through the lens, they require the shutter to be open longer to make an exposure. In doing so, this will accentuate any movement, creating blur.

However, while there may be a temptation to use very small apertures to prolong shutter times, the image quality will be affected by diffraction. This is because the light "diffracts" as it passes through the small opening in the lens, creating slightly soft results.

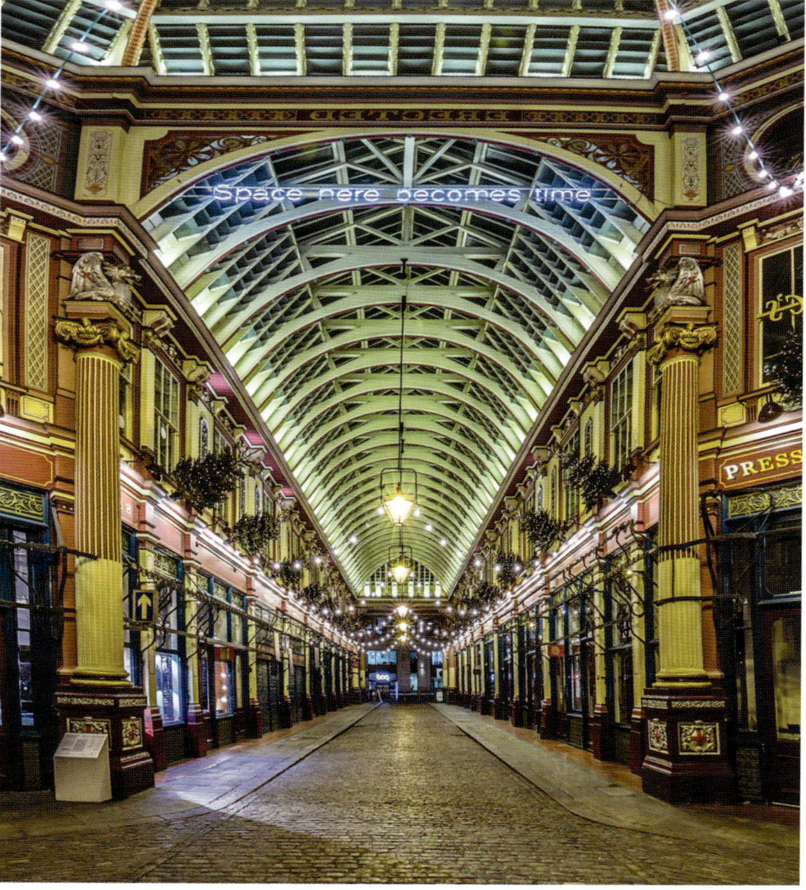

Left: To ensure that the whole of this scene was in sharp focus I used a small aperture setting.

Focal length: 16mm

Aperture: f/16

Shutter speed: 7 sec.

ISO: 200

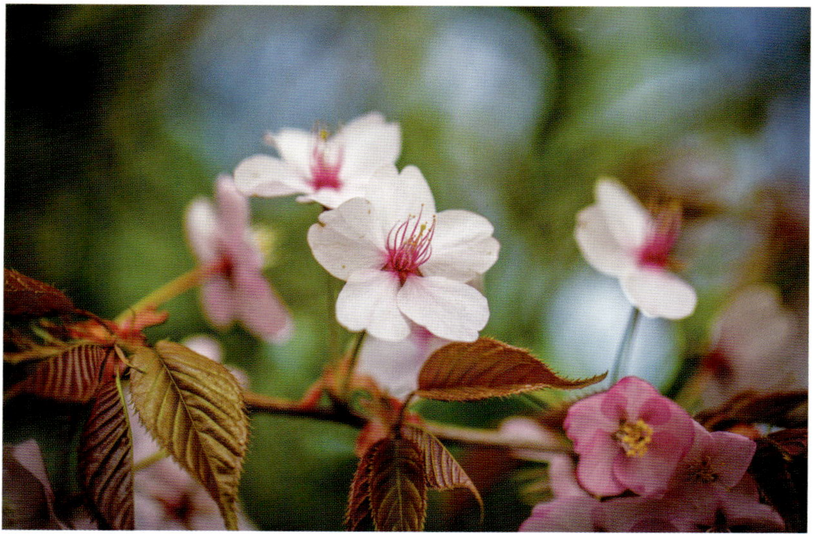

Left: To make the cherry blossom stand out from the convoluted tree branches and leaves behind it, a wide aperture was used to throw the background out of focus. This removes any distractions, so the viewer focuses on the blossom.

Focal length: 100mm

Aperture: f/2.8

Shutter speed: 1/200 sec.

ISO: 200

Shutter Speed

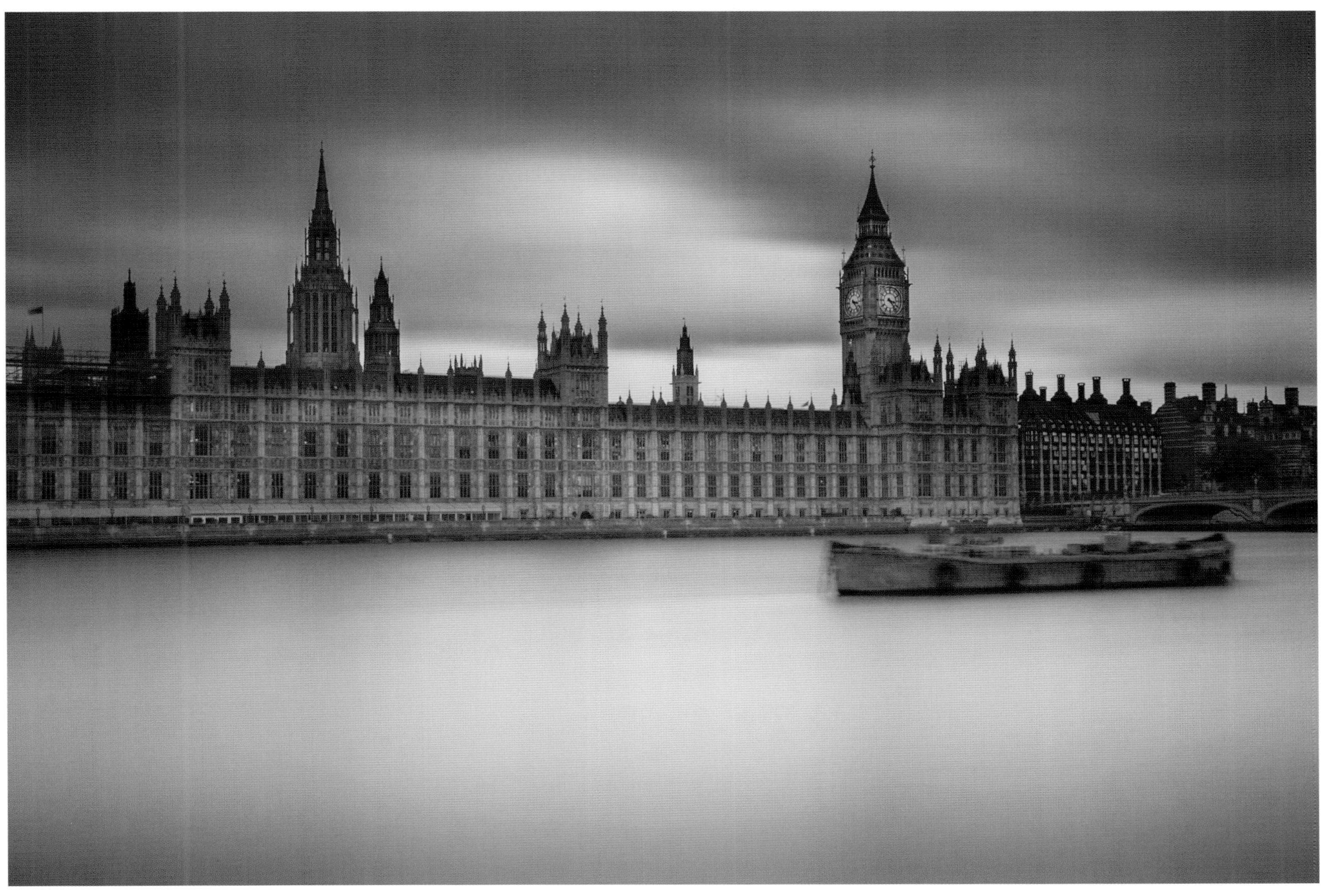

The shutter speed is the amount of time that the camera's shutter remains open, allowing the light passing through the lens to reach the sensor. The longer (or slower) the shutter speed, the more light the sensor receives.

The very nature of long exposure photography requires longer shutter speeds than "everyday" photography. This can be because there is a lack of light in a scene—such as a nightscape or sunset—or the result of deliberately prolonging the exposure time with filters to record more movement within a single image. In either instance, from a compositional standpoint it is vital to consider what elements will remain static in a scene, where movement will naturally occur, and how this will affect the overall image. It is also essential that the camera is held steady.

Above: This image utilized a 10-stop ND filter to extend the daytime exposure to over one minute, without overexposing the scene.

Focal length: 45mm

Aperture: f/14

Shutter speed: 77 sec.

ISO: 100

ISO

The ISO setting in a digital camera is derived from the sensitivity of film to light. It effectively determines how much light the sensor needs to create an exposure: the lower the ISO setting, the more light is required for the exposure, through the use of a larger aperture setting and/or a slower shutter speed.

ISO is an important factor in long exposure photography as it can amplify the camera's ability to record more light information more quickly. This can be very useful in extreme low-light conditions, such as astrophotography, where using an extremely long shutter time will be detrimental to the overall image.

However, there is an inevitable trade-off that has to be considered when increasing the ISO: as the ISO is boosted, the camera becomes more susceptible to digital noise. As you will see later in this chapter, too much noise can degrade the quality of an image, so the ISO needs to be set with care.

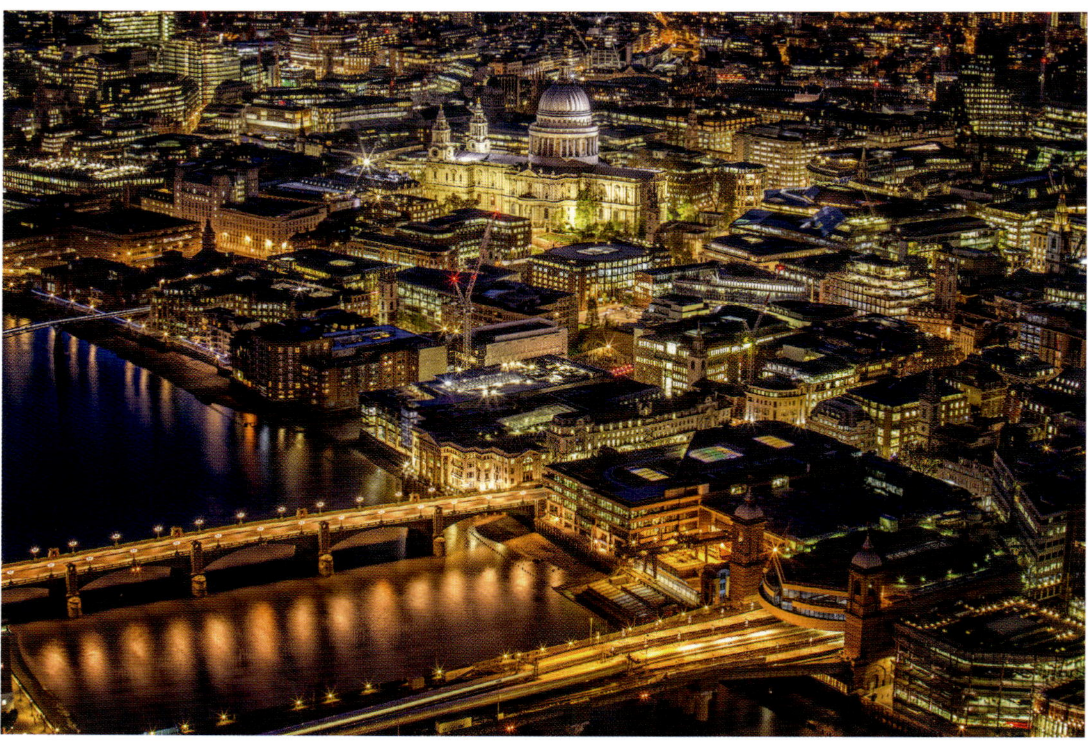

Above: This image of the City of London at night was captured using a high ISO setting, which allowed a shorter exposure time. This was useful as there were a lot of external vibrations that would have resulted in a blurred image if the exposure had been any longer.

Focal length: 70mm

Aperture: f/16

Shutter speed: 11 sec.

ISO: 800

Tip

Some cameras have an Auto ISO function that allows the camera to choose from a specific range of ISO settings. Although this can be useful at times, for long exposure photography it is far better that you take control and choose the ISO specifically for each scene you photograph.

File Formats

The choice between Raw and JPEG file formats—the two formats found on the majority of DSLR and mirrorless cameras—is often portrayed as a trade-off. This generally creates confusion.

A Raw file is simply an unprocessed "digital negative" that records a wide range of data straight from the sensor. This can be retrieved during postproduction, providing you with the flexibility to change minor errors in the color balance, exposure, and so on.

A JPEG file is processed internally by the camera and then compressed into a smaller file. While it can also be edited in postproduction, it does not have the same flexibility for change as a Raw file. Amending a JPEG file also changes its form, and the image quality can degrade quite rapidly each time it is edited and saved.

JPEG files are most useful when no further editing will be done to the final image and/or a small file size is required so the image can be transmitted shortly after capture. However, for most long exposure photography—particularly images taken in low light or under mixed artificial lighting—the power and flexibility of Raw files is a much better option.

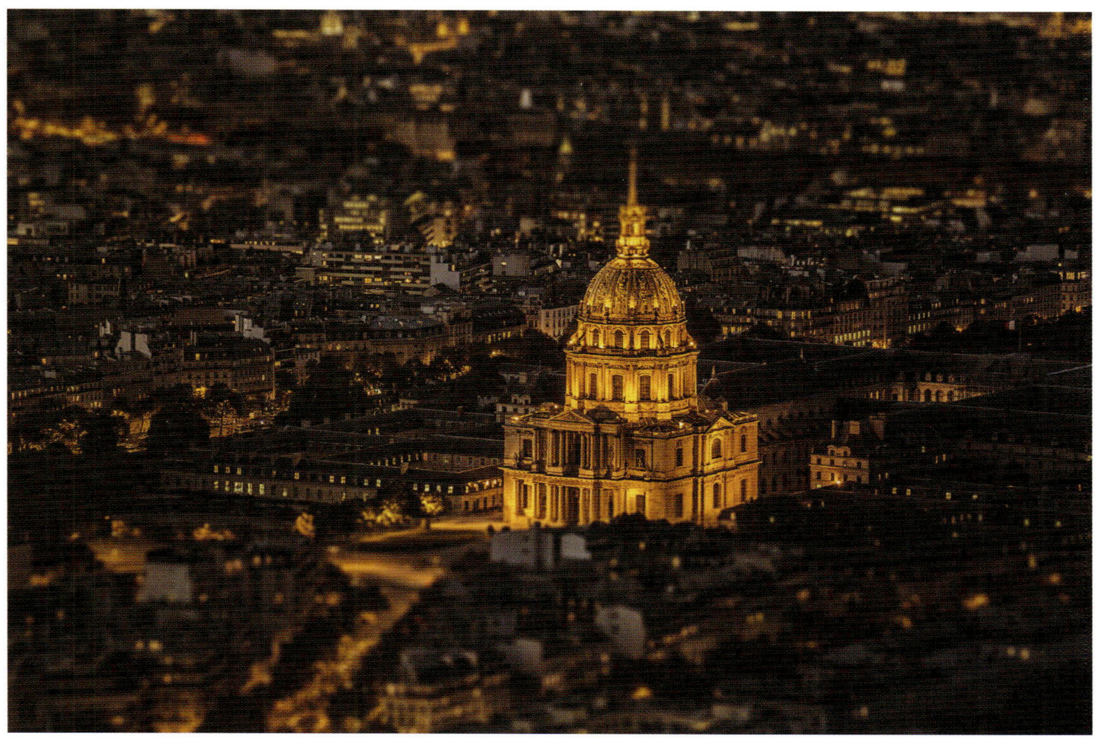

Above: A Raw file allows you to recover more highlight and shadow detail in postproduction than a JPEG. Being able to slightly reduce the highlight exposure and open up the shadows in an image can help produce more balanced photographs.

Focal length: 200mm

Aperture: f/4

Shutter speed: 1/2 sec.

ISO: 200

Exposure Metering

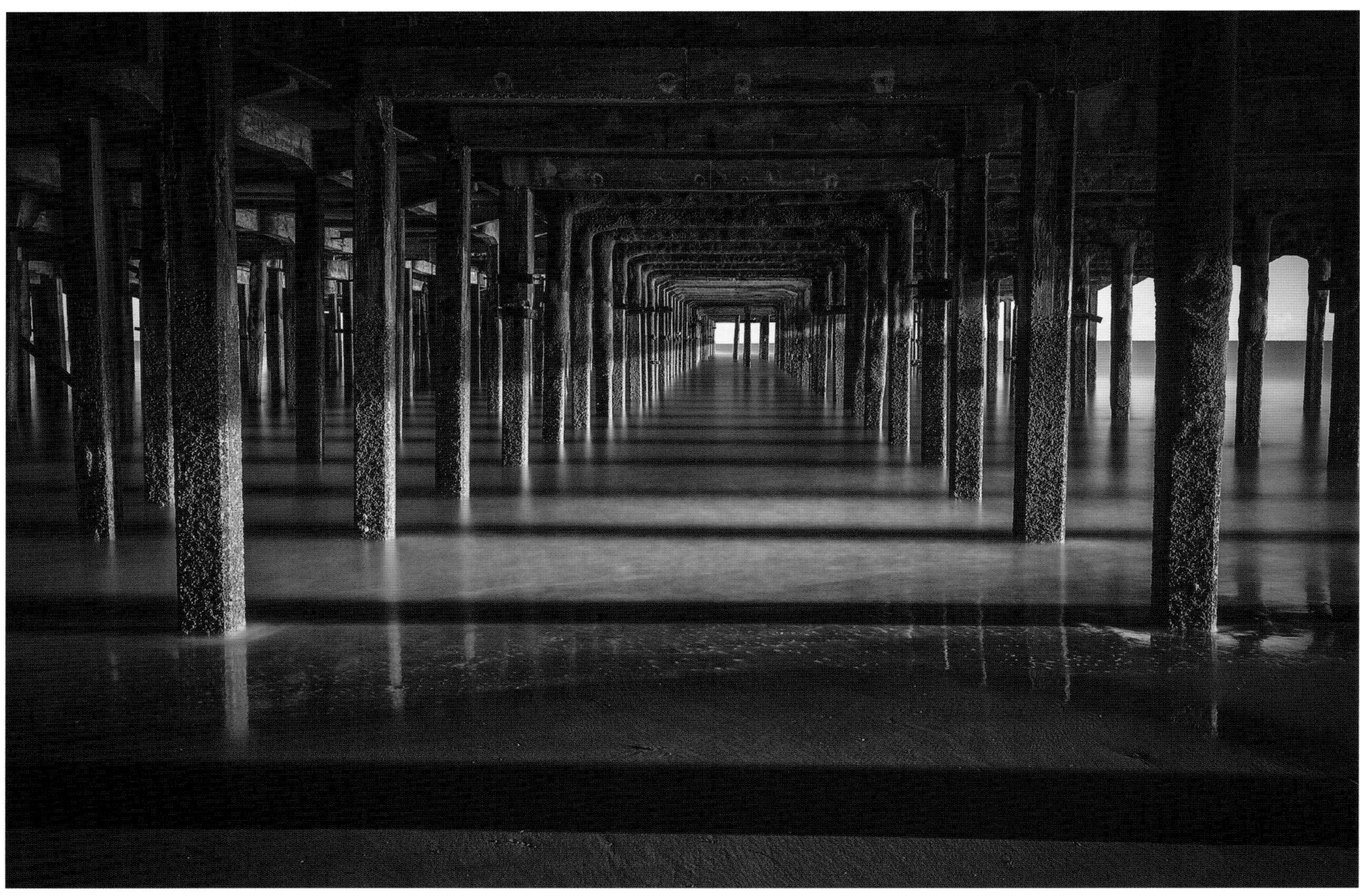

Exposure is the fundamental concept in all photography. Determining the amount of light that is required for each particular image is paramount. Once this has been decided, the camera's exposure controls can be used to ensure that this is captured correctly.

Our eyes are very sensitive, and can adjust to fluctuations in light and dark in very subtle ways. A camera, however, has to rely on a built-in exposure meter to measure the light in a scene.

Exposure metering systems have been developing and improving for decades, so modern in-camera metering systems are generally accurate.

There are still some complex lighting conditions that can confuse the meter, making it harder to obtain accurate readings. When the light levels are low or long exposures are going to be used creatively, for example, the in-camera meter may mistakenly suggest an exposure that is too bright or dark.

Above: Controlling the exposure is essential in the creation of compelling images. Often there is a delicate balance between being able to obtain the correct exposure for shadow area, without overexposing the highlights.

Focal length: 40mm

Aperture: f/16

Shutter speed: 99 sec.

ISO: 100

Metering Patterns

There are three common in-camera exposure-metering options, each of which uses a different "pattern" to assess the light in a scene. Each option can be used to help you achieve the correct exposure in different lighting situations.

Multi-zone

Multi-zone metering goes by many proprietary names (Canon calls it Evaluative metering and Nikon calls it Matrix metering, for example), but they all work on a similar underlying principle.

Essentially, the scene is divided into different sections or zones and the camera determines the exposure for each of these areas individually. It then works out an average overall exposure, often taking the focus point into consideration. Some systems also make an intelligent guess at what the subject might be and amend the exposure accordingly. While not foolproof, this metering pattern usually delivers accurate results in most scenes where there are not extreme contrasting areas of light and dark.

Below: In-camera metering technology is very sophisticated and generally highly accurate. Multi-zone metering is the most widely used pattern, and is the default setting on many cameras.

Focal length: 28mm

Aperture: f/18

Shutter speed: 30 sec.

ISO: 200

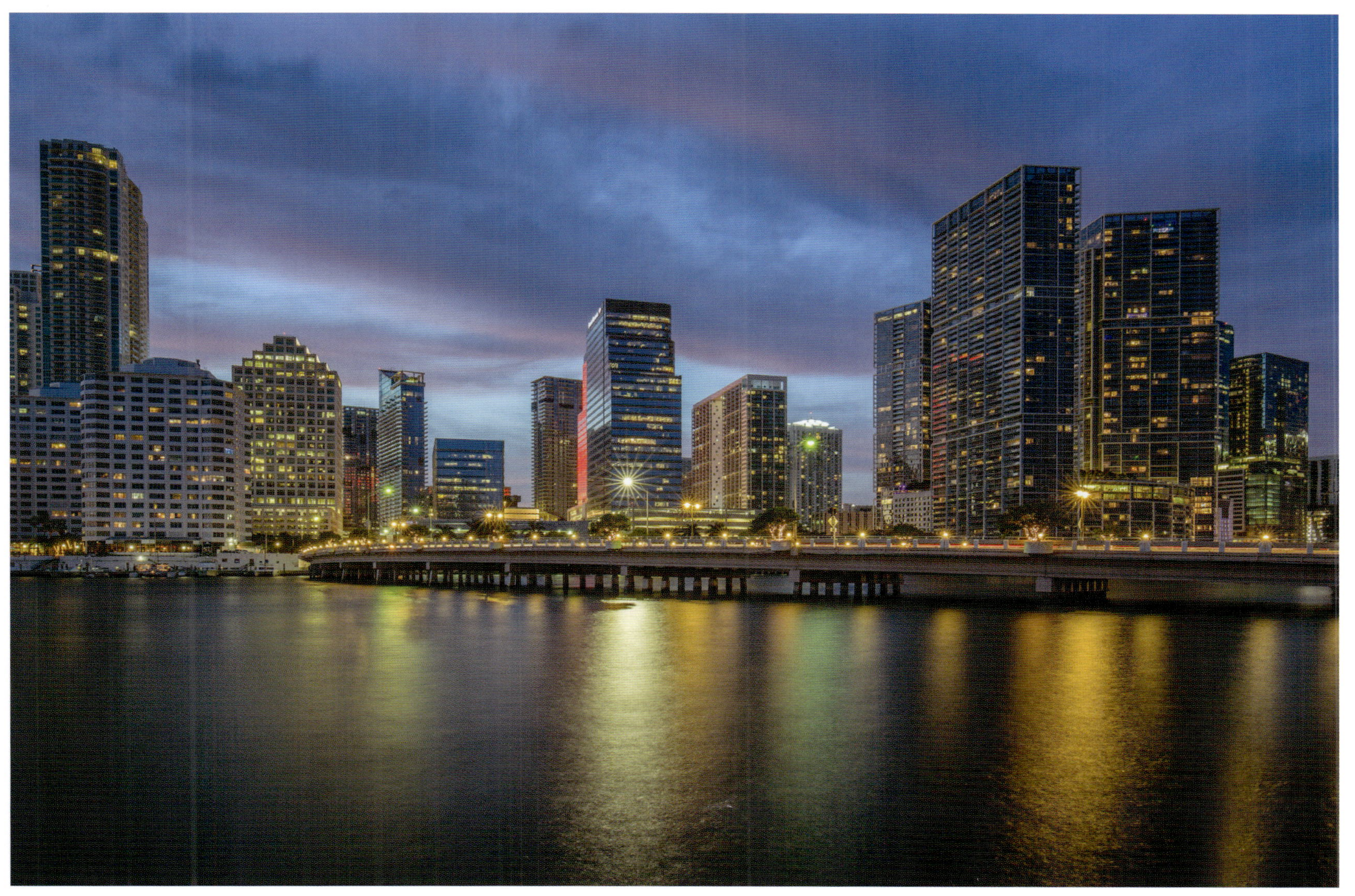

Spot metering

When you switch to spot metering, the camera concentrates on a small part of the scene—usually at the center of the frame—and sets the exposure for that area, ignoring anything outside this zone. This is an extremely useful mode where you have strong contrasts between light and dark, as you can "target" a small part of the scene to measure the exposure from.

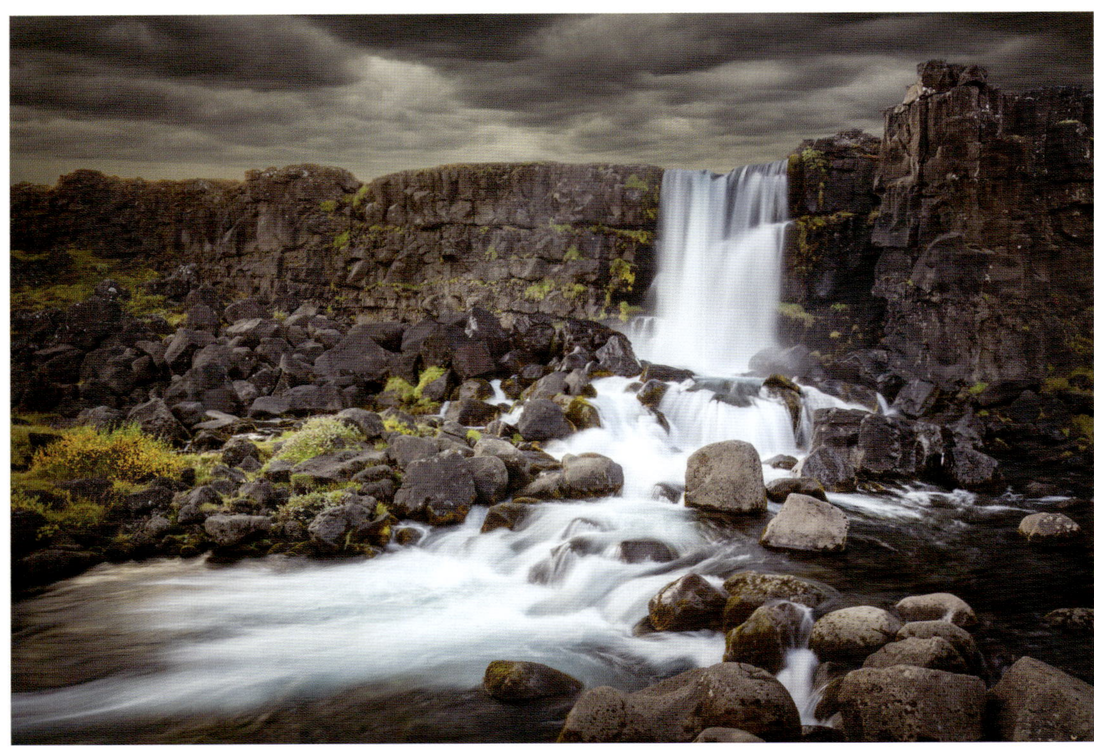

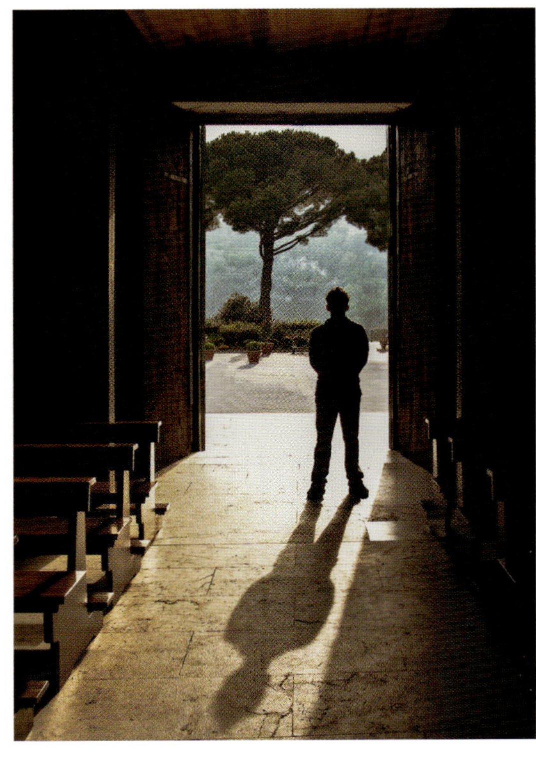

Tips

- Spot metering is often linked to the chosen autofocus point for ease of use when the subject is not at the center of the frame.

- An increasingly common metering pattern is "highlight spot," which lets you set the exposure based on a bright point in an image. This ensures that the highlight detail in that area is preserved, although you may need to "lift" the shadows during postproduction.

Above: It would be easy to overexpose the bright foam from the flowing water in this image and lose all detail. Using spot metering meant it was possible to obtain a well-balanced exposure.

Focal length: 24mm

Aperture: f/18

Shutter speed: 1.3 sec.

ISO: 100

Above: Using the spot metering to expose for the brighter area outside the building helped create a strong and dynamic image.

Focal length: 32mm

Aperture: f/7.1

Shutter speed: 1 sec.

ISO: 200

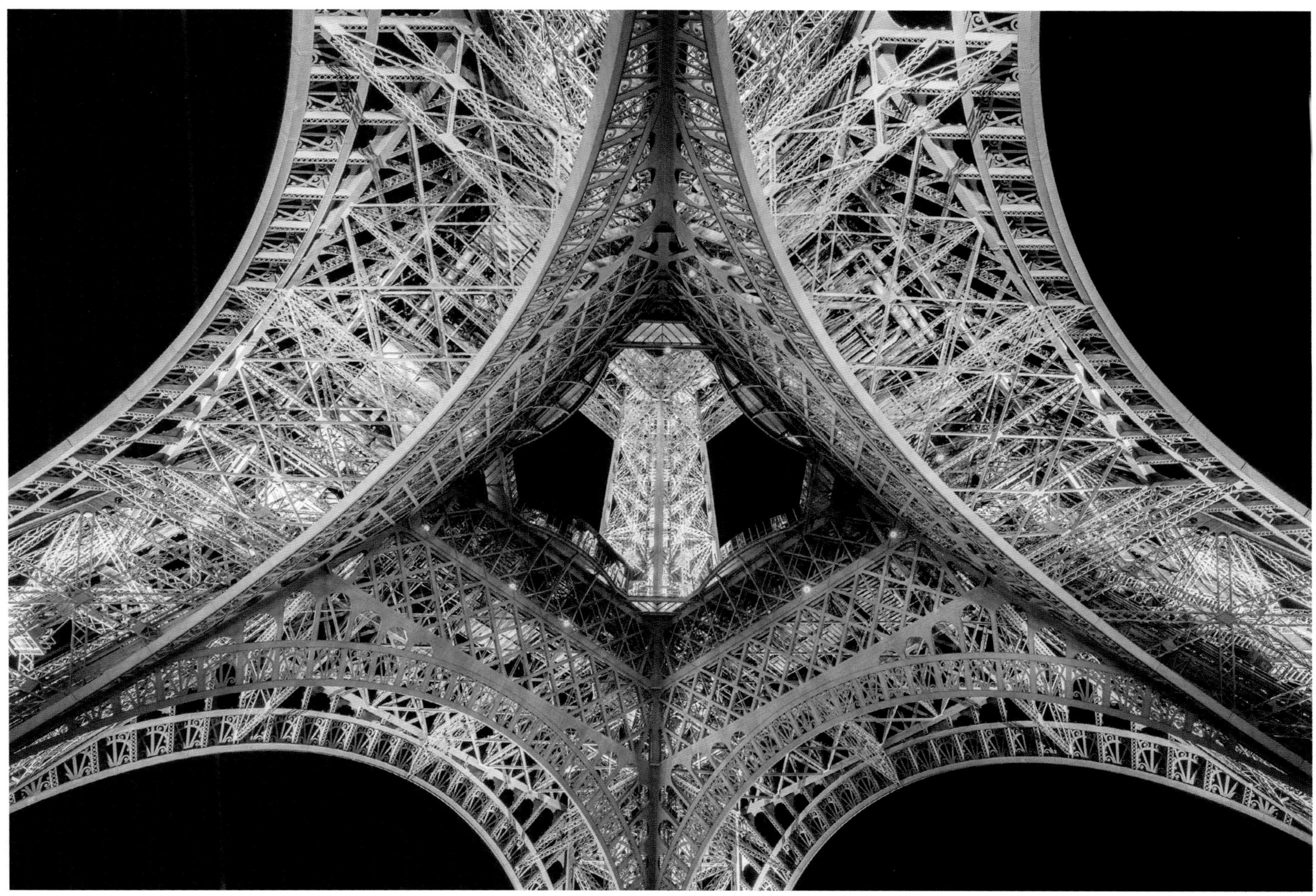

Center weighted

Once the metering "standard," center-weighted metering has now largely been replaced by multi-zone options, although it remains an option on many cameras. In this mode, the metering area is larger than the small section of spot metering, but it doesn't cover the full frame. Instead, the camera reads a large section at the center of the frame; usually covering an area of around 60%. As center-weighted metering ignores the outer areas of the frame it is useful when a central subject is surrounded by particularly bright or dark elements that might adversely affect the exposure.

Above: Center-weighted metering is useful when the main subject is centered in the composition.

Focal length: 16mm

Aperture: f/16

Shutter speed: 15 sec.

ISO: 200

Histogram

A histogram is essentially a graph that shows a visual representation of the levels of brightness in an image. The horizontal (X) axis displays the range of tones in an image from black at the far left to white at the far right. The vertical (Y) axis shows the number of pixels in the image with these tones.

As the LCD screen on the rear of a camera is backlit, it cannot show a true representation of the image taken during playback. This is a particularly important consideration in night photography, as recorded images will look very bright in a darker environment. A natural response is to turn the screen's brightness down, but this will simply make images appear darker than they really are; it will not affect the recorded file.

The role of the histogram is to provide a quick and objective overview of the exposure of the image. A spike at the far left will immediately show that some data has been recorded as true black, while a spike at the far right means something has been recorded as pure white (often indicating that something in the image is overexposed). When data is recorded as true white or true black, it contains no information, so no image detail can be recovered. This is often referred to as "clipping." Some cameras have a setting that will automatically warn of this on image playback, flashing over- or underexposed areas so you can quickly determine if there are any problems. Ideally, it is best to set the exposure so the camera records some shadow or highlight information.

It is important to note that there is a common belief that a histogram should always contain a broad range of data, but this is not technically correct: each scene will have its own unique histogram. For example, a silhouetted object in front of a bright sunny sky will have two spikes of data at each end of the X-axis, but can still be exposed correctly.

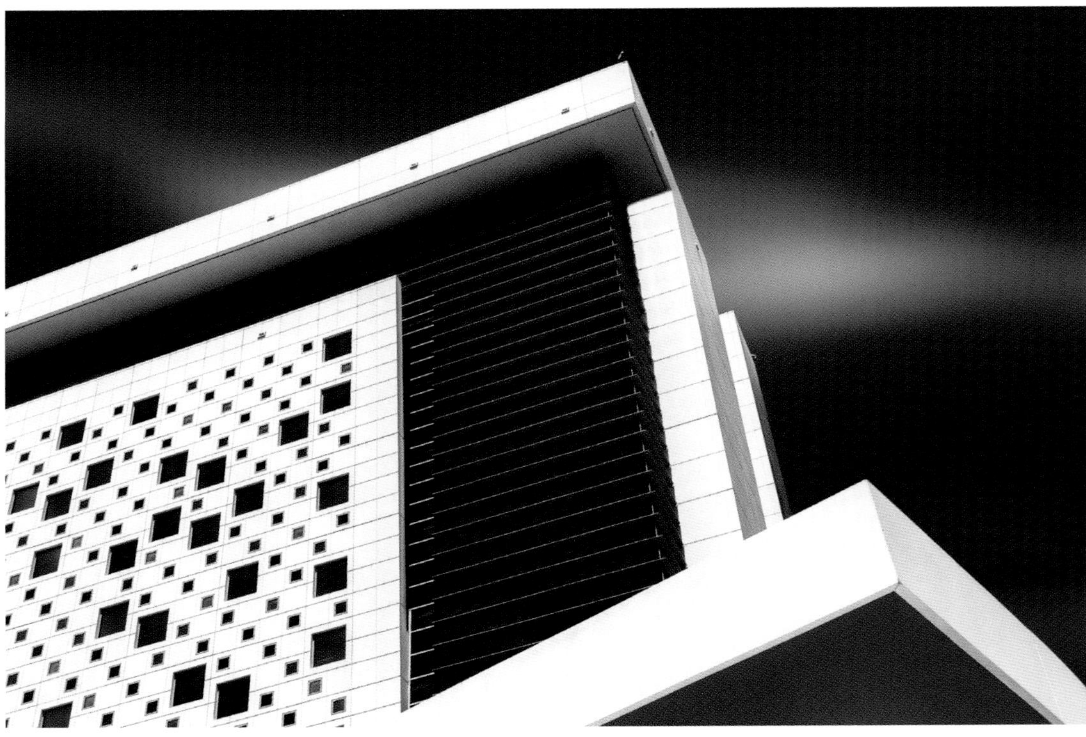

Above & right: A histogram is a useful guide to the spread of tones in the image. In this image there are strong white and black areas, which are represented by large spikes at either end of the X-axis. There is little data at the center, representing the lack of midtones.

Focal length: 45mm

Aperture: f/8

Shutter speed: 90 sec.

ISO: 200

Tips

- The histogram on the back of a camera is very small and can be difficult to read accurately.

- Even if you shoot Raw, the camera's histogram is based on a JPEG preview, rather than the Raw file data. Therefore it should only be used as guidance.

Exposure Compensation

Although in-camera metering is incredibly sophisticated, it is not infallible and can sometimes get things wrong. Despite the best efforts from manufacturers to create more accurate systems, the range of light can sometimes just be too complex for a correct result.

Exposure compensation allows you to manually increase or decrease the exposure to assist the camera where the initial metered results are incorrect. The in-camera control is measured in "stops" of light and can be moved in increments of these stops—usually ½- or ⅓-stop increments. A positive increase will add to the exposure, resulting in a brighter image, while negative exposure compensation will darken the exposure.

Tips

- Exposure compensation is not available in Manual mode, as you are in full control of the exposure settings, so are free to adjust the aperture, shutter speed, or ISO.

- Any exposure compensation adjustment will usually remain set after the camera is switched off. It is therefore a good idea to reset it after each application so it is not inadvertently applied to subsequent shots.

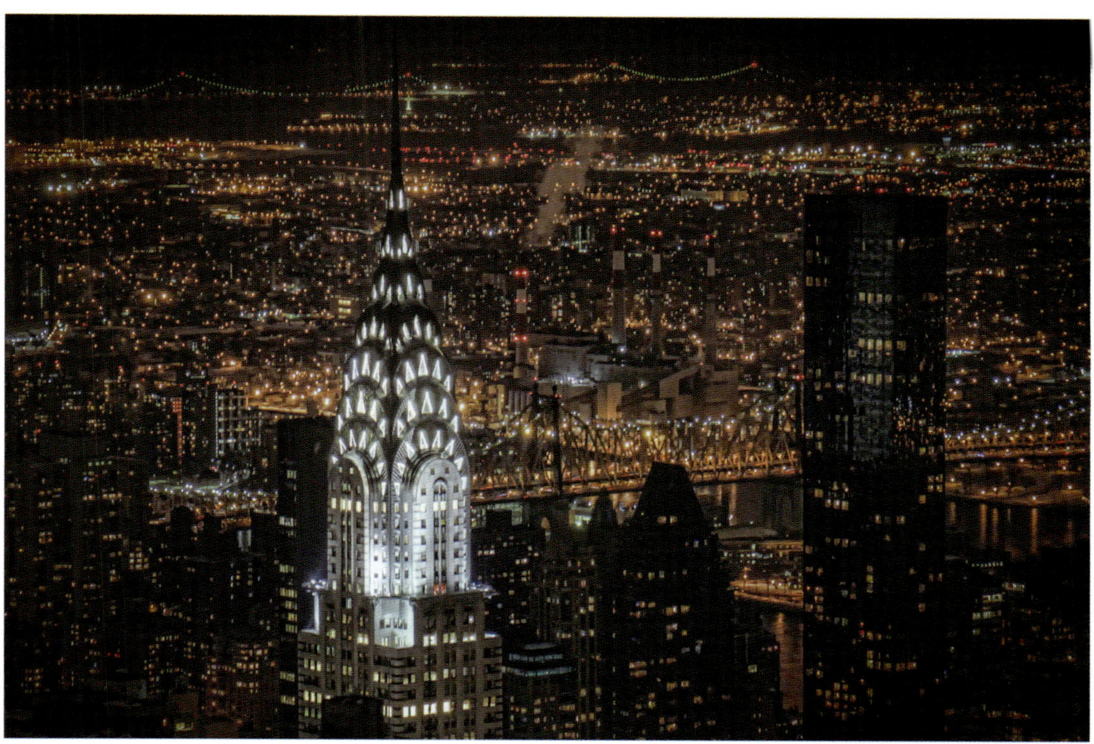

Above: A camera's exposure meter can become confused when there are areas of strong contrast. In this image of New York City, the illuminated Chrysler Building (left) was slightly underexposed as the camera tried to balance out the lights in the scene. Applying one stop of positive exposure compensation quickly countered this, providing a more balanced image overall.

Focal length: 90mm

Aperture: f/5.6

Shutter speed: 2 sec.

ISO: 200

Exposure Bracketing & HDR

There are certain situations where a scene contains extremes of light and dark areas that a camera cannot record accurately in a single image. This is often encountered if you shoot cityscapes at night and it can be very difficult to decide what to expose for; the brighter highlights or the darker shadows. Inevitably, exposing correctly for one will "clip" the other.

In these circumstances the only real solution is to take multiple images at slightly different exposure settings, which is known as "exposure bracketing." Many cameras have an automatic exposure bracketing (AEB) option that allows you to set how many exposures are made (usually it will be three or five) and what the exposure difference will be between them. In this way the camera can be set to take a sequence of images at the "correct" exposure (0), underexposed by one stop (-1), and overexposed by one stop (+1), for example. Once the sequence of images is recorded, it can be viewed on your computer where it is often easier to decide what looks best.

Another option for a bracketed sequence is to blend the images together to create a single photograph with a wider dynamic range. This can be done in-camera in some instances, but for the best results you would need to do it during postproduction. There are many different ways to combine your exposures, ranging from combining them on different layers and manually masking out parts of each image (as described on pages 164–167), through to creating a High Dynamic Range (HDR) image using specialist software.

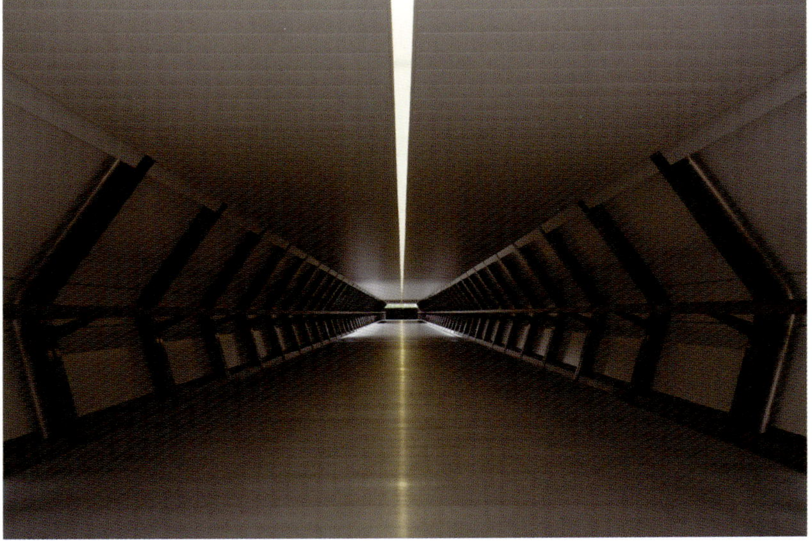

Left: This image was exposed to preserve the highlight detail.

Focal length: 24mm

Aperture: f/5.6

Shutter speed: 1/2 sec.

ISO: 200

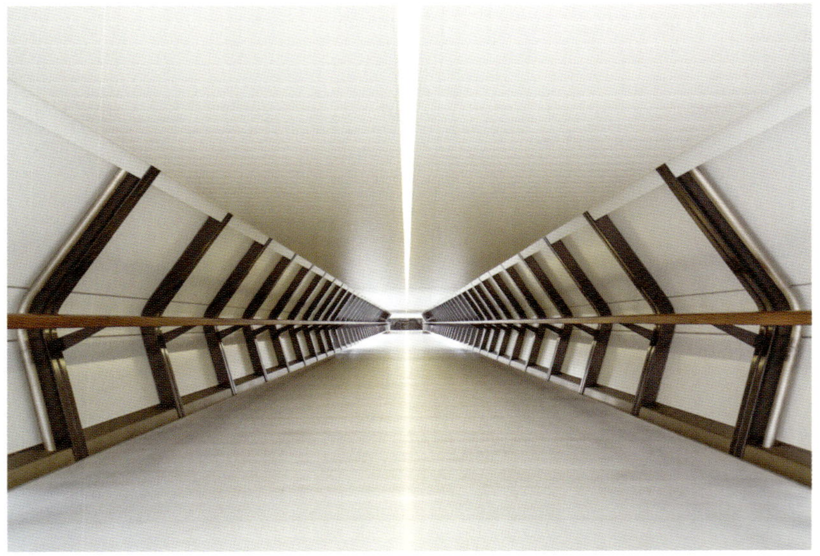

Left: This image was exposed to preserve the shadow detail.

Focal length: 24mm

Aperture: f/5.6

Shutter speed: 3 sec.

ISO: 200

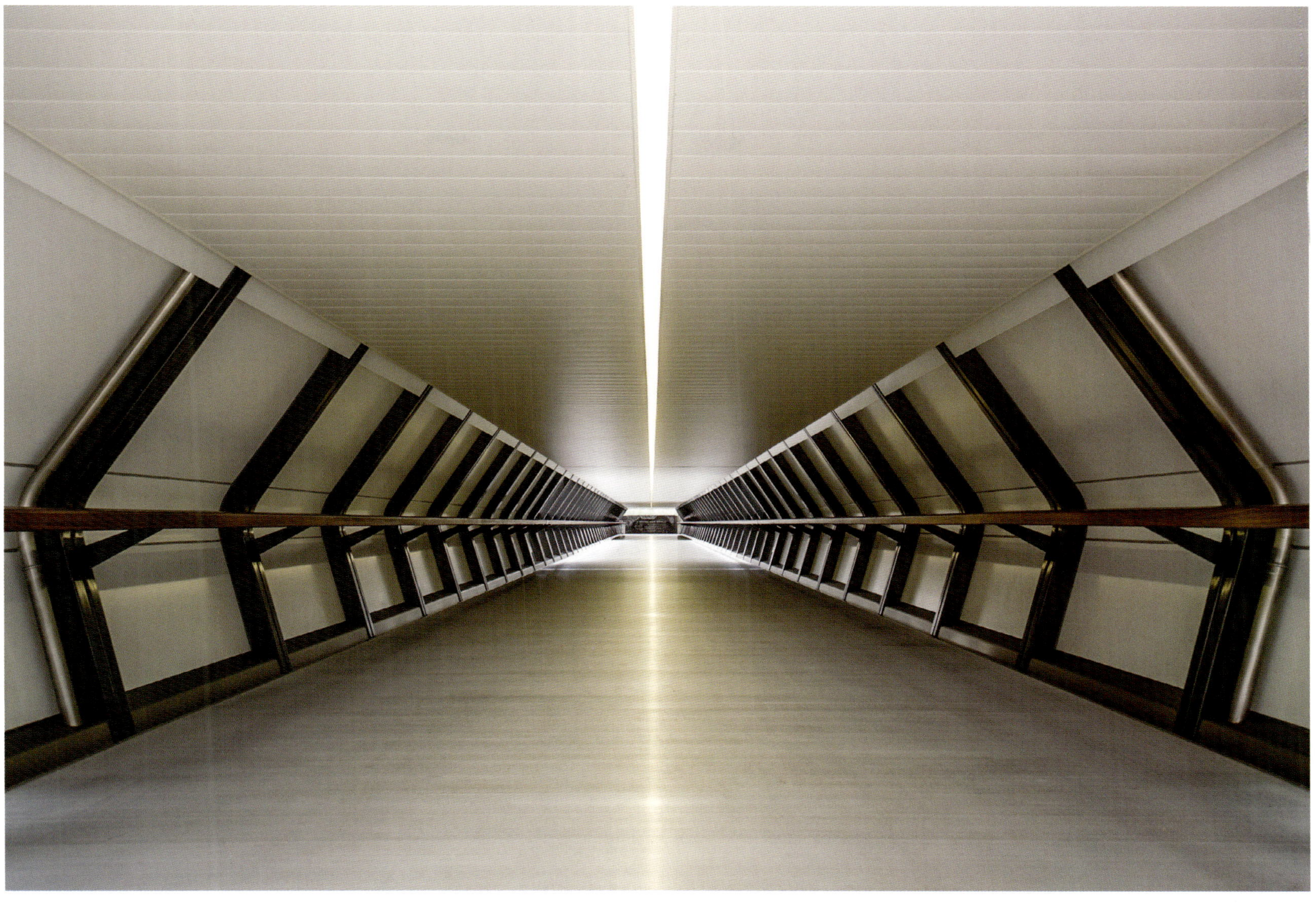

Tips

- When you shoot a bracketed sequence of images, set the camera's drive mode to "continuous" so you can hold down the shutter-release button and make the exposures rapidly. This also helps to minimize any movement if the camera is being handheld.

- HDR processing can easily produce an oversaturated image that looks unreal and "painterly." Image noise can also be exaggerated, leading to an overly noisy composite.

- HDR processing is a global edit that affects the entire image; it cannot be used selectively.

Digital Noise & Other Issues

Aside from camera shake, noise is one of the most common issues that you will encounter in your long exposure images. Noise is the random degradation of pixels that usually appears when long shutter speeds and/or high ISO settings are used. It is usually most evident in the darker areas of an image, which is why it is sometimes referred to as "dark noise."

There are two types of noise: luminance noise, which appears as a coarse underlying texture, and chroma (color) noise, which appears as multi-colored pixels in an image. Both types of noise can be hard to control, especially when higher ISO settings are required. You will see how to deal with noise in postproduction on page 162, but steps can also be taken prior to this to minimize the creation of noise: it usually requires a mixture of equipment, technique, and postproduction to deal with it effectively.

For a start, the camera's sensor plays a part in how noisy your images will be. Generally speaking, the larger the sensor, the less noisy it will be at any given ISO setting. It therefore makes sense to use a full-frame camera if you intend to take the majority of your images in low-light conditions and/or at high ISO settings.

Regardless of your camera, using the lowest possible ISO setting will help keep noise to a minimum. Naturally this is not always possible, but it is best practice to use a low ISO wherever possible, especially if there aren't specific demands in terms of shutter speed and aperture.

To combat long-exposure noise, most cameras have built-in noise reduction (NR). This works by making two exposures. The first is a regular "image" exposure and the second is a "dark frame" that uses the exact same settings—the only difference is that the shutter doesn't open. In theory, the second frame should be pure black, but it won't be, due to the noise generated by the sensor as it heats up during the long exposure. The camera can use the dark frame to offset any noise created in the initial image.

The downside to in-camera NR is that it slows the shooting process, because every exposure you make will require the camera to spend the same amount of time again recording a dark frame. This can be very time-consuming if you are taking images with extremely long exposure times, as well as draining on your battery, so you may prefer to leave in-camera NR turned off and tackle the noise during postproduction.

Below left & below: Noise usually appears in the darker areas of an image and can easily destroy fine detail if it is not controlled (below). Exposing correctly and using a low ISO will help to minimize noise.

Focal length: 21mm

Aperture: f/14

Shutter speed: 28 sec.

ISO: 800

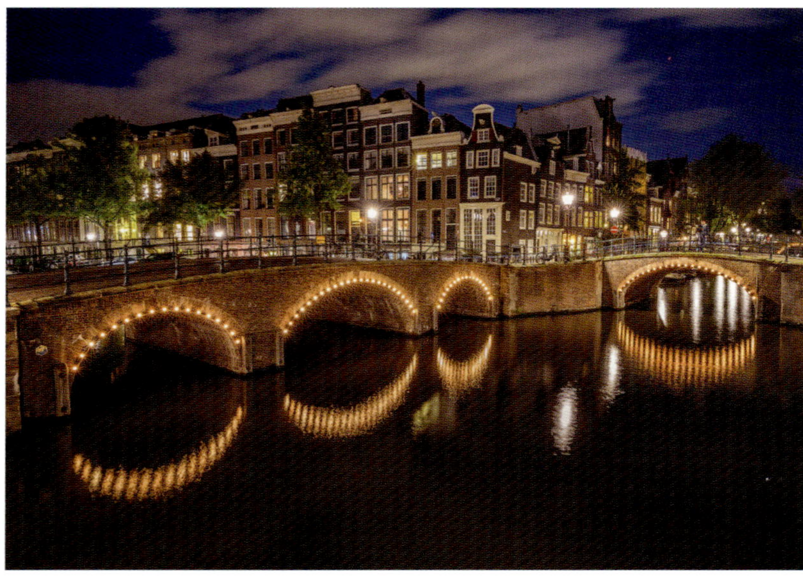

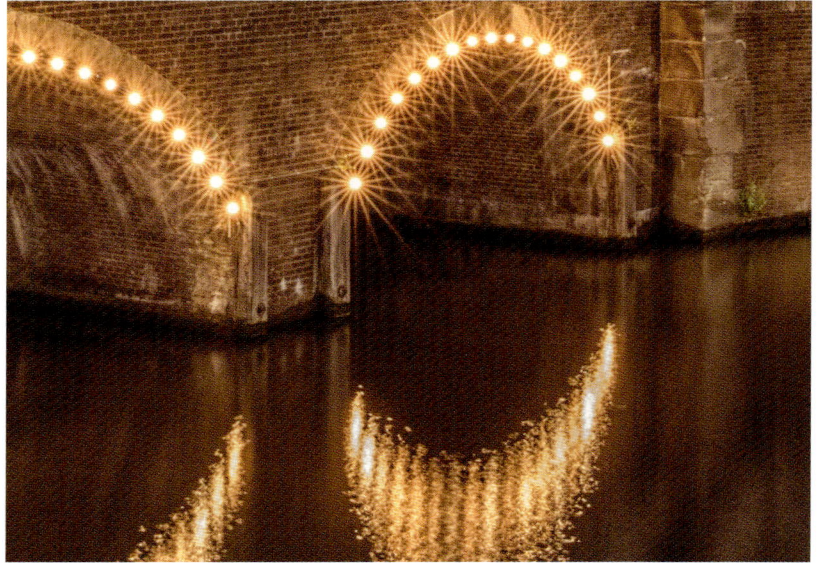

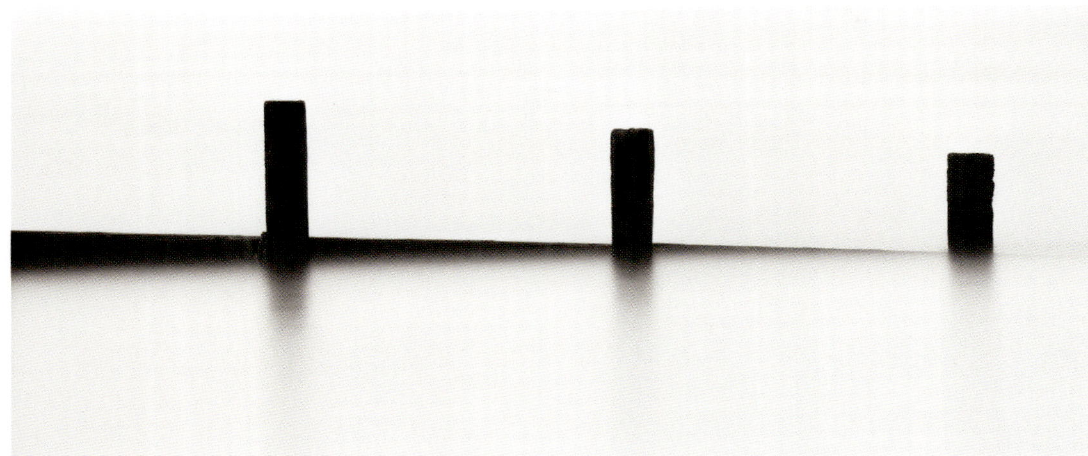

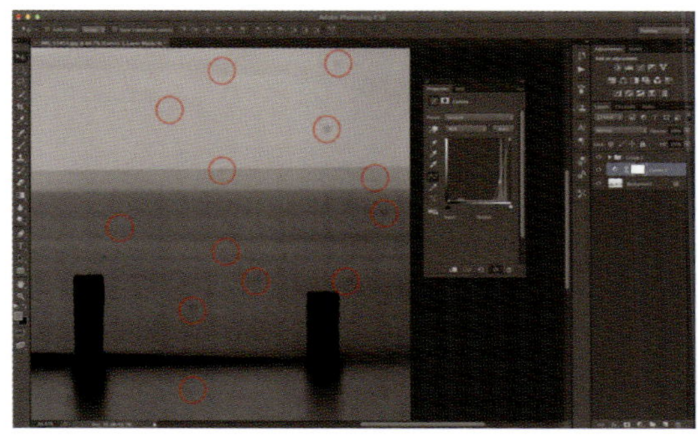

Left & above: This long exposure image was shot during the day with a 10-stop ND filter, resulting in a 90 sec. exposure. As shown in the deliberately darkened detail above, using a small aperture revealed all of the dust on the sensor, which was subsequently removed.

Focal length: 150mm

Aperture: f/16

Shutter speed: 90 sec.

ISO: 100

Chromatic Aberration

Chromatic aberration is a digital imaging artifact that manifests as a colored fringe along high-contrast edges. It can be caused by a lens' inability to bring all the wavelengths of light to focus at the same point (this is most often seen at the edges of the frame, particularly with wideangle lenses) or it can be due to the microlenses in front of the sensor (this is often seen with compact cameras with small sensors). Thankfully chromatic aberration can be removed fairly easily, simply by engaging an option from the menu in most postproduction software.

Dead Pixels

Another issue that can often arise in digital imaging—especially with long exposure photography—is "dead pixels." These are individual pixels that do not record the correct information and appear either as a bright color or white, which looks out of place in the final image. These can be very obvious, especially when shooting JPEG files, but once located they can be cloned out quite easily in postproduction.

Dust Spots

Shooting very long exposures—especially at smaller aperture settings—inevitably makes any dust on the camera's sensor more apparent. While it is a good idea to clean the camera's sensor regularly, it is not always possible or practical to do so (such as when out in a dusty environment). In this instance dust will need to be located and dealt with in postproduction.

Chapter 3
Sunset to Sunrise

Sunsets and sunrises are popular photography subjects for good reason: it is at these times that the colors of nature and the light are often at their best. The skies are usually alight with rich oranges and reds as light travels through the atmosphere and bathes scenes in warm tones. The low angle of the sunlight also adds texture and depth by casting shadows that are longer and more drawn out.

However, when the sun is close to—or below—the horizon, light levels drop and this inevitably leads to longer exposure times. Predawn light and twilight can be especially difficult to capture accurately, as a spectacular scene in front of us can be changing so quickly. Suddenly it is not simply a case of using a smaller aperture for deep depth of field or increasing ISO; as you will see in this chapter, compromises need to be made if you want to capture spectacular imagery at these times of day.

Right: The sun had just dipped behind the mountains at this Scottish loch and the warm hues of the golden hour were reflected all around.

Focal length: 20mm

Aperture: f/4

Shutter speed: 3 sec.

ISO: 100

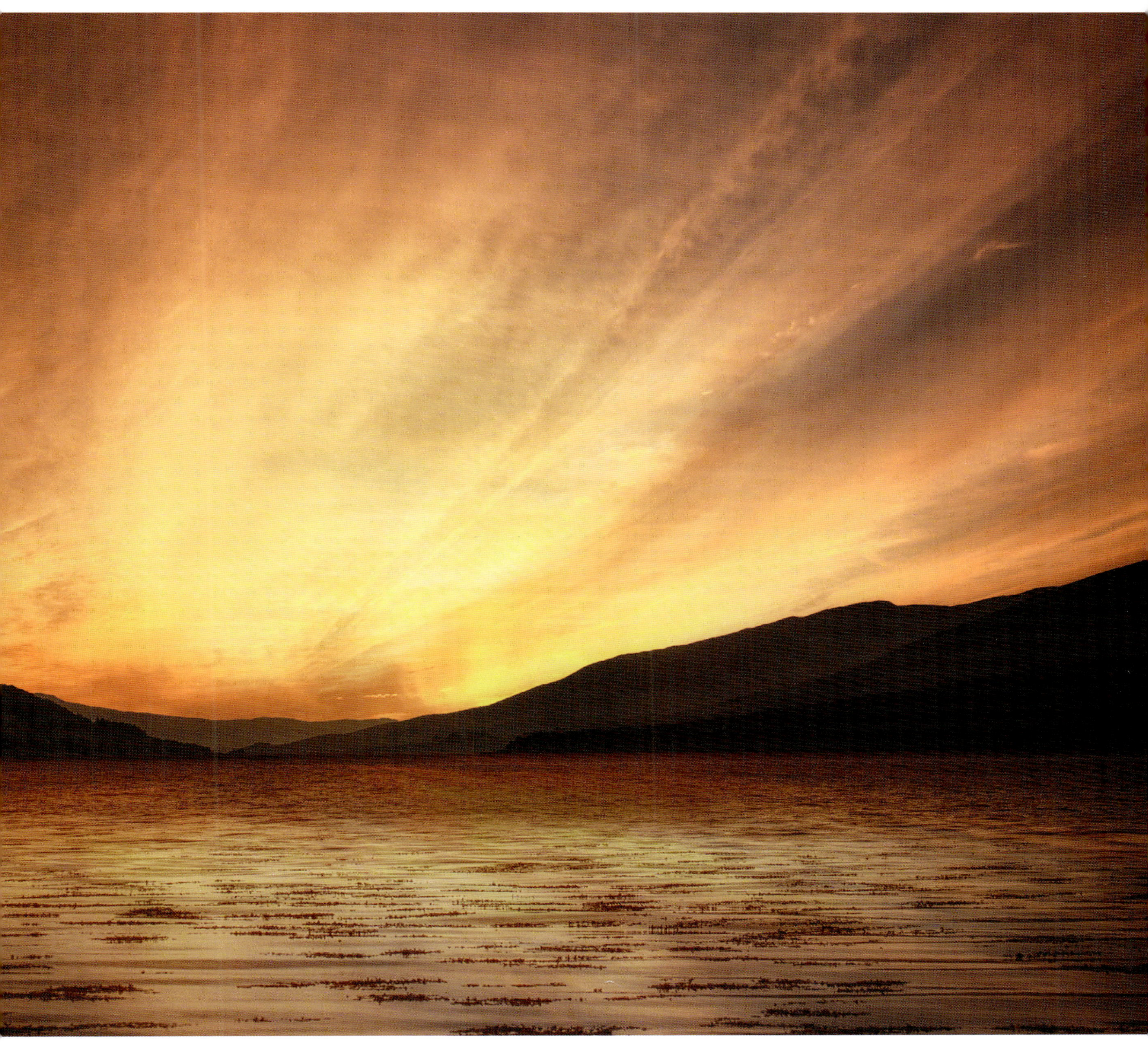

Sunrise & Sunset

The spectacular colors that can occur at sunrise and sunset are capable of transforming an ordinary scene into something sensational. There will be many times when your early morning or late evening endeavors will be in vain, with the golden hues thwarted by last minute cloud, but when it all comes together the rewards certainly outweigh the effort.

However, even when the sky is on fire you need to be careful if you want to get the best results. It is quite easy to end up with images containing washed out, muted tones that are nothing like the scene you were photographing. This is often because in-camera exposure meters have a natural tendency to overexpose the sky, especially if there is some darker ground in the frame.

Below: As the sun appeared above the horizon for this sunrise shot the wind picked up and the clouds were recorded as colorful streaks across the sky.

Focal length: 24mm

Aperture: f/4

Shutter speed: 4 sec.

ISO: 100

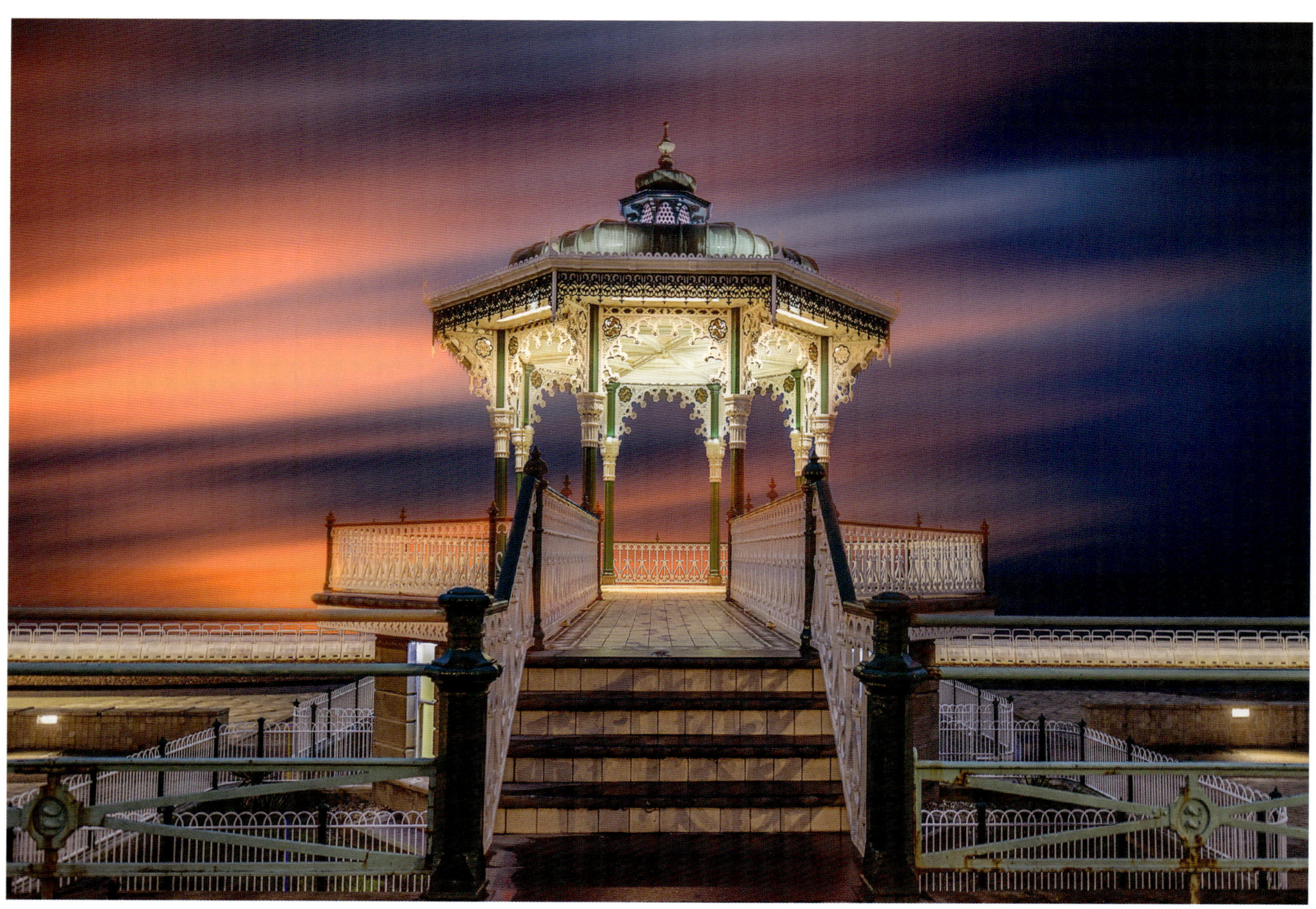

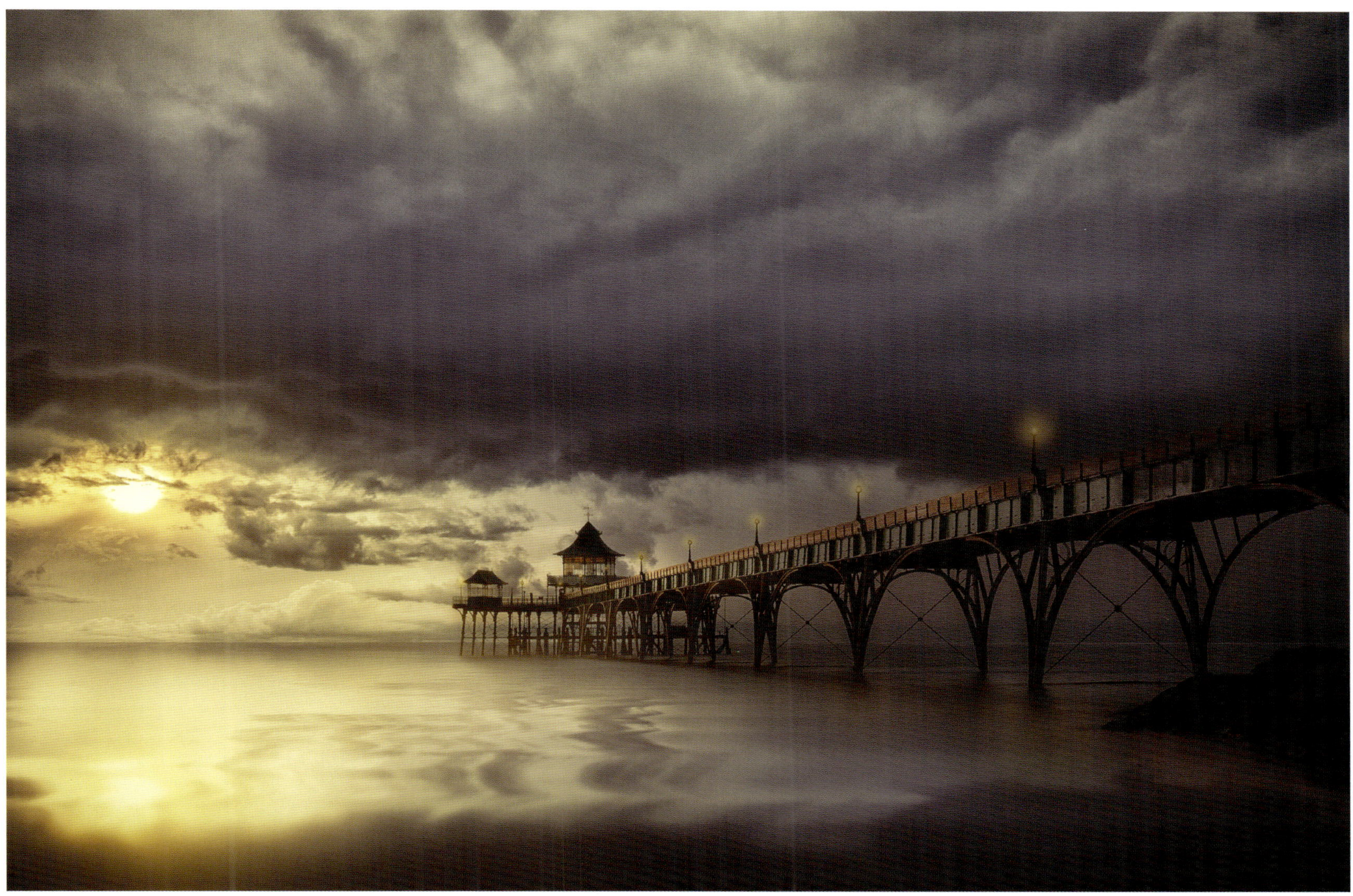

The simple answer here is to use negative exposure compensation to darken the exposure. This will lead to more saturated colors, although the trade-off is that the surrounding scene will become darker and less detailed. Often it is not possible to expose correctly for the details in both the brightest and darkest areas of the scene. When this occurs, you need to decide which part of the scene to expose correctly, or bracket a series of exposures (see pages 36–37) and decide how you want to process them in postproduction. If you opt for a single shot, then the best advice is to expose for the highlights, as it is far easier to recover shadow detail in postproduction.

Tips

- Often, the light show does not end when the sun sets; some of the most amazing light appears just after sunset as light reflects back up into the sky. With a sunrise, pre-dawn light has a similar effect.

- For landscapes, partial cloud cover will often deliver the best results. Too much cloud will naturally obscure the sunrise/sunset, while too little cloud will mean the sky doesn't put on a dramatic light show.

Above: Just the right amount of cloud in the sky can add to a sunrise or sunset. In this case, the sun managed to break free from behind dense cloud at the last minute to create a spectacular sunset scene.

Focal length: 20mm

Aperture: f/7.1

Shutter speed: 2 sec.

ISO: 200

As the sun emerges above the horizon at sunrise, the rich golden hues strike the landscape with warm light. Shooting toward the sun will increase the risk of lens flare (especially if the sun is in the frame), and while a lens hood can help minimize this in some situations, it's also worth trying some shots with flare to see if it enhances the atmosphere. Turning your back to the rising sun will prevent any flare at all, and reveal a scene bathed in golden light.

Sunset is naturally the reverse of sunrise, although the end of the day often presents more striking colors due to haze and pollution building up in the atmosphere, together with the humidity of the evening sky.

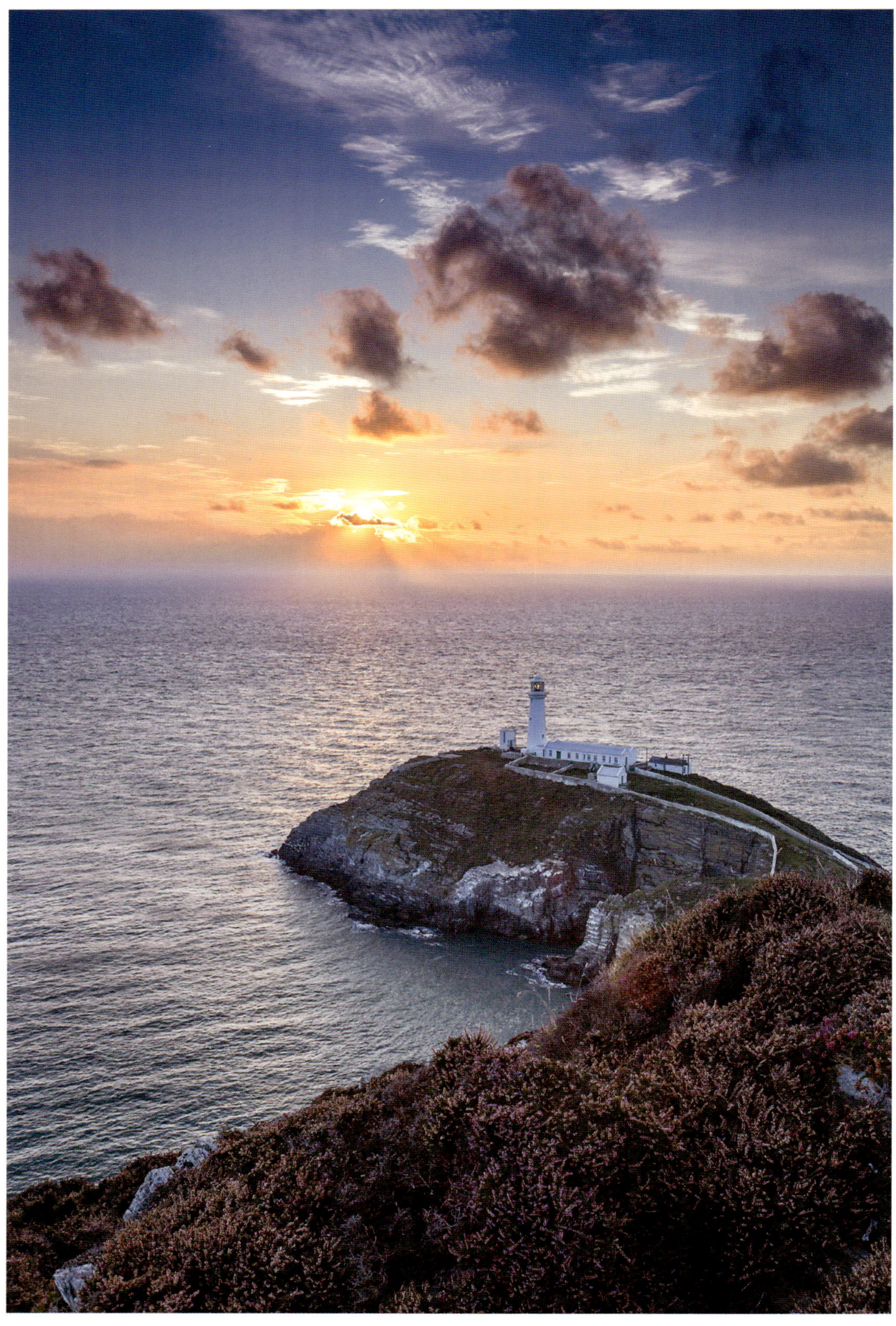

Left: The last light of the day at Anglesey, North Wales.

Focal length: 35mm

Aperture: f/14

Shutter speed: 1.5 sec.

ISO: 100

Silhouettes

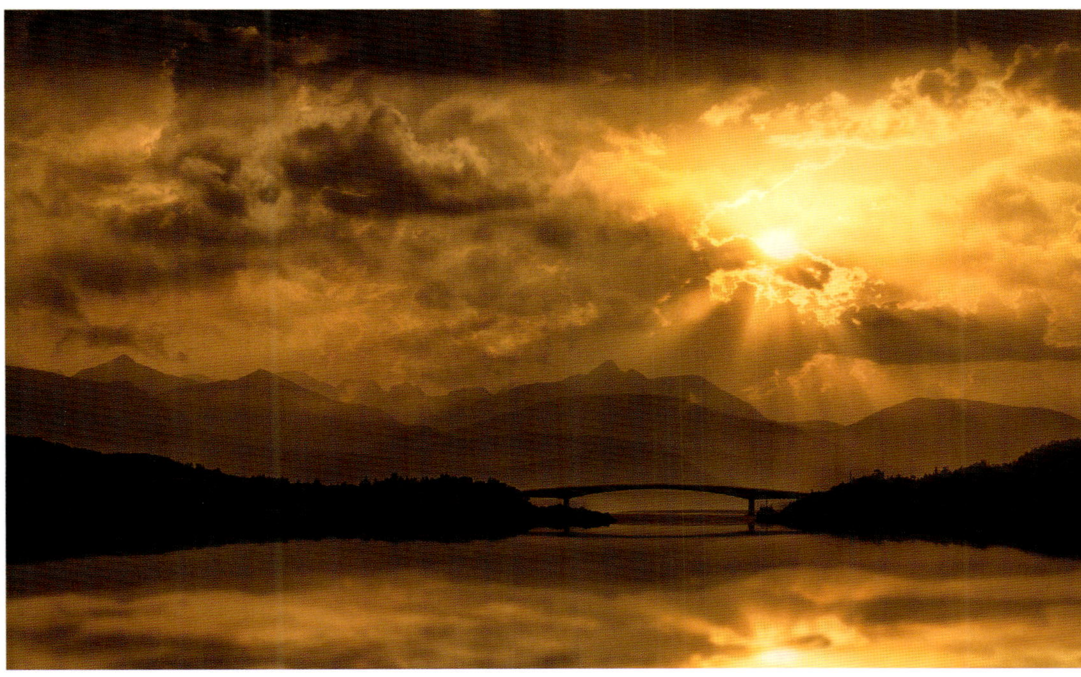

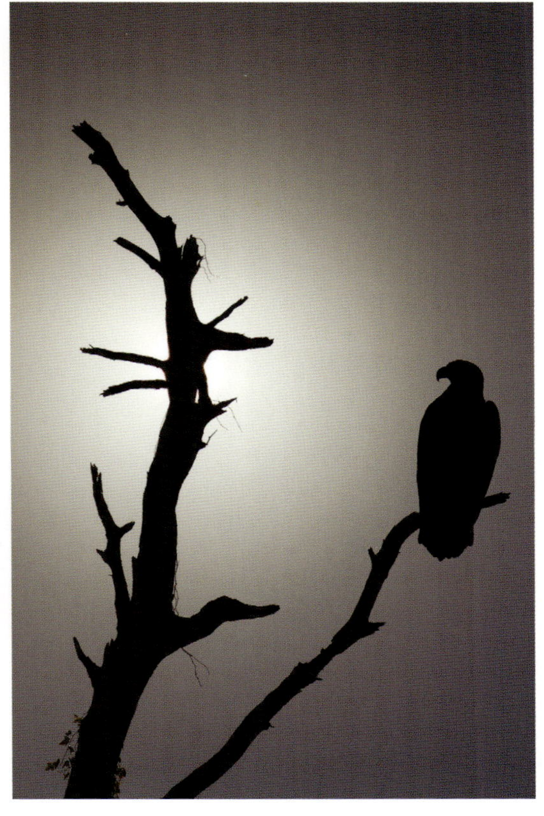

Often, the contrast between bright golden sunlight and the darker shaded areas of a scene is very wide at sunrise and sunset, and the camera will struggle to capture the full range of tones even though your eyes can see it. This is the perfect time to look for stunning silhouettes.

Exposing for the brightest areas in the scene will cause the darker areas to be recorded as black, and the easiest way to do this is to use the camera's spot meter to expose for the area you want to expose correctly (usually the background). Other metering modes will confuse the camera and it will likely try to over-compensate for the darker and lighter areas in an image—you can use exposure compensation to combat this, but spot metering is more reliable.

Above: Exposing for the sunset meant that the mountains and bridge became silhouettes. Even with spot metering it was necessary to apply negative exposure compensation to prevent overexposure of the area directly around the sun.

Focal length: 120mm

Aperture: f/5.6

Shutter speed: 2 sec.

ISO: 100

Above: The outline of the eagle and the tree became more striking in silhouette. I positioned the sun carefully behind the tree to prevent lens flare.

Focal length: 180mm

Aperture: f/7.1

Shutter speed: 1 sec.

ISO: 200

Tips

- Sometimes it can be beneficial to retain a small amount of detail in the shadow areas, rather than rendering them as pure black, so experiment with spot metering and positive exposure compensation.

- Look for subjects with a clearly defined shape, rather than complex or overlapping shapes that will be hard to interpret.

Predawn Light

Predawn light, before the sun rises, is a very soft and gentle light and contains stronger blue tones if it is a cloudless sky. This is a great time to shoot landscapes in particular, as the reflected light from the sky acts like a large diffuser, removing any unwanted shadows from a scene. Urban landscapes will be devoid of cars and people at such an early hour, creating an "unfamiliar" atmosphere, while rural vistas will sometimes have mist and fog that can add a dreamlike quality. The stillness of early morning can also lead to some spectacular reflections in water, which can turn mirror-like with the absence of wind.

The low light levels will require slower shutter speeds and a stable camera, and the white balance will be strongly influenced by the overall

Below: The predawn light filtering through this forest canopy provided a soft, diffused light with a bluish tint. Although it might look like daylight, a long shutter speed was required to capture this scene correctly.

Focal length: 24mm

Aperture: f/10

Shutter speed: 32 sec.

ISO: 200

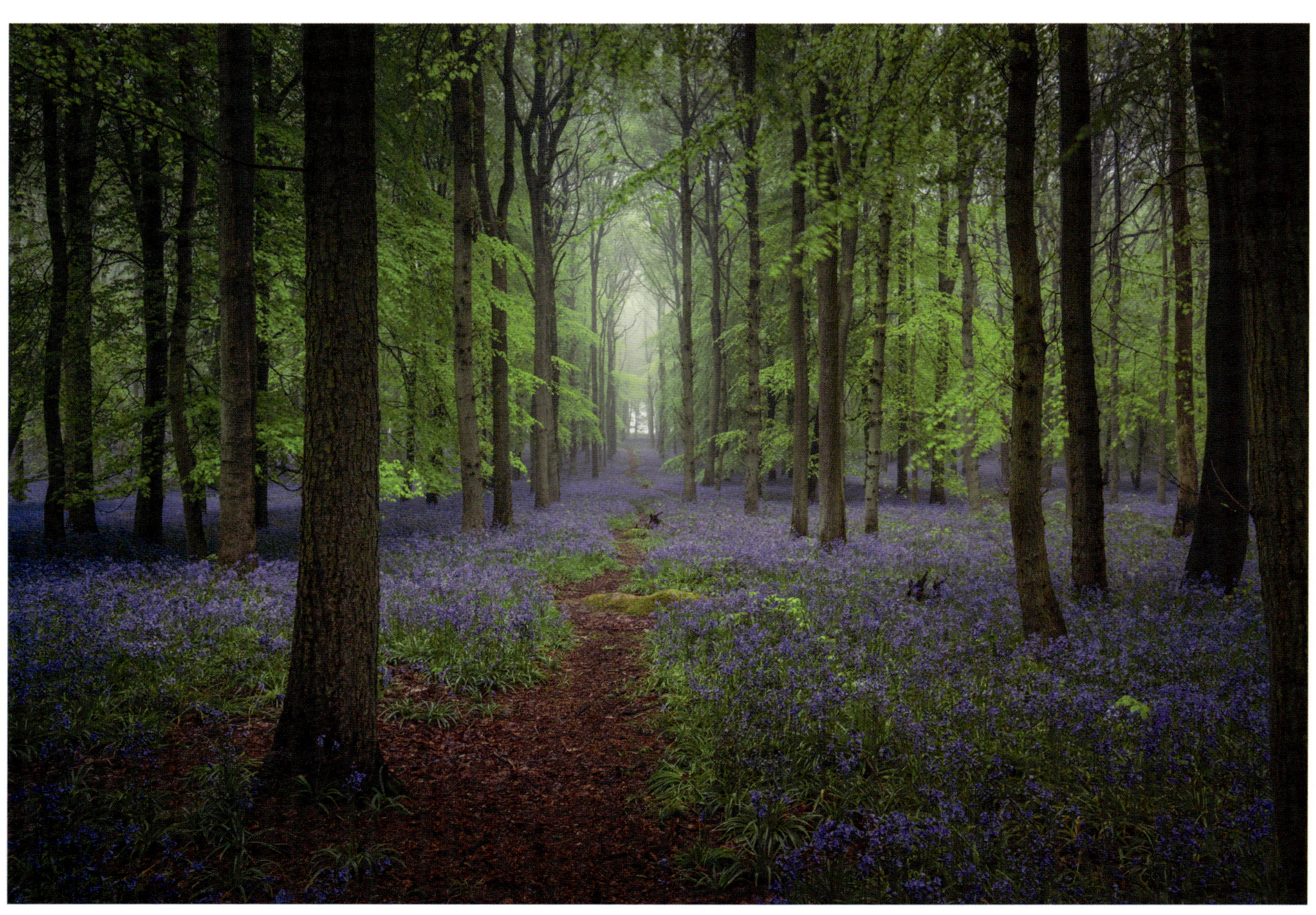

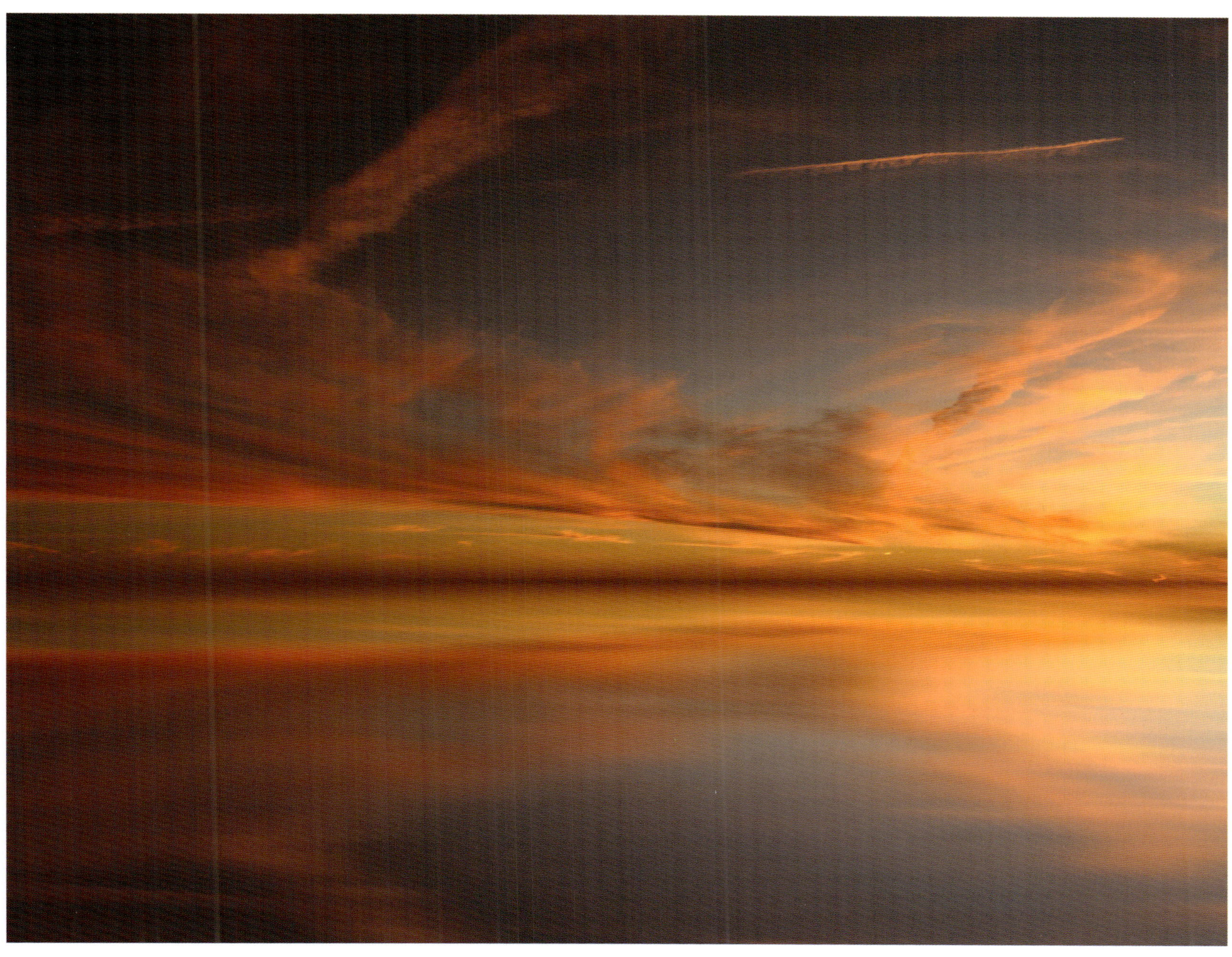

blue tones. If you're shooting JPEGs it is worth experimenting with the white balance to see how different settings affect the final image. The Shade preset option should usually give a more accurate representation of the scene, while Cloudy will add some extra warmth. When shooting Raw, the white balance can be amended in postproduction.

Shooting the predawn light takes a little extra planning, as you will be setting up your equipment and framing your shot in the dark. Further, the light will be changing quickly, so settings will inevitably need to be amended "on the fly." Familiarity with your kit and shooting in Manual mode (with direct control over shutter speed and aperture) will enable you to rise to these challenges.

Above: Wonderful predawn color was reflected on the sea in this shot; a long exposure has maximized the intensity.
Focal length: 28mm
Aperture: f/4
Shutter speed: 2 sec.
ISO: 100

Moonlight Photography

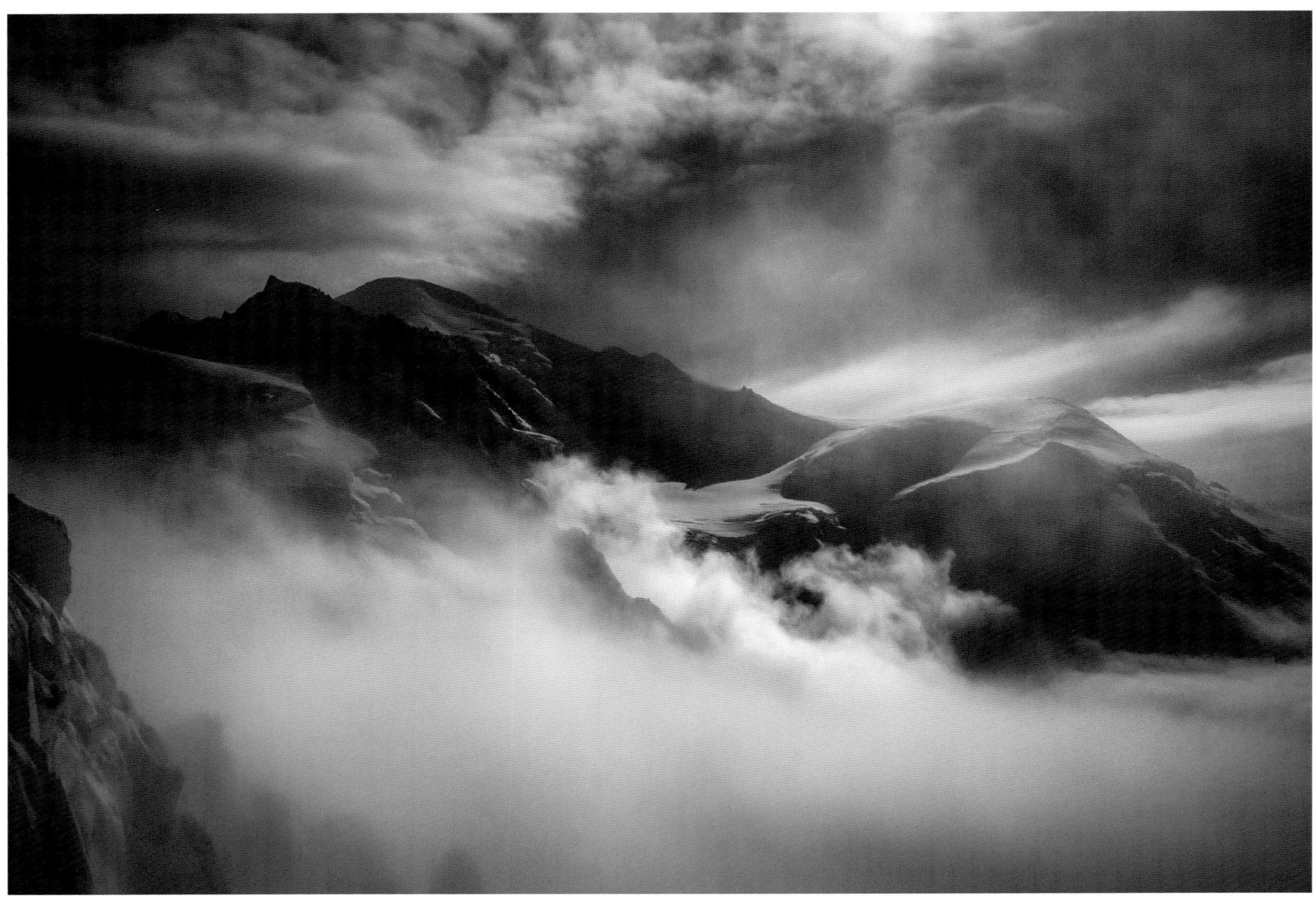

Once the sun has set below the horizon and the moon has begun to rise, landscapes can still be photographed. Although moonlight is not very bright when compared to the sun (it is suggested that it is around 400,000 times dimmer), a full moon high above the horizon can give out a surprising amount of light. More importantly, this less conventional light source has a uniquely beautiful quality to it.

There are inherent difficulties when using moonlight as the primary light source for an image. For a start, it can be very difficult to determine the actual brightness of moonlight. This can fluctuate due to a number of factors, including the apparent size of the moon in the sky and its position, but it is the lunar phase that is the most important factor—there's a significant difference between the brightness of a full moon and a thin crescent.

Above: The long exposure required for this image allowed the rolling clouds to be recorded, illuminated by the moonlight.

Focal length: 16mm

Aperture: f/11

Shutter speed: 49 sec.

ISO: 800

Even though the moon is seemingly bright in comparison to the darkness of the night sky, it is inevitable that longer exposure times will be required for a well-exposed image. However, if the moon is in the frame, it will quickly overexpose with a long exposure and its movement through the night sky will also lead to it becoming blurred. For this reason it is a good idea to shoot images where the moon is either not in the scene or is hidden behind cloud.

Because the brightness of moonlight is so variable, there are no universal exposure settings that apply to all shots, and artificial lights in a scene will also affect the outcome of the exposure. A good starting point is to set the ISO in the region of ISO 800 and choose an aperture that will give you your desired depth of field. The shutter speed will typically be longer than 30 sec. (the maximum automatic duration on most cameras), so you will need to shoot using Bulb mode.

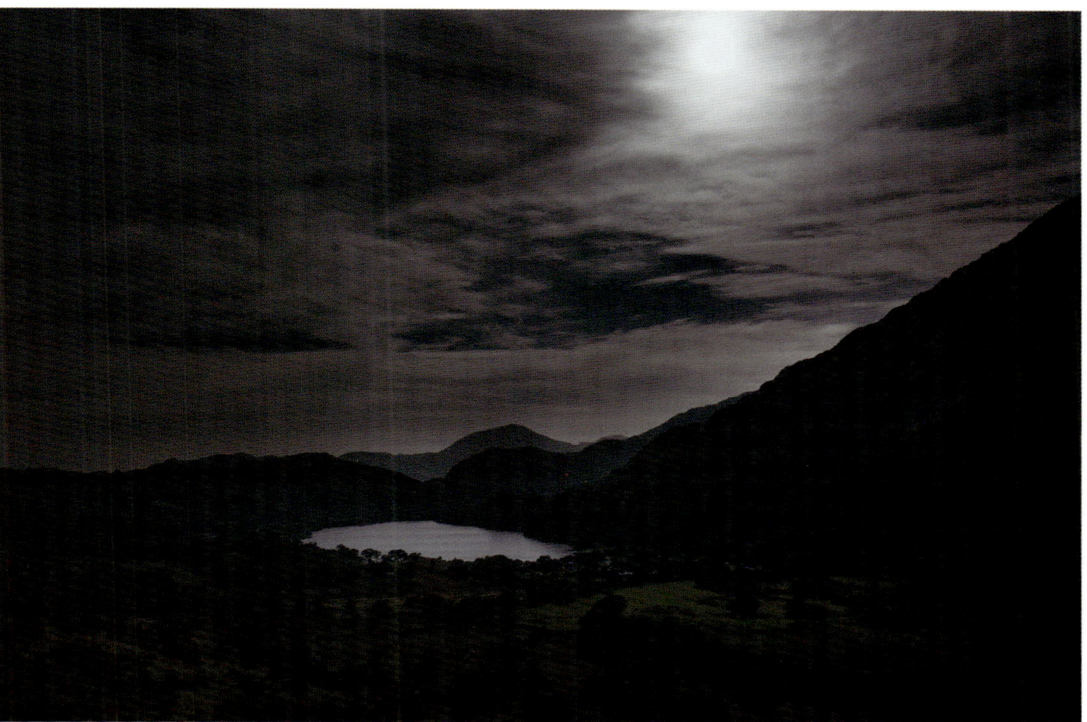

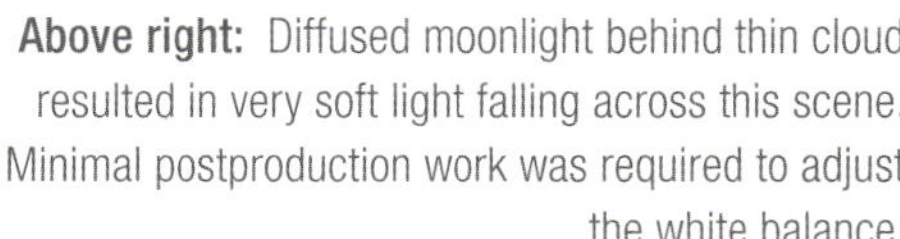

Above right: Diffused moonlight behind thin cloud resulted in very soft light falling across this scene. Minimal postproduction work was required to adjust the white balance.

Focal length: 32mm

Aperture: f/11

Shutter speed: 220 sec.

ISO: 200

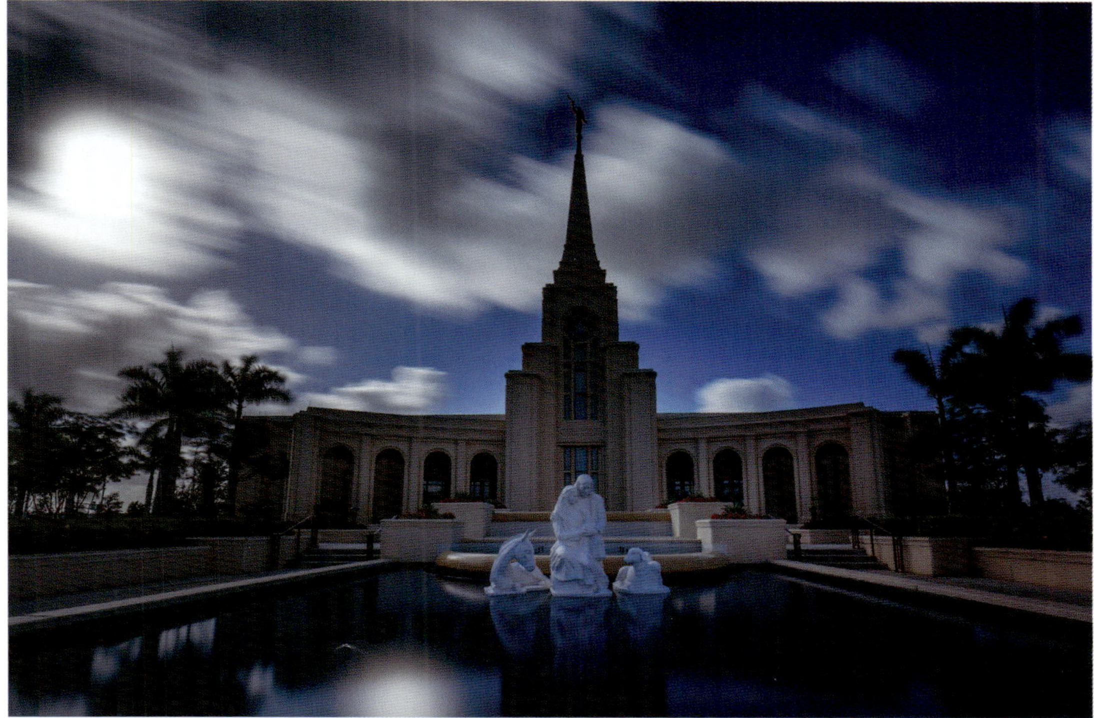

Right: The movement of the clouds appears as streaks, although the moon has been overexposed as the cloud cover was not continuous.

Focal length: 16mm

Aperture: f/11

Shutter speed: 180 sec.

ISO: 100

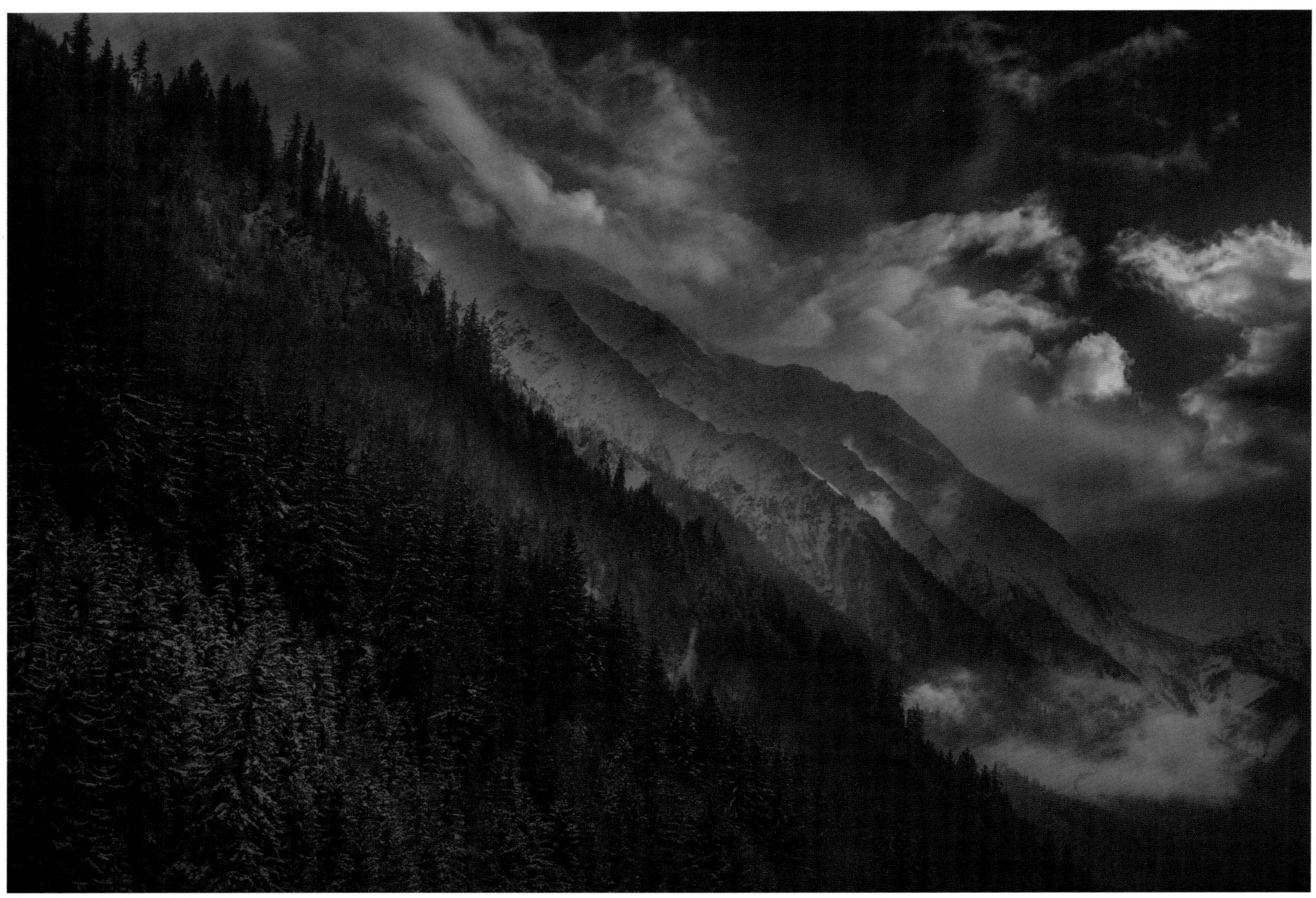

Tips

- There are numerous online resources that can provide information on moon phases, rise and setting times, and clear sky and weather information.

- Moonlight gives off a slight blue color cast; it is a good idea to shoot Raw, so the white balance can be changed in postproduction.

A rough starting point would be to hold the shutter open for 2–3 minutes and assess the histogram. If your images are underexposed, it is usually best to correct this by using a longer exposure time; most landscape imagery requires a deep depth of field, so using a wider aperture to let in more light is not really an option, while increasing the ISO can lead to issues with noise. If, however, your test shot is overexposed you can correct it using any of the exposure controls (a lower ISO, smaller aperture, or shorter exposure time).

Above: When shooting in very dark conditions, the LCD on the back of your camera will appear very bright and can easily make you think that an image is exposed correctly when it is not. It is therefore important to check the histogram instead.

Focusing in the Dark

Sharp focus can often make or break an image, but trying to focus in low light (or no light) can sometimes prove tricky. The camera's autofocus system may struggle—and fail—to find differences in contrast, making it unreliable. Even if your camera has a focus assist function this is not always entirely accurate. In any case, it can be incredibly disappointing to open your images on your computer and discover that they are not focused properly.

There are a few techniques that can help you achieve correct focus. If the point you want to focus on isn't too far away, you can use a flashlight to illuminate it and then use autofocus or focus manually. If you use Live View, "zoom in" on the focus point and you should be able to achieve an accurate result.

An alternative method—assuming it is practical—is to place a flashlight at the focal point in the scene, facing toward the camera. Again, focusing on the light should ensure the scene or subject is focused correctly. Retrieve the flashlight prior to taking the image.

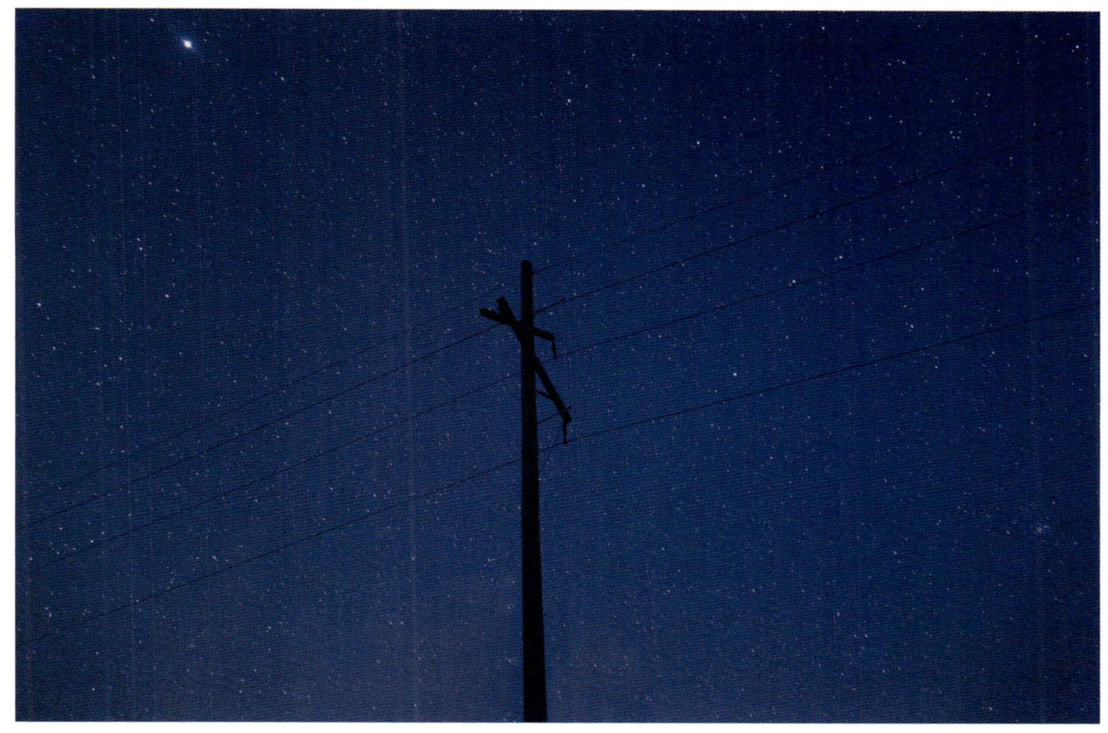

Above: The lack of light in this scene made it difficult to frame and focus. The only way to ensure correct focus on the telegraph pole was to use a bright LED torch to light up a part of it and then to focus manually using Live View mode.

Focal length: 24mm

Aperture: f/4

Shutter speed: 30 sec.

ISO: 3200

FOCUS POINTS

Most DSLRs have different focusing sensors, some of which are "cross-type." These are the most sensitive and should be selected when trying to use auto-focus in low light. Checking your camera manual will tell you where these are on your particular camera model, but on most cameras they are usually the central focusing sensors.

Tips

- If you use autofocus to focus with the aid of a flashlight, switch to manual focus once focus has been achieved. Otherwise the camera will try to reset the focus in the darkness.

- Although some lenses have an infinity focus mark on the lens barrel, this is an imprecise way to set focus. Autofocus lenses have to have some leeway to allow the system to focus slightly beyond infinity. As a last resort, setting the focus manually to this mark and then backing off slightly should yield better results, especially in conjunction with a small aperture setting.

Bulb Mode

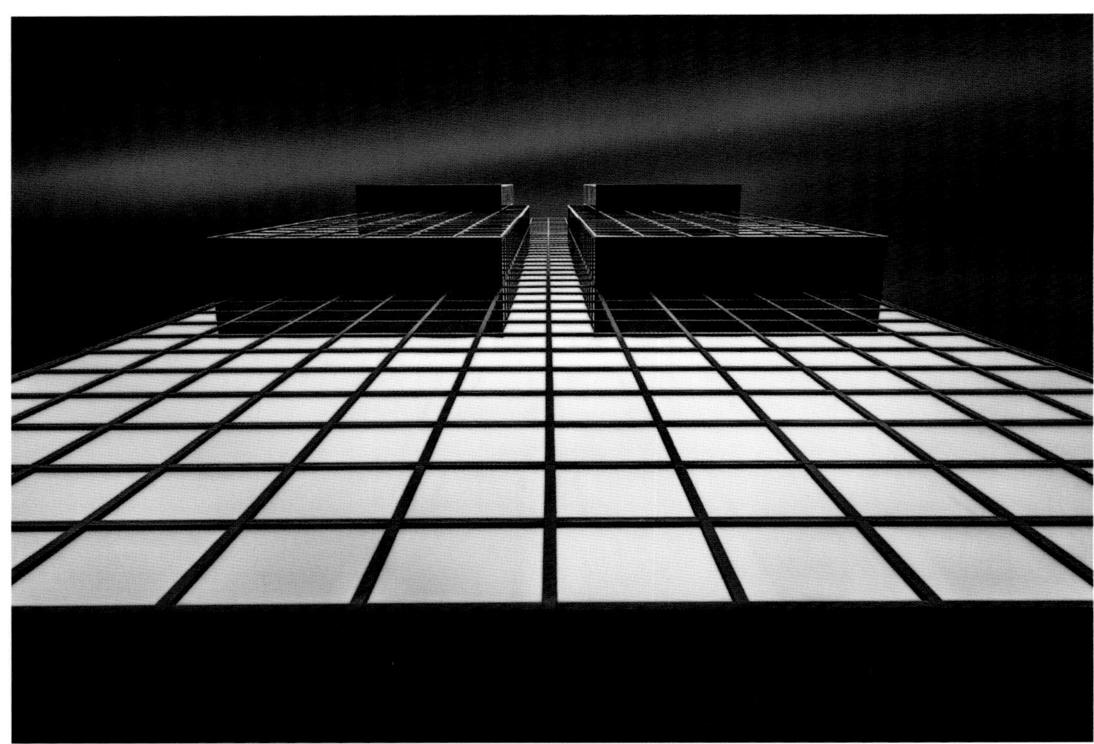

Most cameras have a wide range of shutter
speeds, which usually extends to a maximum
duration of 30 seconds. A lot of the time this might
be enough for your long exposures, but to use
shutter speeds exceeding this you will have to
switch to Bulb mode. This is usually signified with
a "B" on the mode dial or is the next shutter speed
setting after the longest automatic option.

Bulb mode allows you to set the aperture and
ISO, but it's up to you how long the shutter is
held open for. As it is not practical to hold down
the shutter-release button for extended periods
a remote release is essential: you simply open the
shutter with the remote release and lock it open
for as long as you choose. To end the exposure
you unlock the remote release to close the shutter.

Above: If you are using Bulb (or Time) mode, it is essential
that your camera is locked down on a stable tripod to
achieve the sharpest results.

Focal length: 24mm

Aperture: f/11

Shutter speed: 117 sec.

ISO: 200

DETERMINING EXPOSURE TIMES

To determine the correct exposure time for a
Bulb (or Time) exposure, shoot a test image
using a very wide aperture and high ISO. Using
this as your base exposure, the correct exposure
time can be calculated as the aperture is set to
its desired size and the ISO is reduced.

For example, let's say that your base exposure
at ISO 3200 and f/4 is 4 sec., but you want
to shoot at f/11. For every stop you reduce
the aperture by, you need to add a stop to the
exposure time (by doubling the shutter speed).
So, getting to f/11 from your base exposure
would look like this:

f/4 = 4 sec. @ ISO 3200
f/5.6 = 8 sec. @ ISO 3200
f/8 = 15 sec. @ ISO 3200
f/11 = 30 sec. @ ISO 3200

However, you also need to reduce the ISO to
an acceptable level, so more calculations have
to be done. Again, each reduction in ISO loses
a stop and that needs to be applied to the
exposure time, as follows:

ISO 3200 = 30 sec. @ f/11 (as above)
ISO 1600 = 1 min. @ f/11
ISO 800 = 2 min. @ f/11
ISO 400 = 4 min. @ f/11
ISO 200 = 8 min. @ f/11

This gives you the correct settings for your final
exposure: 8 minutes @ f/11 and ISO 200.

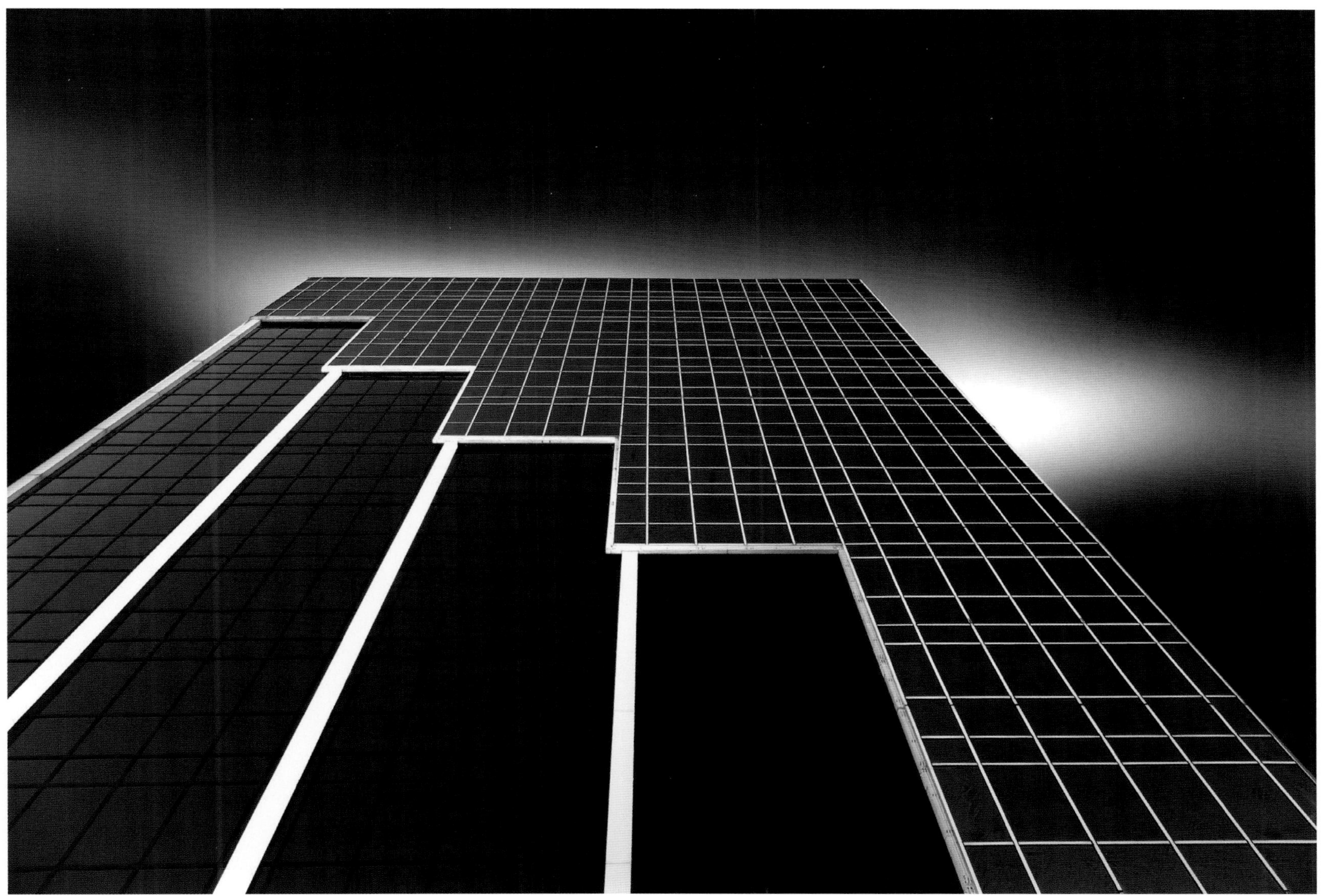

Time Mode

In addition to Bulb, some cameras have a Time ("T") mode that also allows you to make ultra-long exposures. Unlike Bulb, the exposure starts with a single press of the shutter-release button (or remote release) and ends with a second press; there is no need to lock the shutter open for the duration of the exposure. In many ways this is preferable to Bulb mode, although fewer cameras have this option.

Tip

Bulb and Time mode are only available as manual exposure options. You have to set the aperture manually, as the camera does not know how long you intend to leave the shutter open for.

Above: Extremely long exposures can drain your camera batteries quickly, so ensure that you carry spares with you.

Focal length: 24mm

Aperture: f/11

Shutter speed: 124 sec.

ISO: 100

Profile: Sylvia Wright

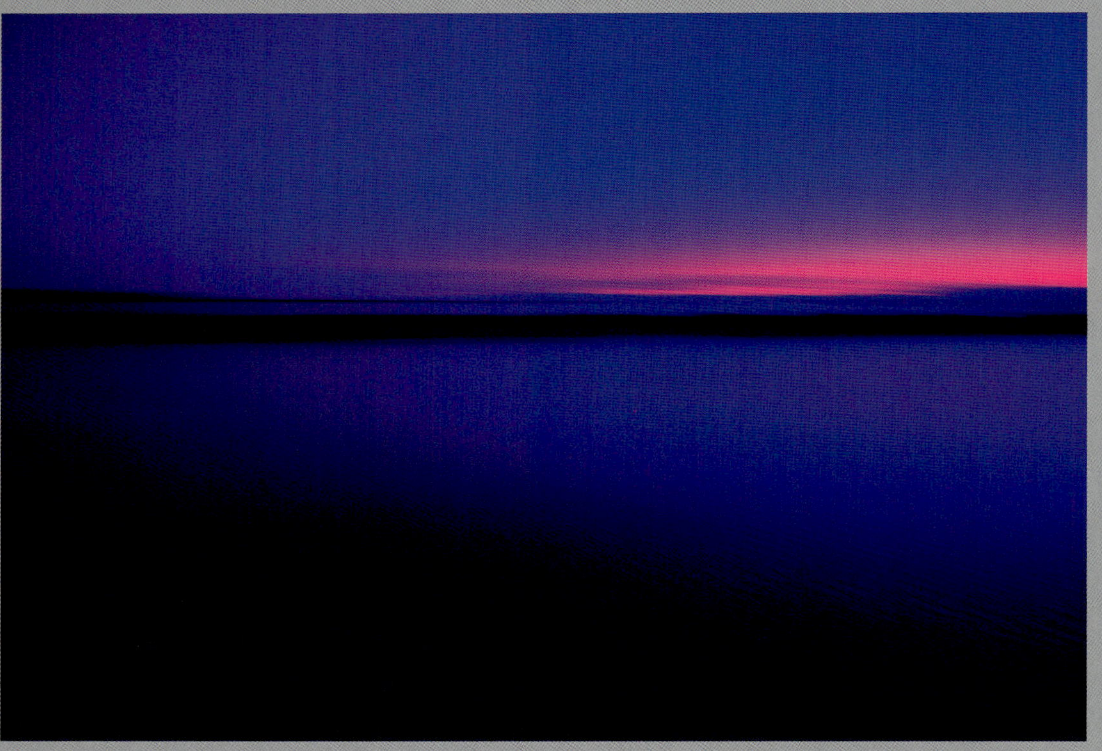

Right:
Focal length: 35mm
Aperture: f/8
Shutter speed: 1/6 sec.
ISO: 1000

Q) What is your specialty?
A) One of my favorite areas to focus on in photography is long exposure; it allows you to be mindful and focus on quality over quantity. Because each image can take a long time to produce, depending on the results you're after, there is a commitment that is required to capture beautiful long exposure images. The results are very gratifying and something that can't be taken with an iPhone or a basic camera.

Q) What drew you to your specialty and why?
A) I am attracted to the ethereal results that long exposures provide. There is a steep learning curve, but once the technical understanding is in place, you can start to focus on the artistic vision you have for the subject and envision it coming to life.

Q) What key equipment do you use regularly?
A) My go-to camera is my Nikon D850 and a sturdy tripod is essential—I carry my carbon Gitzo Exact Traveler G-Lock with me everywhere I go. My Nikon 16–35mm VR ED is an ideal lens for travel photography, including long exposure shots. I exclusively use B+W ND filters.

Q) How do you visualize and compose your images?
A) I initially approach a subject from various angles when I first arrive on the scene. Usually there is something specific that has drawn me to the subject matter so this is a natural starting point. Then I take "regular" photographs of it to see how I like the framing, then experiment with ND filters to get the look and feel I'm after. When circumstances allow, I will go back to a location on numerous occasions, often at different times of the day, to get the ideal shot.

Q) How important is post-production to your imagery?
A) While I like maintaining a natural approach with some of my images, I also really enjoy using Lightroom to "bump up" the saturation, as with my *Showy* series, some of which is shown here.

Q) What is your top tip?
A) Keep practicing! Long exposure photography is best suited to committed photographers who have time to dedicate to their art; it's impossible to make long exposures in a hurry, so it is usually a specialty pursuit.

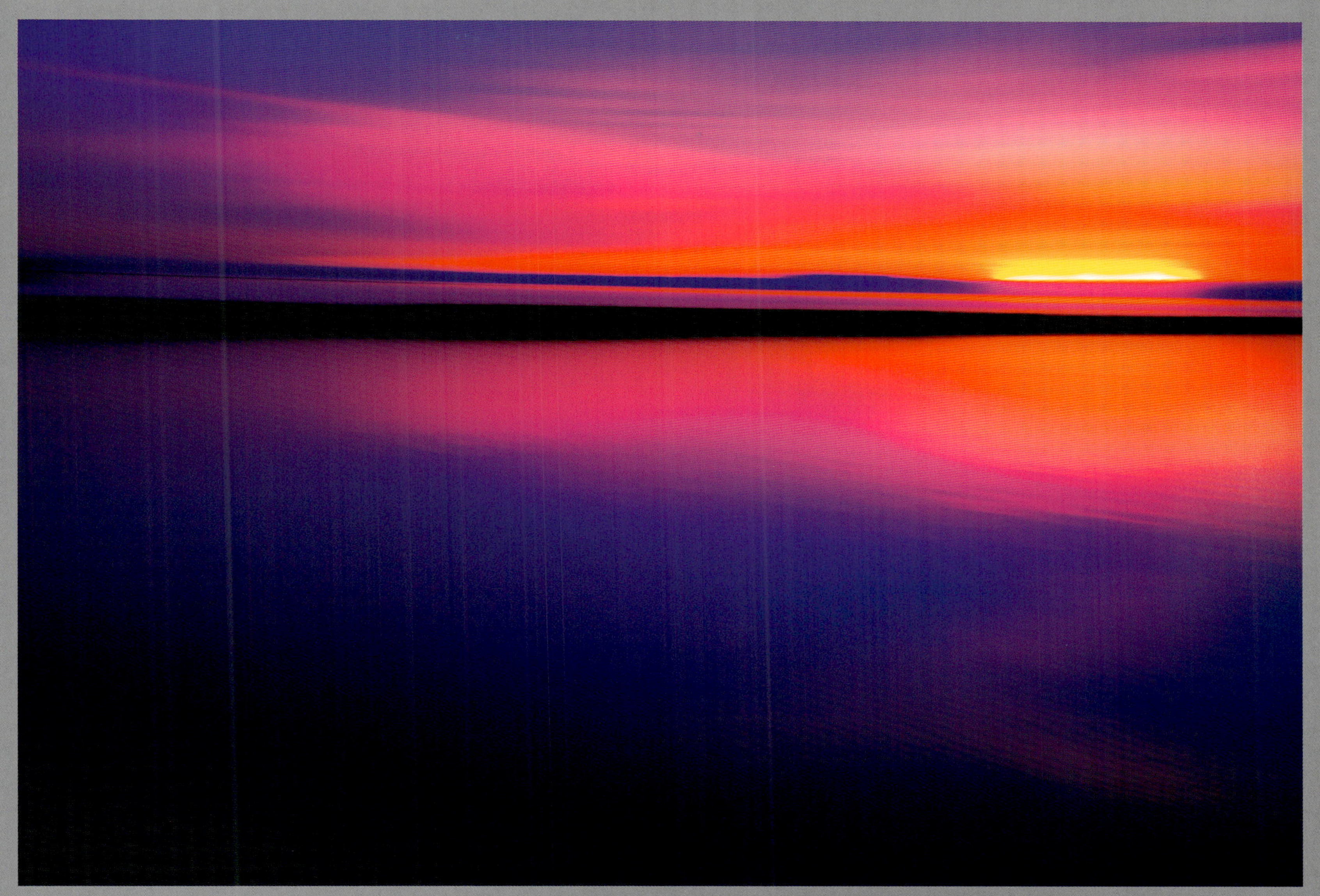

Above:

Focal length: 32mm

Aperture: f/11

Shutter speed: 4.6 sec.

ISO: 64

Chapter 4
The City at Night

The inherent beauty of a city is usually unmatched when the sun begins to set and the lights come on. A visual transformation occurs that provides photographers with endless opportunities to capture the city in a new and vibrant way. There is a heightened sense of energy that is often missing from regular daytime exposures; around each corner there seems to be a dynamic and exciting view that is so different from the daytime scene.

While composing a photograph at night is not that different from during the day, there are some extra considerations that need to be borne in mind. Although there is plenty of photogenic subject matter, there are also numerous new obstacles that can affect your results unless they are considered in advance and dealt with accordingly.

Although it may seem a little tricky to obtain good cityscape images at night, with the right technique and some simple tips it is possible to take great images on almost any night.

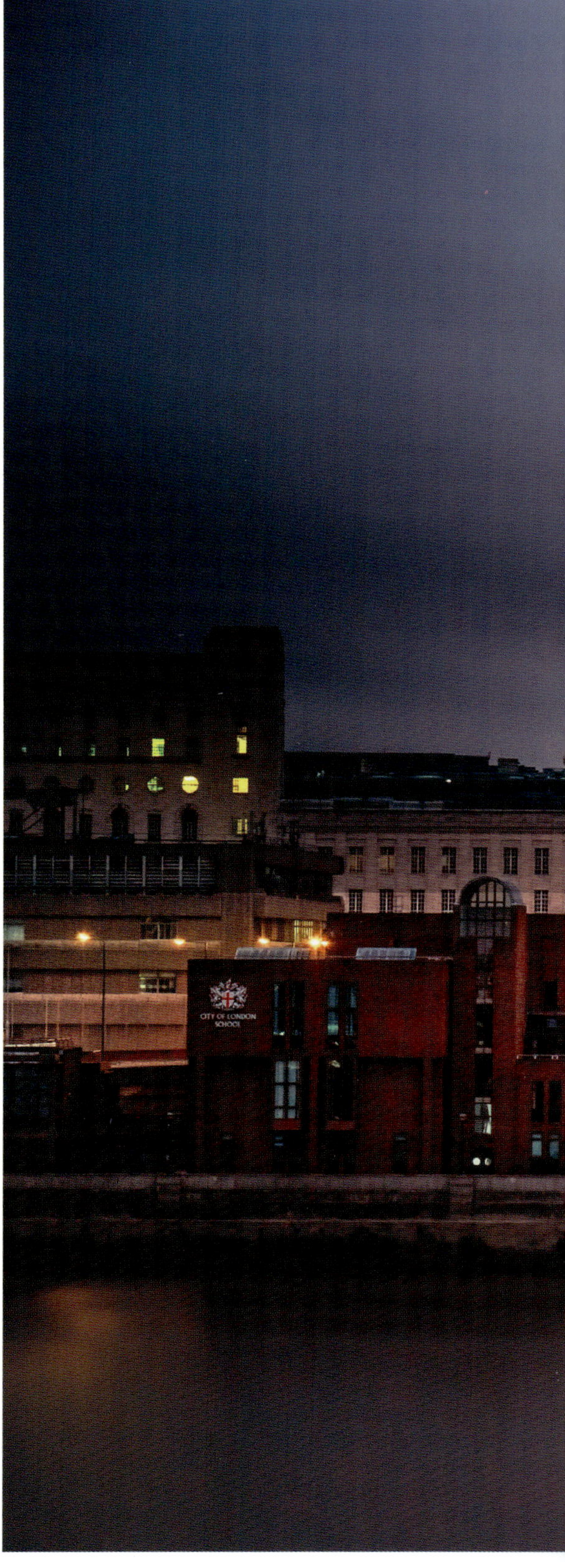

Right: Cityscapes come alive when the lights start to illuminate the scene.
Focal length: 67mm
Aperture: f/5.6
Shutter speed: 129 sec.
ISO: 400

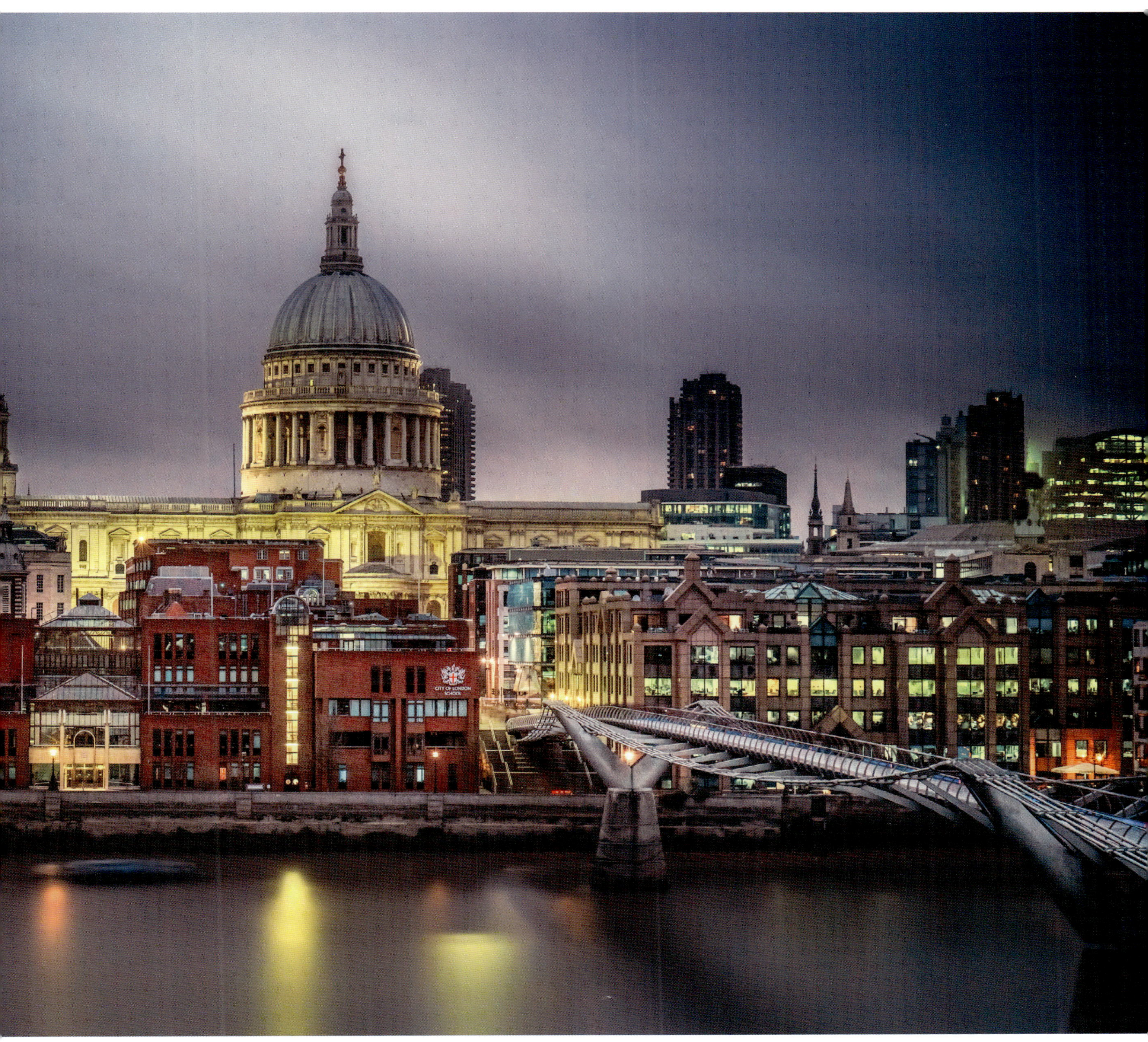

Cityscapes

Choosing when to photograph a cityscape can radically improve the outcome of the image. Too late in the night and it will be a struggle to capture the fine balance between the city lights and the detail of the view itself, while the dark sky will lack texture or color. However, shoot too soon and the early evening glow will dilute the drama of the city lights and weaken the atmosphere.

The best time to photograph is the period from just before sunset, when the sun is dipping down and the colors illuminate the sky, to just after sunset, when the sky turns a deep blue. This is known as the "blue hour" and is the optimum time to photograph most cityscapes. There will still be plenty of light in the sky, so there should be sufficient ambient light to record detail in the whole scene, but the city lights will still sparkle, contrasting with the blue sky.

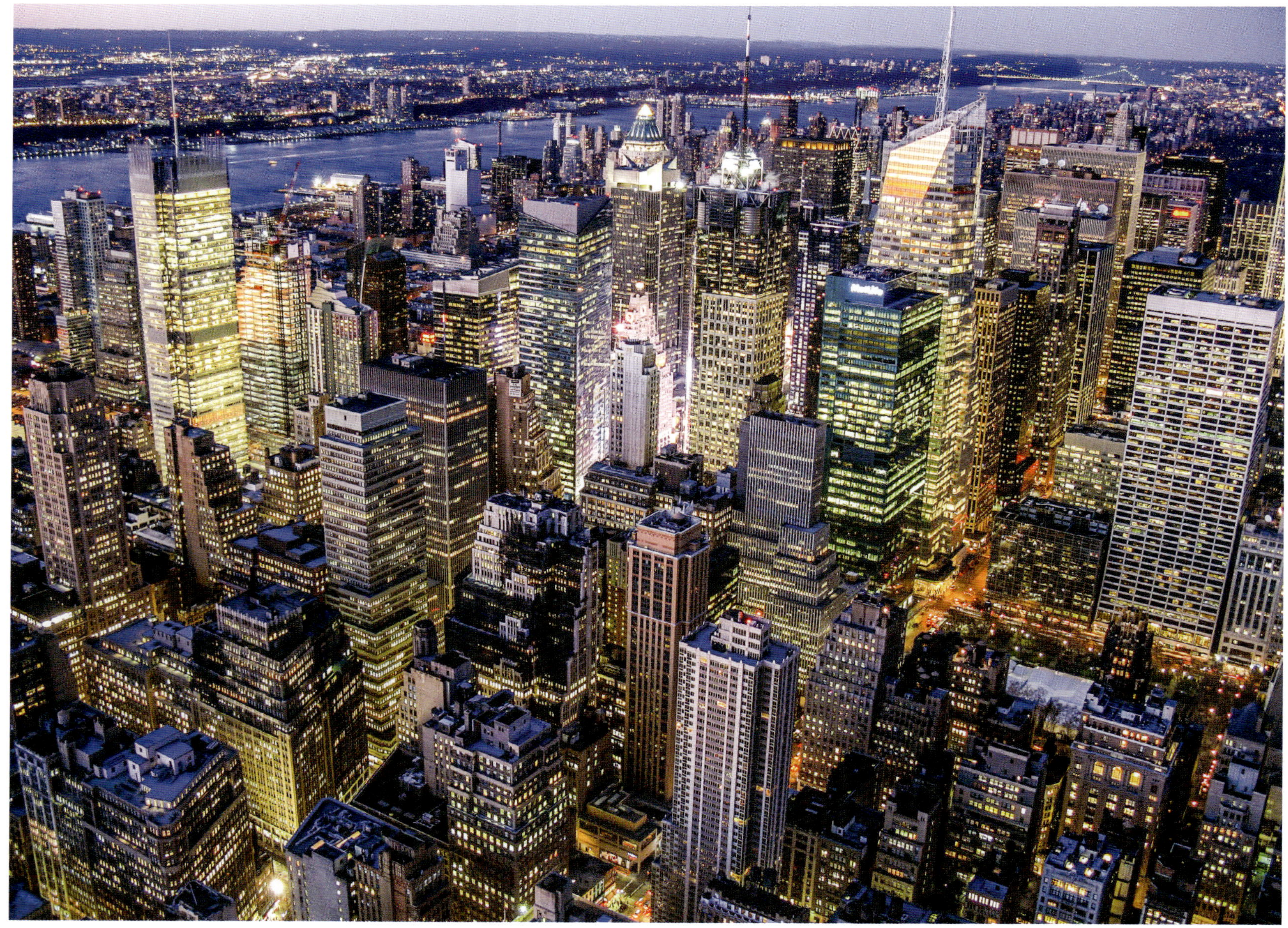

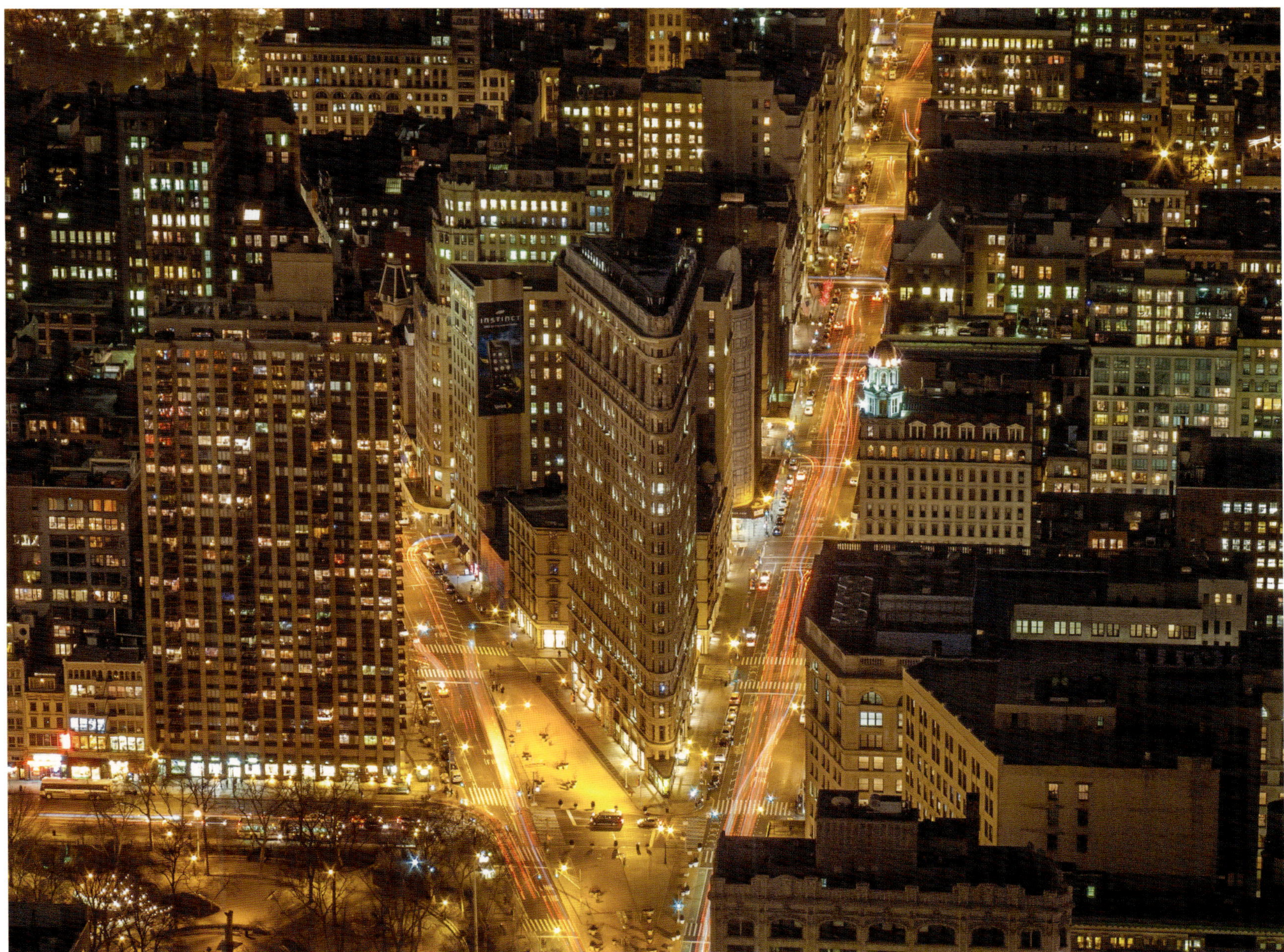

Left: The density of the closely packed buildings in Manhattan provides an incredible view when the sun sets. The mass of lights through Midtown creates an almost dreamlike vision of the city.

Focal length: 16mm

Aperture: f/2.8

Shutter speed: 3 sec.

ISO: 100

Above: The long exposures needed to capture the city at night can result in car light trails being recorded as they speed down the streets. These can often be utilized compositionally as leading lines to draw the viewer's eye into the image.

Focal length: 28mm

Aperture: f/8

Shutter speed: 13 sec.

ISO: 200

Tip

When shooting long exposures of the city at night, it is important that the camera is locked down on a tripod. This will not only help reduce camera shake, but allow a lower ISO to be used as well.

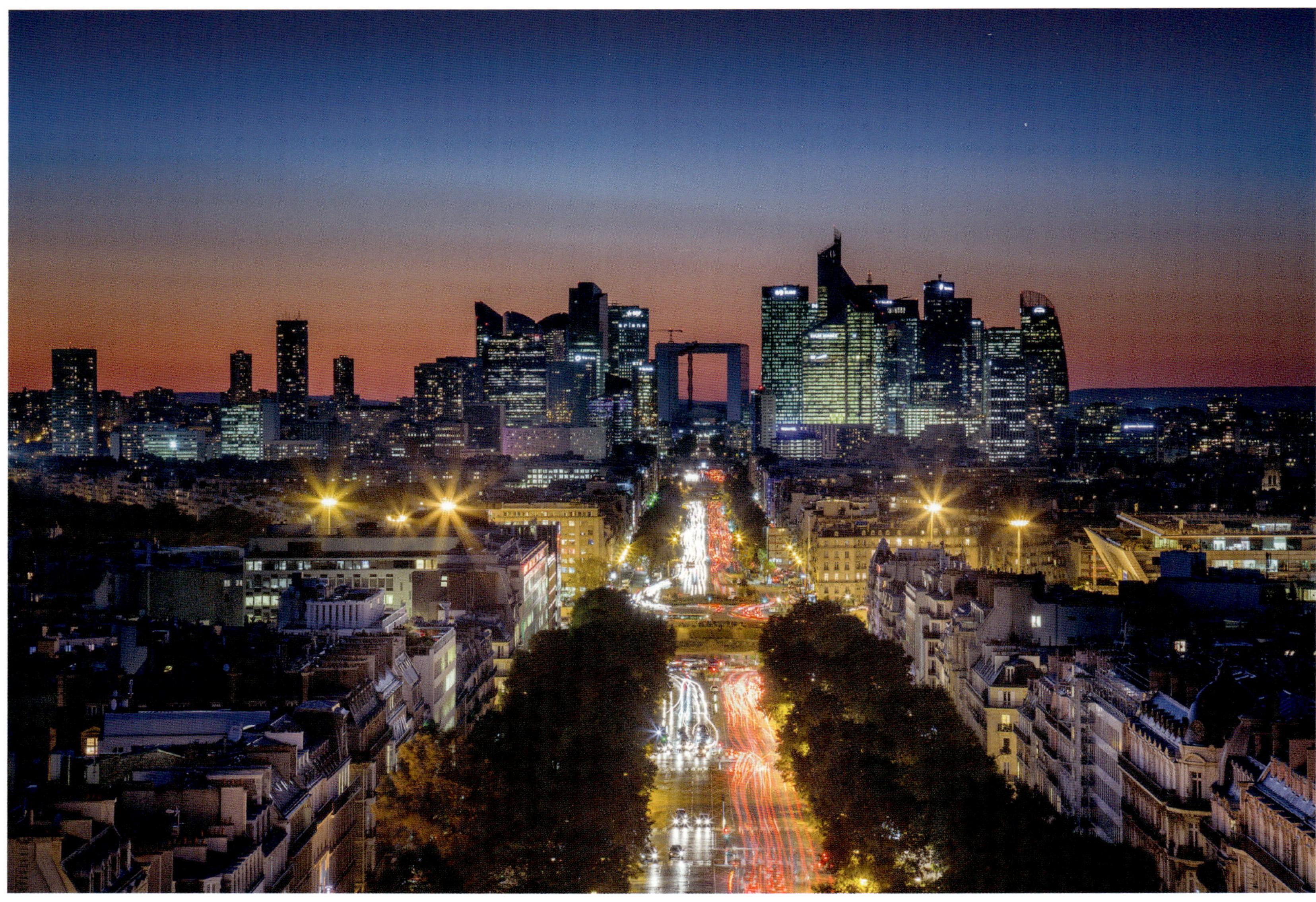

However, sometimes the city lights do not come on fully until much later, when the sky is dark and featureless. Where this is the case, simply leave the camera in position and take a subsequent image when the sky is darker, exposing for the lights themselves. You can then combine the shots in postproduction. It is vital that the camera is not moved between exposures, though, so it will need to be locked down on a stable tripod. You can read how to stack and combine these images on page 164–167.

Composition is an important consideration in all photography and it is no different when shooting cityscapes. It is all too easy to be overwhelmed as the light changes and the city comes "alive," ignoring basic compositional rules in the process.

To avoid this, arrive before sunset and frame your shot in advance. This will allow you to concentrate on the composition, rather than rushing to capture an image quickly as the light changes. Depending on your intended subject, pay particular attention to any stray light that might enter from a point outside of the frame and affect the final composition.

Above: The best time to capture the essence of the city at night is just after the sun sets—there is still sufficient light in the night sky to show color and detail, but it is dark enough to emphasize the colors of the lights.

Focal length: 15mm

Aperture: f/18

Shutter speed: 6 sec.

ISO: 200

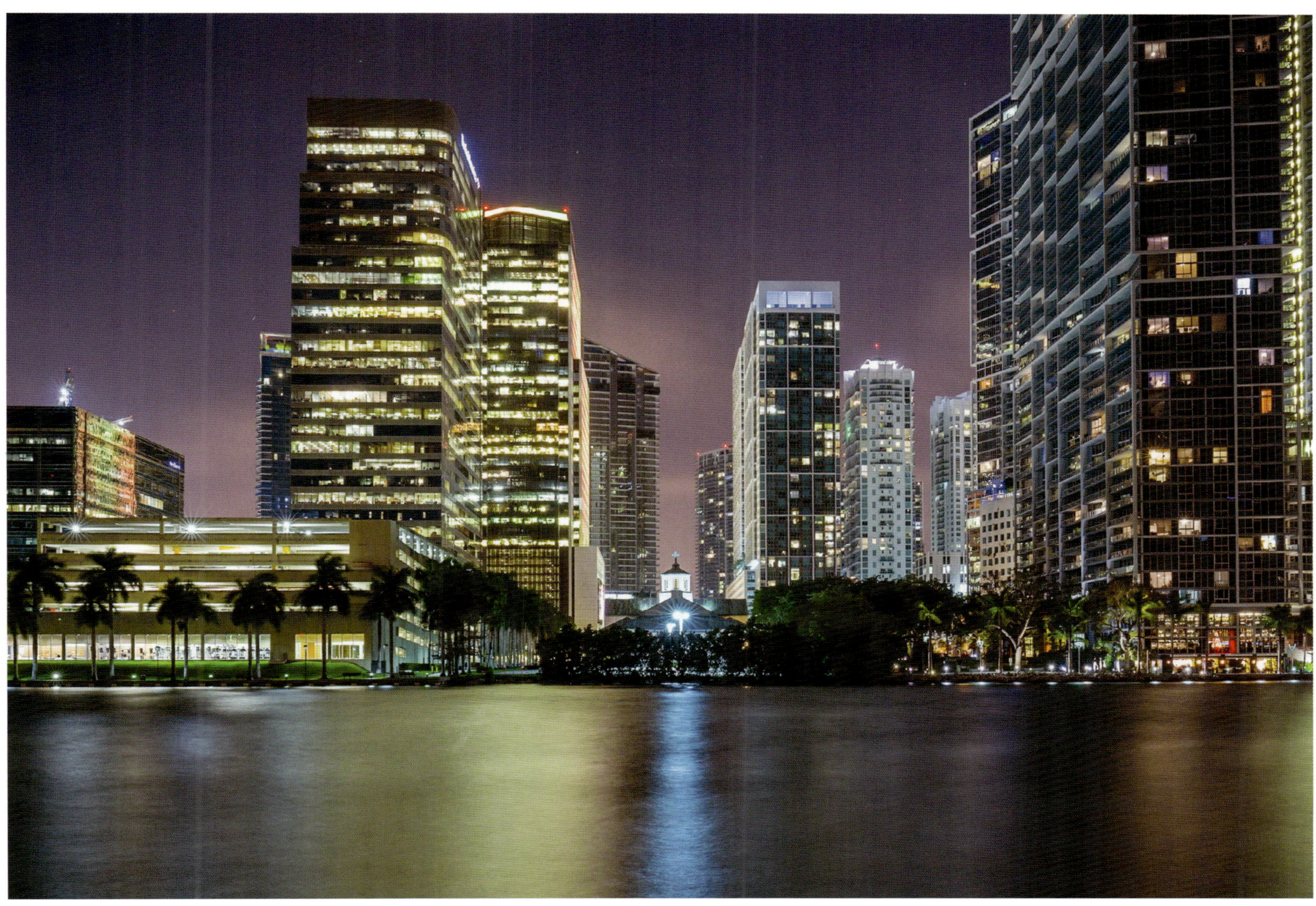

Tip

When taking images at night it is very easy to
overexpose some of the highlights: the dynamic
range of night scenes can be very wide and tricky
for the camera to capture correctly in one single
image. Check the histogram and if your camera
has a highlight warning function, it is useful to
engage and check this as well. It can also be a
good idea to bracket your images so that highlight
and shadow detail can be recovered from the
alternative images.

Street Scenes

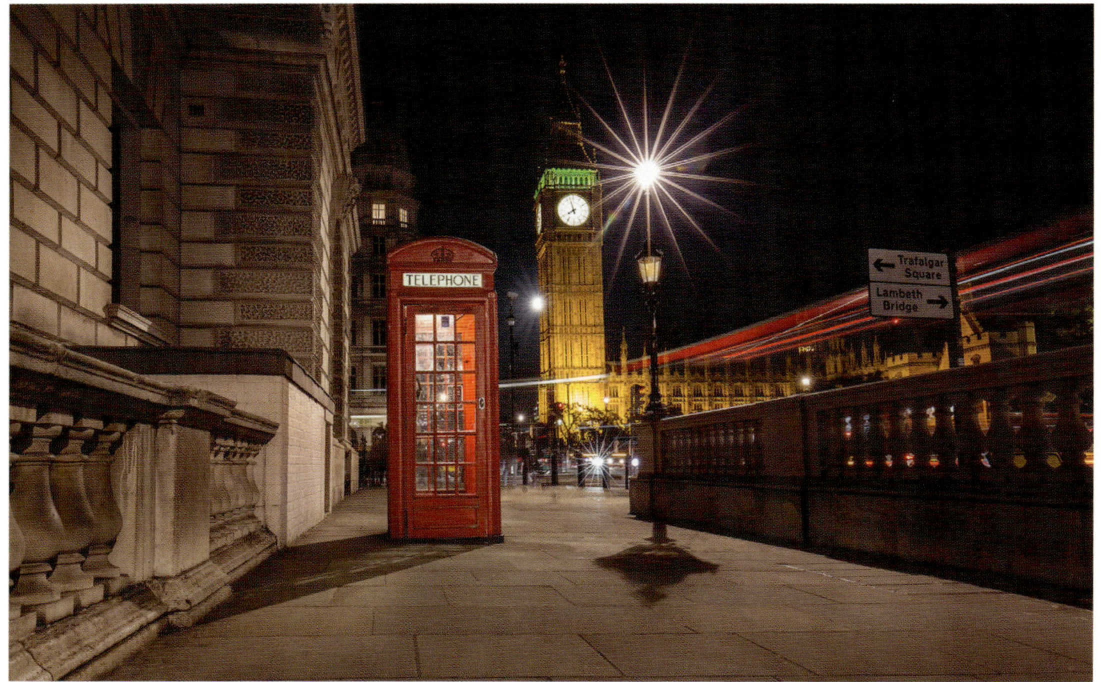

Intimate views of the city can produce powerful images when taken at night. The architecture, streets, and people are lit by a variety of light sources such as traffic, shop displays, and street lighting, and this provides unique opportunities. While a high ISO and wide aperture can help gather more light, for longer exposure work it is vital that the camera remains stationary.

That said, the use of creative blurs and movement can add an additional form of dynamism and help convey the sense of motion and energy of city life. Consider the interplay between the stationary elements, such as buildings that will ground the scene, and transient parts, such as the flow of people or traffic and how they will work together to make a compelling image.

The usual rules of composition also apply, so foreground interest and lines and patterns can be appealing. Looking for the right light in the city—even at night—is vital, as the interplay of contrast and light and shadows will lead to more compelling images. Again, it is important to consider your framing carefully, as the longer shutter times may lead to additional elements entering and leaving the scene, such as people or vehicles.

Above left: Capturing the intimacy of the city at night from street level can provide unique views.

Focal length: 24mm

Aperture: f/20

Shutter speed: 8 sec.

ISO: 400

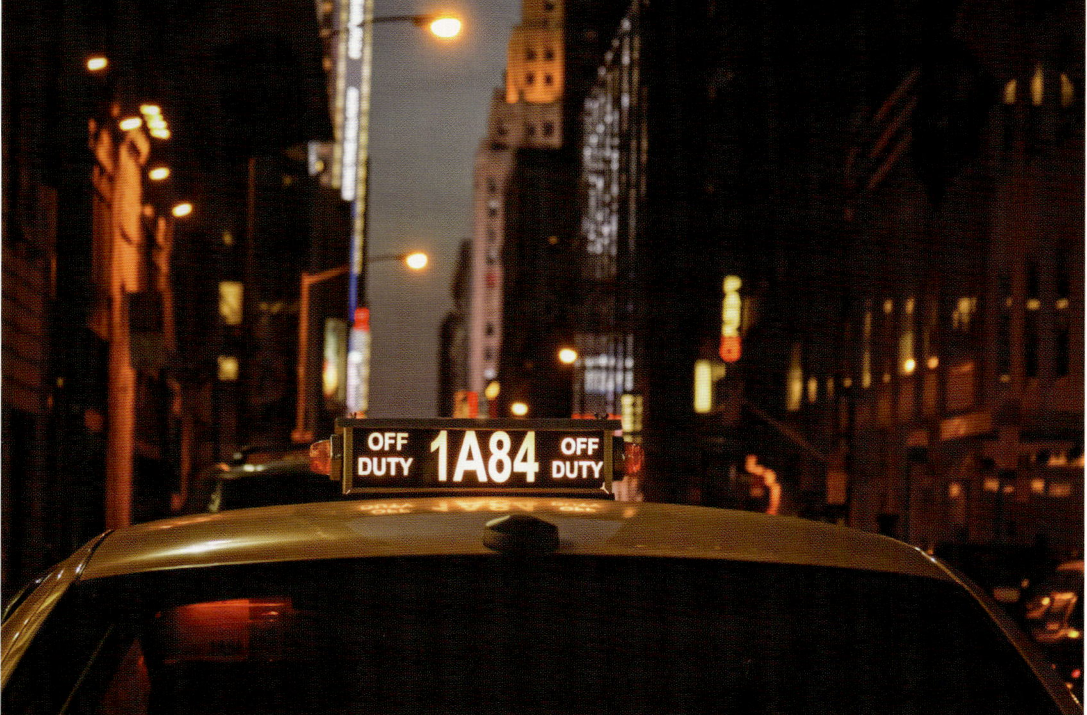

Left: The warmth of streetlights can make an everyday scene look more appealing visually, as this image of a waiting taxi in New York City shows.

Focal length: 85mm

Aperture: f/5.6

Shutter speed: 5 sec.

ISO: 800

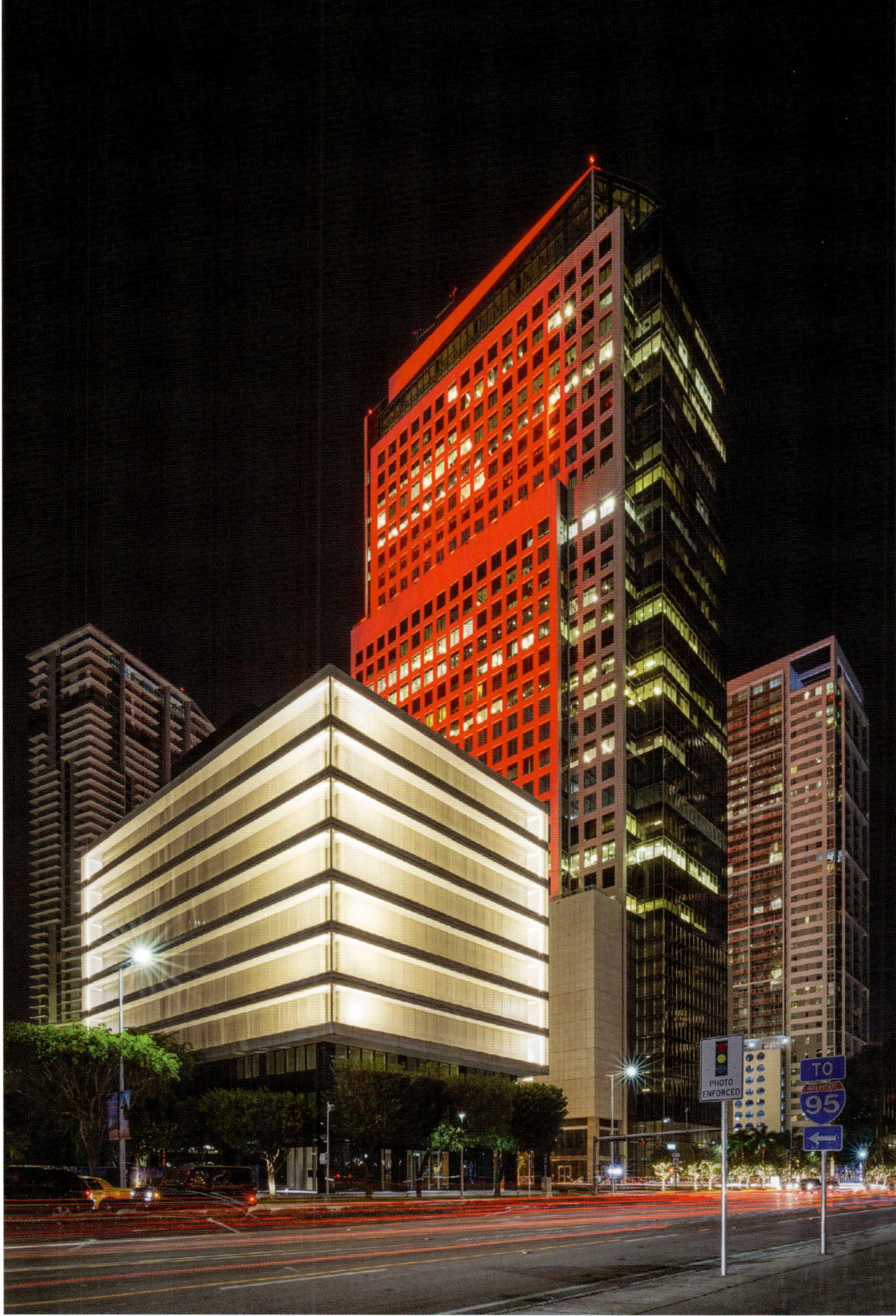

Right: Choosing a street corner at night where cars will travel past will provide additional lights and an added dynamic to your street images. The dramatic lighting on this Miami building adds an extra dimension.

Focal length: 16mm

Aperture: f/20

Shutter speed: 25 sec.

ISO: 100

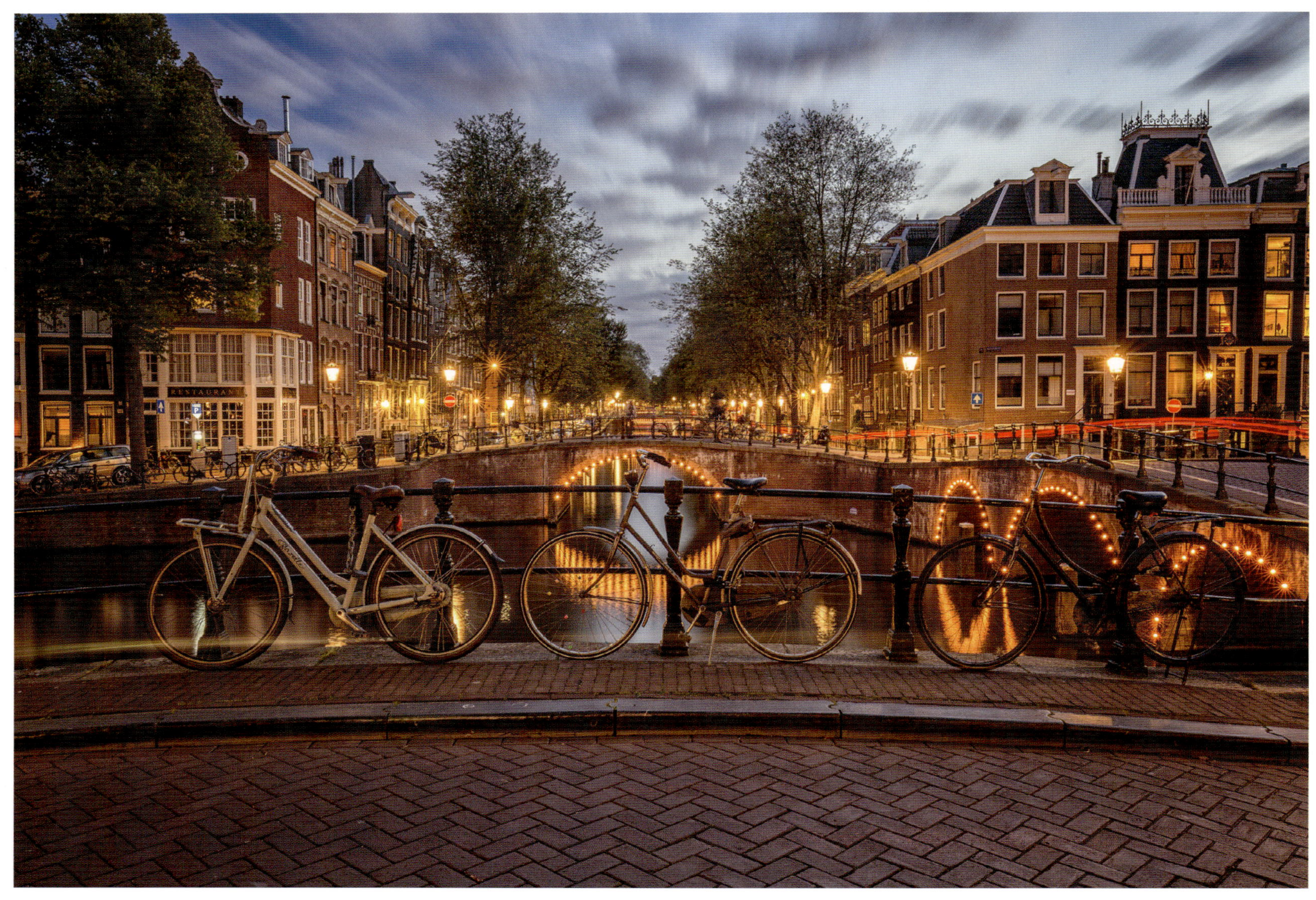

Above: Balancing the natural illumination from the sky and ambient artificial light can allow a lot of detail to be recorded in a nighttime cityscape.

Focal length: 20mm

Aperture: f/14

Shutter speed: 63 sec.

ISO: 200

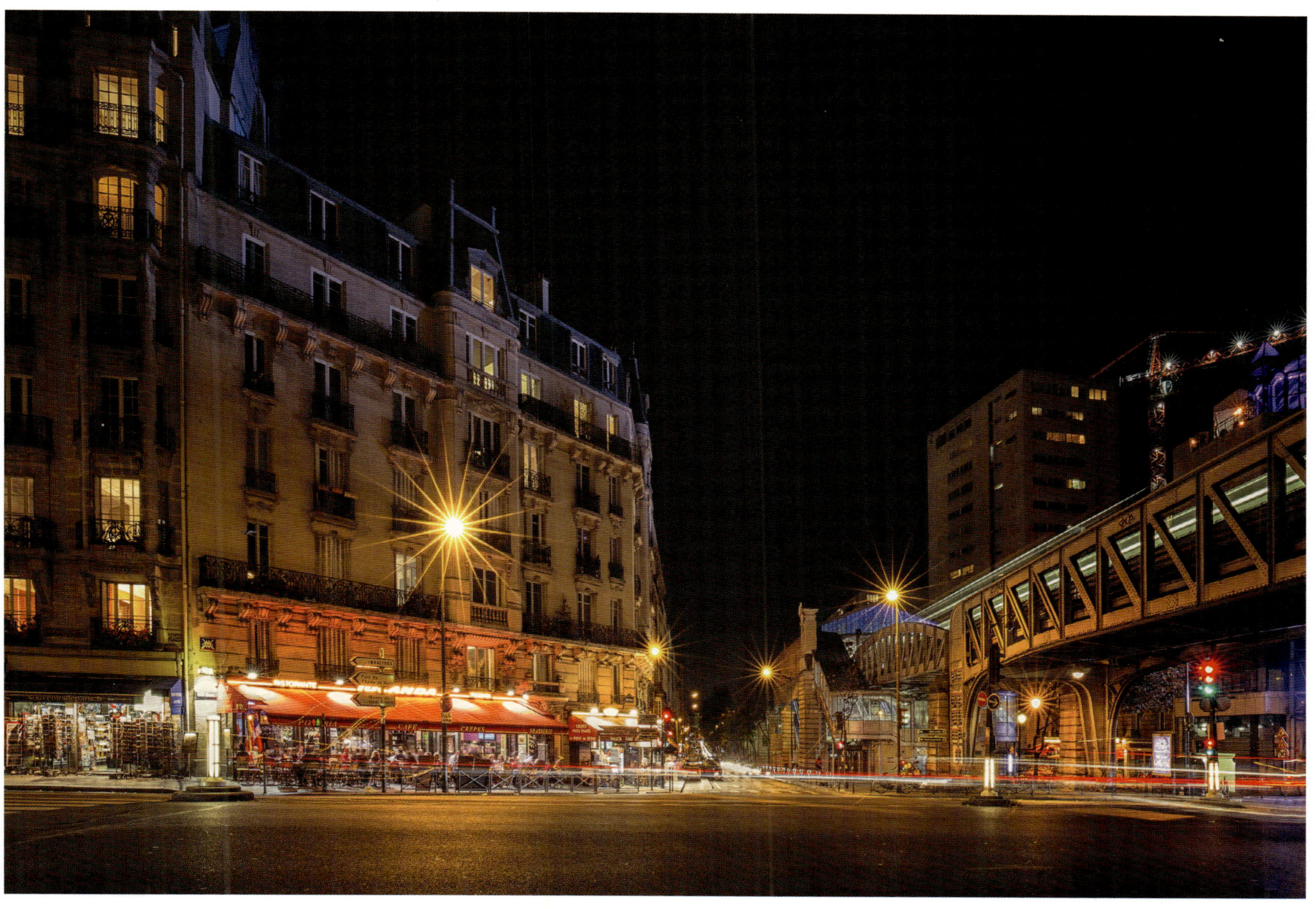

Above: The darker sky in this image of a street corner in Paris emphasizes the colors of the various artificial light sources and really helps them to "pop."

Focal length: 27mm

Aperture: f/18

Shutter speed: 15 sec.

ISO: 200

Neon Lights

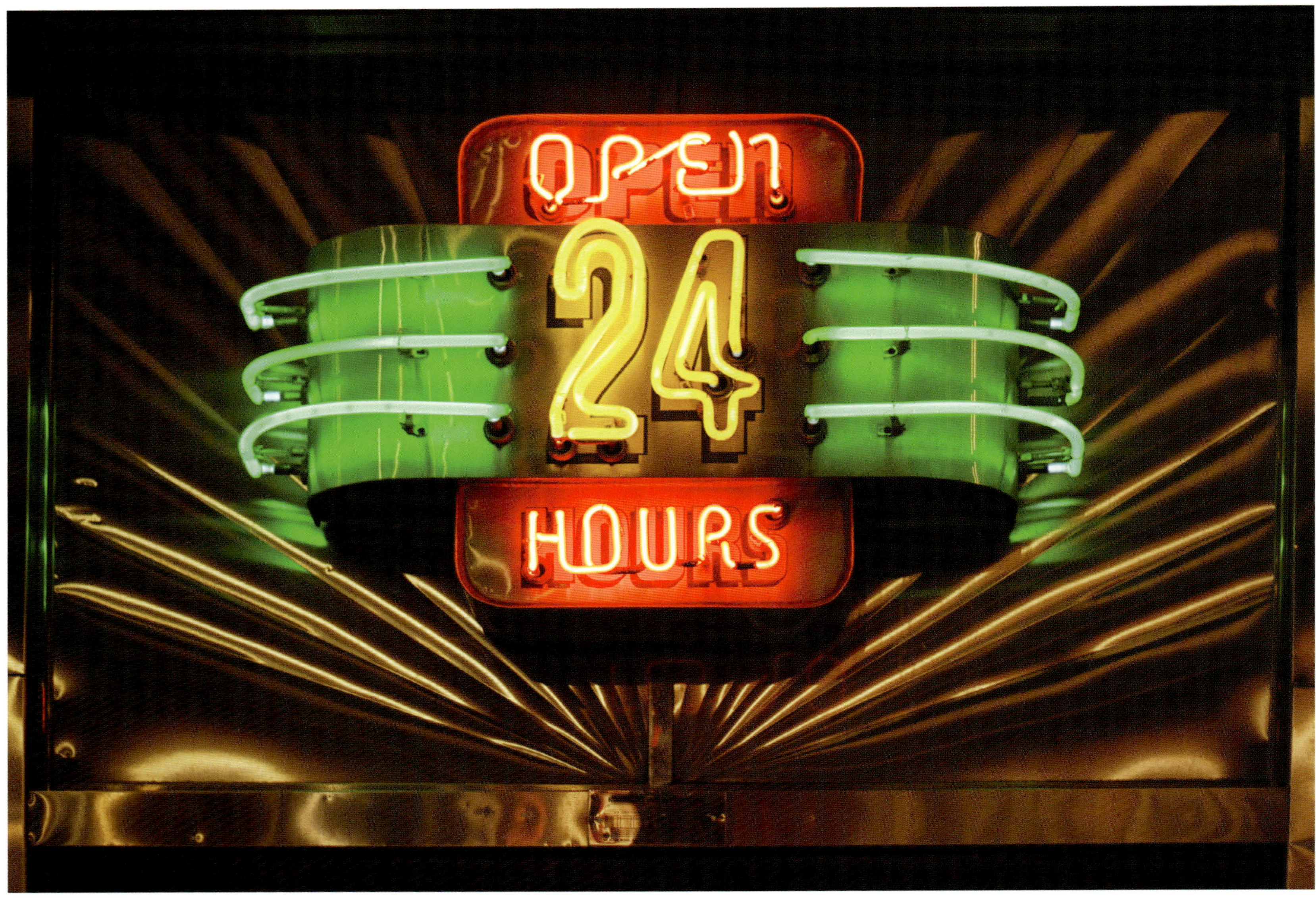

Neon lights have been popular for many decades, and are still commonly used for advertising purposes. At night, these signs draw people's attention due to the intensity of the bright colorful light, but they can prove tricky to photograph. It is often a choice between capturing the brightly lit sign and underexposing the rest of the scene, or exposing the wider scene correctly and overexposing the vibrant neon. In this instance, bracketing your exposures can prove very useful, as it will give you highlight and shadow detail that can be blended manually during postproduction or combined as a High Dynamic Range (HDR) image.

A tripod will naturally help keep the camera stable, enable the use of a lower ISO, and—if you are shooting a bracketed sequence of exposures—

Above: Capturing the full array of the colors of neon lights and correctly exposing for the wider scene can often prove difficult. Sometimes it can make a more compelling image to zoom in on the neon sign itself.

Focal length: 50mm

Aperture: f/5.6

Shutter speed: 1 sec.

ISO: 200

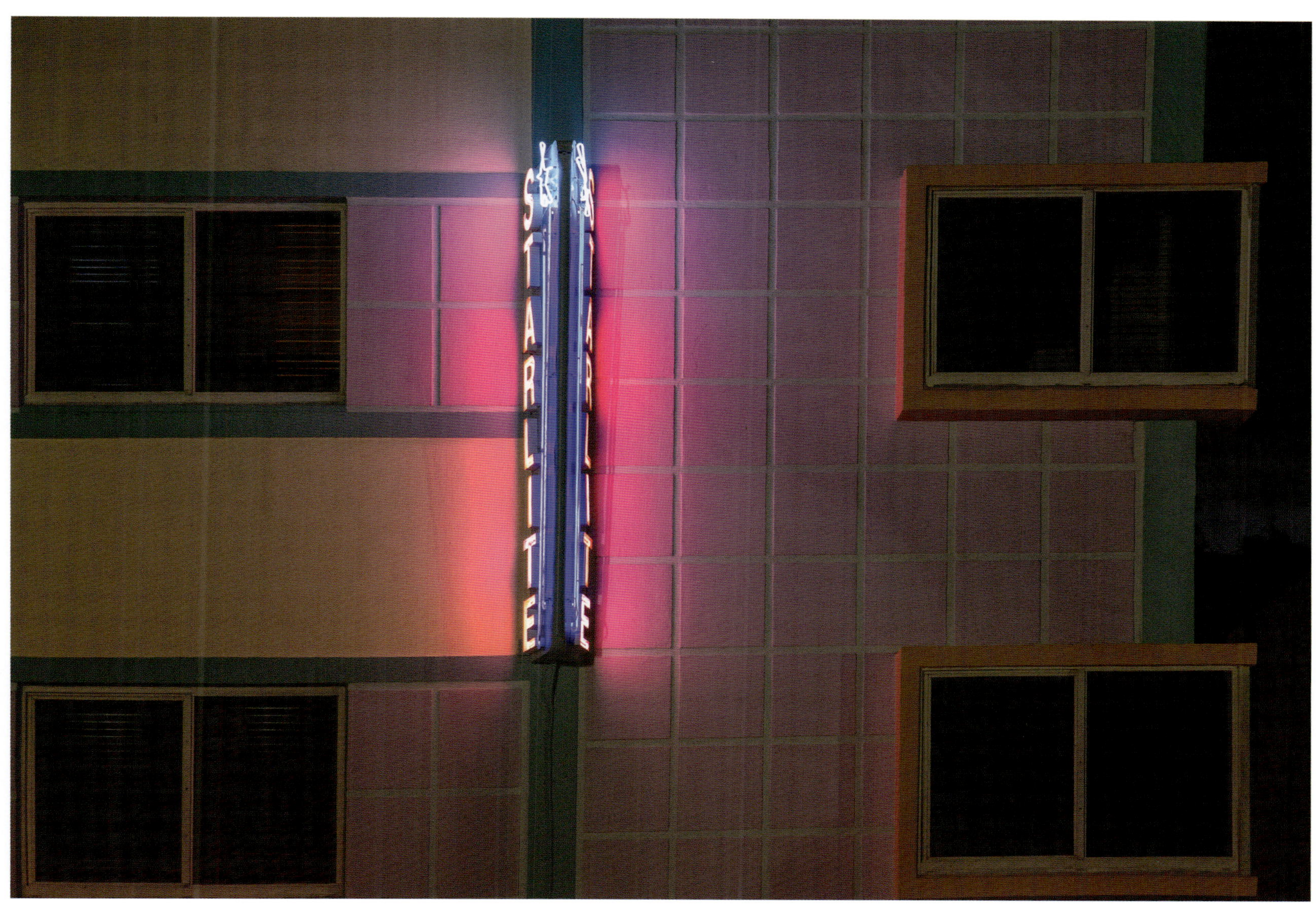

ensure that your frames are all aligned. The shutter speed will naturally depend on the scene, but start with an aperture of around f/8 or f/11 when shooting a neon sign face on; if the sign is large or at an angle, a smaller aperture may be needed, which will inevitably affect the shutter speed.

As the bright neon is often the subject of the image and the light source, the camera meter may get confused and try to underexpose. Check the histogram and consider amending the shutter speed or applying exposure compensation. Again, it is very useful to shoot Raw files, so the white balance can be fine tuned in postproduction.

Above: Photographing this neon sign indirectly allowed its pink glow to be captured on the walls of this building.

Focal length: 105mm

Aperture: f/5.6

Shutter speed: 3 sec.

ISO: 400

Light Trails

Towns and cities all have one thing in common; traffic. Using longer exposure times, the vivid colors of the vehicle lights can be recorded as light trails, adding an extra dynamic layer to an otherwise static image. The seemingly endless source of lights can also provide an additional compositional element, such as leading lines that can be used to help guide the viewer into and through your image.

The best time to photograph light trails is right after sunset, when there is still a little light left in the sky and any street lighting has just come on. This allows extra detail in the surrounding areas to be captured, providing a more balanced image.

As each scene will have different exposure requirements, there are no universal settings that can be applied to all, but a shutter speed of around 5 sec. at f/11 (at ISO 100) will provide you with a good starting point. If the trails are too dark, increase the shutter speed or increase the aperture slightly, but bear in mind that increasing the aperture will also affect the depth of field of the image. Keep the ISO as low as possible.

As with all long exposure photography it is vital that the camera remains still, preferably locked down on a tripod. Using your camera's Bulb mode with a remote release will allow precise control of the shutter and the ability to time the exposure with the flow of traffic. Watch for changing traffic signals or a steady flow of cars as a cue for when to trigger the shutter.

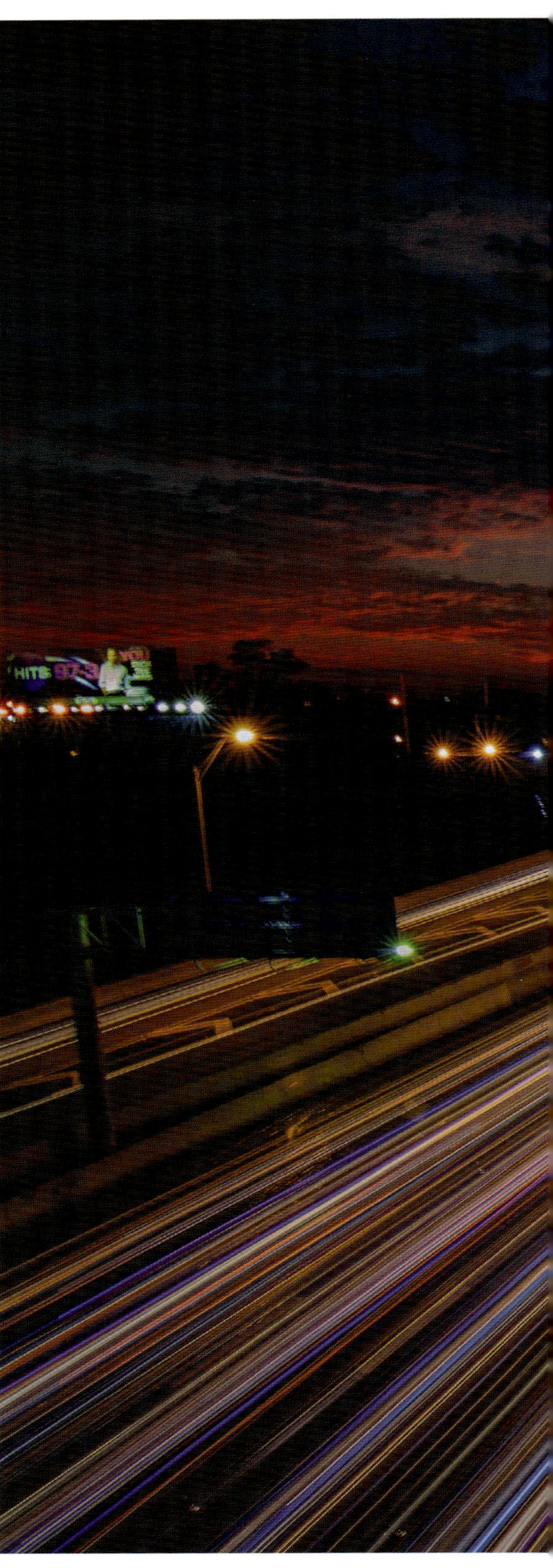

Tips

- As with most night photography involving high contrast and bright lights, lens flare can be an issue. Use a lens hood to help reduce the risk of this happening.

- Remove all filters from your lenses to prevent light reflecting back into the camera creating unnecessary flare.

- To exaggerate the effect of the light trails, consider taking a number of images at the same exposure, without moving the camera. These images can be stacked during post-production to reveal the trails and boost their spread and brightness in the final image.

- If you want flowing, solid trails you need to start your exposure before the vehicle enters the frame.

- Slow-moving vehicles will require longer shutter speeds to create flowing trails.

SAFETY

Extra care needs to be taken when you are photographing moving traffic at night. If you are close to the traffic make sure you are in a safe, protected position and can be seen clearly by drivers.

Right: Looking down on a road from above can lead to some striking compositions, while putting you in a safe shooting position, away from the traffic. A small aperture was used here to ensure that the image had adequate depth of field.

Focal length: 16mm

Aperture: f/22

Shutter speed: 25 sec.

ISO: 100

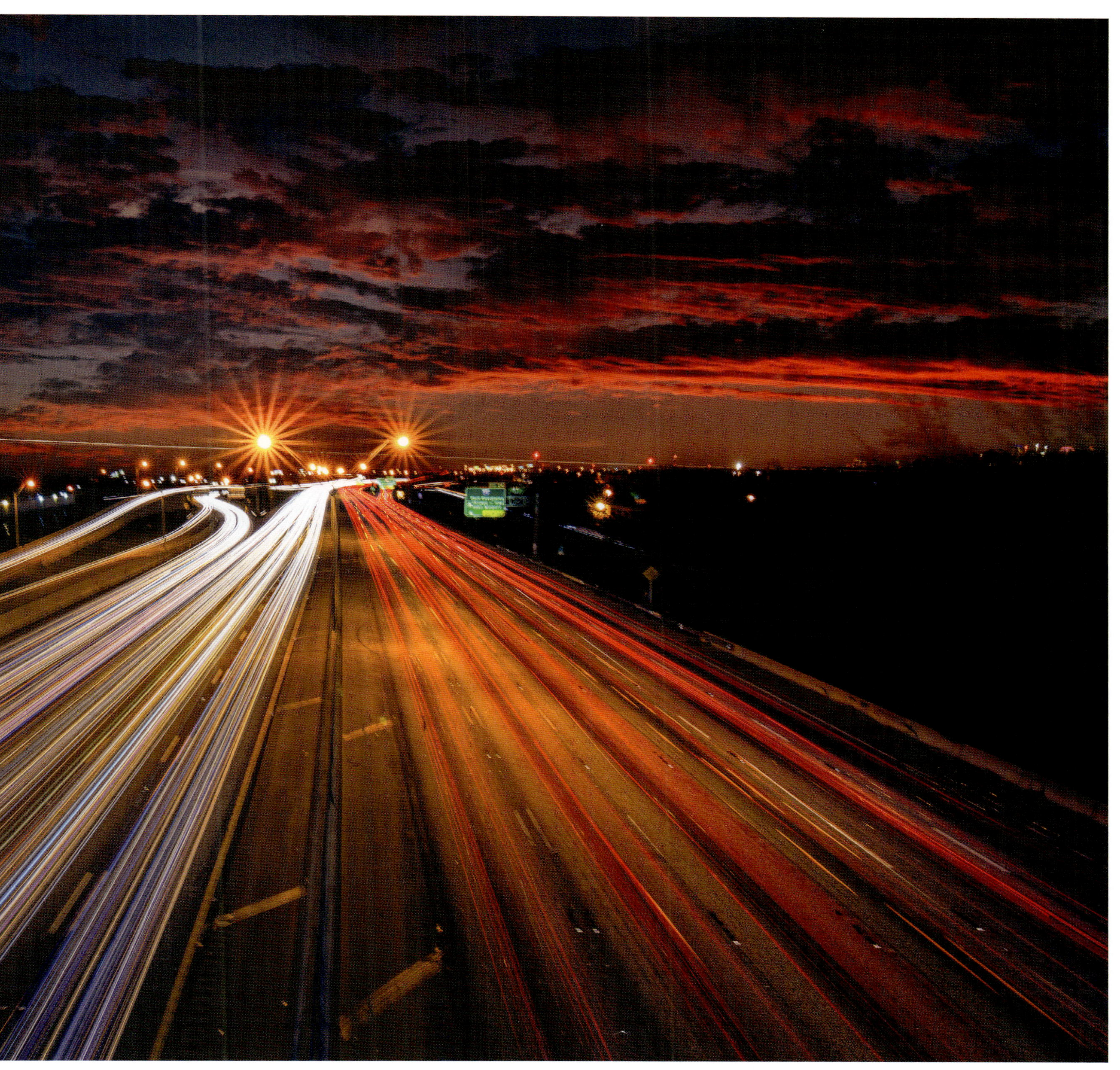

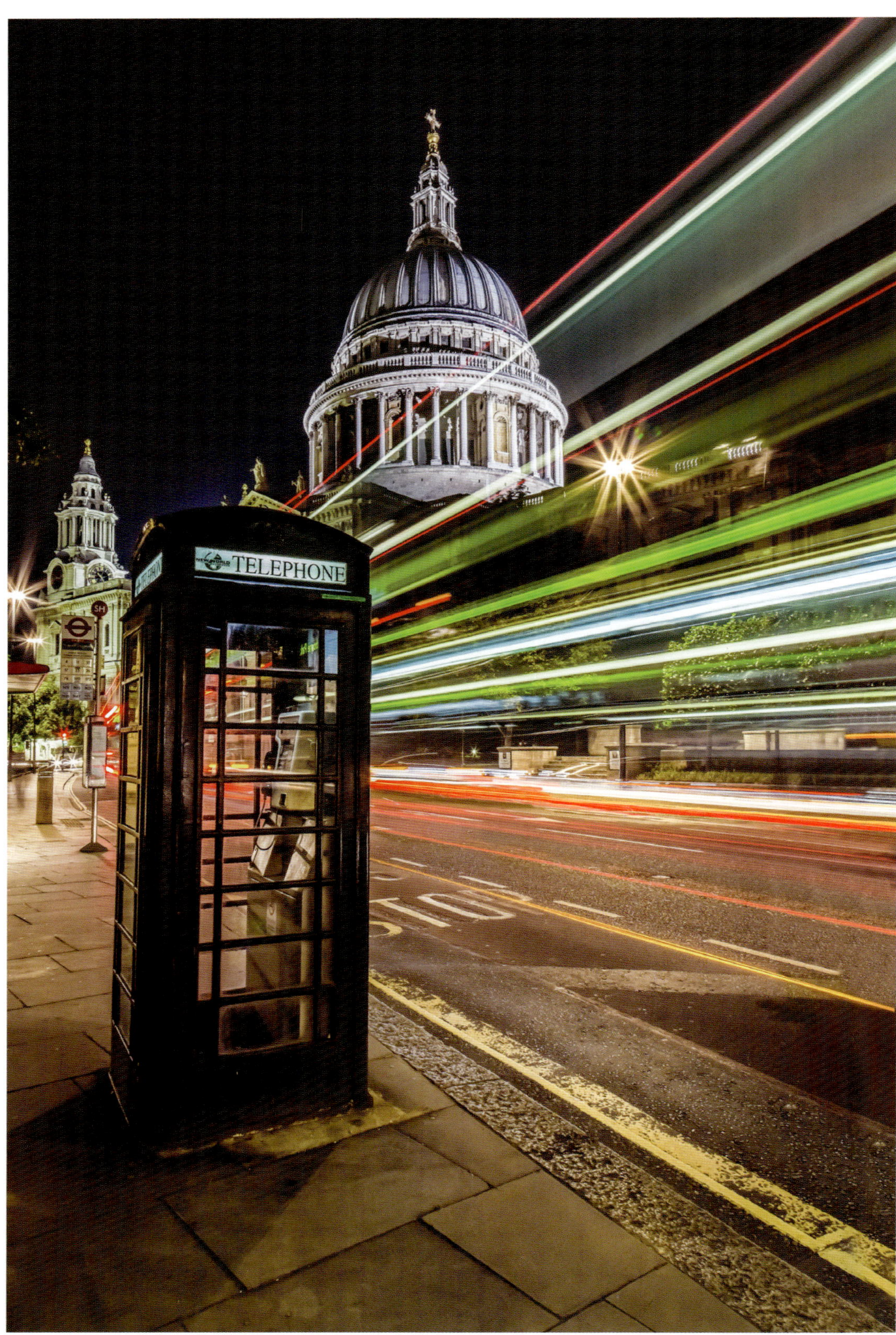

Left: The light trails in this image lead the viewer toward an iconic telephone box and cathedral in London. Buses, coaches, and other tall vehicles provided additional levels of trails in the image.

Focal length: 24mm

Aperture: f/20

Shutter speed: 20 sec.

ISO: 100

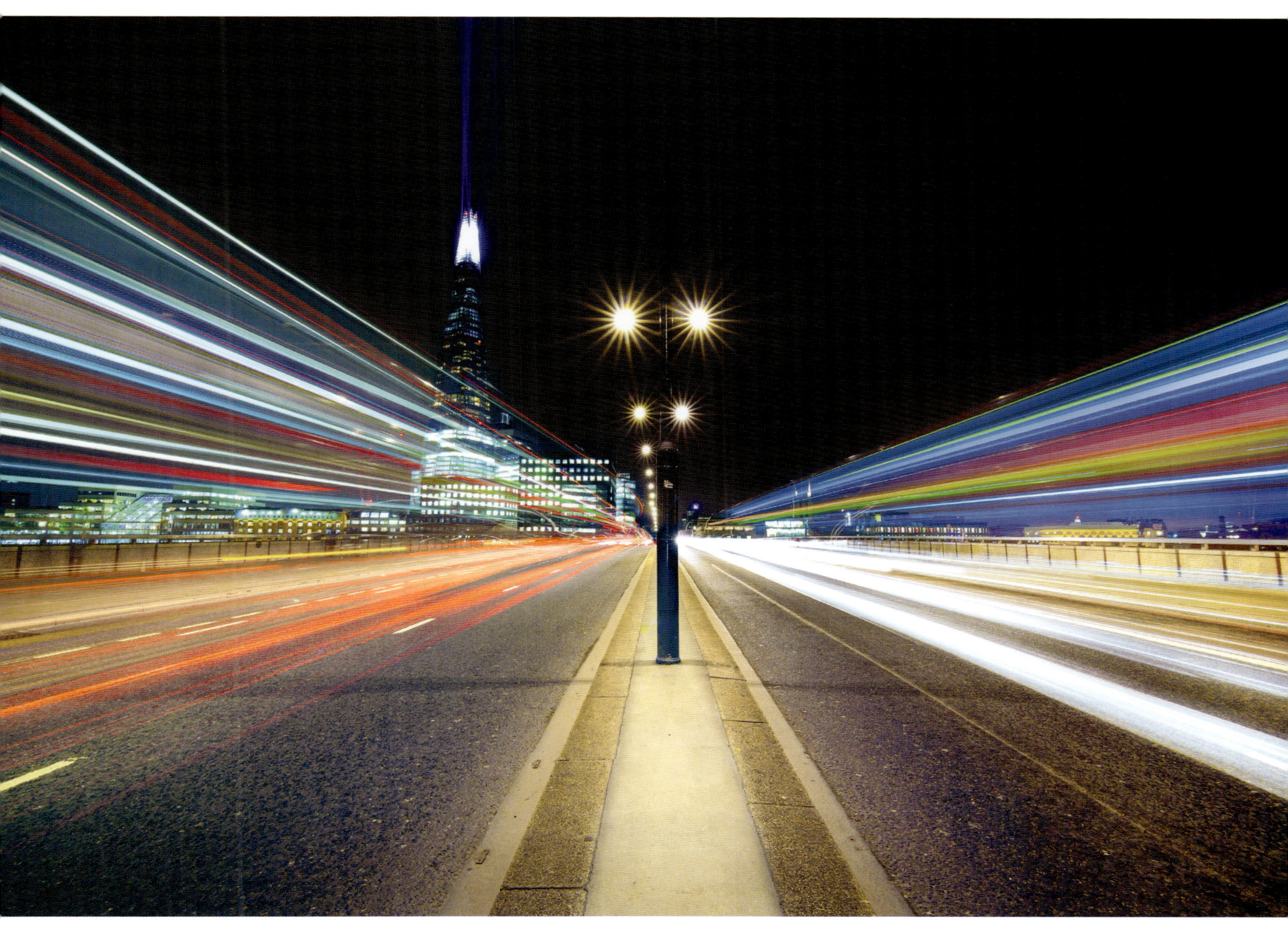

Above: Busy city roads have a multitude of cars, which makes for great light trail imagery. The pedestrian island in the center of this road provided the ideal shooting angle as well as protection. The light beams from the top of the skyscraper add an additional source of light trails.

Focal length: 16mm

Aperture: f/10

Shutter speed: 13 sec.

ISO: 100

Lens Flare

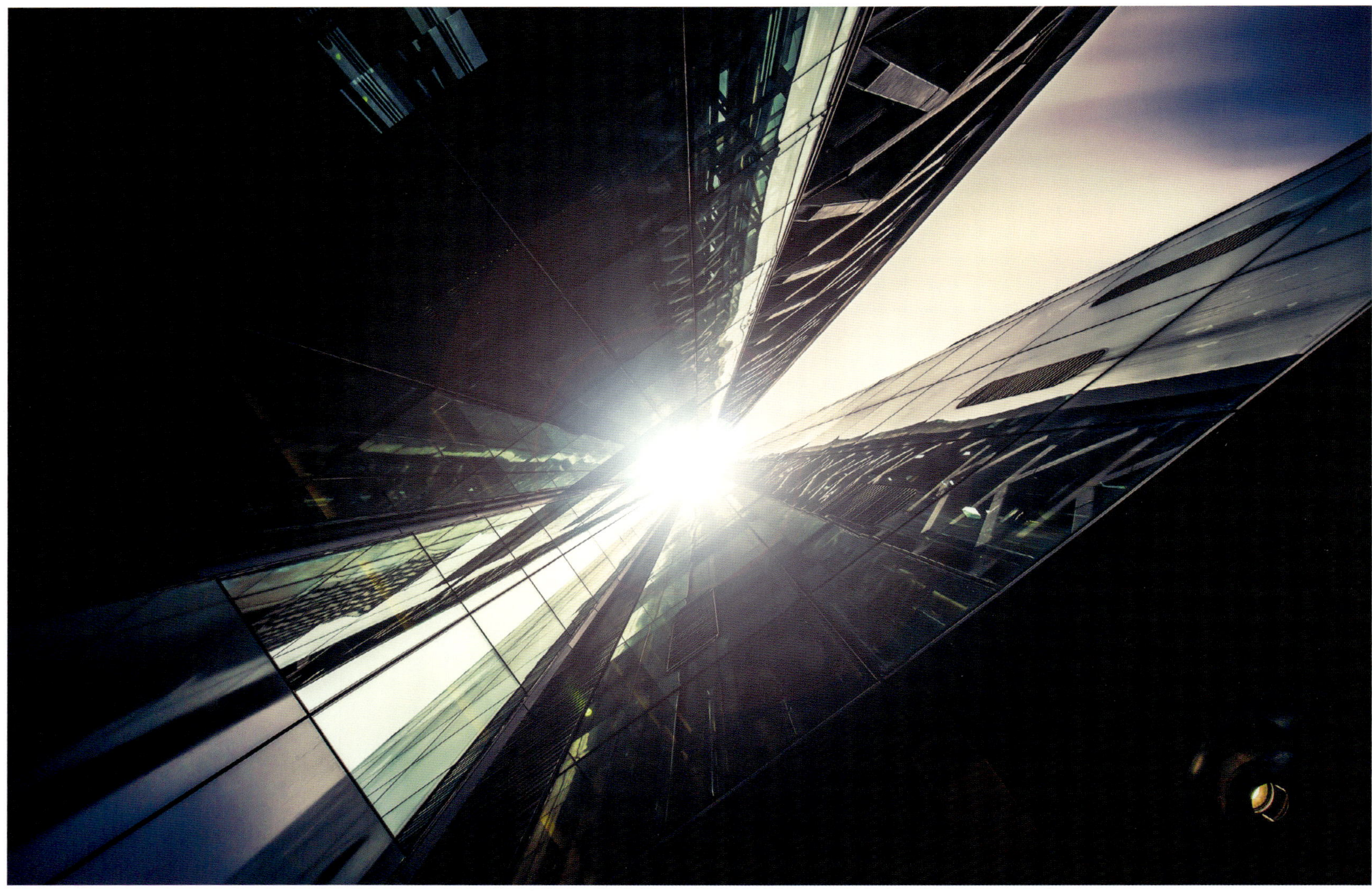

Cities at night are lit up by a variety of light sources at a wide range of heights and angles: shop fronts, car lights, building windows, and streetlights to name a few. Consequently, it can prove extremely difficult to prevent stray light from hitting the lens and creating flare, either in the form of distracting artifacts over part of the image or an overall reduction in contrast.

The main way to try to deal with lens flare is to always use a lens hood. This doesn't guarantee that flare will not occur, though, so it is vital to check your images after they've been captured to ensure they are flare free.

If flare still appears, try altering your shooting angle slightly to block the non-image-forming light from hitting the lens. An alternative approach is to use your hand or something else, such as a dark cloth or piece of card, to shield the lens. Obviously, you need to ensure that this shade stays out of the frame when you make your exposure.

Above: Shooting directly into the sun has created some obvious flare here, with both artifacts and reduced contrast present. However, careful positioning of the camera has limited this to the bright central area of the image where it doesn't detract from the image.

Focal length: 16mm

Aperture: f/16

Shutter speed: 49 sec.

ISO: 100

Aperture Star Spikes

"Aperture spikes" is another name for the star-shaped effect created by point light sources, where light rays appear to emanate from the light itself. The number of spikes created is determined by the number of aperture blades inside the lens, so the more aperture blades a lens has, the more light rays will appear.

To create this effect you simply have to close down the aperture. This is because the effect is caused by diffraction: as light is forced through a small aperture it "bends" around the edges of the aperture blades, creating the distinct starburst effect. The smaller the aperture setting, the more pronounced the starburst will be, but you need to be careful, as too much diffraction will start to soften the image overall. A good starting point is f/16; the aperture will be small enough to create spikes, but without affecting image quality. However, diffraction can vary between lenses so it's worth experimenting.

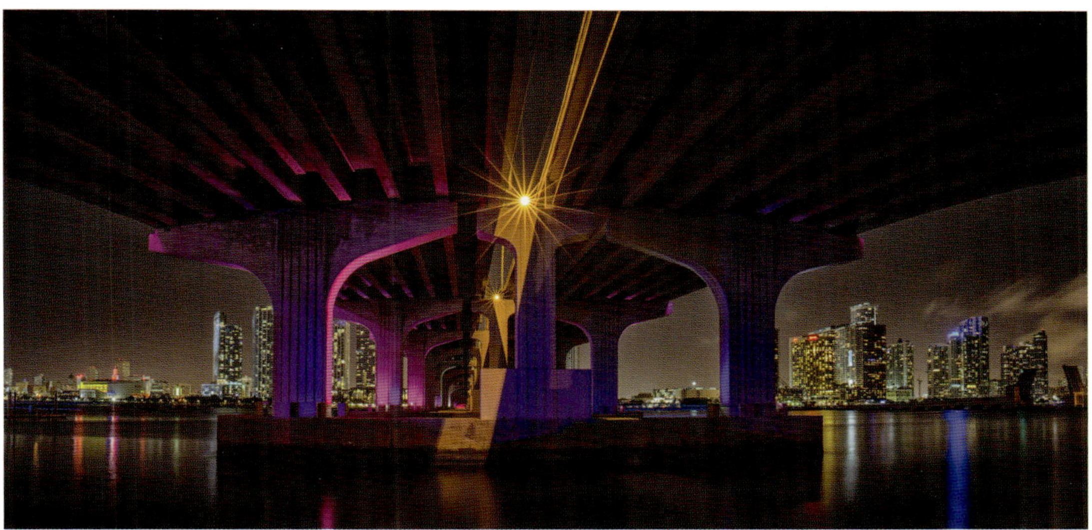

Above right: For this shot I carefully positioned the camera so that the streetlights above this bridge in Miami were centered; a small aperture was used to create the spikes.

Focal length: 16mm
Aperture: f/16
Shutter speed: 46 sec.
ISO: 800

Right: Any point light source can create an aperture spike. In this image of the London Eye and River Thames, a full moon was bright enough to create a starburst and add a unique element to the image.

Focal length: 28mm
Aperture: f/20
Shutter speed: 69 sec.
ISO: 100

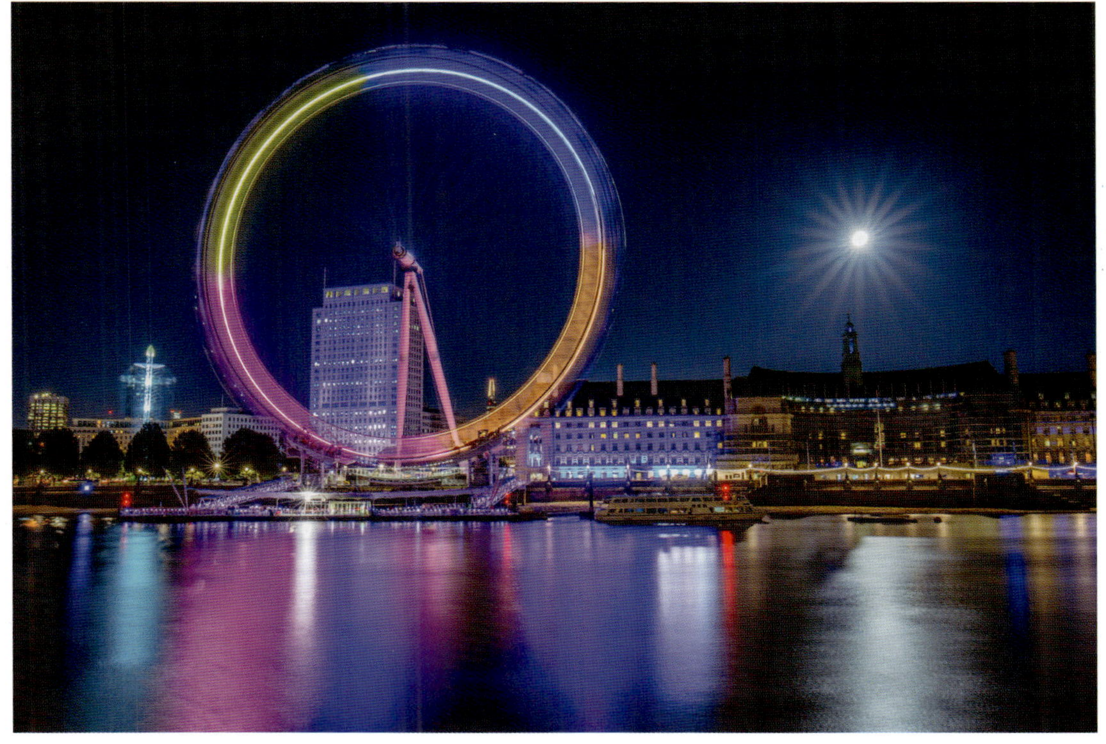

Bridges & Reflections

Finding a viewpoint beside a body of water can add depth to a nocturnal city image, as any lights reflected on the water's surface are likely to become smooth bands of soft color thanks to a long exposure time. The longer the exposure, the smoother the water will become, and when there is minimal wind or current it can become a glossy, mirror-like surface reflecting the cityscape.

Bear in mind that after rain, puddles of water will also be available to use creatively. Even the sheen of water on roads and sidewalks can create a semi-reflective surface in your images, so look for compositions that make the most of these to reflect their surroundings.

Bridges can also serve as interesting subjects at night. They usually have a multitude of lights, which will again reflect in the water. The dynamic angles and linear designs of most bridges can also act as strong compositional lead-in lines to draw a viewer's eye to a more distant cityscape.

Below: Faster-moving water, such as the River Thames in London, will rarely be still enough to create a true mirrored reflection, but the bright colors of the scene are still reflected on the water, helping to add energy to the image.

Focal length: 35mm

Aperture: f/8

Shutter speed: 30 sec.

ISO: 100

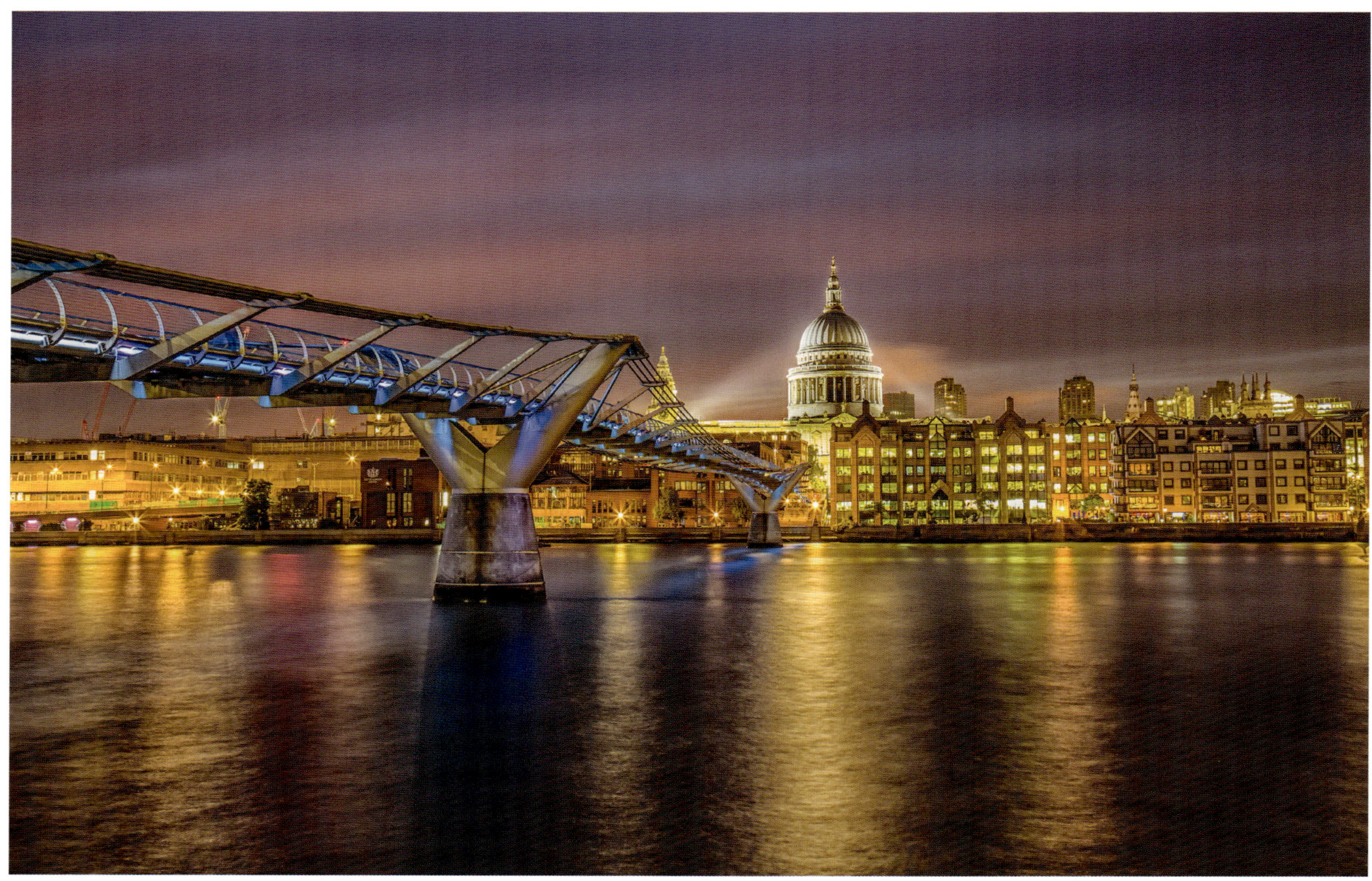

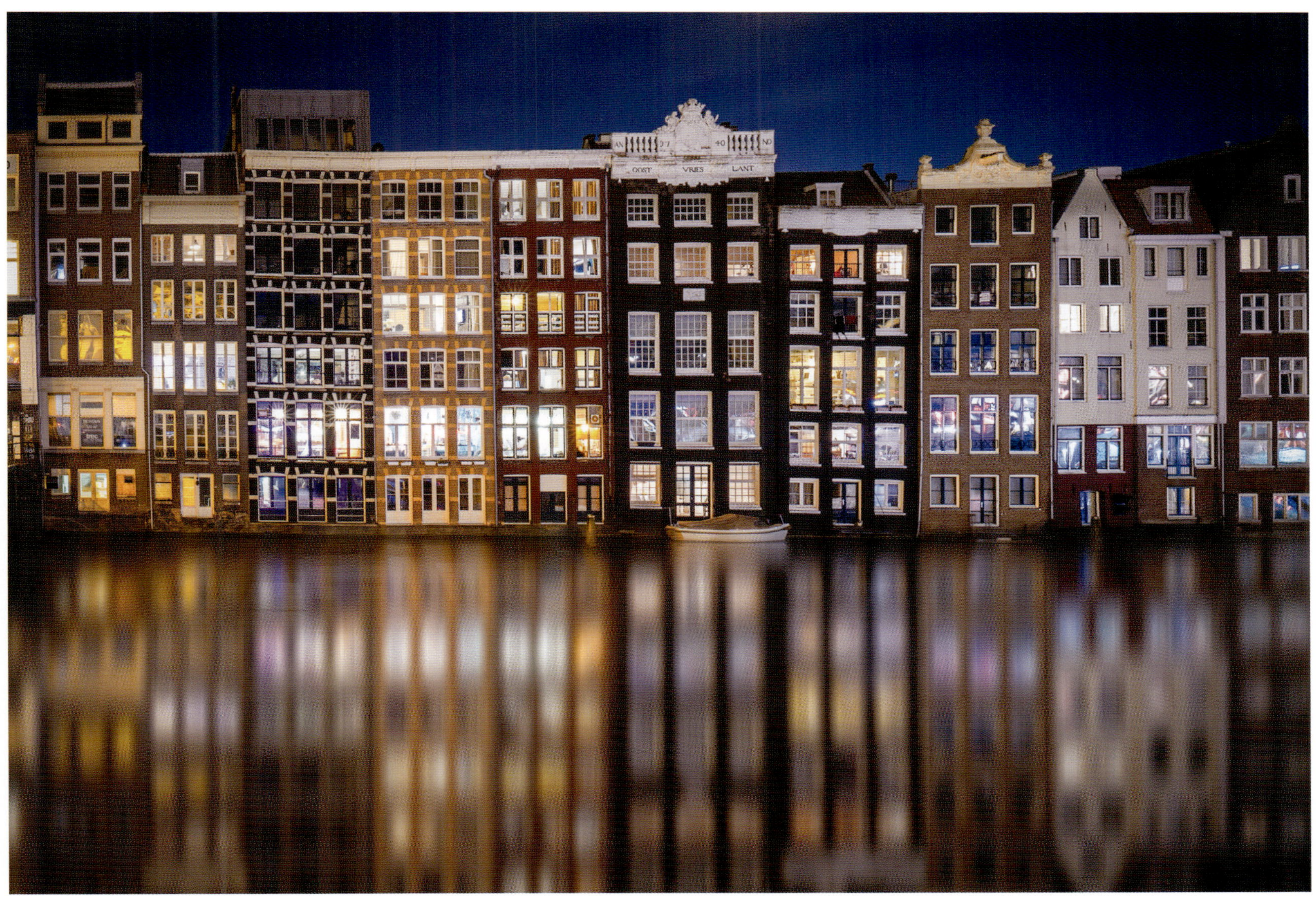

Above: The illuminated windows in these houses in Amsterdam provide a colorful array of reflections on the canal below.

Focal length: 33mm

Aperture: f/16

Shutter speed: 78 sec.

ISO: 200

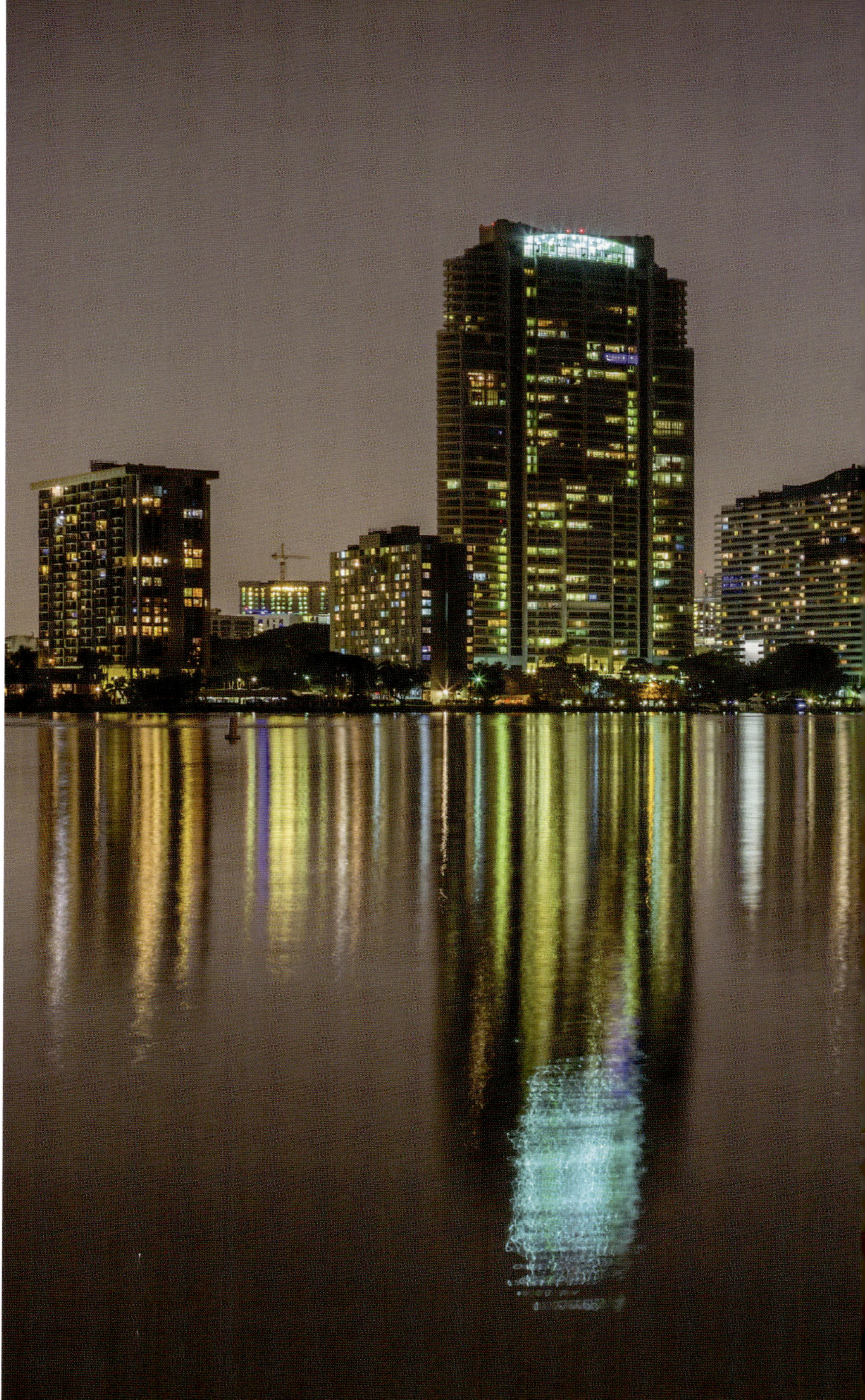

Right: This image of downtown Miami is made all the more vibrant by the relatively still waters of the bay providing colorful reflections of the scene.
Focal length: 45mm
Aperture: f/14
Shutter speed: 13 sec.
ISO: 400

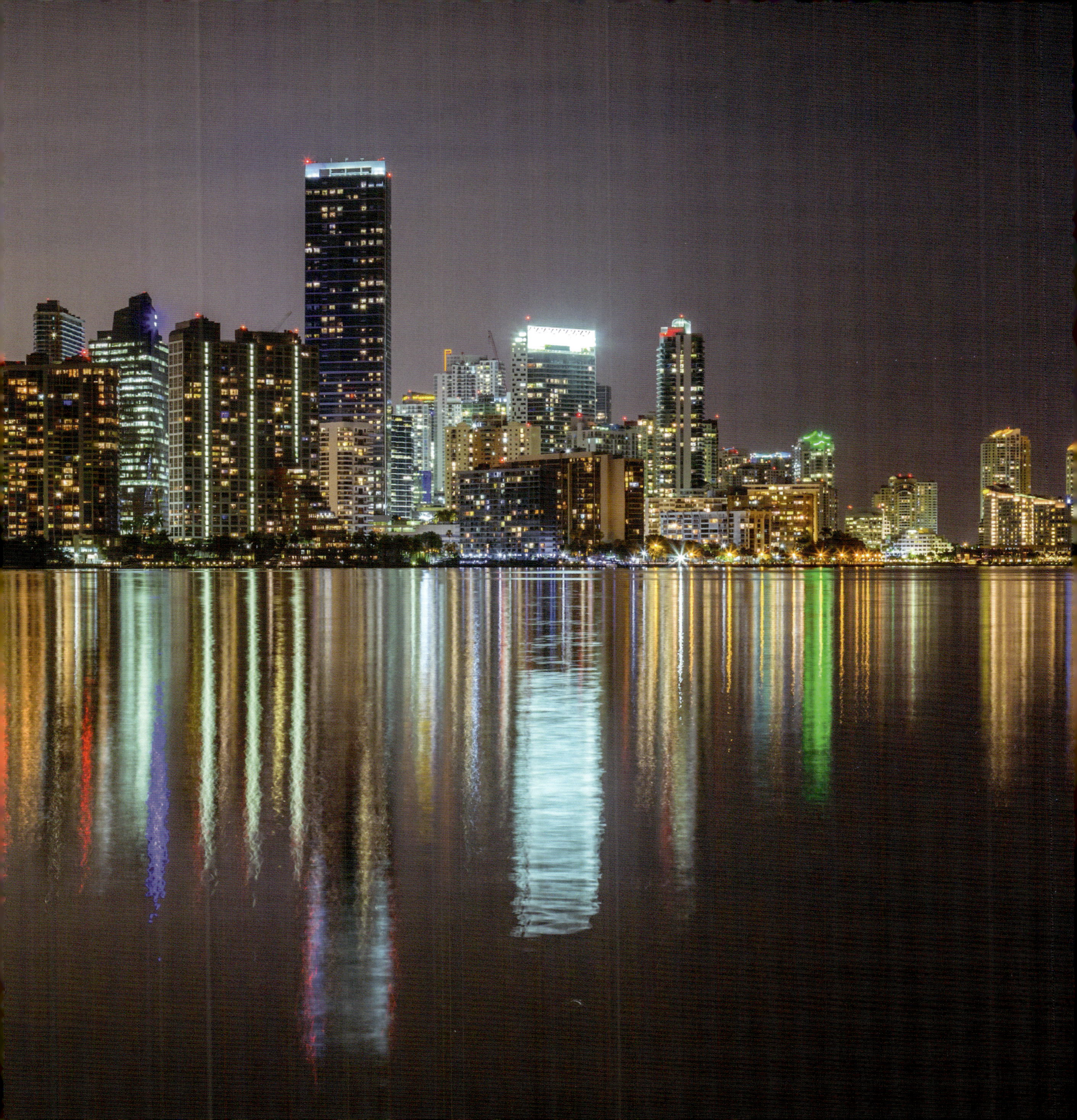

White Balance

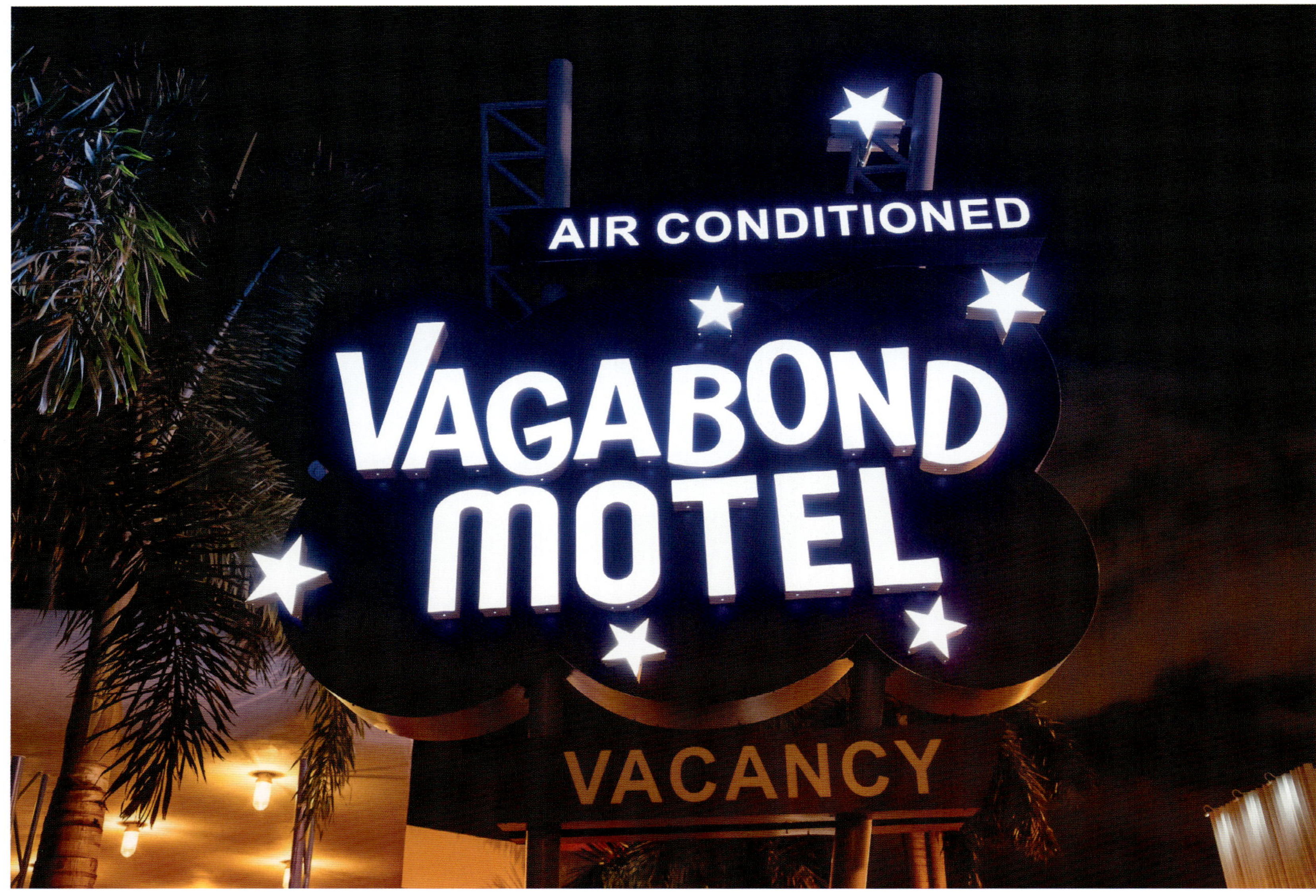

An important issue when photographing the city at night is the color of the lights and how these will affect the look of the image. The color of light varies with different light sources and is measured on the Kelvin scale (K); warmer shades have a low color temperature (1000–4000K), while cooler blue and white tones are at the high end of the temperature scale (10,000–12,000K). Regular daylight is estimated to be around 5500K.

White balance is simply the process of telling the camera what kind of light source is providing the primary light, so it can correct any color cast that may occur due to the temperature of the light. Most cameras have a number of built-in settings to cover most common lighting scenarios, but city lights often come from many different sources, with a variety of color temperatures and intensities. This makes it difficult to set a decisive white balance, so

Above: This vintage hotel sign had a different color temperature to the orange street glow behind. As it was shot in Raw the preferred color balance could be set in postproduction.

Focal length: 16mm

Aperture: f/2.8

Shutter speed: 15 sec.

ISO: 100

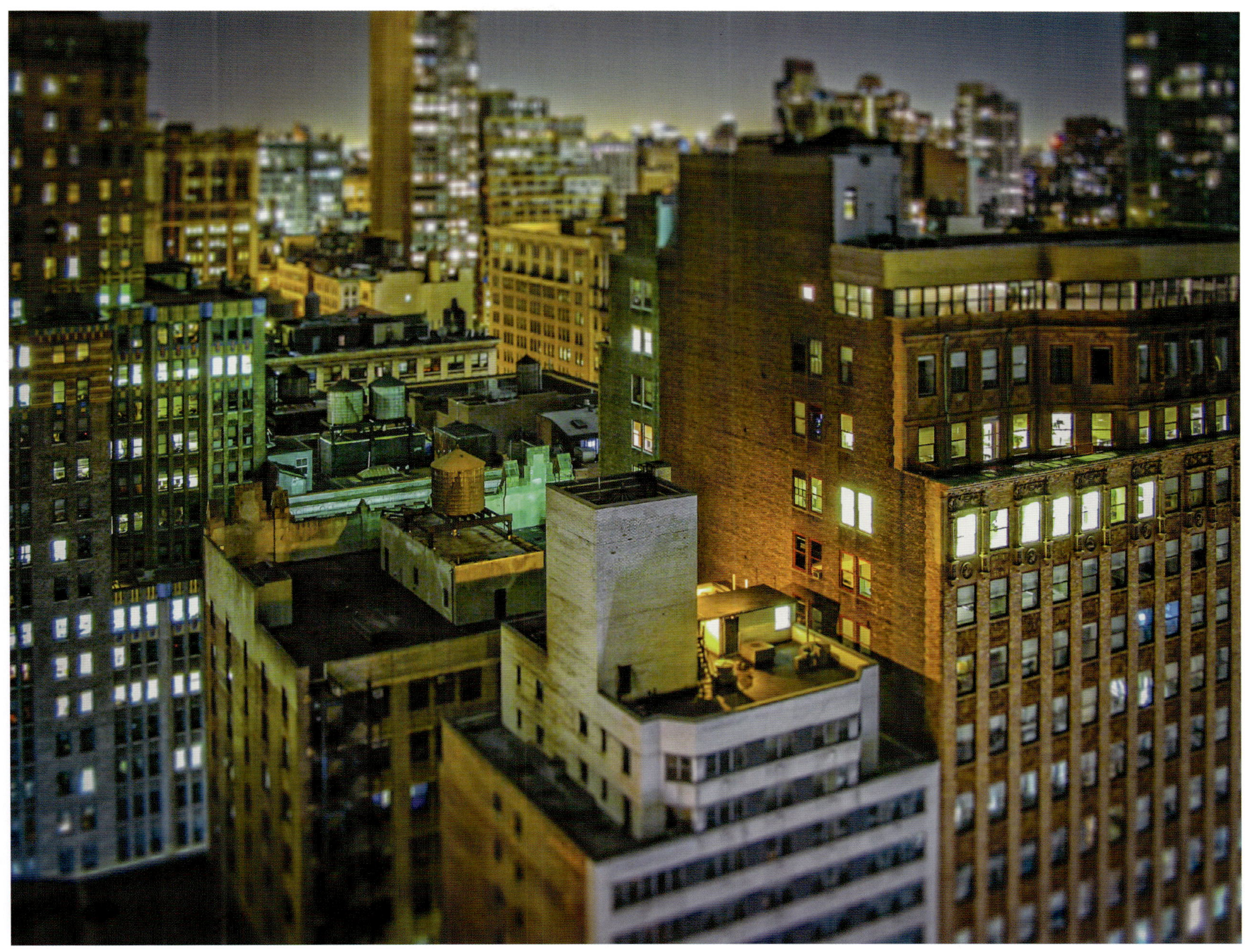

it's best to experiment with various settings to see which one provides you with the most accurate or creative color for a particular scene or image.

Although you can experiment with different white balance options in-camera, if you shoot Raw you can also change the white balance after a shot has been taken, when you process the image. As there is no degradation of the image data you can make as many changes as you like to find the best balance; this is just one reason why Raw is recommended for photographing the city at night.

Above: This scene of rooftops in New York City shows the variation of colors from different artificial light sources. Although this can easily confuse the camera's white balance algorithms, the range of lights helps provide an interesting look.

Focal length: 24mm

Aperture: f/16

Shutter speed: 45 sec.

ISO: 200

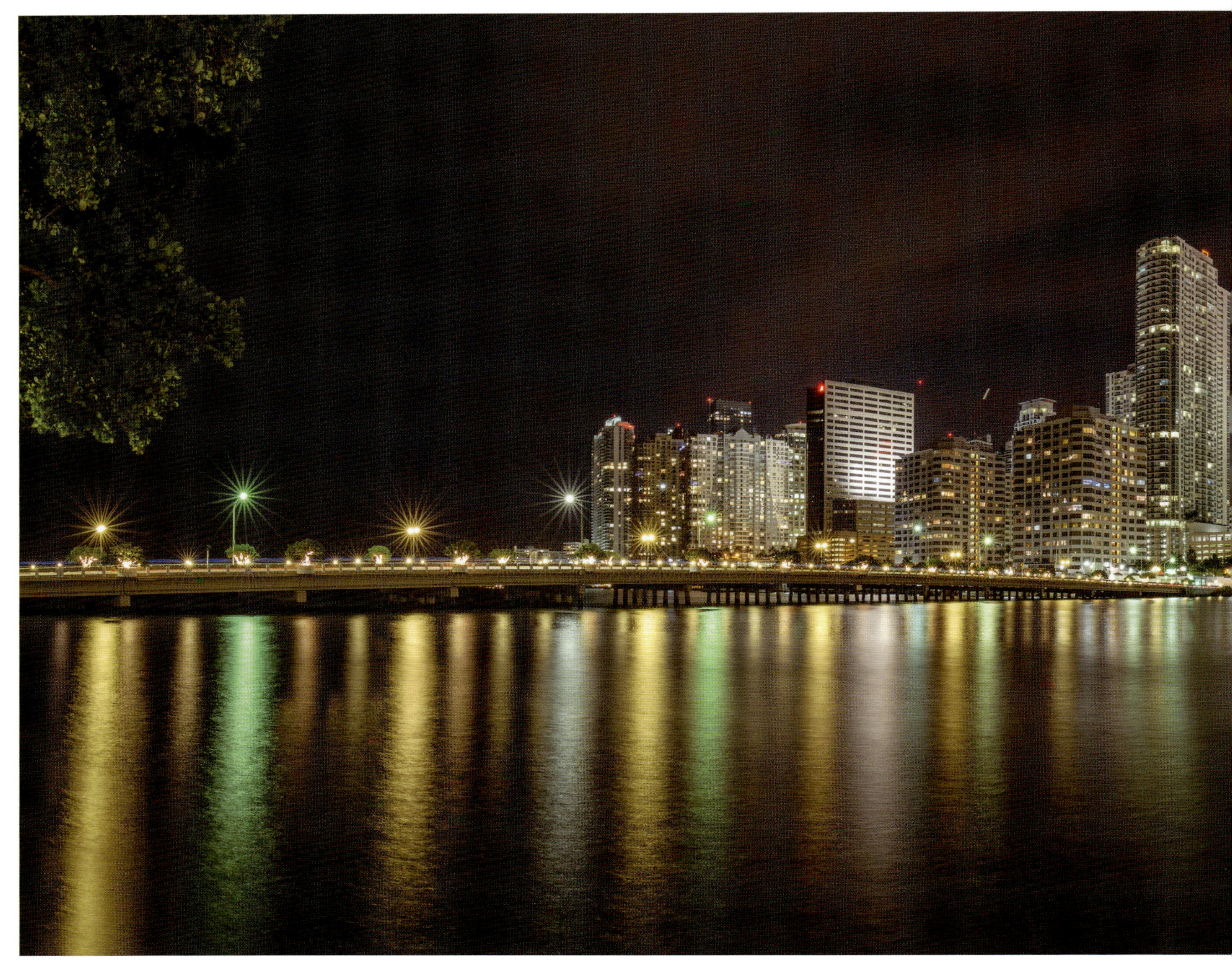

Above: This view of Miami shows the multitude of colored lights that shine throughout many cityscapes. The various colors can be difficult to capture accurately, so it is better to shoot Raw: achieving the correct white balance in-camera with a JPEG is extremely difficult.

Focal length: 32mm

Aperture: f/7.1

Shutter speed: 11 sec.

ISO: 400

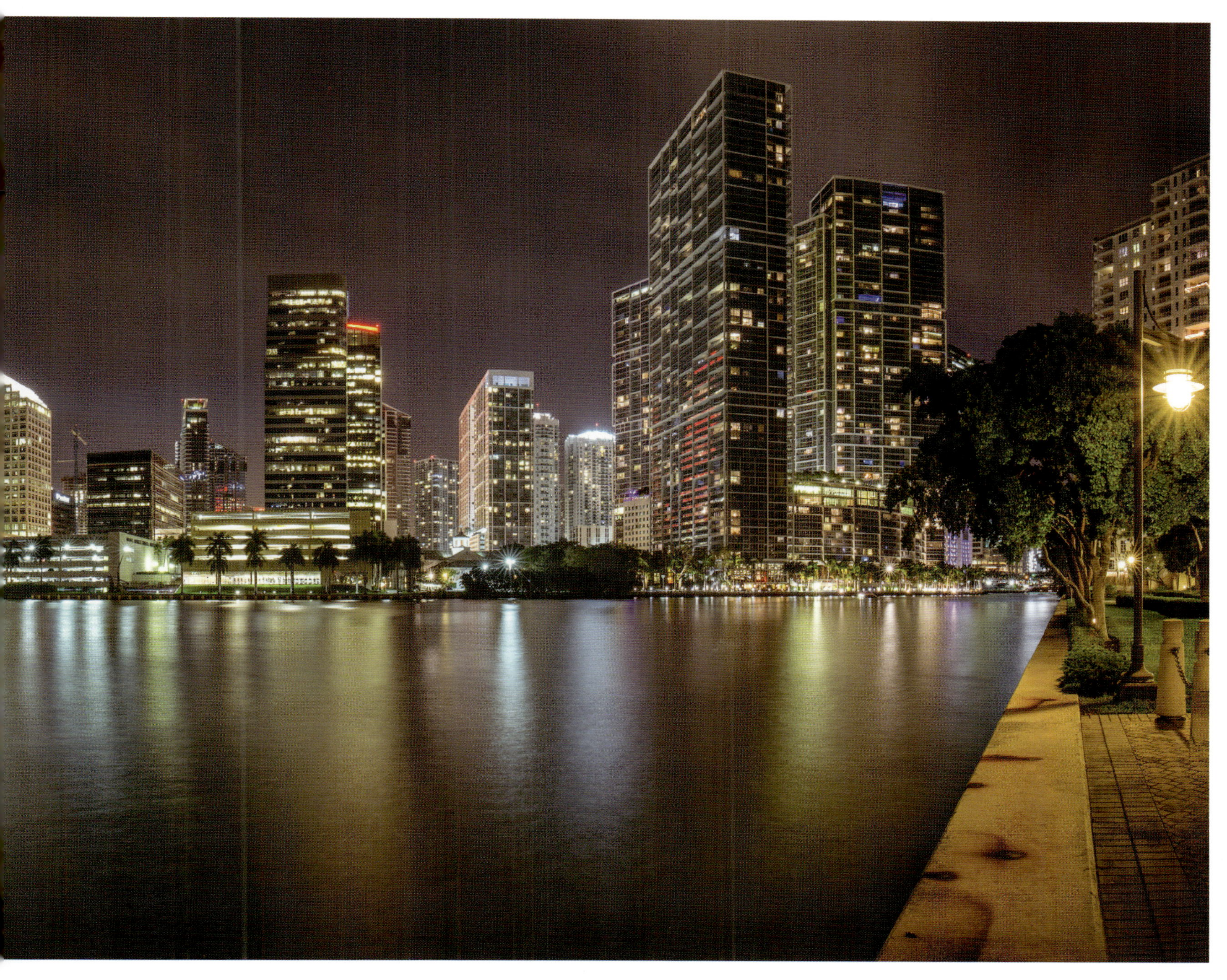

Chapter 5
Photographing the Heavens

The complexity and beauty of the night sky has provided wonderment in the minds of people throughout history. Whether it's the stars, the moon, planets, or other phenomenon, such as lightning, the night sky provides a vast alternative "landscape" for beautiful views of the natural world.

It is natural that photographers want to capture the phenomenon of "the heavens," and there is certainly something magical about being out in the wilderness, witnessing the wonders of the night sky. Photographing these mystical views can produce rewarding and attractive images, and recent technological improvements have made it easier than ever for clear, sharp images to be captured without the need for expensive, ultra-specialized equipment. However, a little preparation and a few additional skills are still needed if you want to guarantee success.

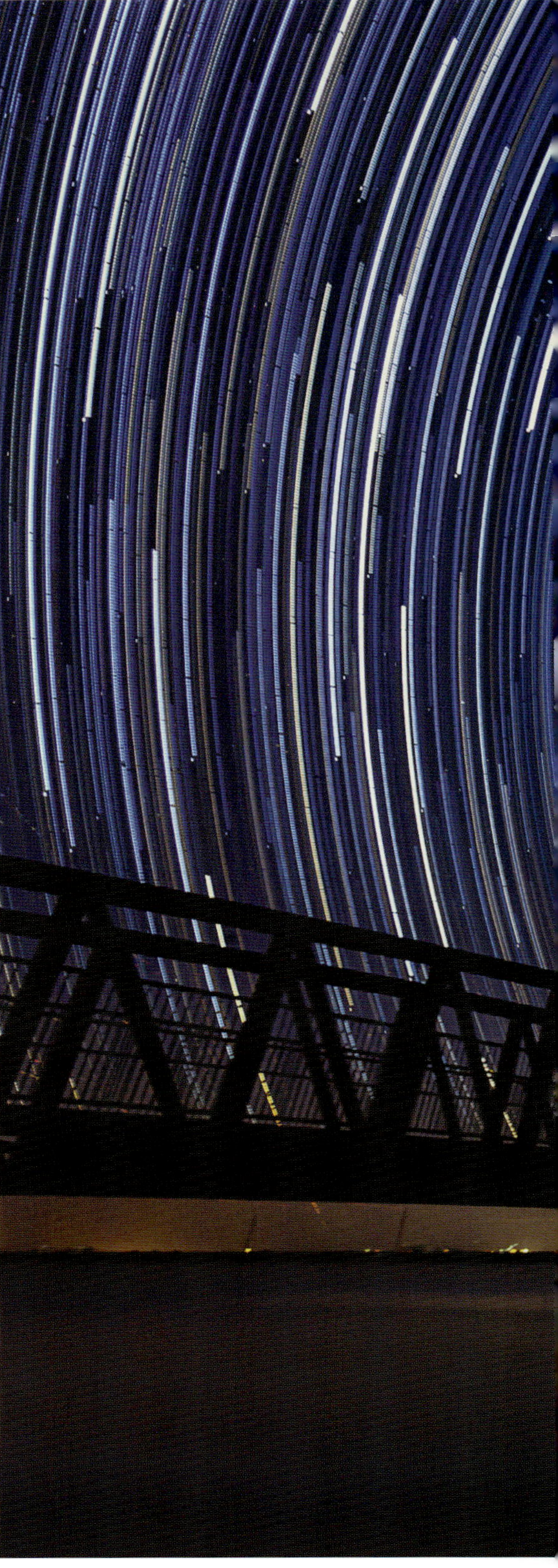

Right: This star trail image was captured in the Florida Everglades and consists of around 180 exposures taken every 30 seconds. Despite being in such a rural place, the glow of urban lights is still present and the green lights from fireflies have also been captured.

Focal length: 16mm

Aperture: f/4

Shutter speed: 30 sec.

ISO: 1600

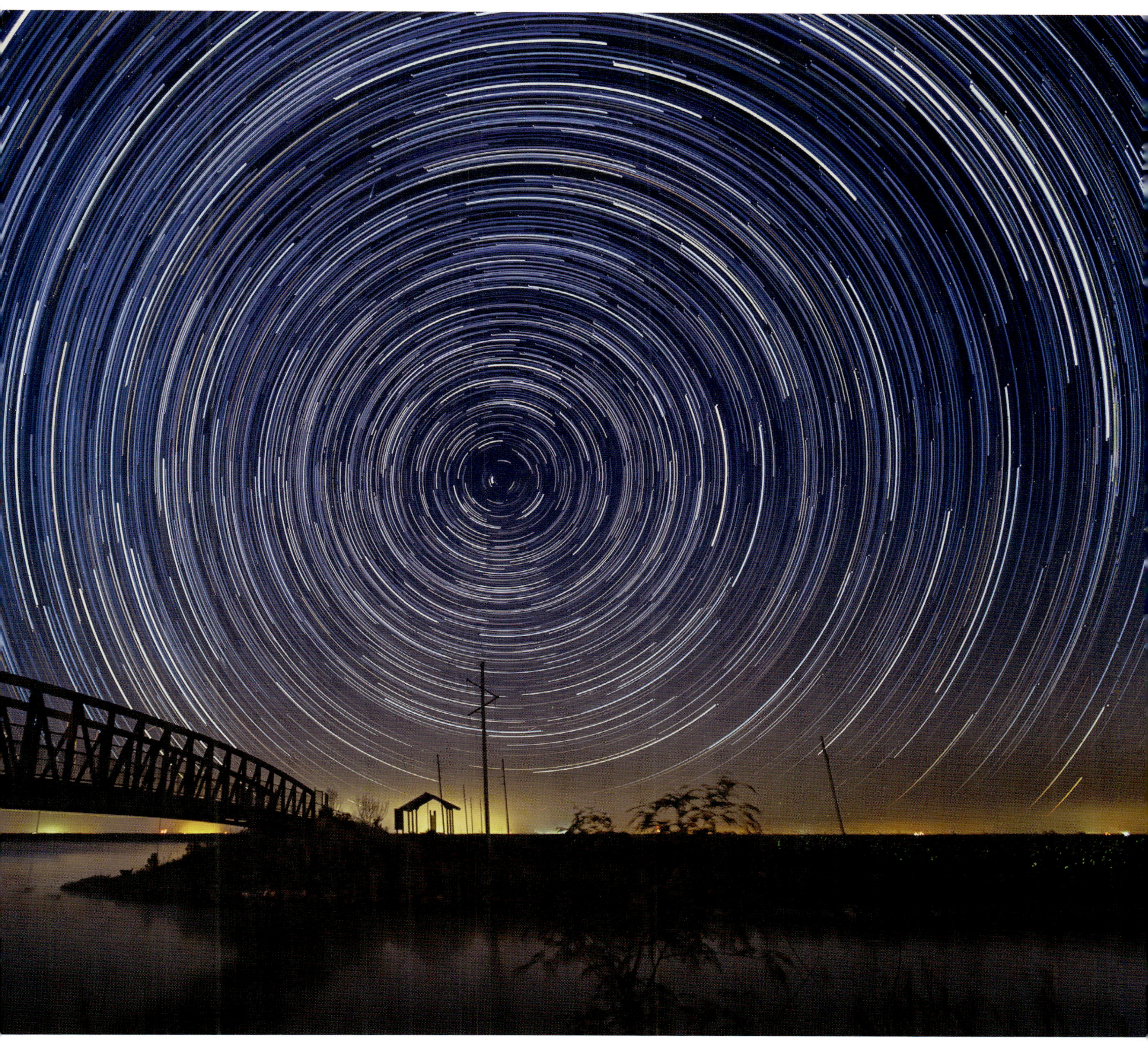

The Moon

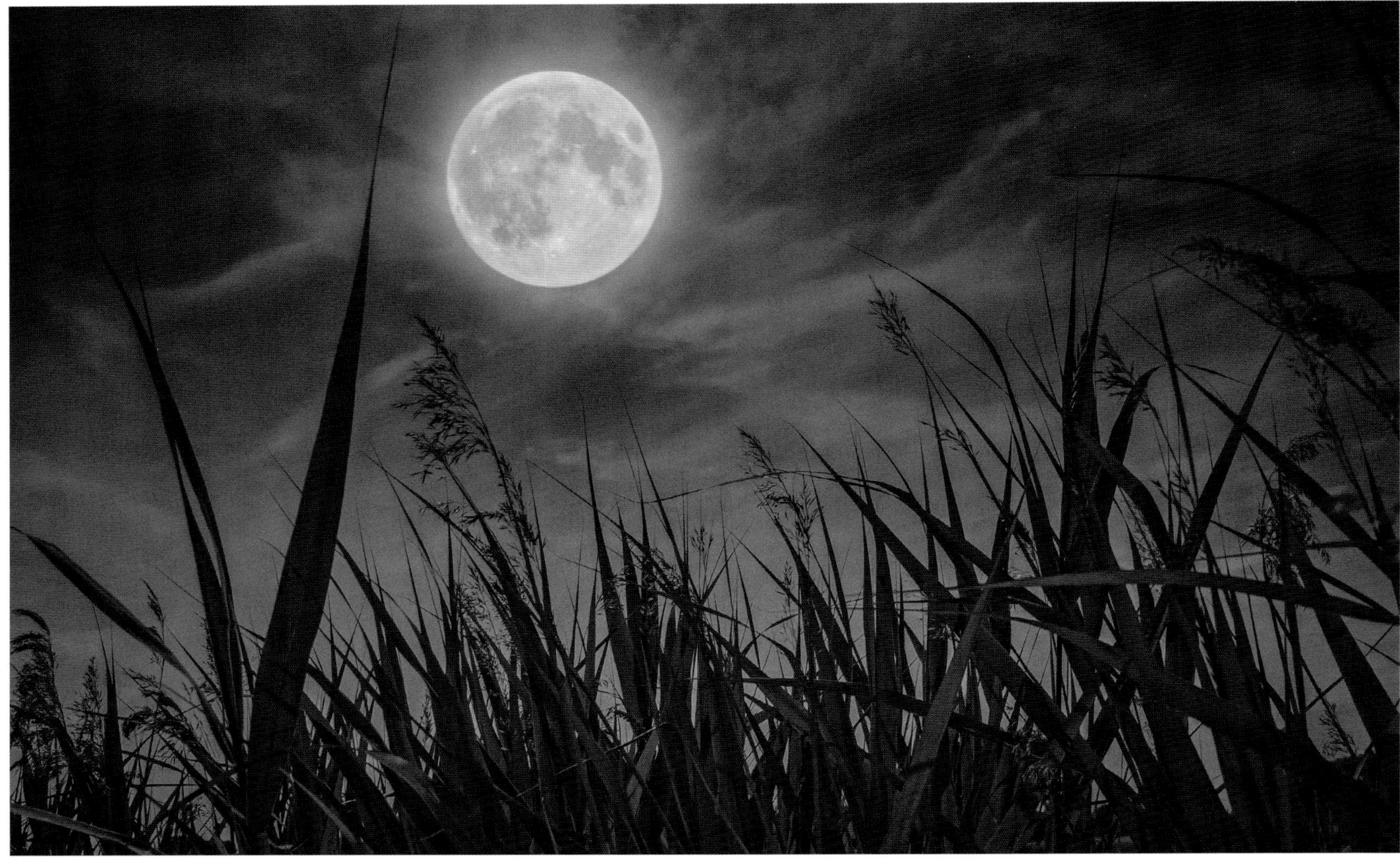

The moon is often photographed against the dark night sky, which leads to a common misconception that a very long shutter speed is required to expose it correctly (hence its inclusion in this book). However, the moon is relatively bright, as it is reflecting the light from the sun; it is the surrounding sky and environment that is extremely dark. As such, taking nighttime images that have the moon in the frame will involve a trade-off: you can underexpose the background or overexpose the moon, but you can't correctly expose both. Bracketing a series of exposures to combine in postproduction is the only way to obtain a well-balanced image.

If your image is focusing solely on the moon, you will need to use a focal length of at least 300mm—ideally longer—so you can fill the frame as much as possible. As with photographing all celestial objects, it is essential that the camera remains motionless, especially when long telephoto lenses are used, as the slightest vibration will be magnified, resulting in a blurred image. A stable tripod, mirror lock-up, and remote release are essential.

Above: Getting down low can provide you with a unique perspective and can often create dynamic photographs. This image is a composite of two separate frames: the foreground was taken with a wideangle lens, then without moving the camera, a separate exposure for the moon was taken with a telephoto lens. It would not have been possible to capture such clear detail in the same frame with the same lens.

Tips

- For moon "portraits," where it is filling the frame as much as possible, an aperture in the region of f/5.6 and a shutter speed around 1/250 sec. is a good starting point, combined with a low ISO setting (ISO 200–400). Take a test shot and assess the histogram: if the image is too dark, increase the ISO; if it is too bright, increase the shutter speed. As the moon is always moving, using too slow a shutter speed will record this movement and result in a blurred image.

- The contrast between the moon and the dark sky will likely confuse your camera's multi-area metering, so try taking a spot meter reading from the moon instead.

- The moon will appear larger the closer it is to the horizon, so you may find that it helps to take images as it rises or sets. There are numerous apps that will give you the time and direction of the moonrise or moonset in your location.

Below: This is a composite of the different stages of a lunar eclipse. The moon turns red for the same reason that a sunset has warm colors; the low angle of the light source and atmospheric pollution.

Focal length: 280mm

Aperture: f/5.6

Shutter speed: 1 sec.

ISO: 400

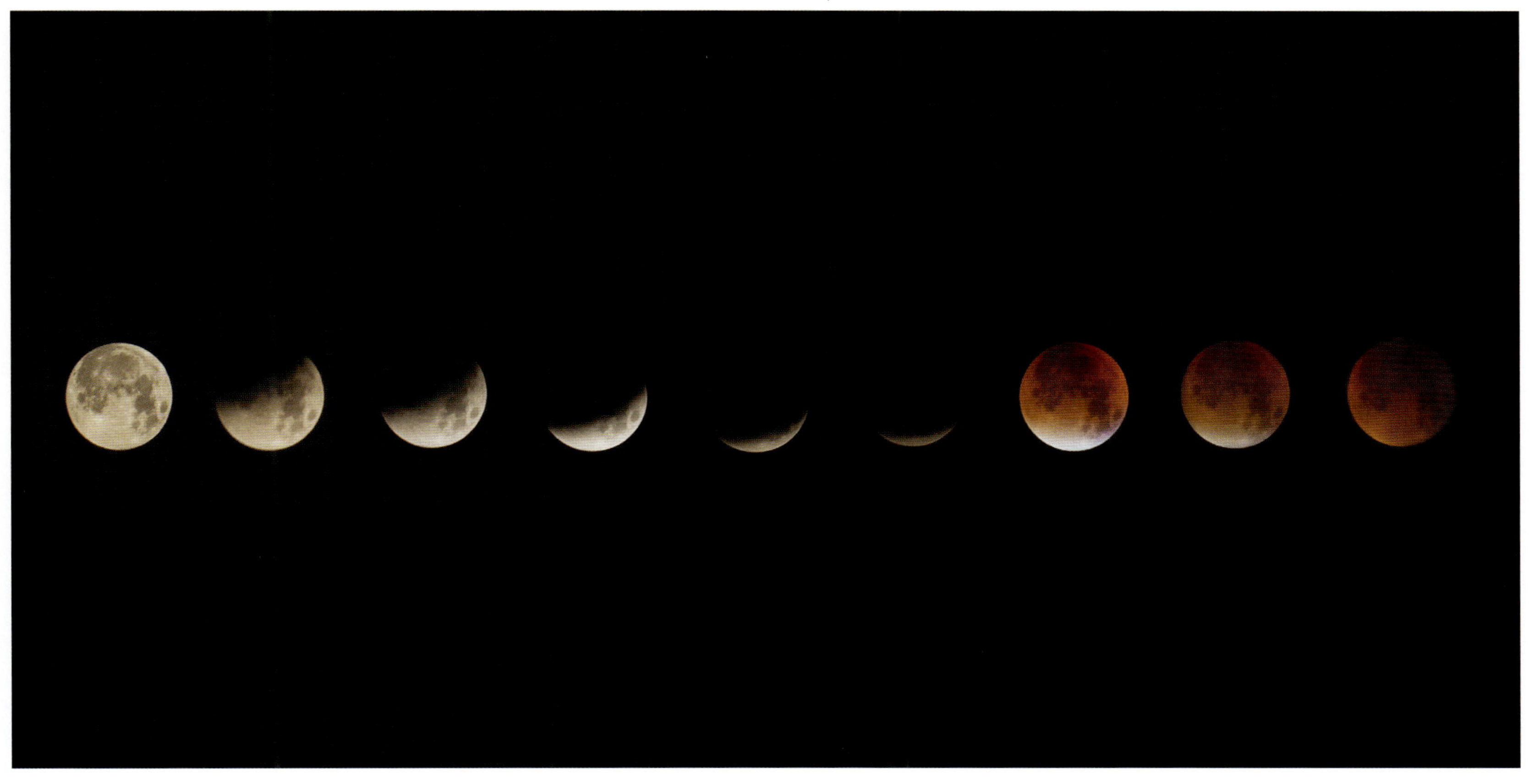

Stars

On a clear night, a star-filled sky can provide a spectacular natural background. To capture stars sharply, the key is to get as much light to your sensor as quickly as possible. A fast lens will help here, although depth of field issues may come into play if you use a large aperture and want both the stars and some foreground to be in focus. In this situation it may be necessary to take a separate frame for the foreground, using a smaller aperture to obtain sufficient depth of field, and combine this with your star shot in postproduction.

An alternative way to photograph the stars in the night sky is to celebrate their apparent movement in the form of star trail images. Although it would seem that the easiest option is to leave the camera shutter open for as long as possible, this method does not achieve the best results. As the sensor is active for a long duration, heat builds up creating high levels of image noise, and there is also the risk of accidentally moving the camera, and of condensation forming on the lens and ruining the image.

Instead, the preferred method for capturing star trails is to take a number of shorter, individual exposures and then stack them together in postproduction. This leads to less image noise (due to shorter exposure times), plus the ability to use a higher ISO and larger aperture. It also means the individual frames can be edited to remove airplane trails, car lights, or any other unwanted distractions.

To shoot stacked trails, switch your camera to Manual exposure mode, set your lens to its widest aperture, the ISO to 1600, and the shutter speed to 25 seconds. Take a test shot and adjust the ISO if you need to change the exposure.

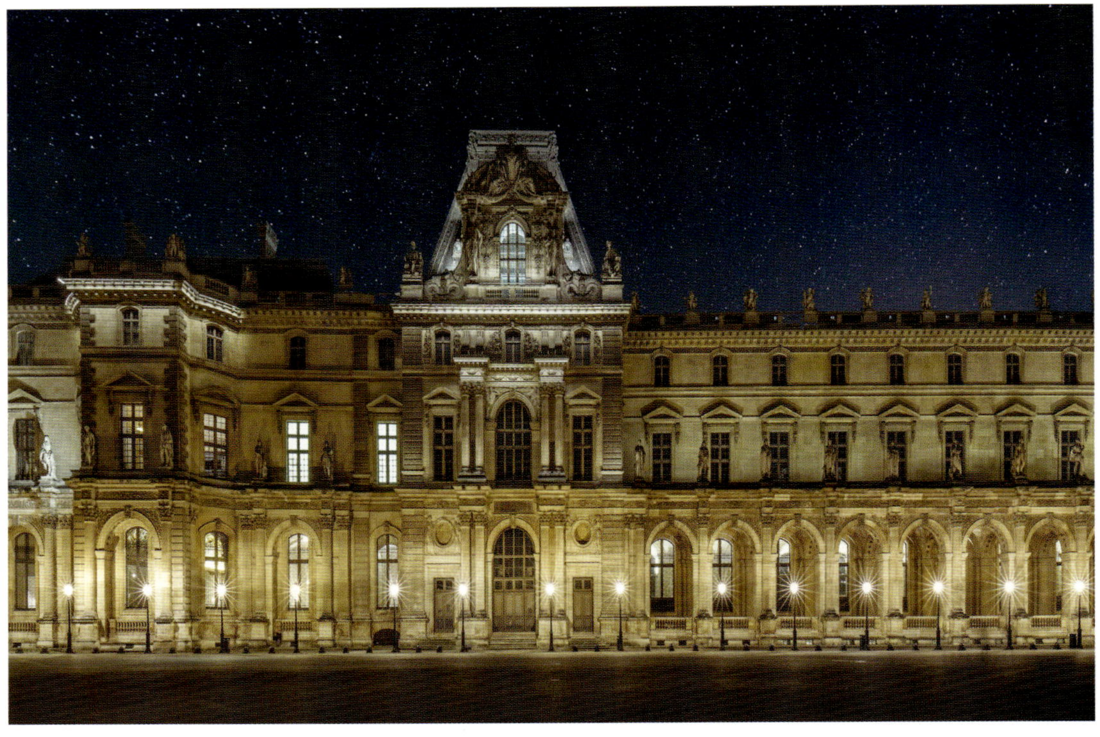

Above: This image is a composite of two separate images. The first exposure relied on a very high ISO and relatively brief shutter speed to capture the stars and ensure the lights near the building didn't overexpose the sky. The building was then photographed using a lower ISO to ensure sharp detail and low noise, with a small aperture used to create the aperture spikes on the lights.

Tips

- Turn your camera's long exposure noise reduction function off, as this will take another frame for the same duration of the initial image and render the camera unusable for this long period.

- Make sure you have fully charged batteries and spares. Colder night temperatures can drain batteries more quickly.

- Start with a blank memory card as star trail images usually require large numbers and may fill up a card quickly.

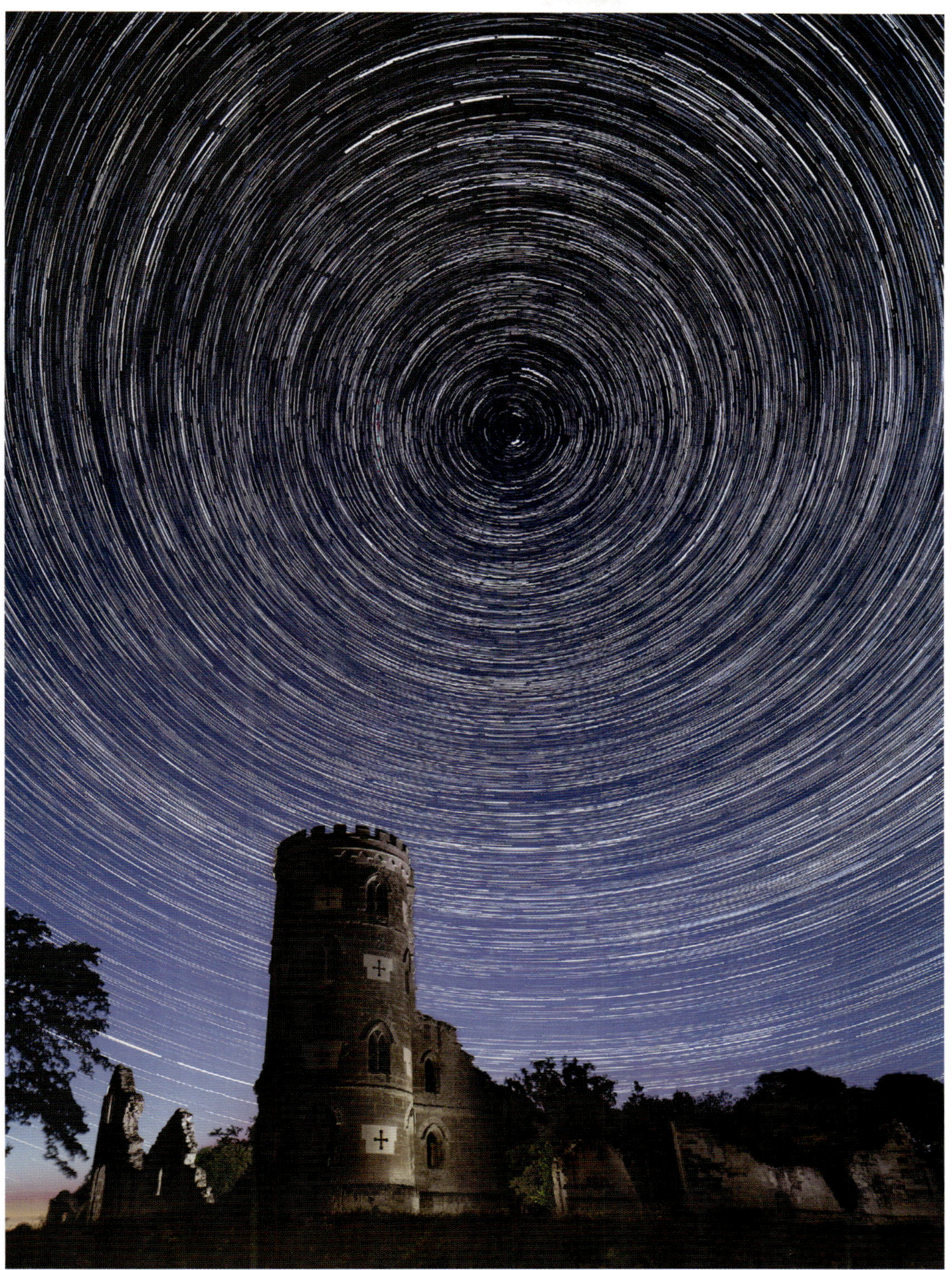

Left: More than 200 separate images were stacked to create this star trail, which shows stars rotating around the North Star. During the exposures, a flashlight was used to light up the buildings in the darkness so that some detail could be recorded.

Focal length: 24mm

Aperture: f/4

Shutter speed: 25 sec.

ISO: 1600

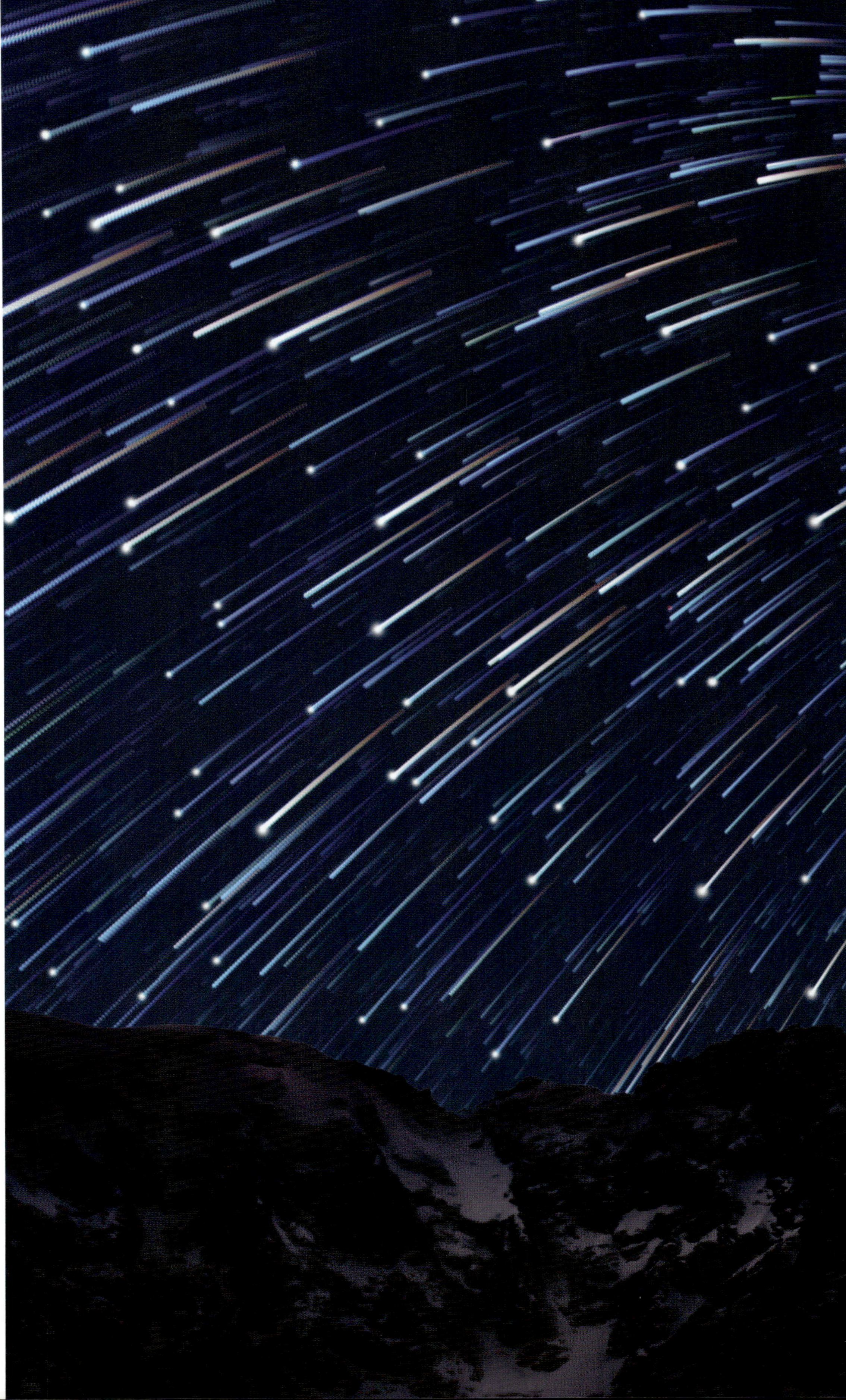

Right: The "vortex" effect on the star trails in this image was created in Photoshop (the natural orbit of the stars will not create such a pattern!). The technique used follows the basic stacked star-trail method explained on the previous pages, but the Free Transform function is used to tweak the individual layers. Place the tool's cross point where you want the rotation point to be—this will usually be where the North Star is. Then, amend the rotation value to 0.1 and the scaling to less than 100%. As each star-layer is applied to the image using these settings, they will be slightly out of natural position, creating a vortex effect.

Focal length: 16mm

Aperture: f/4

Shutter speed: 30 sec.

ISO: 6400

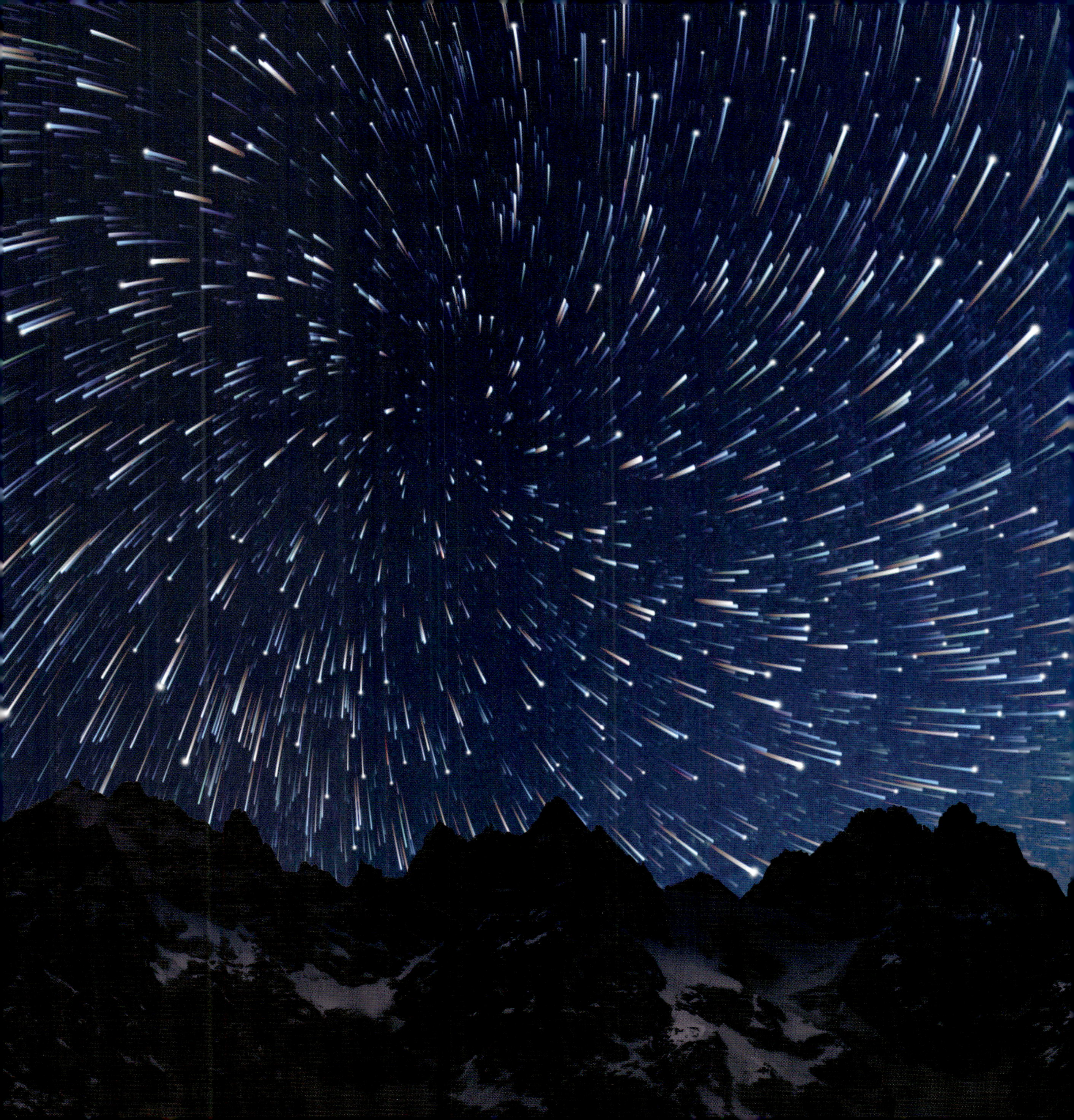

The Milky Way

Photographing the Milky Way (or more accurately the "galactic core" of the Milky Way) is relatively straightforward once you can locate it, but a basic level of preparation is required.

To start with, you don't want any cloud cover, so you have a clear, uninterrupted view of the sky. In addition, you need to find a location with minimal light pollution, which may prove to be one of the hardest challenges; even a faint glow from distant city lights can brighten the night sky sufficiently to wash out your images when exposures lengthen.

The brightness of the moon will also affect the brightness of the sky and the number of stars that can be captured in your images. It is important to check the lunar calendar and seek out a new moon, so there is minimal light interference. It is recommended that you only try to photograph on nights where the moon is less than a quarter in the sky.

Even with the right conditions, locating the core of the Milky Way can be challenging. It is unlikely that you will be able to simply look into the sky and see it with your own eyes, so it is advisable to use a website or app to point you in the right direction. This will enable you to plan out in advance the precise location and predicted movement of the Milky Way, which can also help you prepare your composition in terms of ground-based interest.

In terms of camera settings, start with the lens set at its widest aperture and a high ISO (in the region of ISO 1600–3200). With a shutter speed of around 20–25 sec., you should get a sharp capture without blur (blur usually becomes evident when exposure times reach 30 sec. or longer). Check the results closely on the camera's LCD at 100% to ensure that there is no motion blur; if there is, reduce the shutter speed. If the image is too bright or dark, reduce the ISO accordingly.

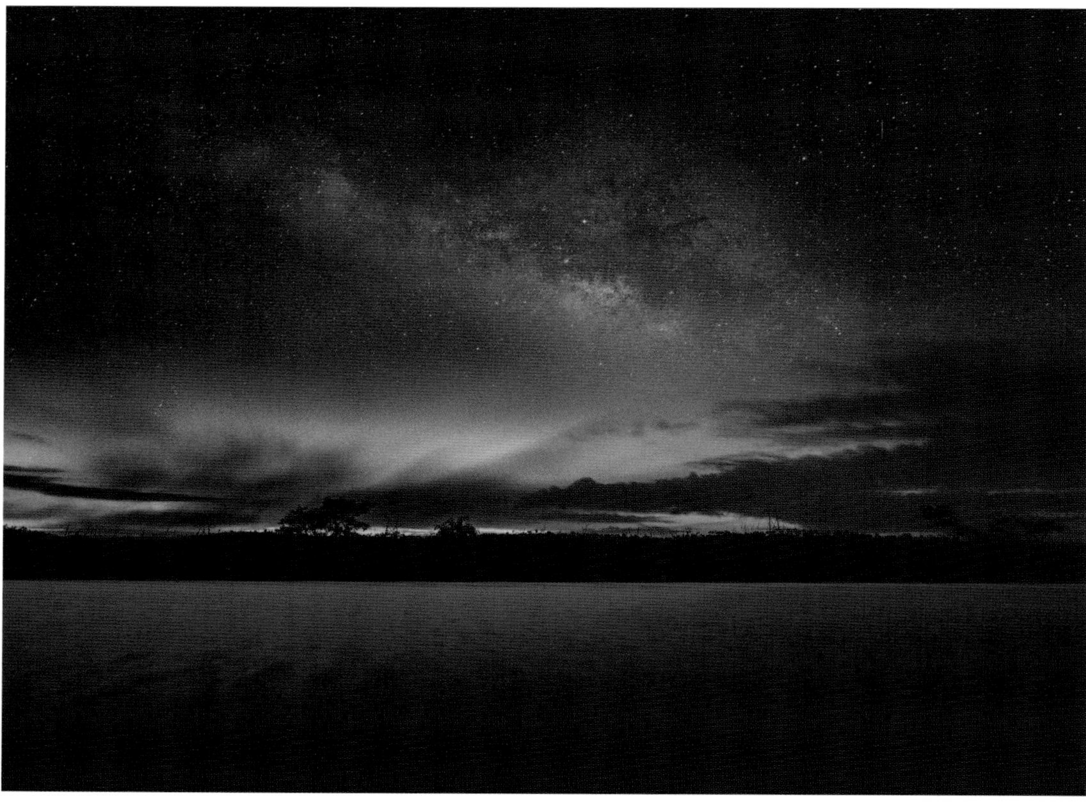

Focusing can be tricky, as your camera's AF is very unlikely to pick out the stars, but an easy option is to focus your lens manually at infinity and then turn on Live View and zoom in to maximum magnification. Adjust the focus until one star appears as a solid point of light.

Above: The essence of the galactic core of the Milky Way can be captured even when there is not a truly dark sky.

Focal length: 17mm

Aperture: f/4

Shutter speed: 26 sec.

ISO: 1600

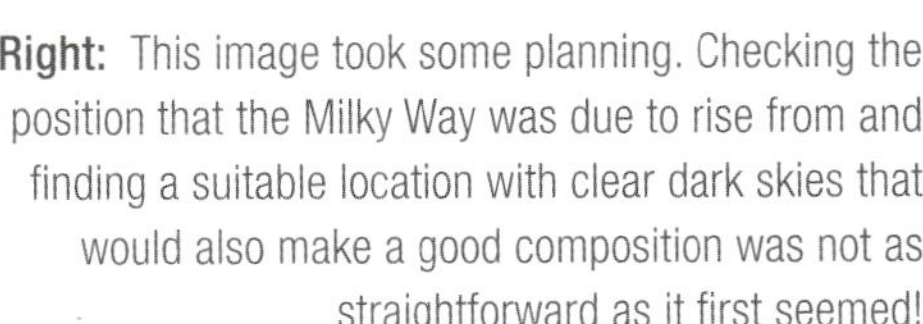

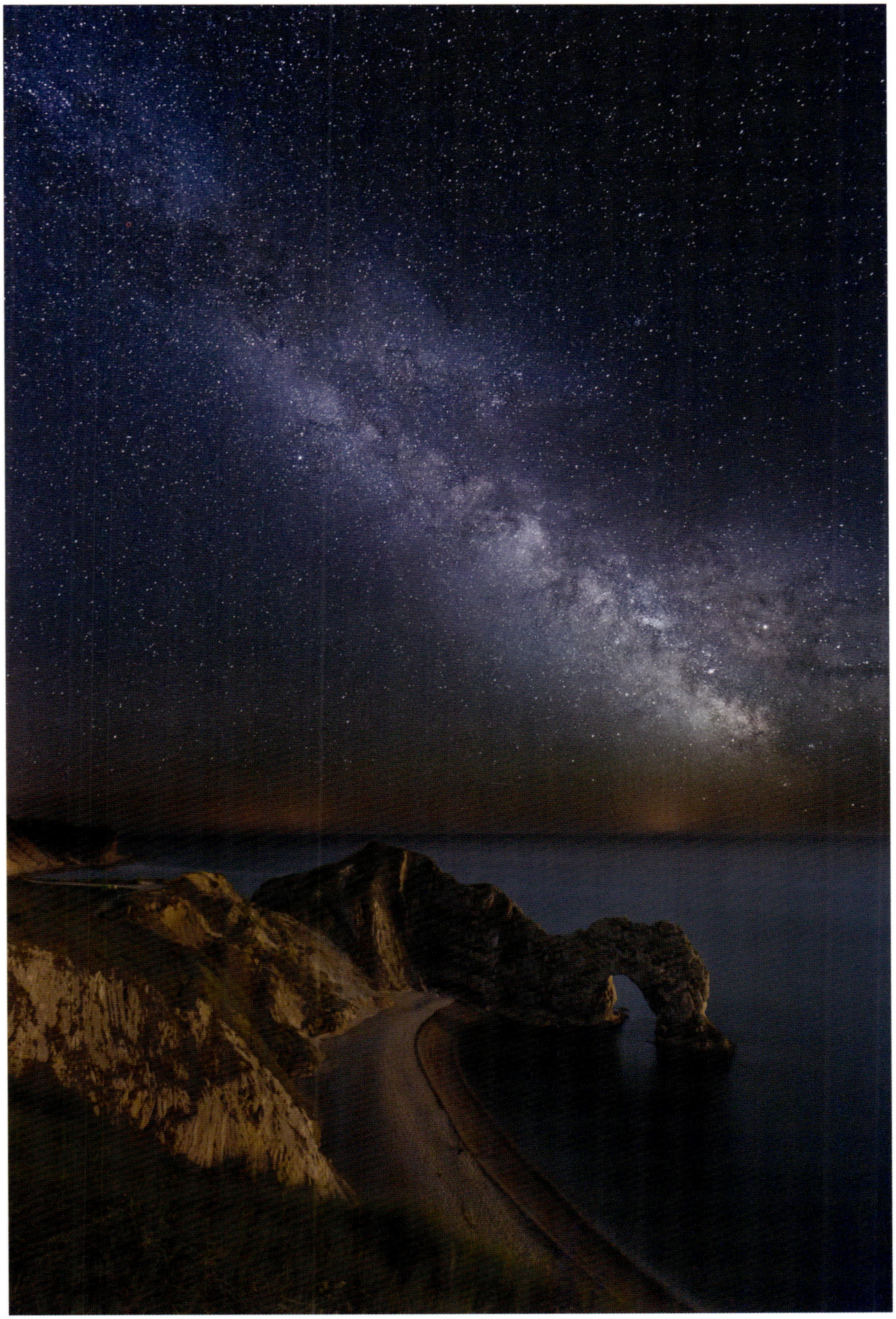

Right: This image took some planning. Checking the position that the Milky Way was due to rise from and finding a suitable location with clear dark skies that would also make a good composition was not as straightforward as it first seemed!

Focal length: 16mm

Aperture: f/4

Shutter speed: 25 sec.

ISO: 6400

Fireworks

Photographing fireworks can result in spectacular images, and it is not too difficult to achieve good results. Focus and framing will be the most difficult aspects to deal with, as the trajectory of fireworks is not always predictable and the camera will have to be fixed on a tripod. Some degree of guesswork and anticipation will be needed to predict where the first explosion will occur, so try to arrive early and determine where the launch-site is; if you know where the fireworks are being launched from you will have a better idea of where they are likely to burst.

Focusing can prove a little tricky, but once the first firework explodes you can focus on the explosion. Autofocus should be reliable enough for the first frame, but then switch to manual focus and "lock" the focus for subsequent fireworks.

It is unlikely that you'll be able to meter accurately for fireworks, so this is another scenario where shooting in Bulb mode will help. As with lightning shots, set an aperture of around f/11 and an ISO in the region of 200–400. Using a remote release, time the firing of the shutter with the launching of the fireworks and close it after they have detonated and the color streaks have disappeared fully.

Take a test shot and check the image. If it's underexposed, reduce the aperture by a stop or two and try again. If the fireworks are too bright, reduce the ISO or set a smaller aperture.

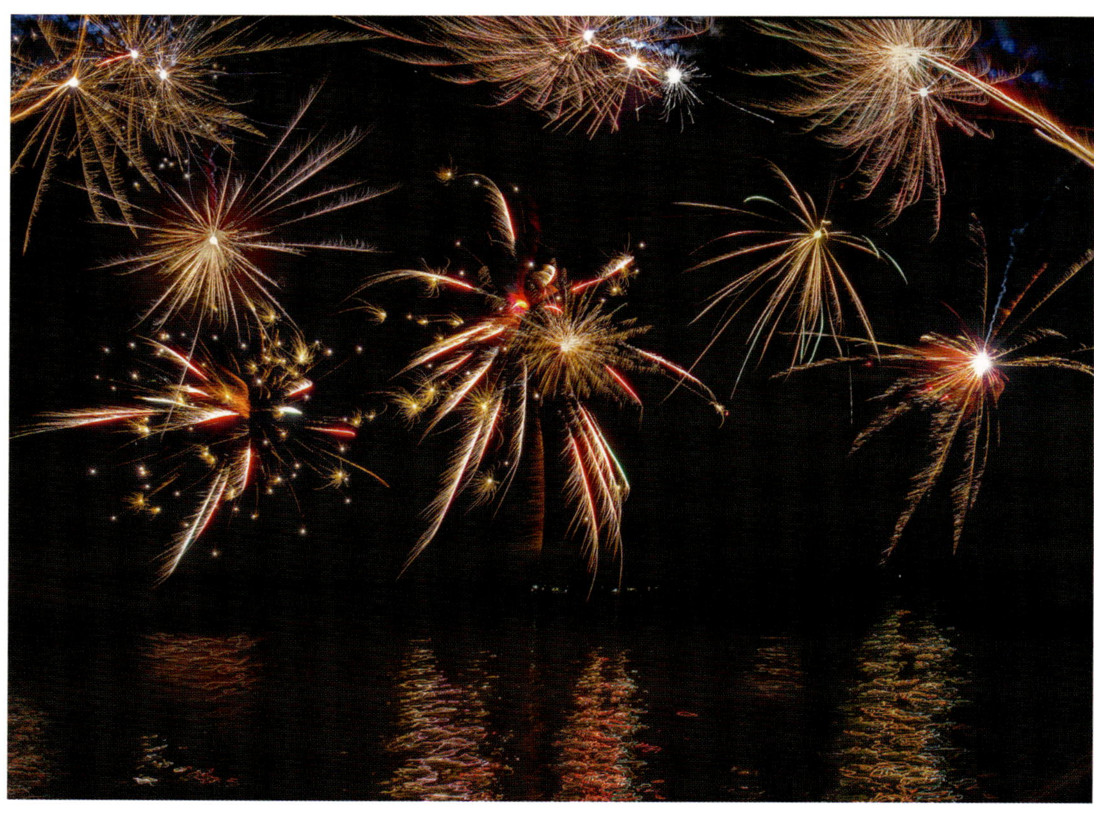

Above: This is a composite of multiple exposures of fireworks all launched from the same place. Combining shots like this can create a stronger image when there is minimal foreground interest or light in the sky.

Focal length: 16mm

Aperture: f/7.1

Shutter speed: 2 sec.

ISO: 800

Tips

- If your camera does not have Bulb mode, manually set the shutter speed to 15–20 sec. and trigger the shutter as fireworks are launched. If the explosions finish quickly then use a piece of black card (or your hand) to block the lens until the exposure ends.

- Shoot with a wider lens than you actually need, so you don't end up losing some of the fireworks from the frame. Crop your images in postproduction.

- Most often firework displays have a large barrage launched as a finale. This can lead to striking photographs.

Lightning

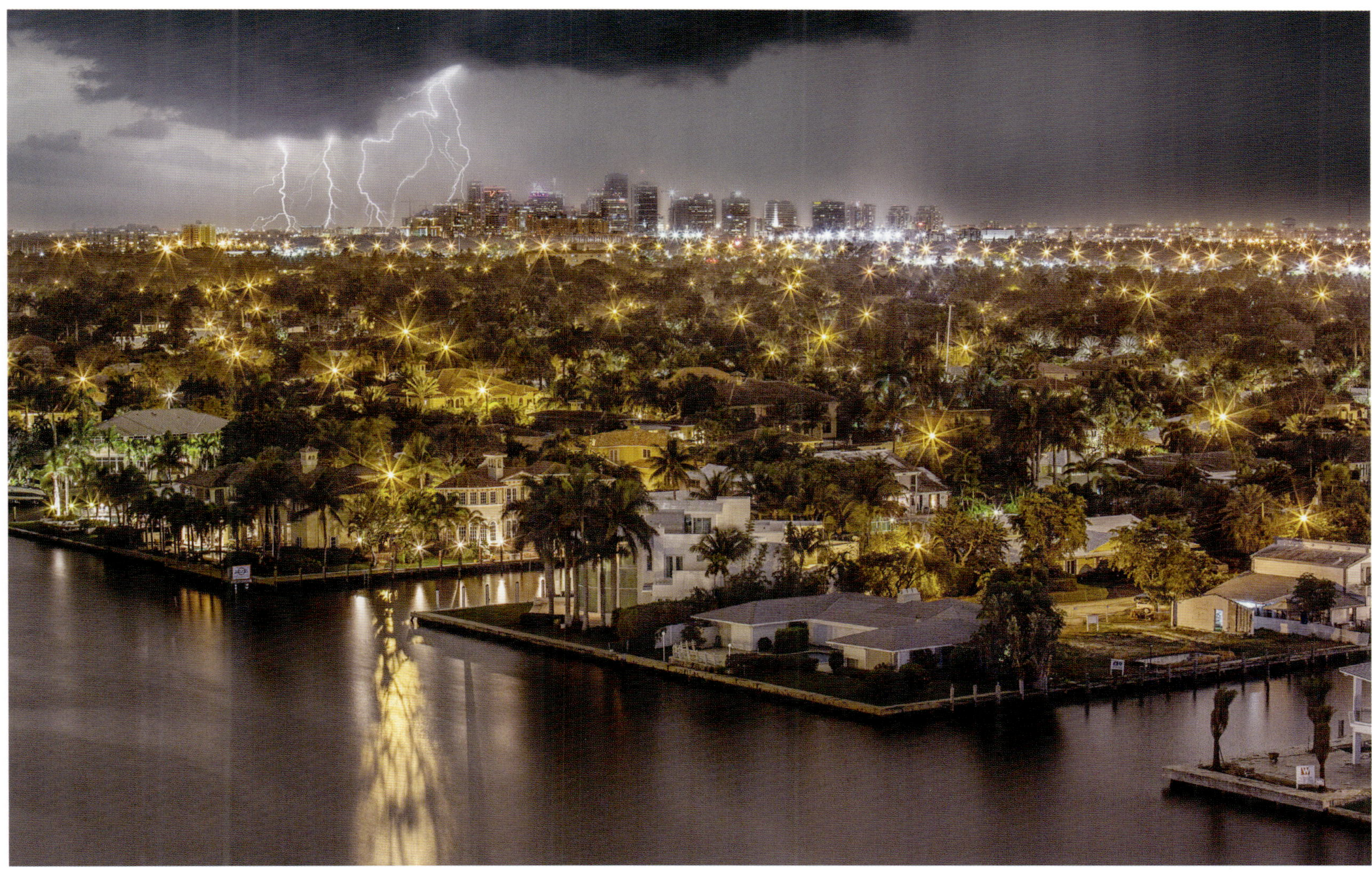

Although photographing lightning is not technically difficult, challenges arise when it comes to composing an image: guessing where and when lighting may strike or how a storm may move can be very difficult and unpredictable!

Although there is specialist equipment available that will trigger the camera's shutter automatically as lightning strikes, a simpler solution is to set the camera on a tripod and use Bulb mode; set the aperture around f/11 and the lowest ISO possible. The trick is to keep the shutter open for as long as you can without overexposing the scene, predicting when the lightning will strike. Although you will have many empty frames, you should eventually get lucky and catch a bolt of lighting or more.

This will obviously work best when the ambient light levels are low; twilight is a great time for this reason. Depending on the light, you might also want to consider taking an additional frame to correctly expose the scene so you can merge the files in postproduction.

Above: Lightning is difficult to predict. Once you can see the movement of the storm, using a longer shutter speed allows for multiple captures of the lightning bolts.

Focal length: 24mm

Aperture: f/7.1

Shutter speed: 5 sec.

ISO: 400

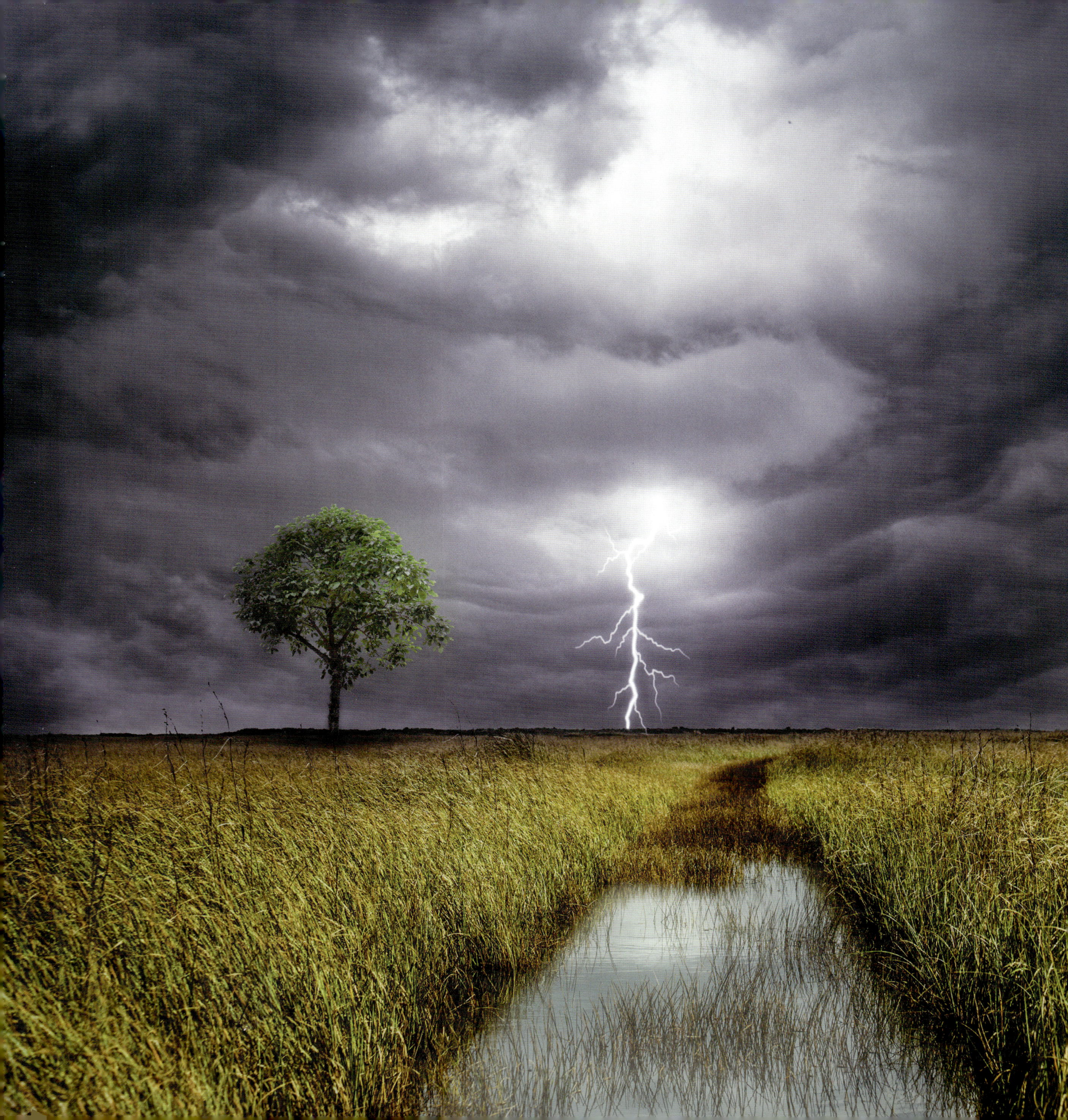

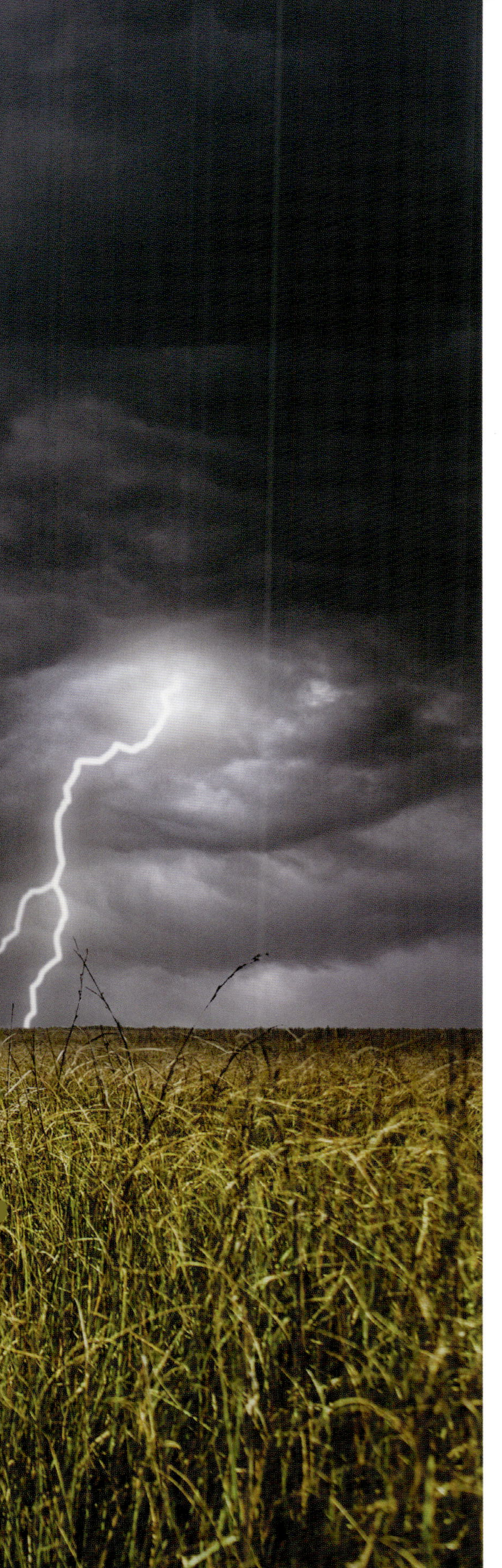

Left: Photographing lightning can be life threatening. There was a lightning shelter nearby when taking this image, so a hasty retreat could be made if the storm got too close.

Focal length: 70mm

Aperture: f/5.6

Shutter speed: 3 sec.

ISO: 400

SAFETY
Lightning is very dangerous. It is important to take shelter if the storm is unpredictable and lightning is striking close by. You should also beware of torrential rain downpours that can damage your equipment.

Chapter 6
Painting with Light

The word photography derives from the Greek meaning "writing with light." It is clear that light is the most important element in all photography and the idea behind light painting is that you have complete control over the light, and by extension, complete control over the resulting image. As you will see, this can come through the use of different lighting tools; by controlling the color of the light; or choosing specifically how and where to light certain elements within a scene.

Painting with light is relatively simple and there are two broad approaches: the first is where a light source is used to paint light onto the subject, without appearing in shot, and the second is where the light itself becomes the subject of the image. Deciding how to use these techniques—and to what effect—will help you create truly individual and often visually stimulating photographs.

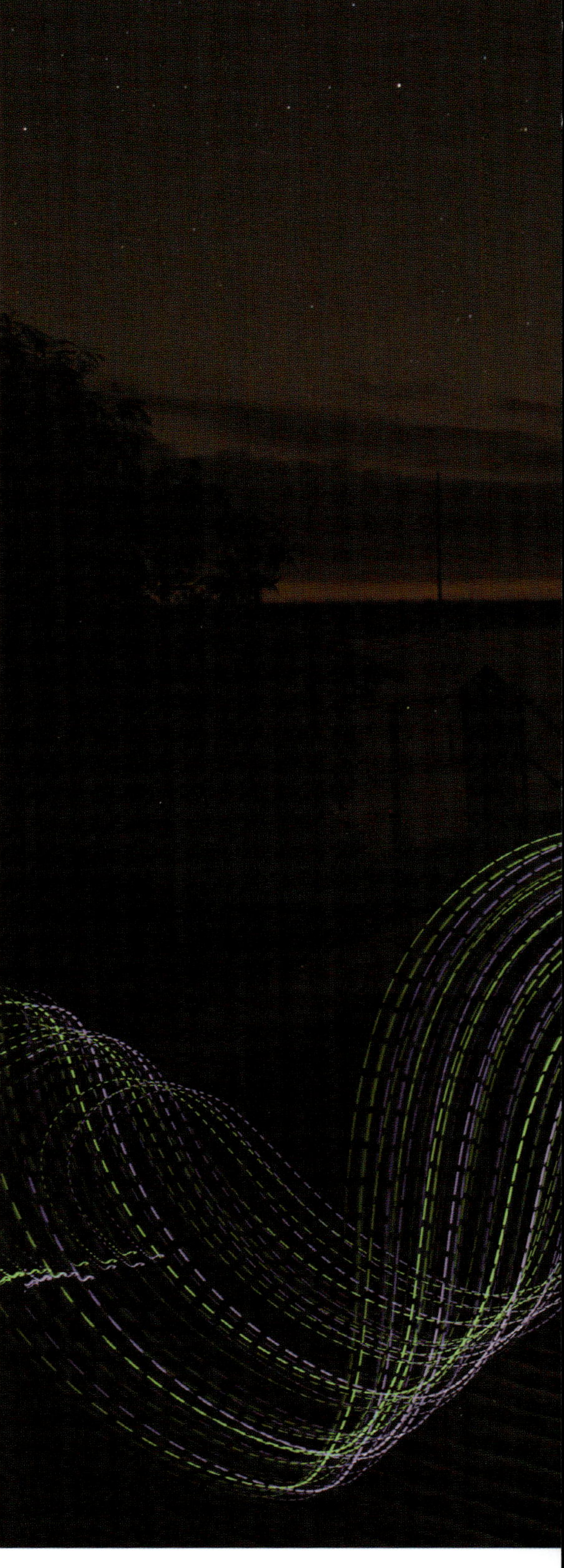

Right: The wide variety of light sources available means that there are almost limitless creative possibilities for light-painting imagery.

Focal length: 24mm
Aperture: f/4
Shutter speed: 10 sec.
ISO: 1600

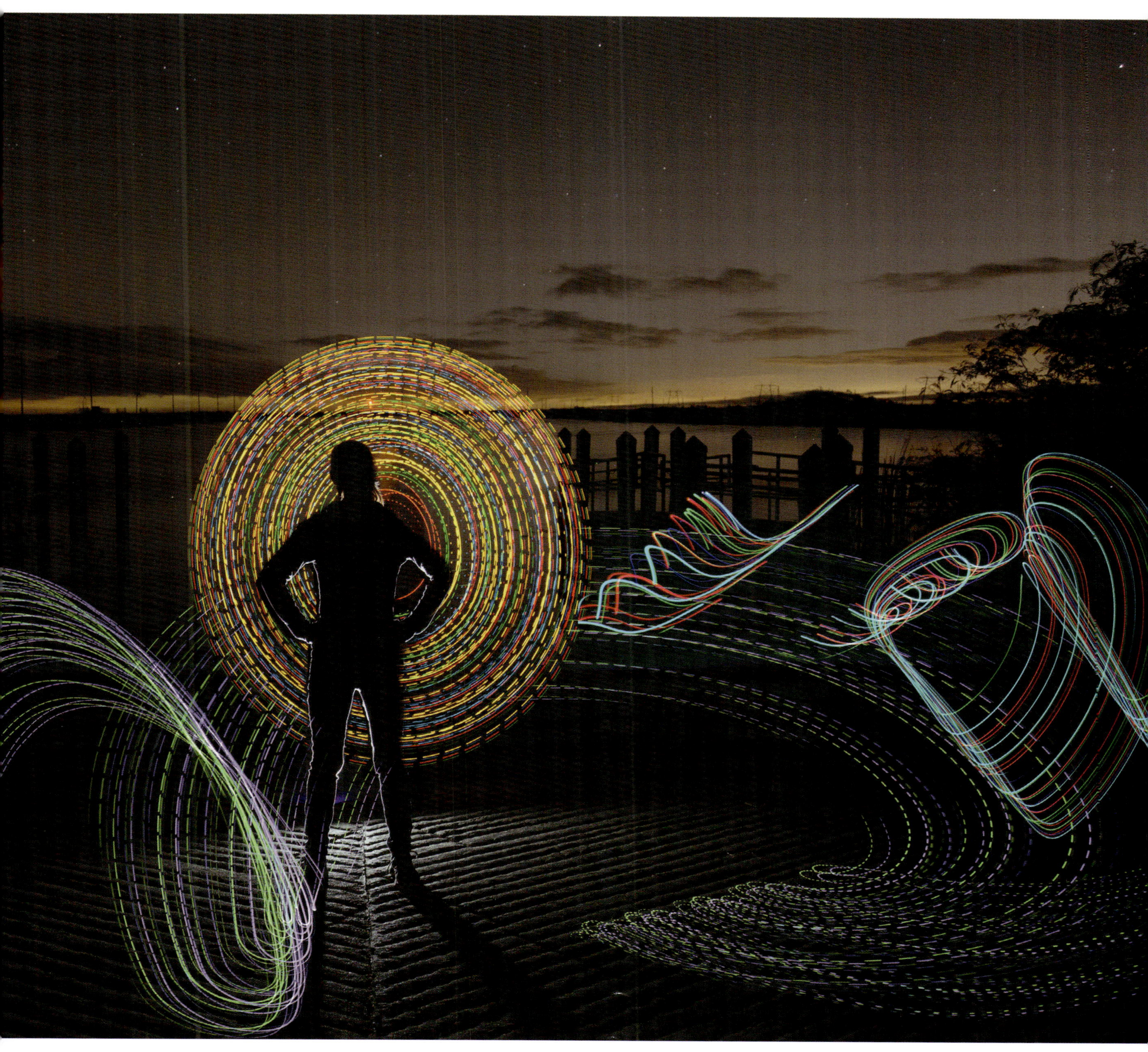

Light Sources

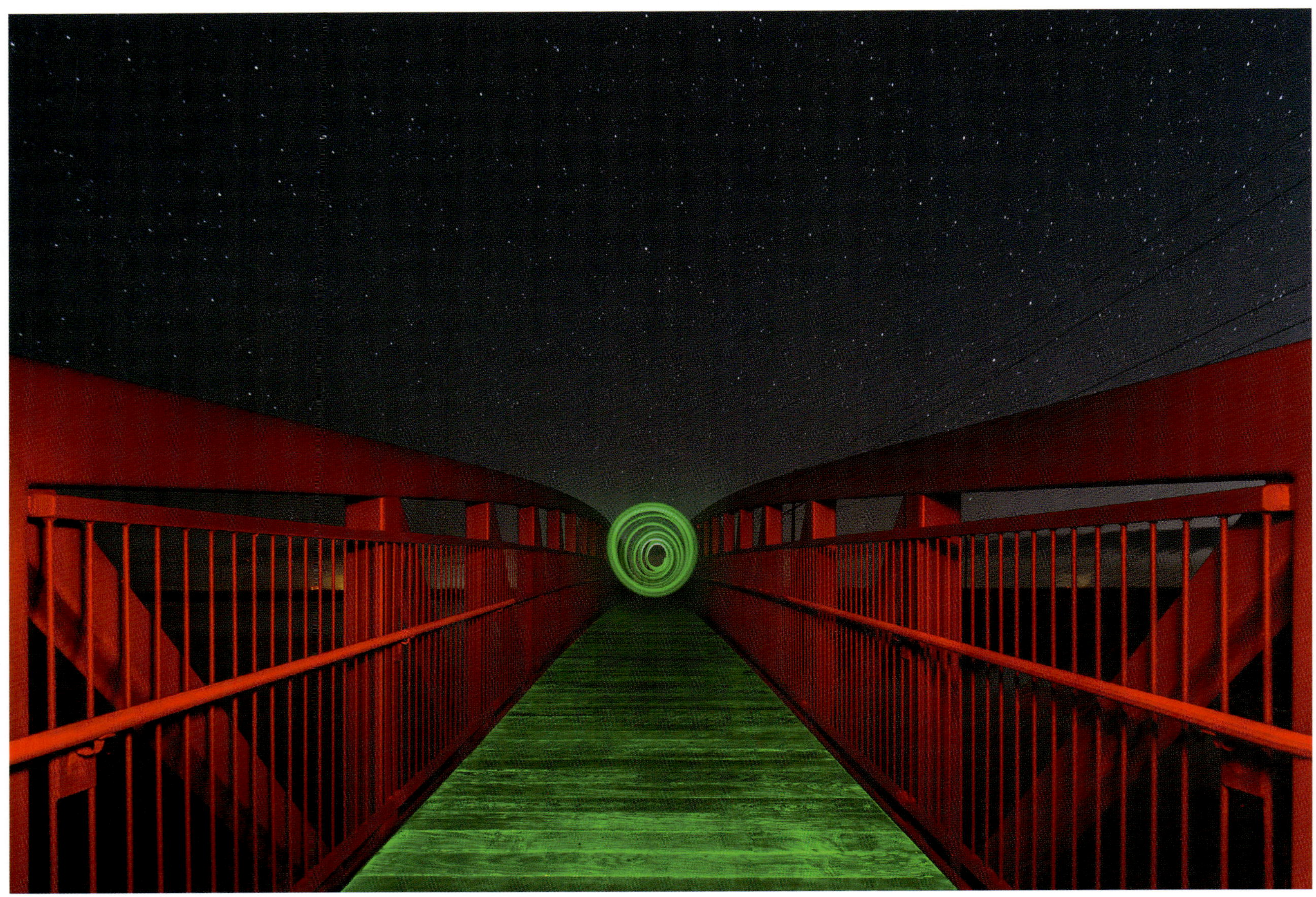

The possibilities when it comes to choosing a light source for your light painting are really only limited by your imagination. There is an immense variety of light-emitting devices available, and the number of ways in which they can be adapted for your photographs is equally broad. Ultimately, though, they break down into two categories:

Flash

An off-camera electronic flash that you can fire manually can be used for light painting, but it is not the easiest light source to use. A flash with manual power settings will give you the most control, and a snoot or other accessory that can be used to narrow the spread of light will also prove useful unless you simply want to use the flash to light up a large area in one go.

Above: This nocturnal location shot used a number of techniques. Flashlights with red and green gels were used to light up the bridge, and then the green light was spun on a cord to create a circular focal point.

Focal length: 16mm

Aperture: f/4

Shutter speed: 30 sec.

ISO: 400

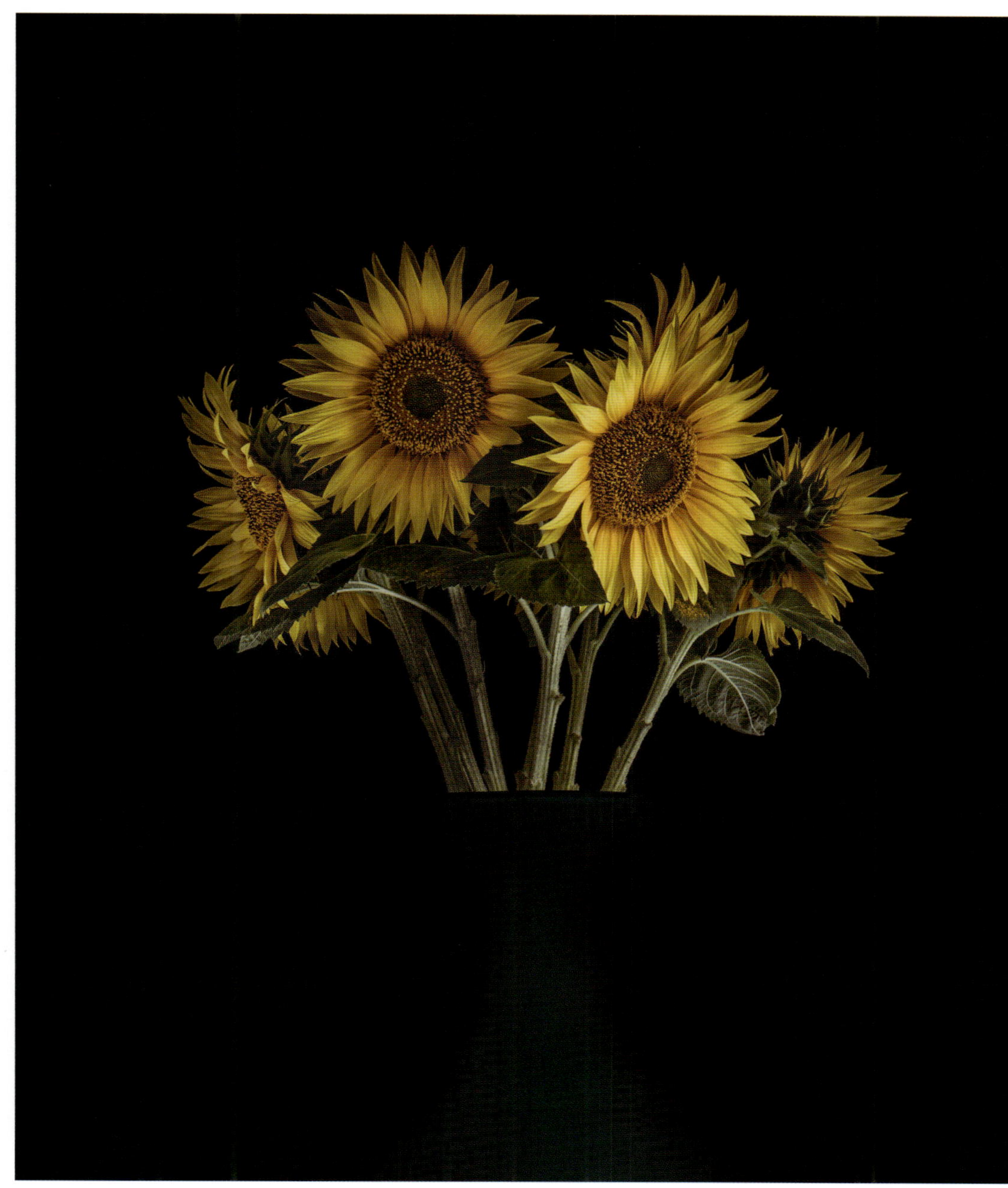

Above: For this still-life image, sunflowers were placed in a dark room with a piece of black velvet behind them. Using a low-powered flashlight, the flowers were "painted" with light to build up the exposure. It typically requires a lot of trial and error to achieve acceptable results.

Focal length: 50mm

Aperture: f/7.1

Shutter speed: 41 sec.

ISO: 200

Continuous light sources

Continuous light sources are the easiest tools to use for light painting. Options range from simple flashlights to multi-colored LEDs, to modern "light wand" designs that allow you to control the strength, color, and power of the light, as well as its width and spread; there are even specialist tools that you can program to emit a light "image" so you can literally create and photograph a picture made entirely of light. These are not the only tools available, as any constant light source can be used to paint with light.

Tips

- If you're using a continuous light source, take care when turning the light source on and off so no uncontrolled light spills into the image or scene. With a flashlight, it is a good idea to shield the light with the palm of your hand.

- With flash, a remote trigger can be used to fire it from a distance. This can allow you to use the flash to light one particular area in the image from afar, such as the inside of an abandoned car or behind a tree in a forest.

- Use colored gels on your light to change the lighting effect.

Light Painting Settings

In the first instance, light painting can be a little frustrating, as there are no general camera settings that apply to all situations; some degree of trial and error is required and it can take a number of test shots to achieve the desired effect. Also, as the subject or scene will be very dark (you may even be shooting in total darkness), you need to visualize the outcome of the painting.

The camera should be fixed on a tripod with the desired scene focused and composed. If you are shooting at night, follow the focusing tips on page 51; indoors you can simply turn the lights on to setup your shot, then turn them off before you make your exposure.

Set your camera to Bulb mode, dial in a low ISO, and choose your aperture based on the depth of field you require. The duration of the exposure will depend on the brightness of the light source used, and also on the available ambient light.

Open the shutter and start to paint your subject with your light. Try to light the subject (or the area) using slow methodical lighting strokes. If the light source remains stationary for too long on one point, there is the risk of creating an overexposed "hotspot" in the image; fluid, continual movement of the light source is essential for best results.

After you have made your exposure check the image histogram. If the image is underexposed then you can either raise the ISO, increase the brightness of the light source or work with it closer to your subject (if possible), or hold the shutter open for longer so you can paint more light onto the scene. This process is purely down to trial and error, and it will help if you make notes as you go so you can see what improves your shots.

If your image is overexposed then you should lower the ISO, decrease the intensity of the light source (by changing its power or working distance), or reduce your exposure time and work more rapidly.

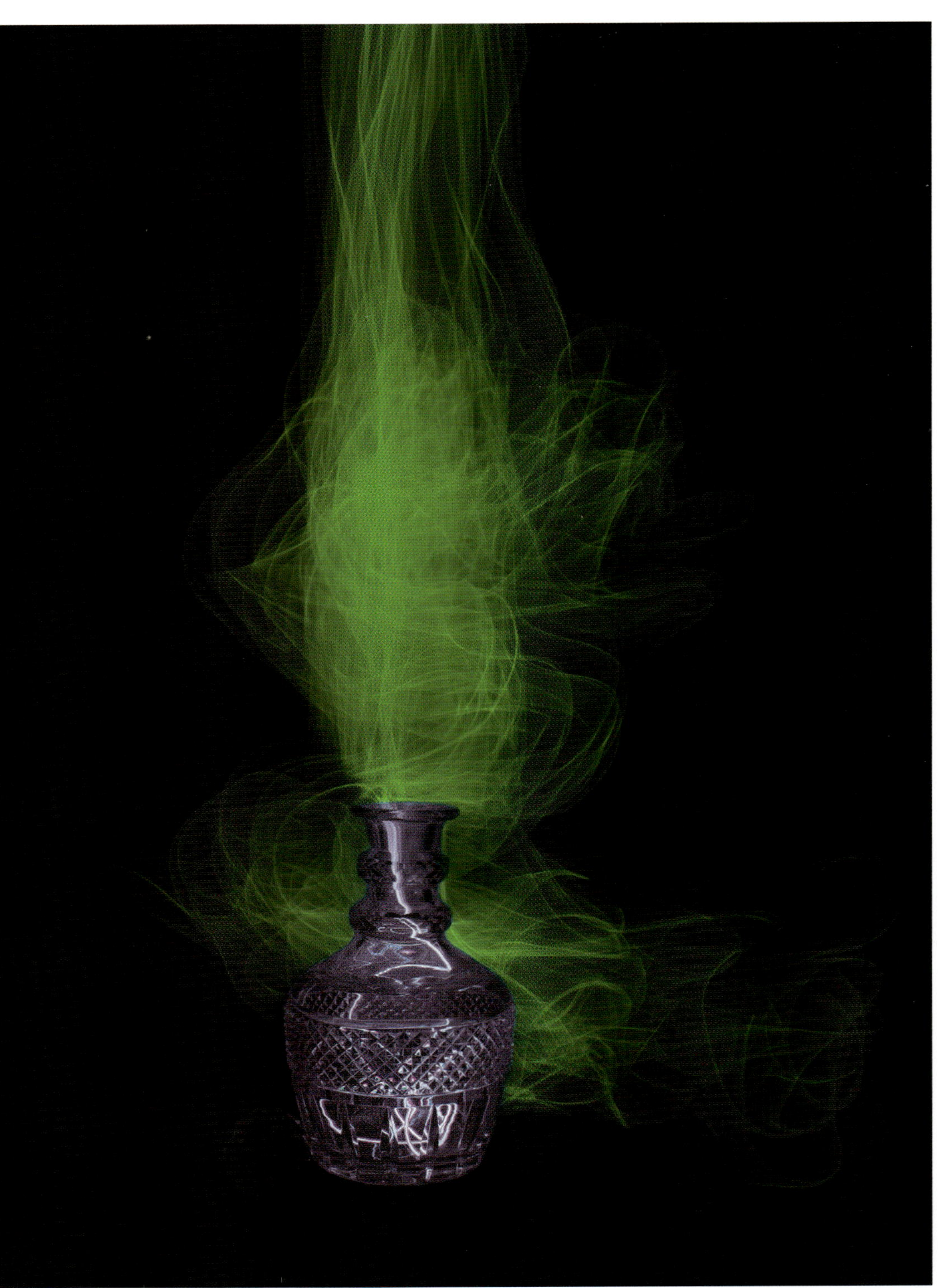

Tips

- If you want to photograph a large or complex scene using this technique, consider "image stacking." With the camera fixed in position, make a number of separate exposures, lighting a particular area or section of the subject in each one. The various exposures can then be combined during postproduction.

- The process outlined here assumes you are using a continuous source. Working with flash is essentially the same: hold the shutter open in Bulb mode and fire the flash manually to illuminate specific areas in the scene. As long as the person firing the flash doesn't remain still for too long, they will not be captured in the image. For best results, they should also dress in dark clothing.

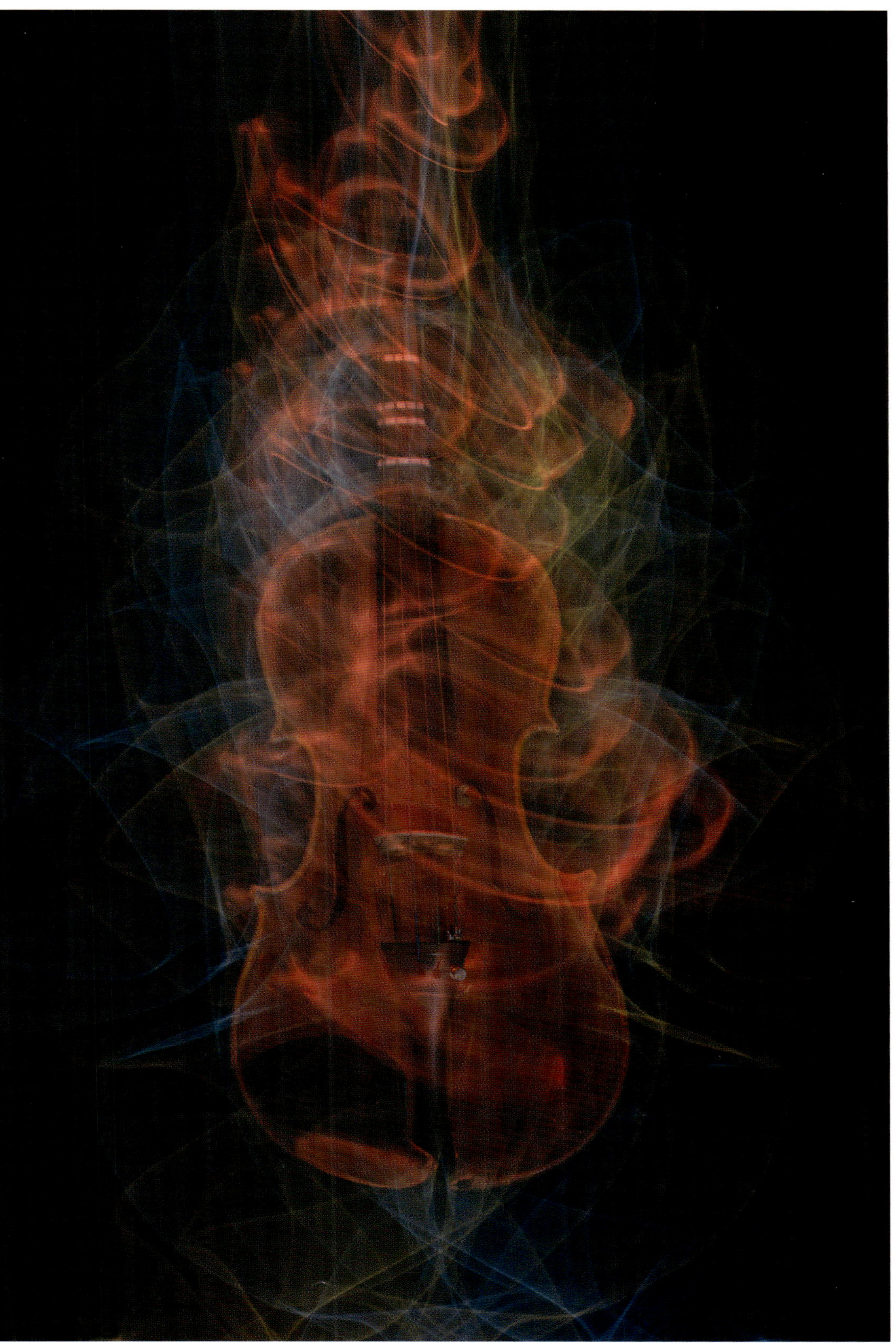

Left: The glass decanter in this image was painted using a flashlight with a purple gel. Neon wire was then moved in a slow vertical motion to replicate the look of smoke emanating from it.

Focal length: 24mm

Aperture: f/11

Shutter speed: 27 sec.

ISO: 200

Right: The violin in this image was positioned against a piece of black velvet, with the camera on a tripod. The shutter was triggered in Bulb mode and the instrument was "painted" with a small flashlight fitted with different colored gels.

Focal length: 35mm

Aperture: f/8

Shutter speed: 37 sec.

ISO: 200

Light Writing

Light writing is a creative and fun technique. Fixing the camera on a tripod, the idea is to use a light source to write or draw in front of the camera while the shutter remains open. The premise is pretty simple, but it can be tricky to do it effectively!

You can start with the light painting settings outlined on page 100, but exposure time becomes a bigger challenge, as it will depend on the scene and how you want it to appear. A creative decision will have to be made as to whether the background is to be revealed behind the writing or if the aim is just to capture the light writing itself. If you want to expose the background, then a longer exposure time will be needed and a small amount of ambient light may be beneficial. Shorter exposure times and total darkness is a better combination if you only want to record the writing.

When it comes to making your exposure, it can be difficult to keep the writing level so extra care should be taken. To minimize the chance of the writer appearing in the frame they should wear dark clothes.

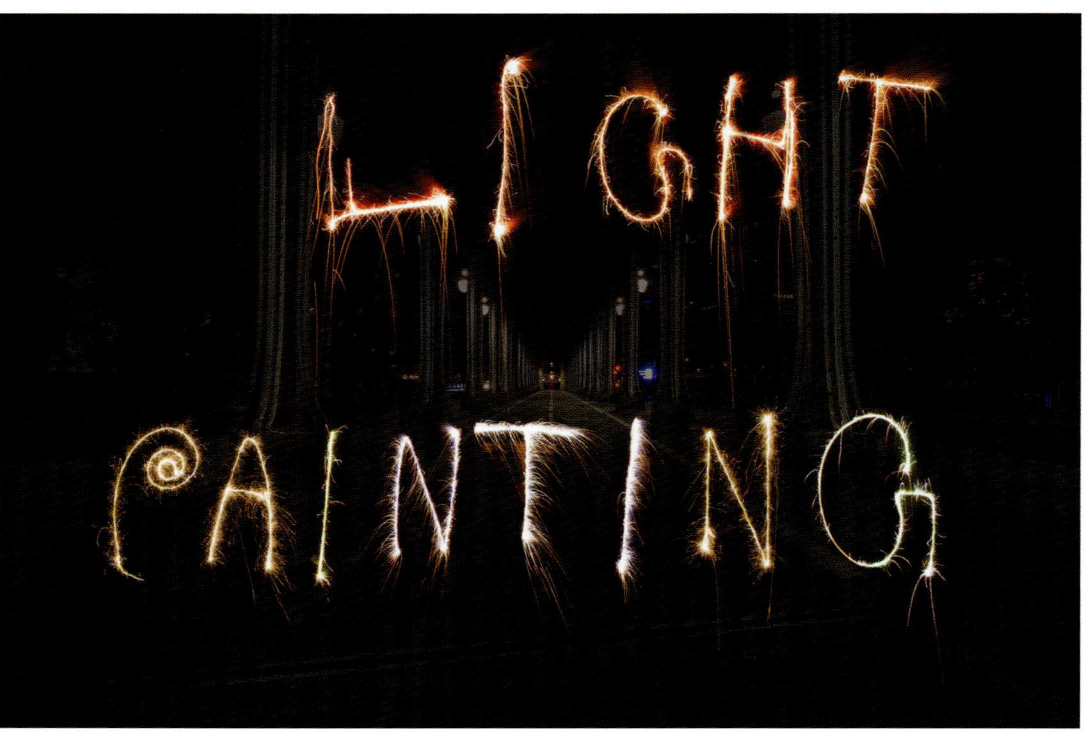

Above: The letters in this image were written out individually with sparklers (using a 3.2 sec. exposure for each letter) and then combined with the background layer in Photoshop.

Focal length: 55mm

Aperture: f/8

Shutter speed: 3.2 sec.

ISO: 200

Tip

Strictly speaking you will need to write backward, so the letters appear the right way round to the camera. However, it is far easier to write normally and then flip the image horizontally in postproduction!

SPARKLERS

Sparklers are a fairly common light source for light writing. You will need to take extra care, though, as they are very hot and can easily burn you if they're used without care and consideration. Bear in mind that the sparks can also ignite any flammable materials on the ground or around you.

Steel Wool

This technique (also known as "spinning") creates a unique look to nighttime images. Unlike other light-painting techniques, where specific areas of a scene are deliberately lit, steel wool photography adds a chaotic, industrial feel as sparks fly around in a scene.

The basic idea is that a small clump of steel wool is placed in a metal whisk and clipped into place. A cord or chain is attached to the base of the whisk and the steel wool is ignited. The steel wool will glow orange and emit a large number of sparks as it's spun in a circular motion. The light produced from the circular motion can be used very effectively to light up an archway or other derelict structure, while the sparks create dramatic fiery light trails through the image.

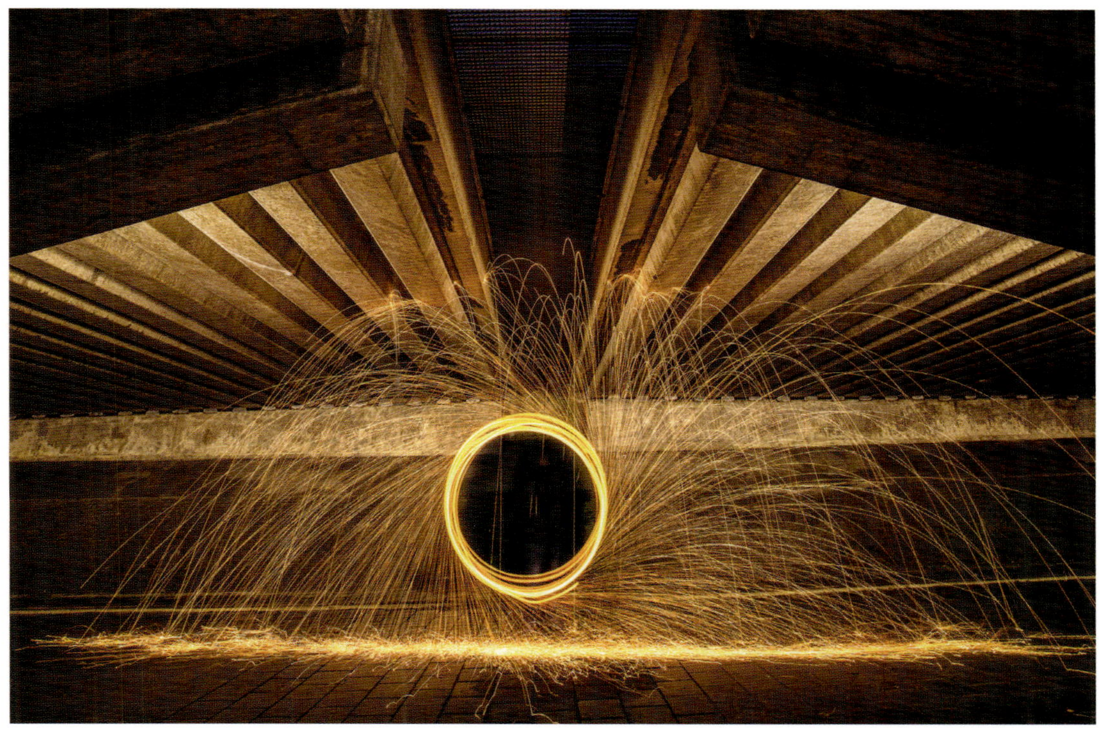

Above: A dark underpass provides the "grungy" backdrop for this steel wool shot.

Focal length: 16mm

Aperture: f/10

Shutter speed: 3 sec.

ISO: 100

WARNING!

The temperature of burning steel wool is very high: there is a serious risk of starting a fire or injuring people or equipment if you fail to take adequate precautions. Protective gear such as a hat and goggles should be worn and care needs to be taken that all sparks are extinguished after the image is taken so any fire risk is diminished. You should also take care in choosing a location: dry grassland can ignite easily.

Physiograms

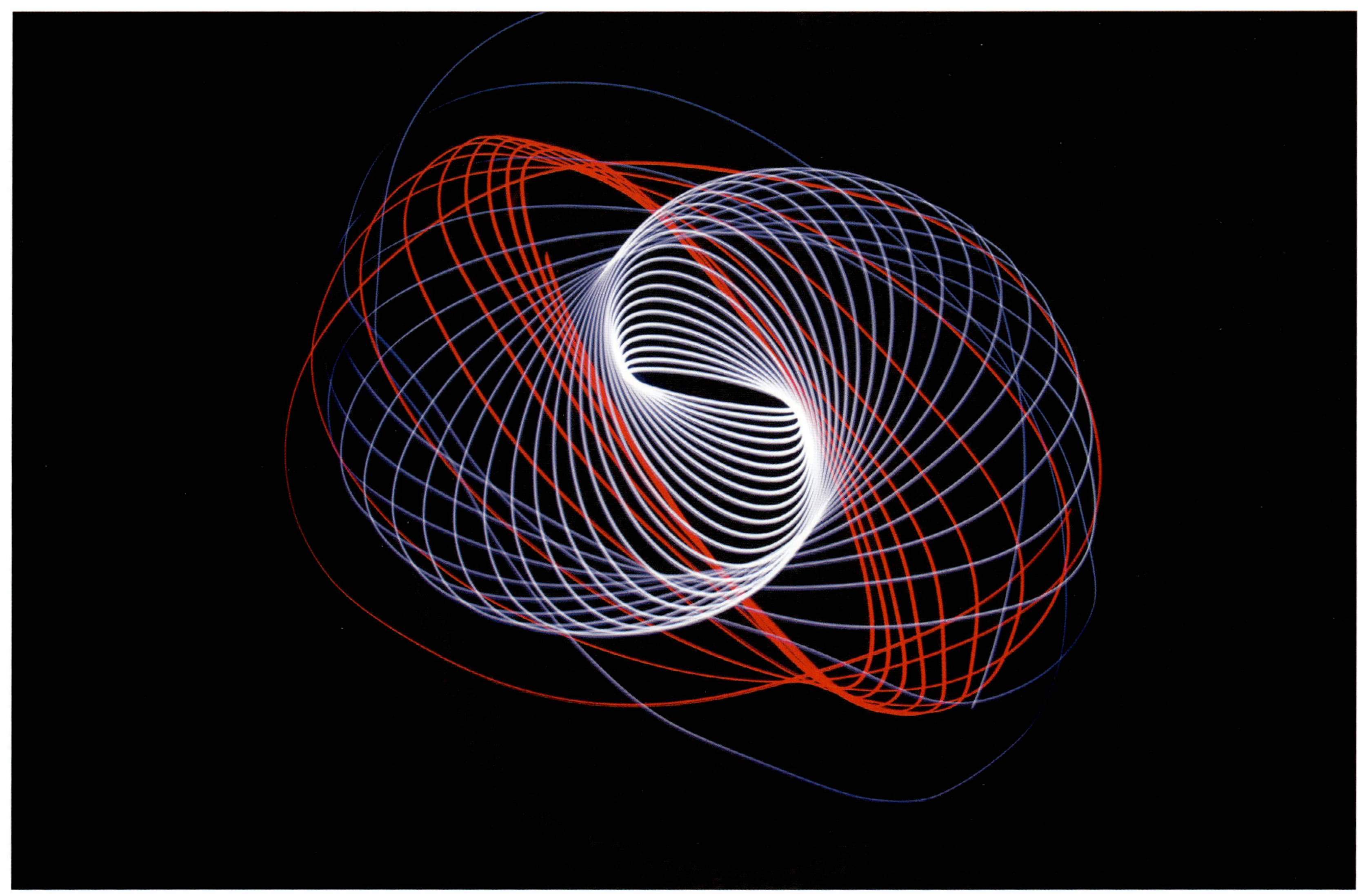

A physiogram is an abstract geometric pattern that is made by swinging a light source like a pendulum and photographing its movement. These are quite simple to create, but each pattern produced will be unique; with creativity and imagination you can generate extremely intricate and ornate patterns.

The concept is straightforard. Take a small flashlight and cover the front of it with black card or tape with a very small hole in it to reduce the light beam it emits. Attach the light to a cord so it is suspended, pointing downward. Then, place the camera directly below the light (aimed upward) and focus manually on the beam of light. Set the camera to Manual mode with an aperture of f/11, shutter speed of 30 sec., and a low ISO. Turn off any external lights so the only visible light is from the flashlight. Then, gently swing the flashlight and trigger the camera using a remote release. The camera will record the light's movement as a long exposure light trail.

Tips

- To make more intricate shapes and designs, consider rotating and changing the angle of the swing so the shape and pattern change.

- Use colored gels to change the color of the light source.

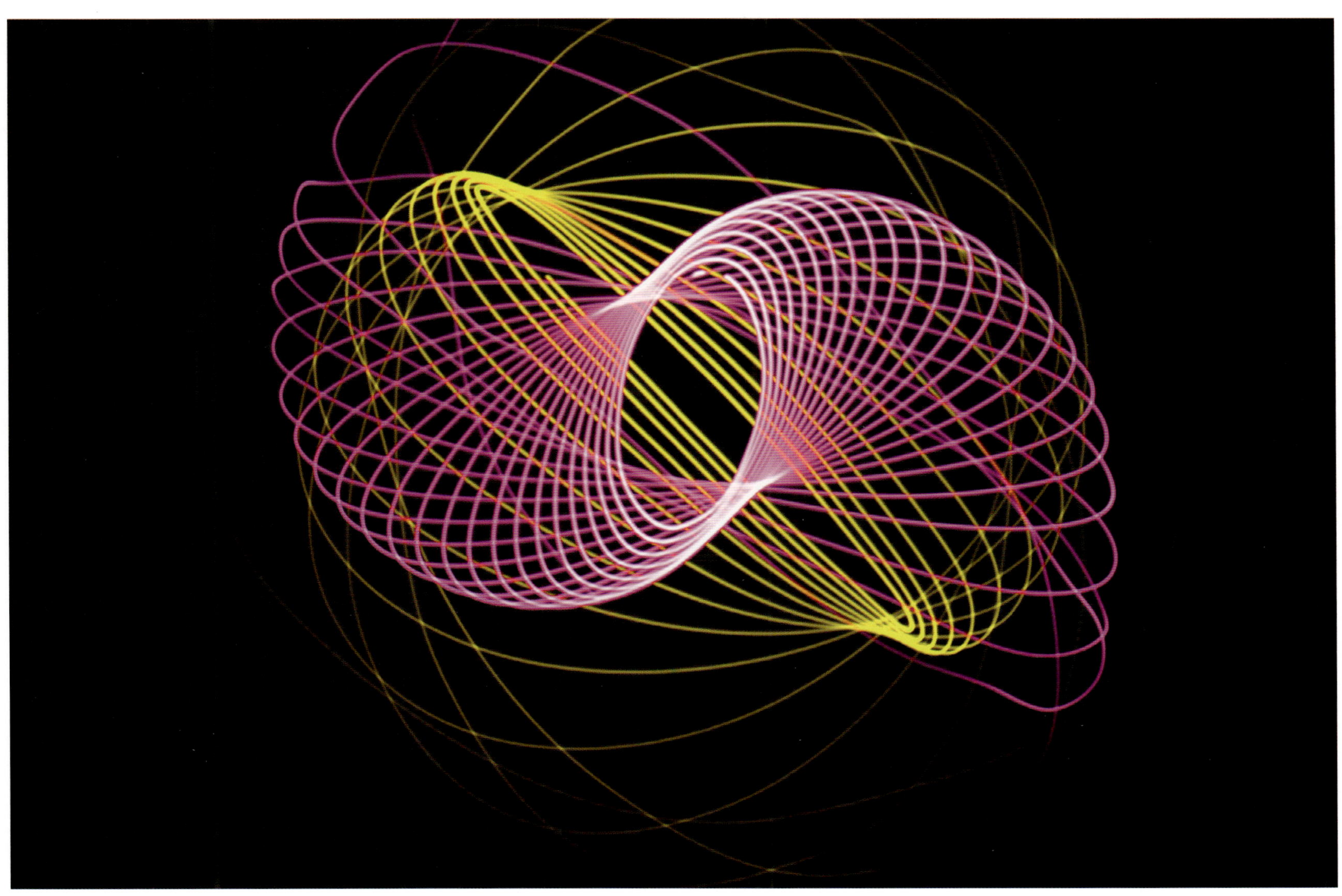

Above left & above: To create the different colors in these images I used colored gels over the light. I extended the exposure time so I could change the gel half way through the exposure, covering the lens with a piece of black card while I swopped colors. I then removed the card and continued exposing with the second color. The great thing about physiograms is that no two images will be the same, as the speed, direction, and revolutions of the light inevitably differ.

Above left:
Focal length: 24mm
Aperture: f/10
Shutter speed: 81 sec.
ISO: 100

Above:
Focal length: 24mm
Aperture: f/10
Shutter speed: 77 sec.
ISO: 100

Tip

Experiment with two or more light sources, or combine multiple physiograms to create more complex patterns.

Additional Techniques

The variety of light-emitting devices available is huge, and the ways that these can then be adapted to create complex and unique patterns is immense. Here are just a few alternative options for you to consider:

Fairy lights

A string of battery powered, colored "fairy lights" can lead to very inventive and unique imagery. These lights can also be attached to an array of different items to produce individual patterns through different means of movement.

Neon wire

Neon wire is a low-cost light source that emits a colored light through a thin flexible plastic tube. The tube can be bent into imaginative shapes to imprint into scenes or it can be moved; moving the wire in a slow, shaky motion can create a fog-like colored "mist" that can be used to add texture and atmosphere to certain scenes. This is especially effective in forests or by water.

LEDs

The power of LEDs enables a multitude of colors to be selected or changed easily. The low-power usage of LEDs, and the fact that they do not get hot with use, makes them ideal for light painting. They can easily be affixed to ropes or sticks to create dazzling light pattern displays. Some specialist "light wands" allow changes and patterns to be selected with an app on your smart device, so complex lighting arrangements can be pre-programmed.

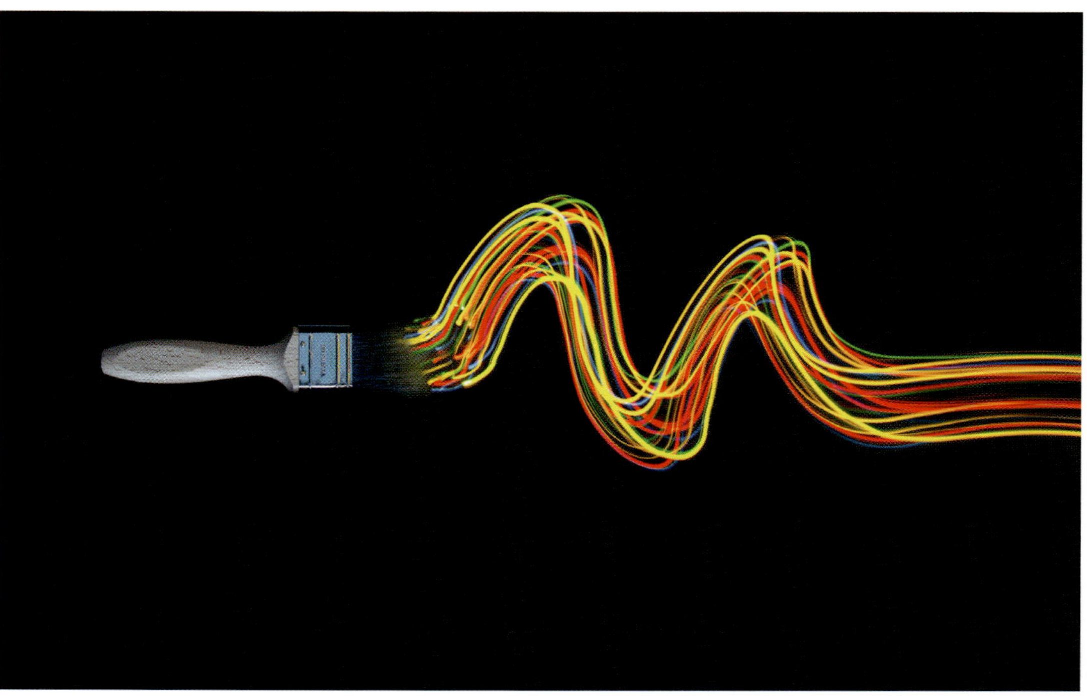

Above: This paintbrush was positioned on black velvet and a small string of battery operated lights was used to create a flowing light trail.

Focal length: 28mm

Aperture: f/7.1

Shutter speed: 2 sec.

ISO: 200

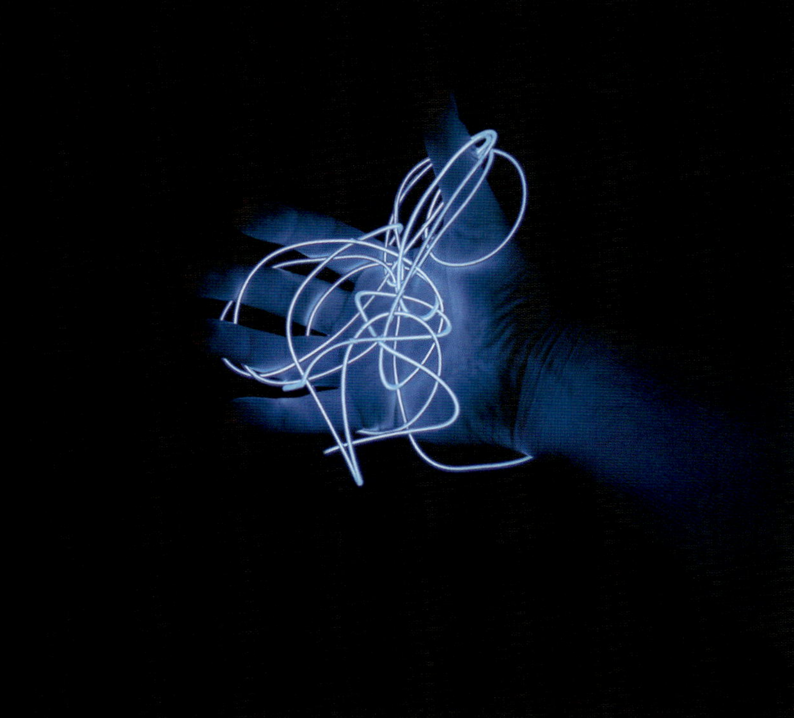

Left: Neon wire can be used in multiple ways to create unique images.

Focal length: 35mm

Aperture: f/9

Shutter speed: 5 sec.

ISO: 100

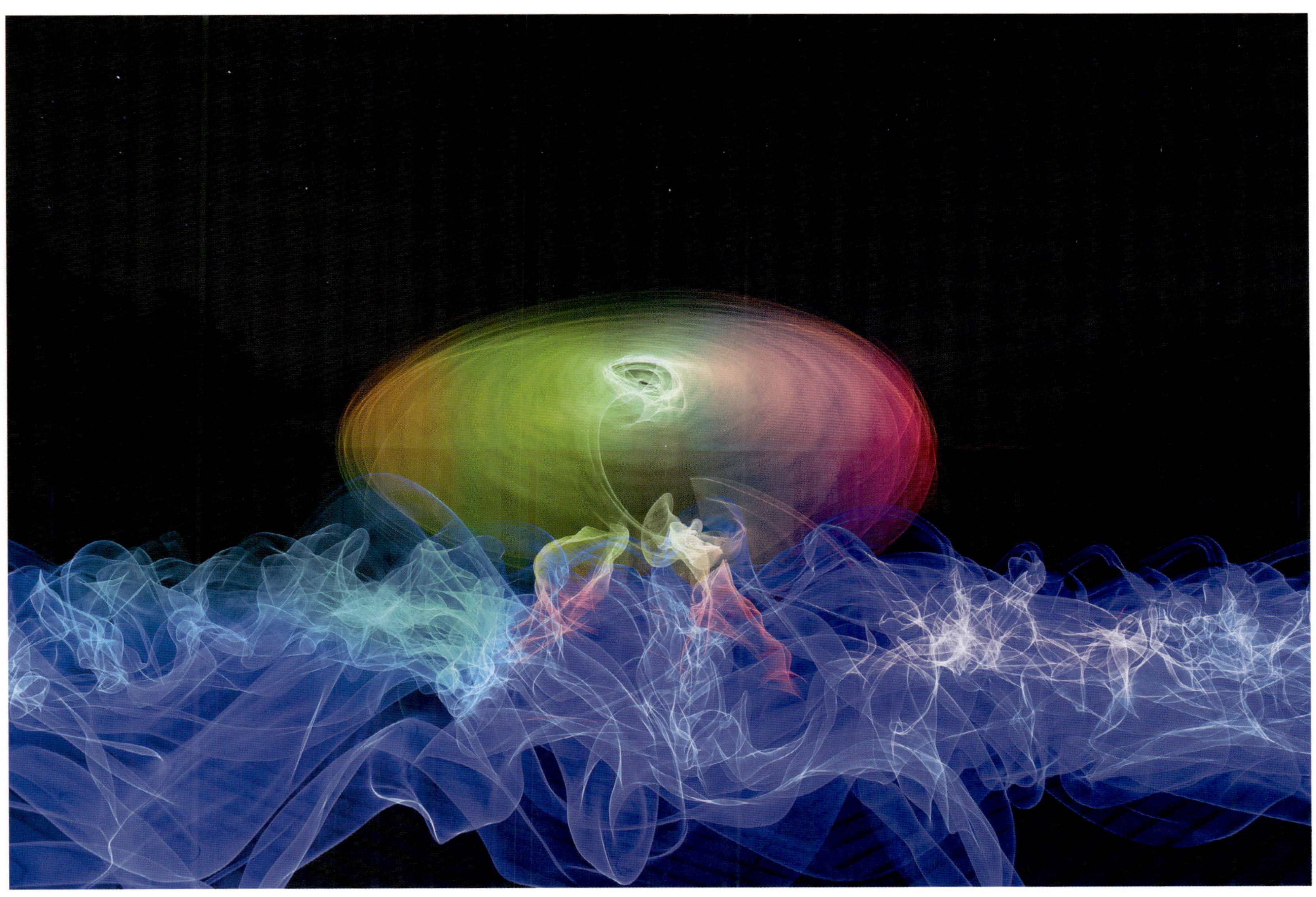

Moving the light

Some of the most compelling light painting imagery comes when the movement of the light source(s) is smooth and regular. This can include swinging or rotating the light source, either on its own or by attaching it to a cord of some sort, and avoiding any jarring movements.

Above: Attaching a string of colored lights to a cord that is spun creates a unique pattern. The blue fog-like lights are from neon wire that has been moved slowly through the scene. The people moving the lights were dressed in black so they were not recorded by the camera.

Focal length: 16mm

Aperture: f/8

Shutter speed: 16 sec.

ISO: 800

Profile: Janne Parviainen

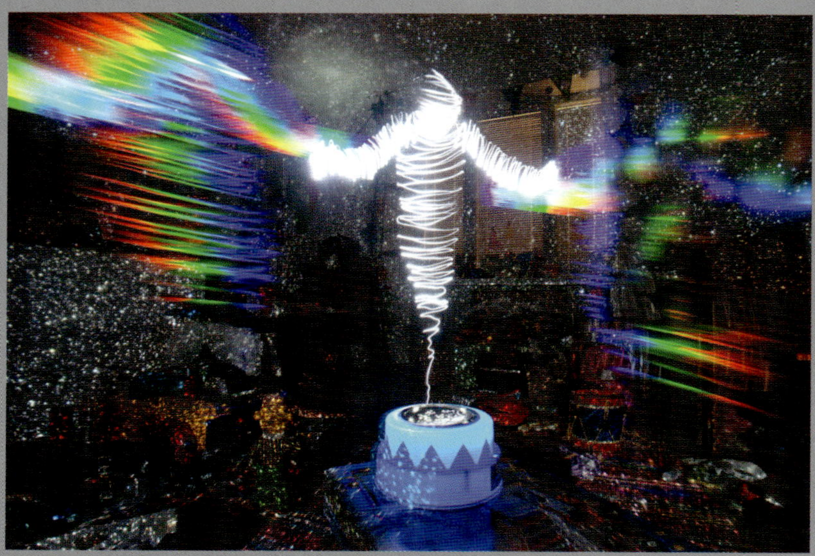

Above:
Guiding Hand
Focal length: 17mm
Aperture: f/14
Shutter speed: 1311 sec.
ISO: 100

Above:
Late Night Show
Focal length: 27mm
Aperture: f/5
Shutter speed: 1237 sec.
ISO: 100

BIOGRAPHY

Janne Parviainen is a Finnish light artist who currently lives and works in Helsinki. His work has featured in countless books, magazines (including *National Geographic*), and online articles, and has been shown in both solo and group exhibitions, light art festivals, and museums around the world.

www.jannepaint.com

Q) What is your specialty?

A) I specialize in light painting, often using exposures in excess of 20 minutes. I use this time to form a variety of figures and luminescent skeletons, and to create topographic maps of spaces, in which I trace entire rooms with light.

Q) What drew you to your specialty and why?

A) In 2008 I was walking home late at night with my pocket camera in my hand and took some long exposure shots with it. The street lamps created beautiful light trails, which caught my attention.

Following on from that I placed the camera on a table and tried to draw in front of it using different lights. I was absolutely mesmerized at the possibilities offered by light painting and bought a DSLR camera so I could develop my technique.

Q) What key equipment do you use regularly?

A) My gear is very simple: I use are a Sony Alpha 850 with a Minolta 16–35mm lens and a Sony Alpha 200 with an 18–55mm lens.

For the light painting I use small, colored LED flashlights. I have a lot of different lights that I use for lighting up the scenery or focusing in the dark. LED lights are essential to my art because they are very small, which allows me to accurately trace and create things with them.

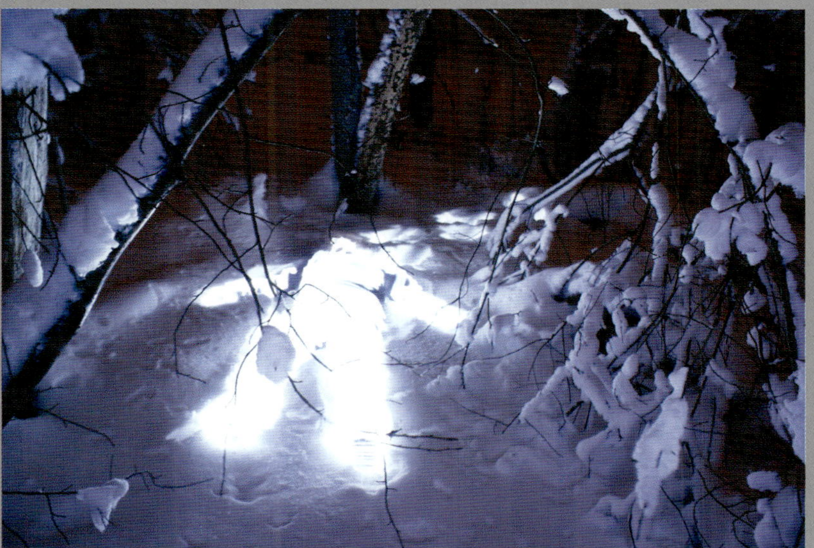

Above:
Return To Forever
Focal length: 27mm
Aperture: f/6.3
Shutter speed: 202 sec.
ISO: 100

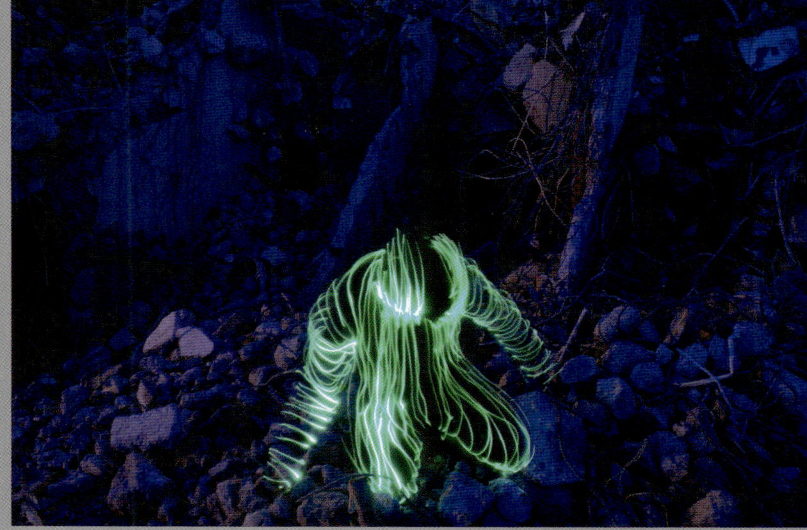

Above:
Roads That Lead Nowhere
Focal length: 27mm
Aperture: f/16
Shutter speed: 150 sec.
ISO: 100

Q) How do you visualize and compose your images?

A) I usually have an idea in mind, but then look at ways that I can take it further based on the location or objects I'm using. A lot of the time I have to improvise, as you tend to bump into unexpected situations while shooting; sometimes I'll even shoot a new idea entirely. When searching for potential locations I try to find places that inspire me to create a story, and I also like to use materials I find in the locations.

I almost always have to take multiple shots before I'm happy with the outcome because in light painting taking test shots is the only way to see what has to be changed in a photograph in order to get it right.

Q) How important is postproduction to your imagery?

A) The idea of my light painting is that all of my photos should be straight from the camera, without any postproduction. It is sort of "professional pride" for me to get the image right in camera.

Q) What is your top tip?

A) The most important thing is to be original. Emulating other people is OK when you start out, but after a while it's like writing a book that's already been written—people aren't interested in that. Develop your own style and think what you want to tell people with your photography. A photograph is a photograph, but if it touches your heart it can be much more than that!

On a practical level you should also remember to light up the background of your shots. When you start out painting with light it is easy to concentrate only on painting or drawing your subject and forget about the background.

Chapter 7

Daylight Exposure

During the day there is usually an abundance of light, so even on an overcast or cloudy day the basic settings of aperture, shutter speed, and ISO will combine to produce accurate results with a relatively short exposure time. However, using a few simple techniques and filters will enable you to capture a much longer period of time in a single frame, without overexposing the image. In doing so you will emphasize any movement that is taking place in the scene in front of you, revealing things that cannot be seen with the naked eye. This can add a dynamism to your pictures that otherwise wouldn't be recorded in a single momentary photograph.

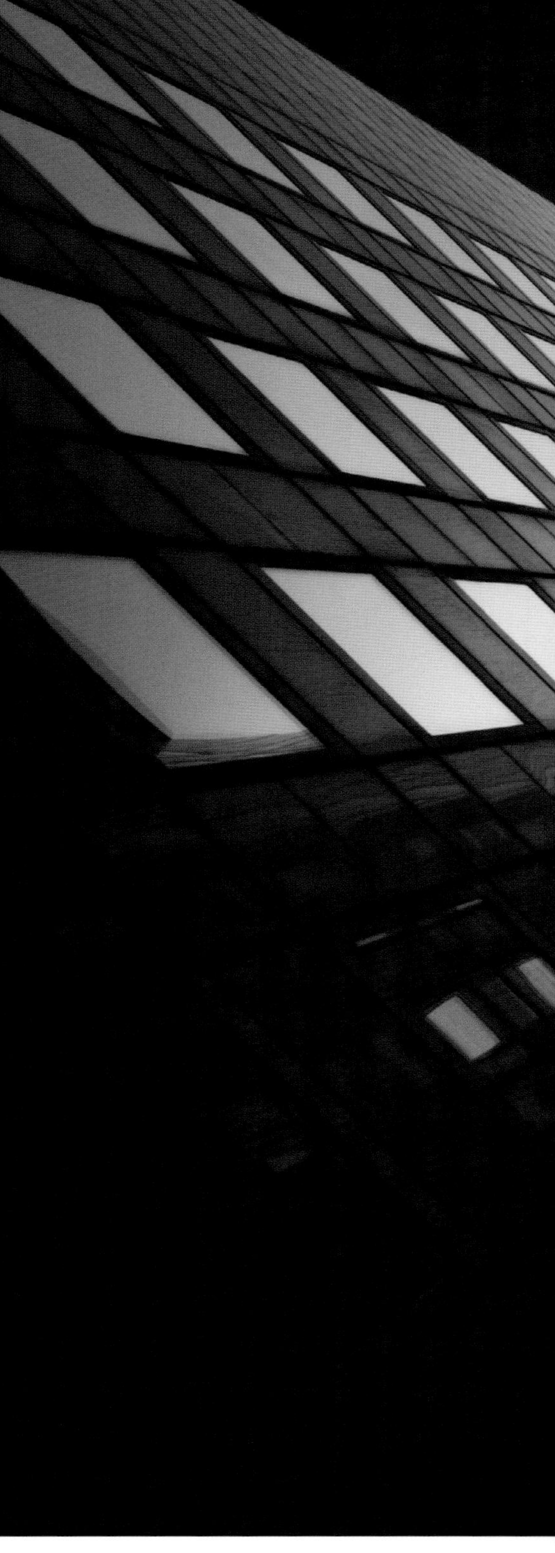

Right: The walkway between these two buildings creates a central focal point for this long exposure image. Taken with a 10-stop ND filter, it was possible to capture the subtle movement of the cloud and the light reflecting on the buildings.

Focal length: 16mm

Aperture: f/16

Shutter speed: 96 sec.

ISO: 200

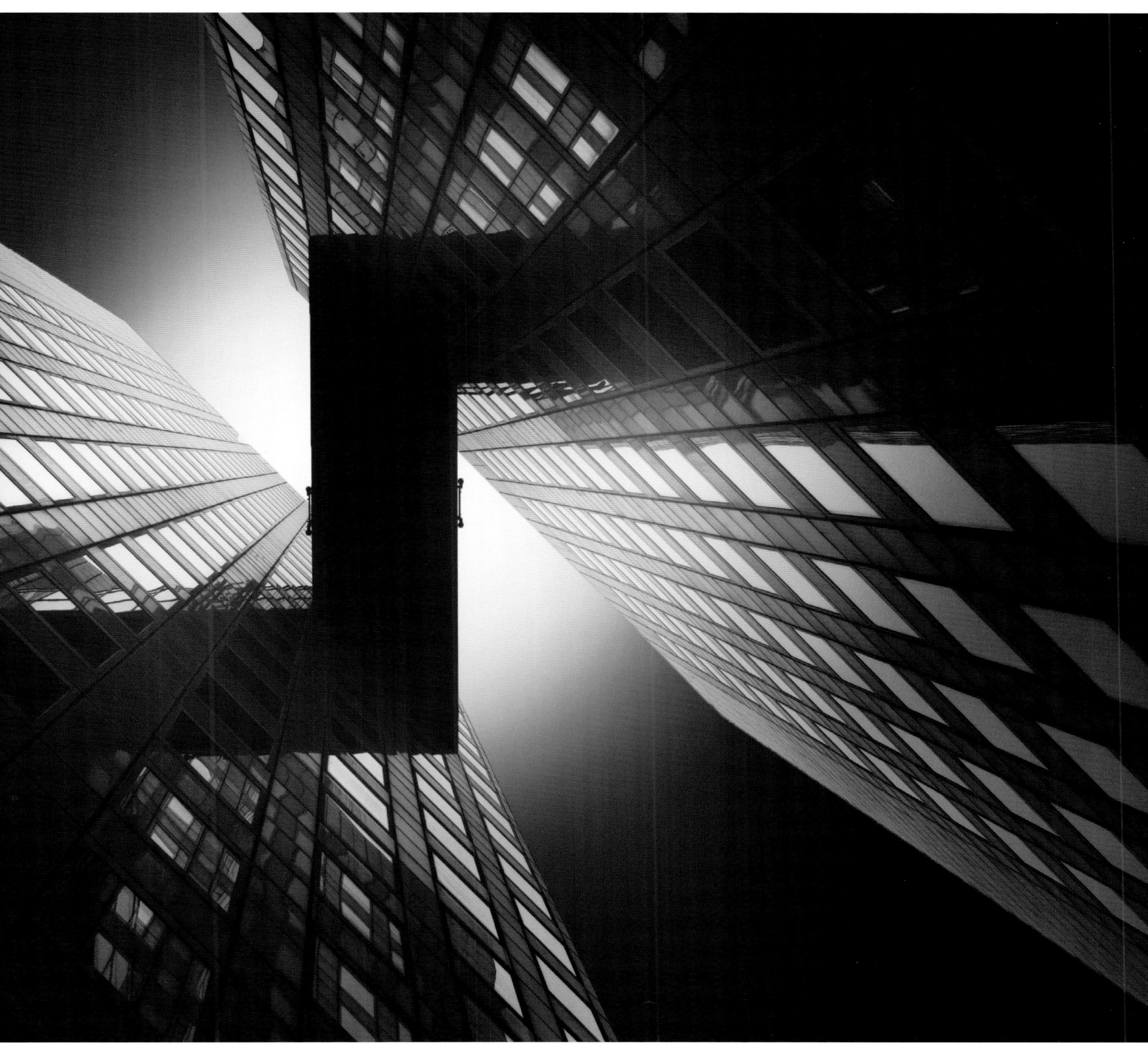

Polarizing Filters

A polarizing filter is probably the most essential all-round filter for outdoor photographers, as its effects are broad when used correctly and cannot be replicated in postproduction.

Its main uses are to heighten contrast (particularly between white clouds and blue sky), increase saturation, and reduce glare from reflective shiny surfaces. This can be very effective when it comes to removing reflections from wet rocks and from the surface of water.

Polarizing filters work at their best when used at a 90-degree angle to the sun. Care should be taken if they are used at a slightly different angle as the effect may only be seen in part of the image. This can be especially noticeable in the sky areas and extra care should be taken where using a polarizer to take a panoramic image.

Tips

- A polarizing filter can help to saturate colors and remove glare on cloudy days, as well as when the sun is out.

- When it's used at maximum strength, a polarizing filter reduces the amount of light entering the lens by around two stops. This can help you use a slower shutter speed during daylight hours, but the polarizing effect may not always be desired.

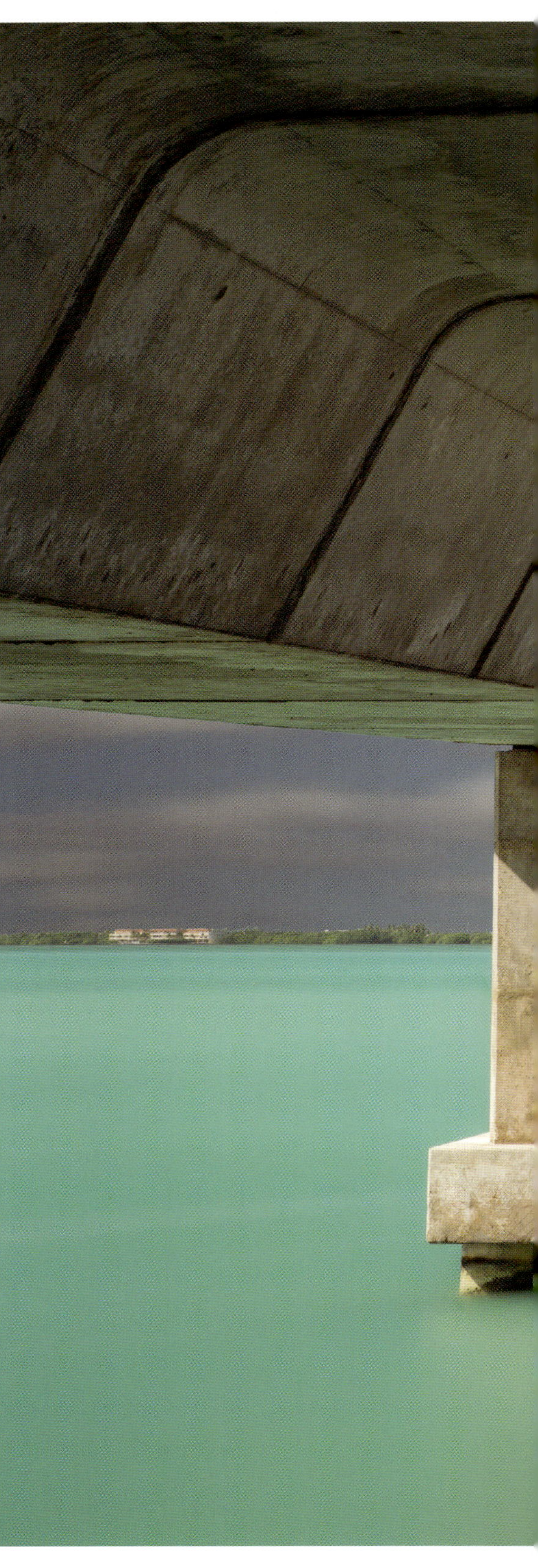

Right: This image, taken in the Florida Keys, combined a polarizing filter with a 6-stop neutral density (ND) filter. The ND filter allowed a long shutter speed, which flattened the water, while the polarizer removed the glare from the water's surface.

Focal length: 65mm

Aperture: f/16

Shutter speed: 65 sec.

ISO: 100

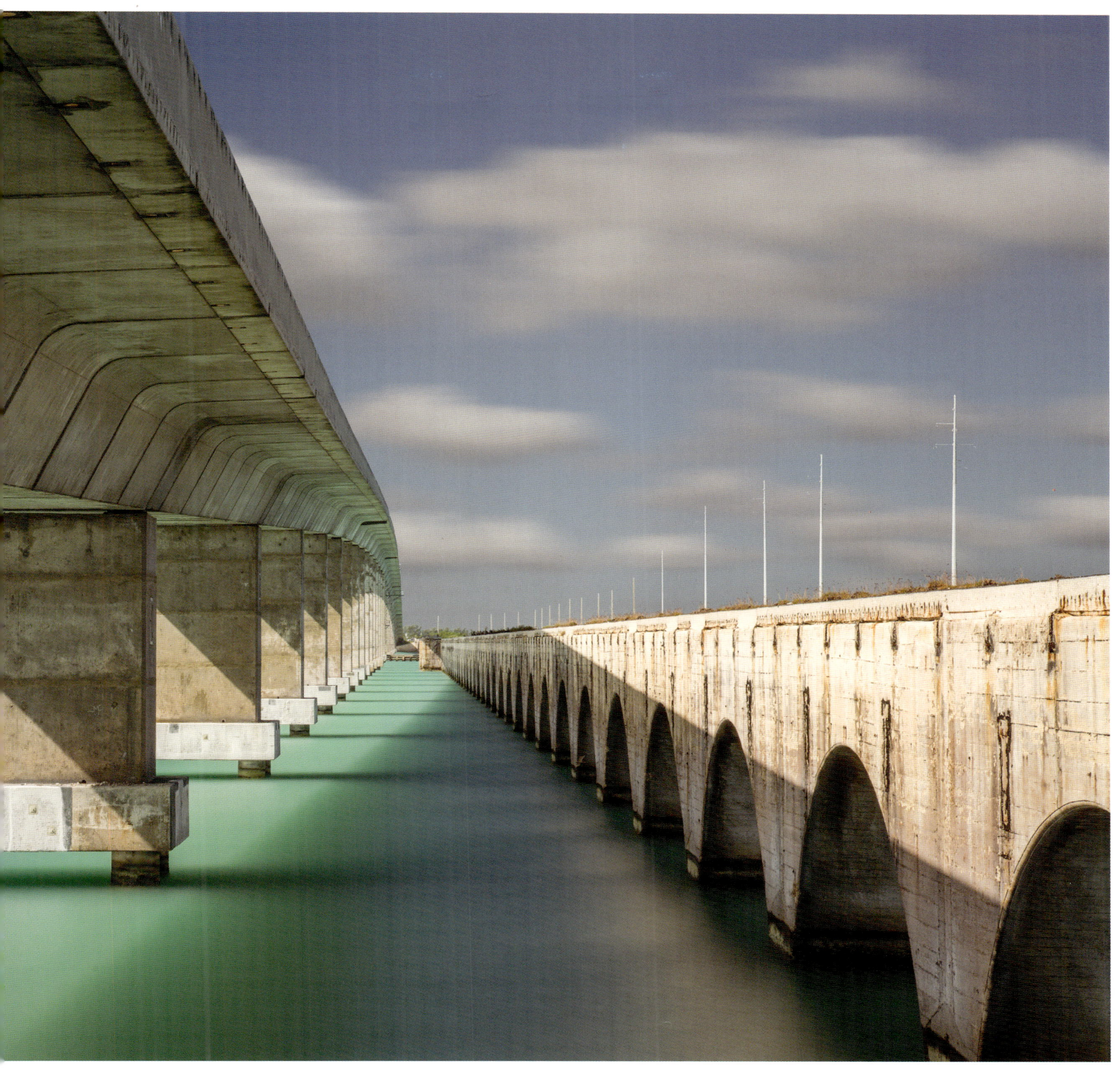

Neutral Density Filters

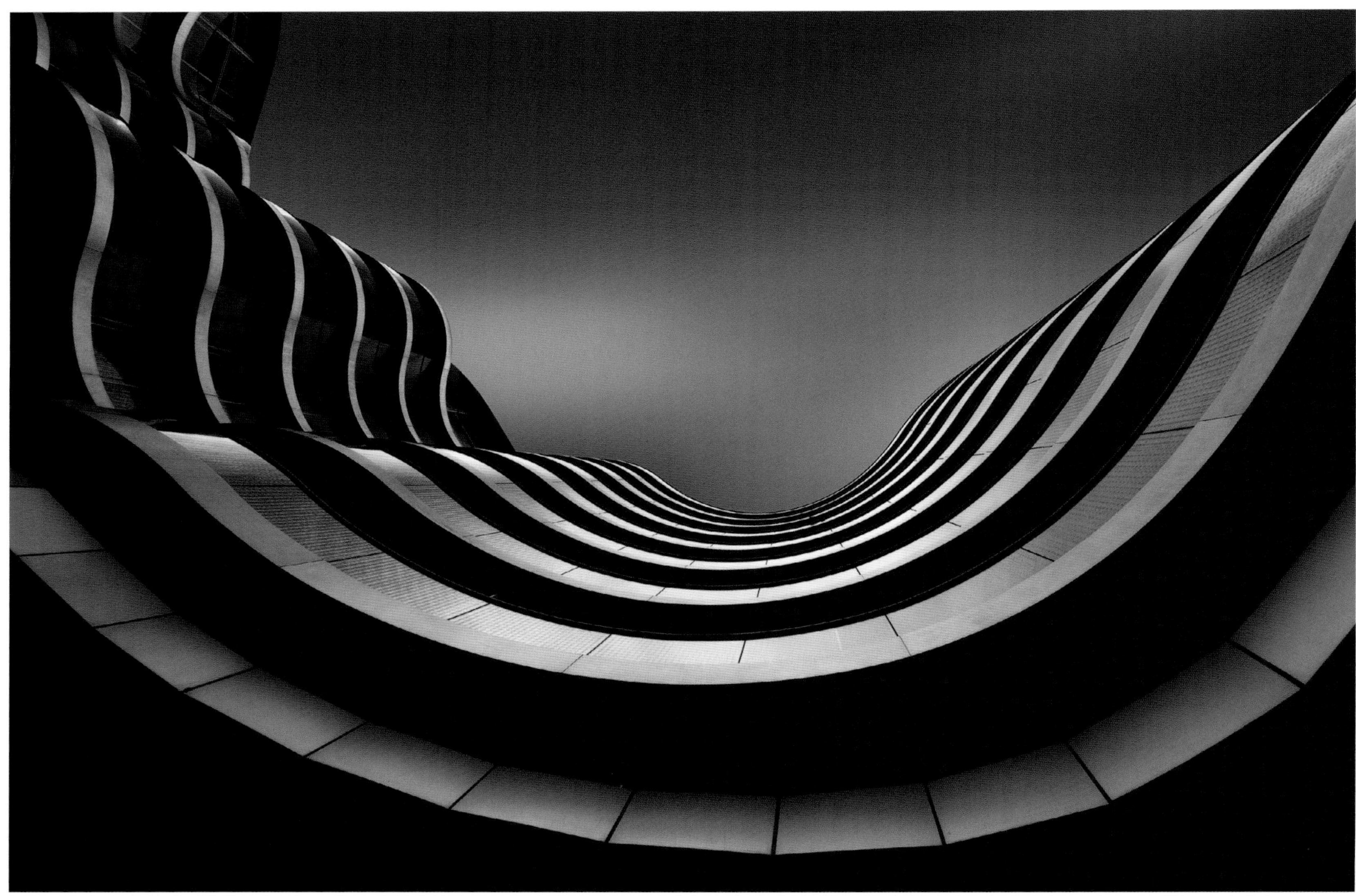

Extending exposure times to create very long exposures in daylight can be difficult without the right equipment. Often, novice photographers will simply reduce the aperture setting to its minimum. While this will extend the exposure time, it is often not enough to provide very long shutter speeds in daylight, and there is also the natural image degradation that occurs due to diffraction; using very small apertures such as f/22 or f/32 will result in reduced image quality.

The answer is to use a neutral density (ND) filter. In the simplest sense this is a piece of darkened glass that reduces the amount of light entering the lens. ND filters come in varying strengths, measured in stops, so a 2-stop ND filter reduces the amount of light passing through it by two stops. Or, to put it another way, a 2-stop ND filter lets you to extend the shutter speed by two stops.

In addition to plain ND filters, which affect everything being photographed, landscape photographers often use graduated ND filters. As the name suggests, the filter graduates from ND to transparent, so the filter can be positioned to darken the brightest parts of the scene, while leaving the other areas uncovered. This is ideal for balancing the exposure of a bright sky with a darker foreground, but it will not necessarily extend exposure times.

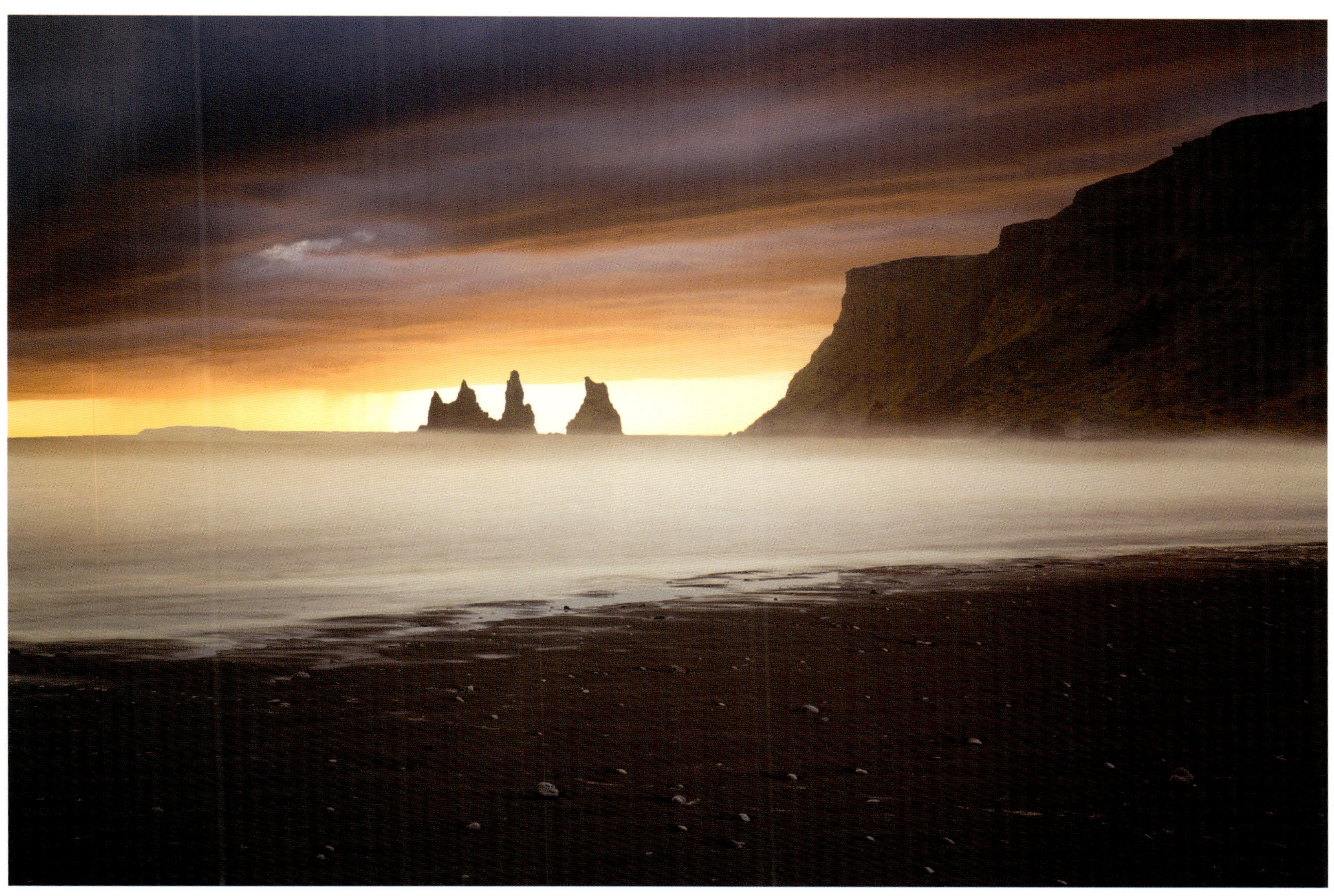

Above left: The unique curvature of this building has been accentuated through the use of an ND filter, which has blurred the sky and removed the distractions of the clouds from view.

Focal length: 16mm

Aperture: f/11

Shutter speed: 22 sec.

ISO: 100

Above: For this image, taken in Iceland, I used a 6-stop ND filter to blur the motion of the waves. A graduated ND filter was also used to help balance the exposure of the spectacular sunset with the foreground.

Focal length: 58mm

Aperture: f/13

Shutter speed: 13 sec.

ISO: 100

Tip

ND filters can also be used when you want to use a wide aperture to minimize depth of field in bright conditions; they do not only have to affect shutter speed.

STOP REDUCTION	OPTICAL DENSITY	ND NUMBER
1	0.3	ND2
2	0.6	ND4
4	1.2	ND16
6	1.8	ND64
10	3.0	ND1000

Above: The strength of an ND filter is measured in stops, but this may be expressed as an optical density value or ND number, depending on the filter manufacturer. This grid shows how the numbers compare.

Filter Types

Neutral density filters come in two forms: round filters that screw into the filter thread on the front of a lens and system filters where a square or rectangular filter fits into a holder attached to the lens. Both systems have their advantages and disadvantages.

Round filters

Screw-in filters are quick to fit to a lens, are quite robust, and the design means that light can't get behind the filter and cause flare. However, if you have lenses with different filter thread sizes you will either need multiple filters or have to use "stepping rings" to use a single filter on your various lenses; if different strength filters of varying sizes are required the costs and bulk can mount up quickly.

Bear in mind that although screw-in filters can be stacked together, they are more likely to vignette (darken in the corners), which can affect the final images taken. Some ultra-wideangle lenses will inevitably vignette when just a single filter is applied, although filter makers are now manufacturing thinner filters to deal with this issue.

System filters

Unlike screw-in filters, system filters are larger than the lens barrel and are dropped into a filter holder that clips onto the front of the lens. This filter holder can be attached to any lens using a low-cost adaptor ring and can accept a number of different filters simultaneously, enabling you to combine ND filters with graduated ND filters and a polarizer. As the filter holder can be rotated, the filters can be more easily aligned to specific subjects in the frame.

The downside is that filter systems are bulky and the filters are large. These larger filters are often glass (although there are resin and plastic filters available) and are more prone to breaking or getting scratched than screw-in filters. They can also be more expensive.

Tips

- It is possible to purchase variable ND filters (screw in filters only) that can be rotated to increase or decrease the level of density. Although convenient, they are generally more expensive than "fixed strength" filters and are not necessarily truly neutral. They will not usually work with a polarizing filter either.

- If you intend to use graduated ND filters it is far better to use a filter system as the filters can be rotated and slid up and down in the filter holder to position them accurately.

- Combining multiple screw-in filters can lead to vignetting (darkening) at the corners of your images. A simple fix is to shoot the scene with a slightly wider focal length and then crop out the vignetting in postproduction.

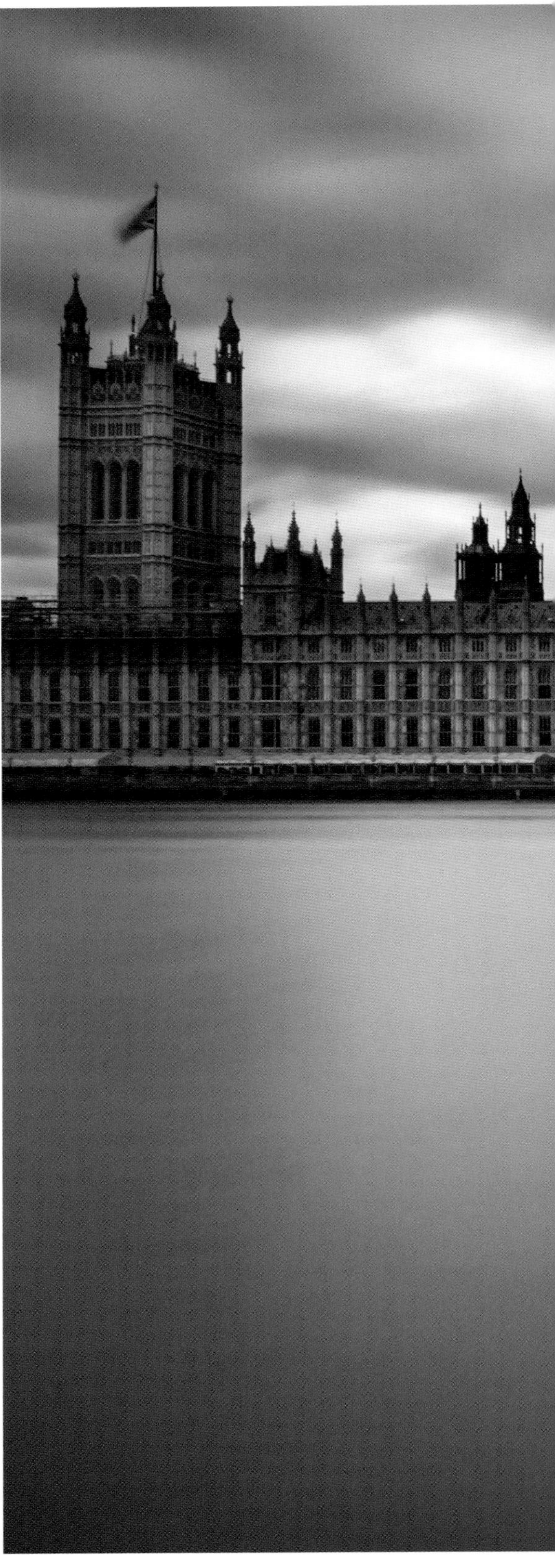

Right: For this iconic London view I used a 6-stop ND filter to smooth the water and ensure the focus of the image is on the architecture of the Palace of Westminster.

Focal length: 24mm

Aperture: f/14

Shutter speed: 33 sec.

ISO: 100

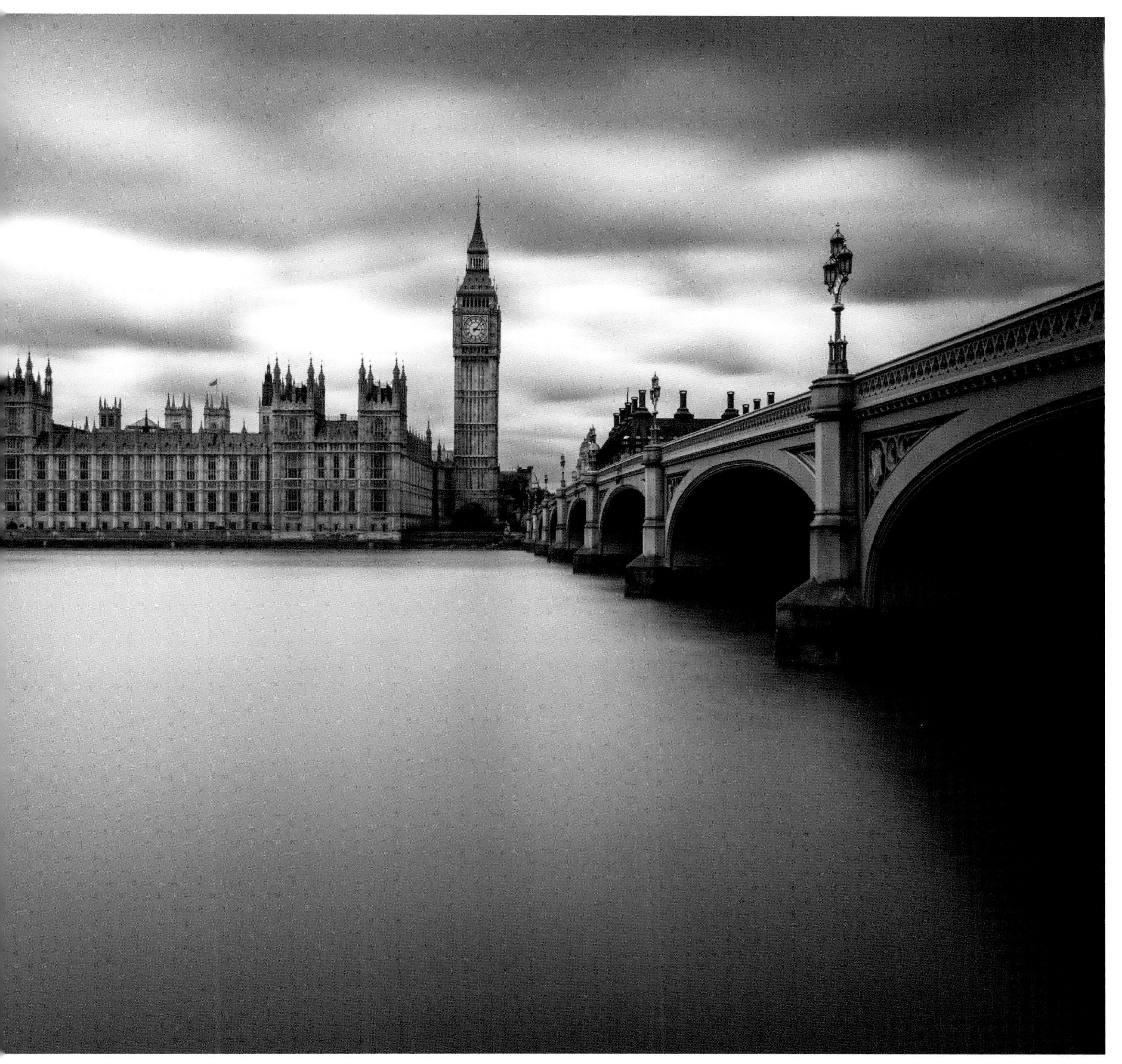

Ultra-long Exposures

Ultra-long exposures are incredibly popular and can present the viewer with something they simply cannot see themselves. Compressing long periods of time into a single frame requires dense filters. In the past, this meant using homemade welding-glass filters, but these have now been replaced by "extreme" ND filters from filter manufacturers, which offer increased light reduction, minimal color degradation, and improved optical performance.

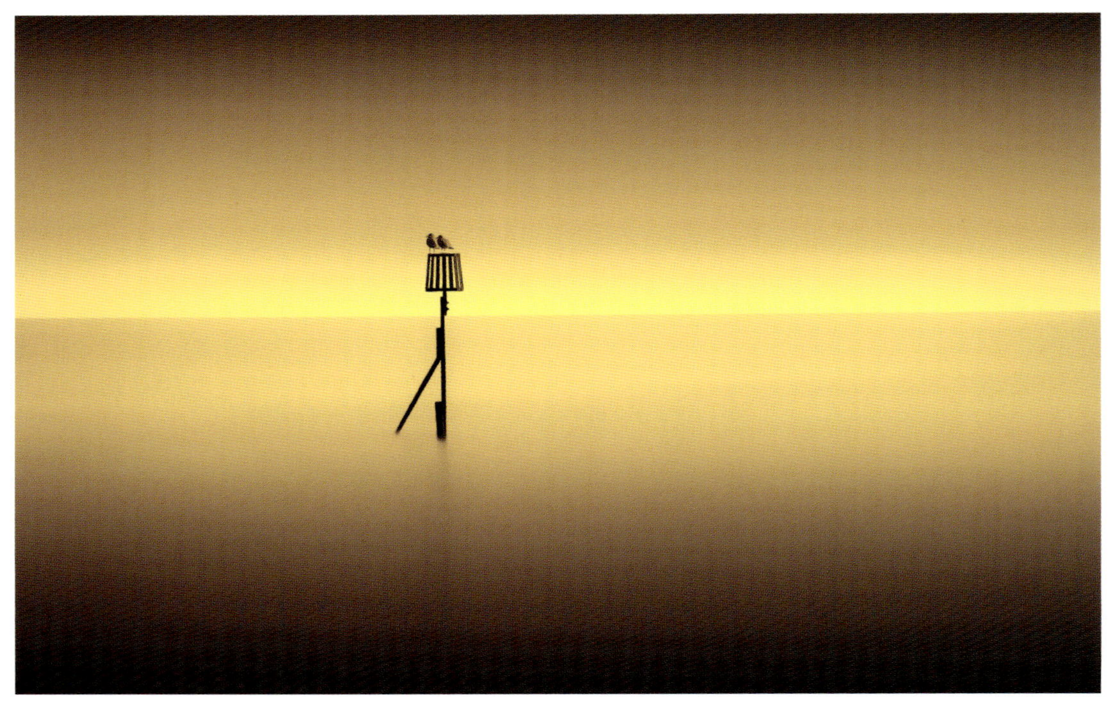

Right: The sunset exposure was taken through a 10-stop ND filter. Fortunately, the two gulls remained stationary for the duration of the capture, allowing them to be recorded in the image.

Focal length: 67mm
Aperture: f/11
Shutter speed: 113 sec.
ISO: 100

EXTREME ND FILTER USE

Using these filters requires a slightly different approach to "straight" photography. Although there is no right or wrong way to taking extreme long exposure photographs, working through the following steps will help you avoid some of the common mistakes that can ruin an image:

1 Before you attach your filter, and with the camera locked on a tripod, frame your shot and focus. This can either be done with autofocus or manually—either way, once the correct focus is achieved, switch the camera/lens to manual. If you don't, the camera's autofocus will try—and fail—to refocus when the ND filter is in place.

2 Turn off any image stabilization, as this can sometimes introduce a slight blur when the camera is on a tripod.

3 With the camera set to Aperture Priority mode, decide on the depth of field required for the scene and set the aperture. Keep the camera at its lowest ISO and take a test shot: the camera will automatically work out the recommended shutter time.

4 Check this resulting test image and decide whether any adjustment is necessary; the aim here is to determine the correct shutter speed for your aperture and ISO without the filter in place.

5 Affix your ND filter and switch to Bulb mode. Calculate the exposure time required with the filter in place: there are plenty of apps that you can download that will help with this, or you can use the grid on page 120 as a guide. Note that the aperture and ISO should stay the same as your test shot.

6 Use a remote release to trigger the camera and make your exposure.

7 Once the exposure has been made, review the image and check the histogram to ensure no clipping has occurred (it can be worth comparing this histogram with that of your test shot, as the two should be very similar). Any exposure issues can be resolved by reshooting with a longer exposure time (to counter underexposure) or a shorter exposure time (to tackle overexposure).

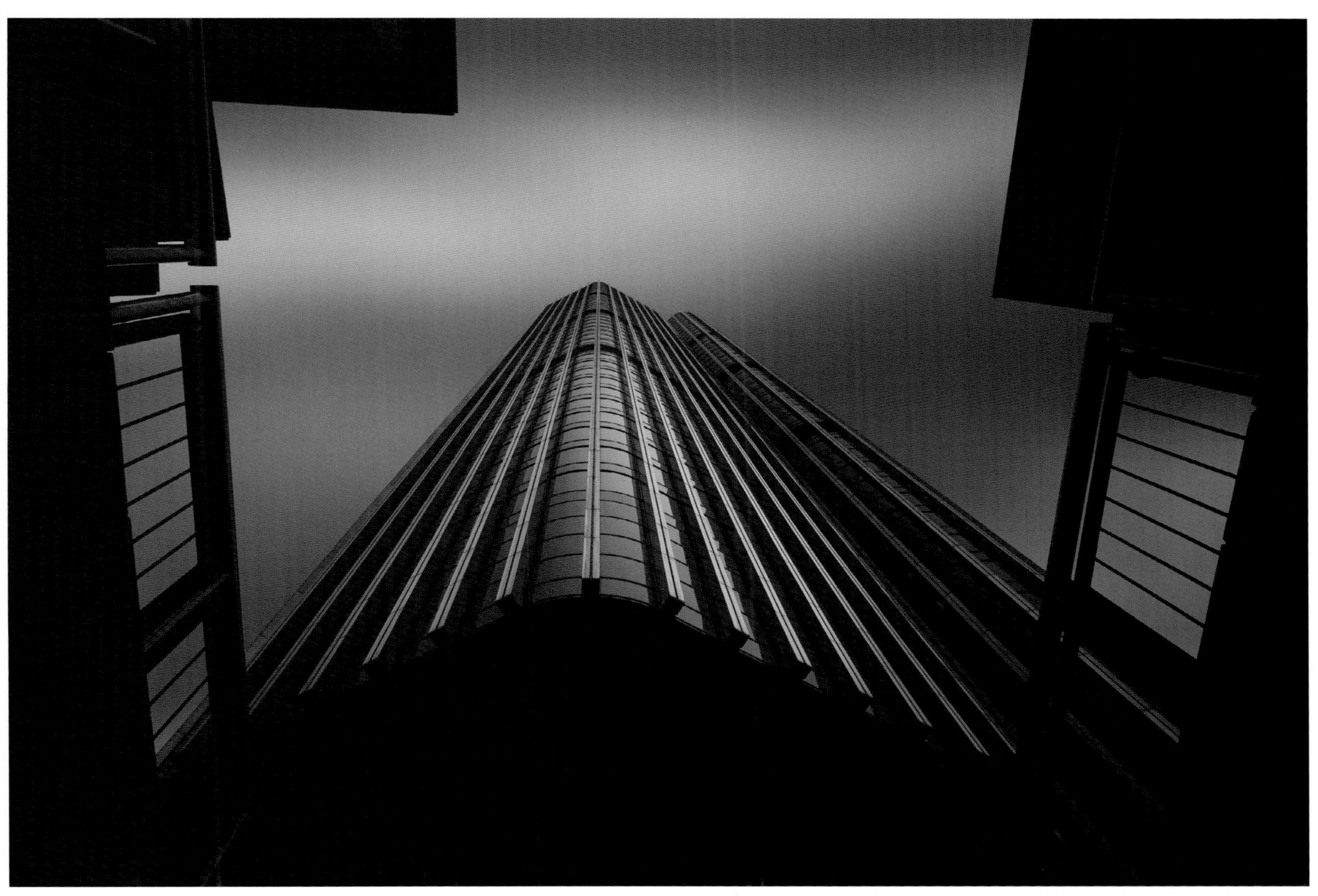

Above: A 10-stop ND filter creates a nice blur in the sky in this image. The strength of the filter made it extremely difficult to capture any detail in the shadow areas, so these have been recorded as silhouettes. However, this adds to the atmosphere.

Focal length: 24mm

Aperture: f/13

Shutter speed: 57 sec.

ISO: 100

UNFILTERED	6 STOP ND	10 STOP ND
1/4000 sec.	1/60 sec.	1/4 sec.
1/2000 sec.	1/30 sec.	1/2 sec.
1/1000 sec.	1/15 sec.	1 sec.
1/500 sec.	1/8 sec.	2 sec.
1/250 sec.	1/4 sec.	4 sec.
1/125 sec.	1/2 sec.	8 sec.
1/60 sec.	1 sec.	15 sec.
1/30 sec.	2 sec.	30 sec.
1/15 sec.	4 sec.	1 min.
1/8 sec.	8 sec.	2 min.
1/4 sec.	15 sec.	4 min.
1/2 sec.	30 sec.	8 min.
1 sec.	1 min.	16 min.
2 sec.	2 min.	32 min.
4 sec.	4 min.	64 min.
8 sec.	8 min.	128 min.
15 sec.	16 min.	256 min.
30 sec.	32 min.	512 min.

Left: To determine the shutter speed needed when you attach your extreme ND filter simply take an exposure reading *without* the filter in place and then cross-reference this on the grid shown here.

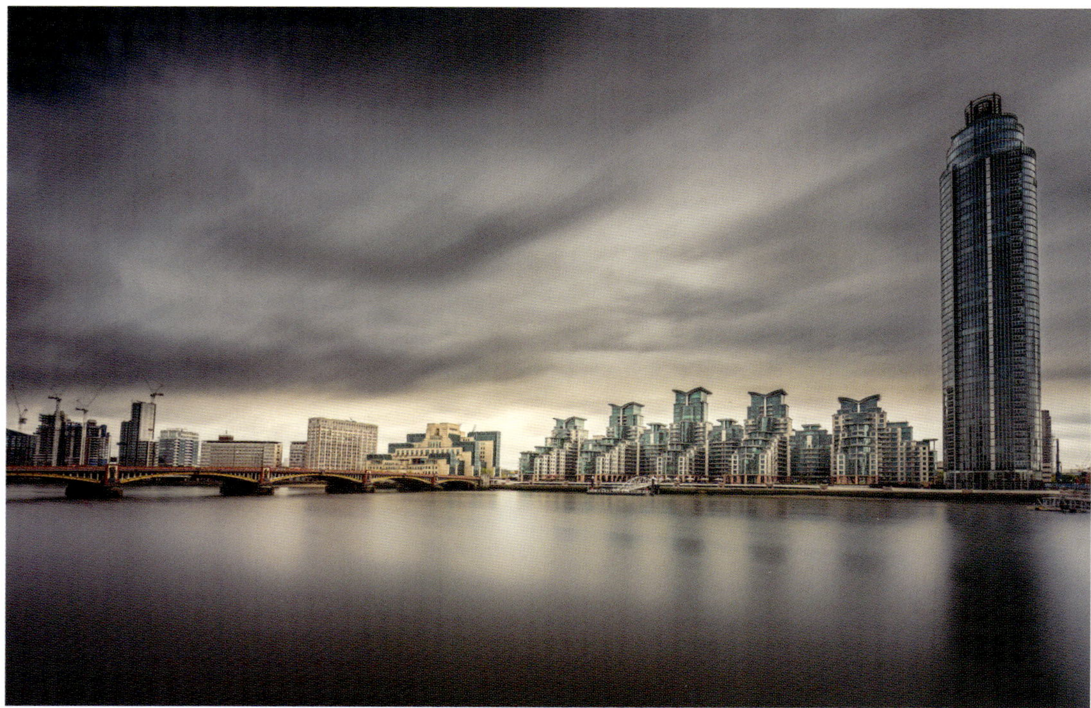

Left: Using an extreme ND filter not only accentuated the movement of the clouds and water in this shot, but also recorded the changing light as the sun appeared momentarily through the clouds.

Focal length: 16mm

Aperture: f/7.1

Shutter speed: 97 sec.

ISO: 100

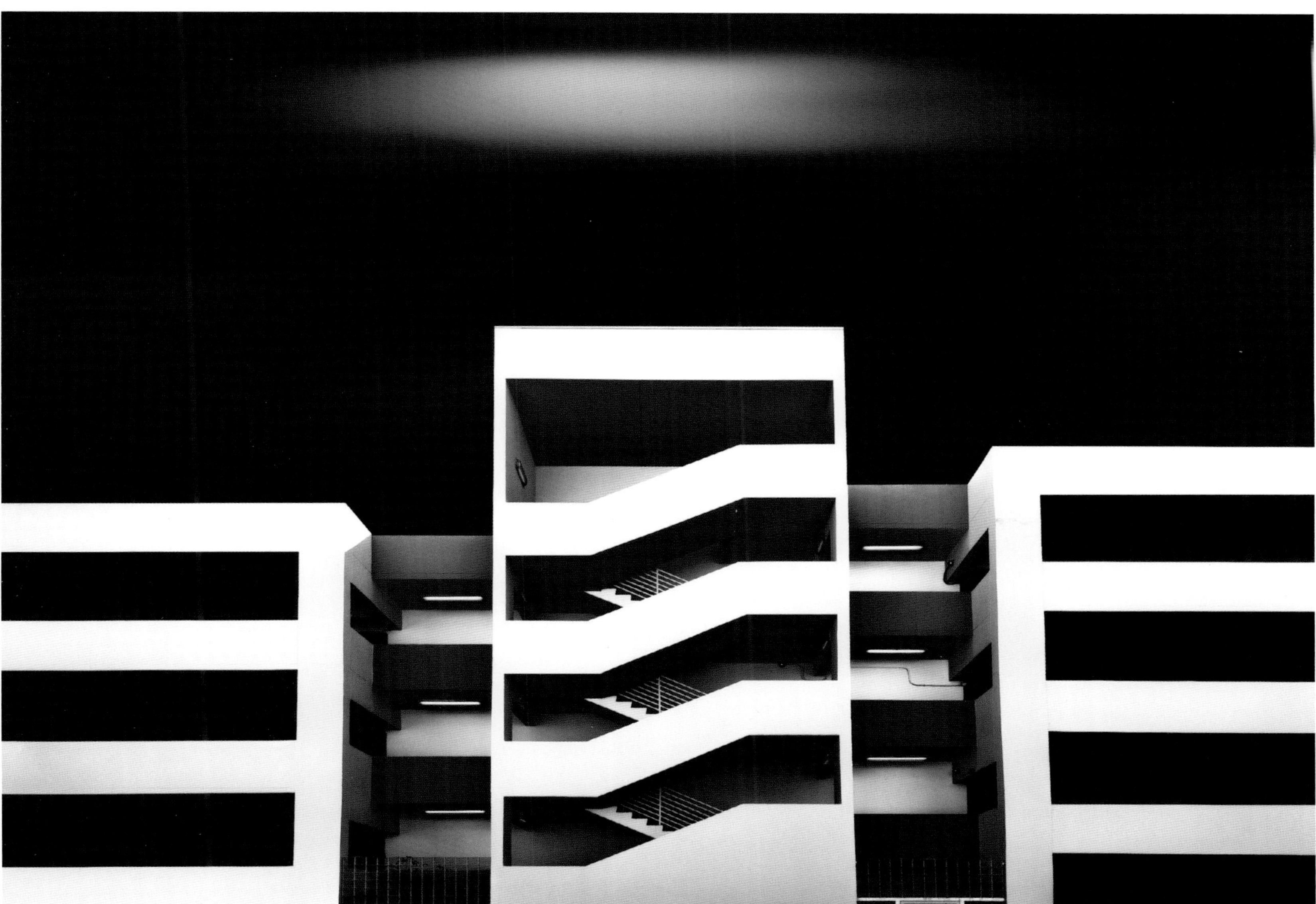

Above: The single, slow-moving cloud in this image required an ultra-long exposure time to capture its movement. This was only possible using an extreme ND filter (in this instance a 10-stop filter).

Focal length: 24mm

Aperture: f/6.3

Shutter speed: 127 sec.

ISO: 100

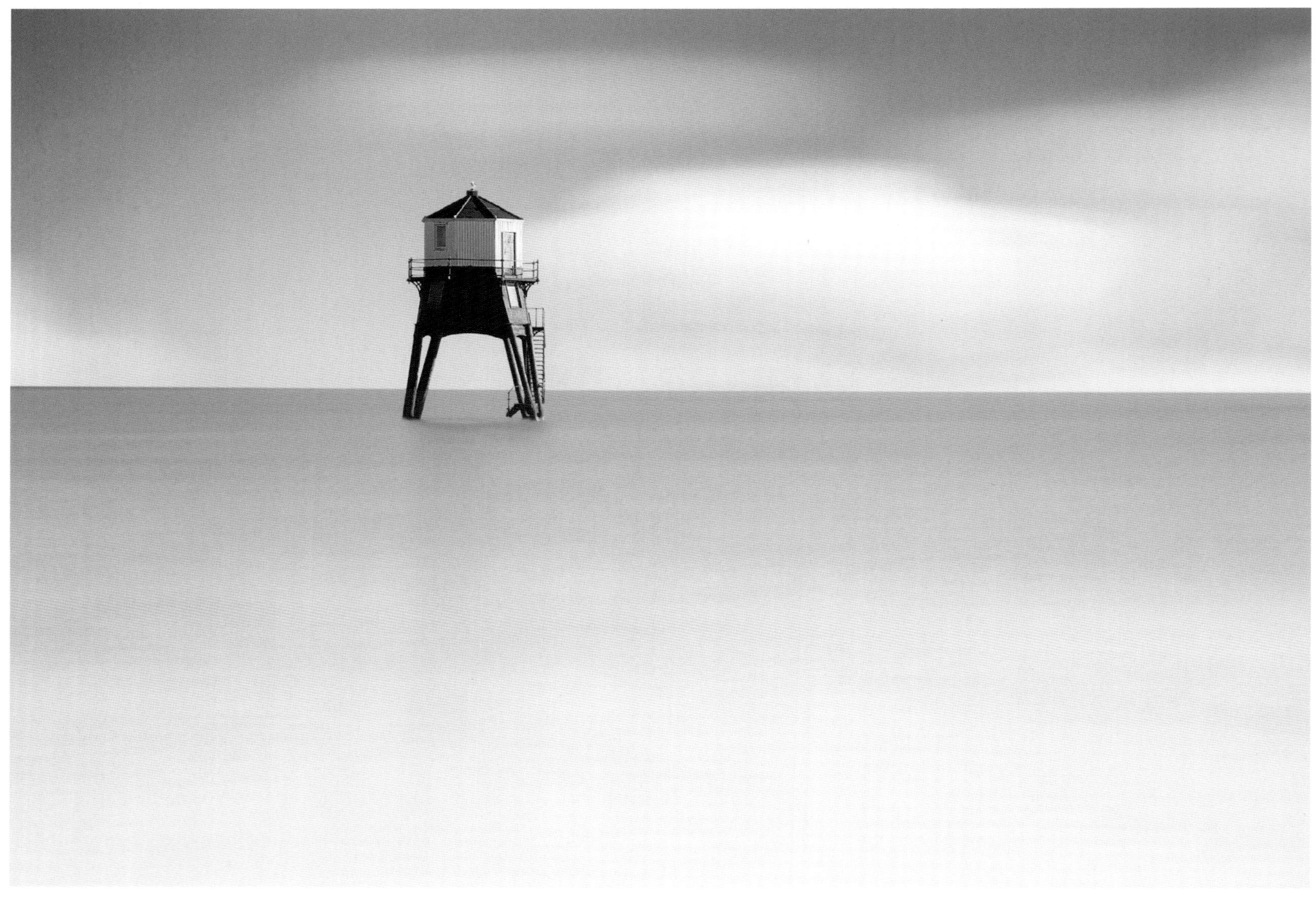

Tip

It is important to ensure that the horizon in an image is perfectly straight; crooked lines can be an unnecessary distraction. To achieve this, use your camera's electronic level or Live View grid overlay function as a guide (if it has either of these features). Alternatively, some tripods have a built-in spirit level that will help ensure the camera is level.

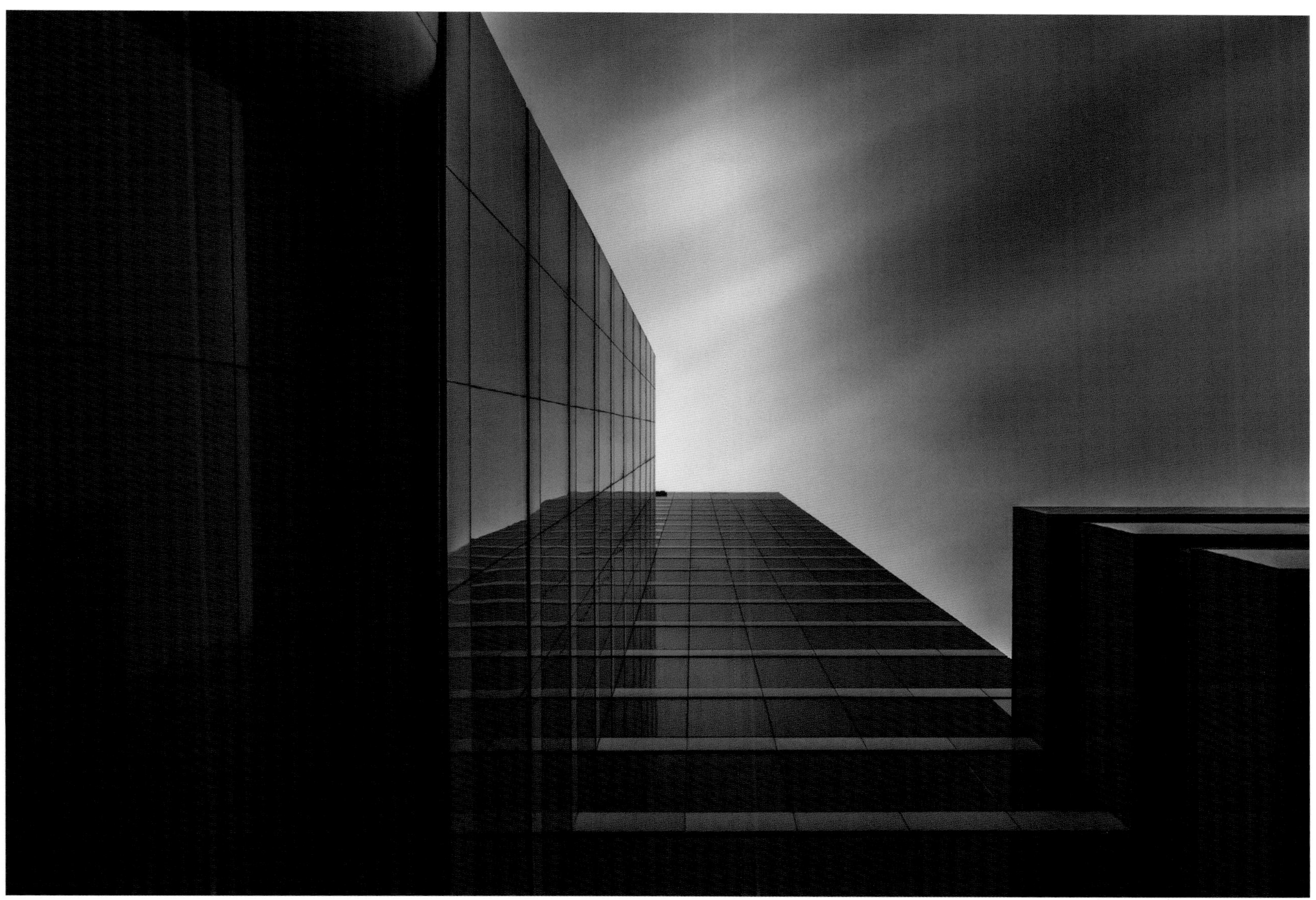

Tip

It can often be useful to use a polarizing filter together with ND filters to control reflections on glass. These reflections can be used compositionally by using the polarizer to either accentuate them or remove them.

Above: The extreme ND filter used in this image wasn't perfectly neutral—it had a slightly blue color cast. However, that has worked well in this instance, as it accentuates the modern feel of the glass skyscraper.

Focal length: 24mm

Aperture: f/18

Shutter speed: 40 sec.

ISO: 100

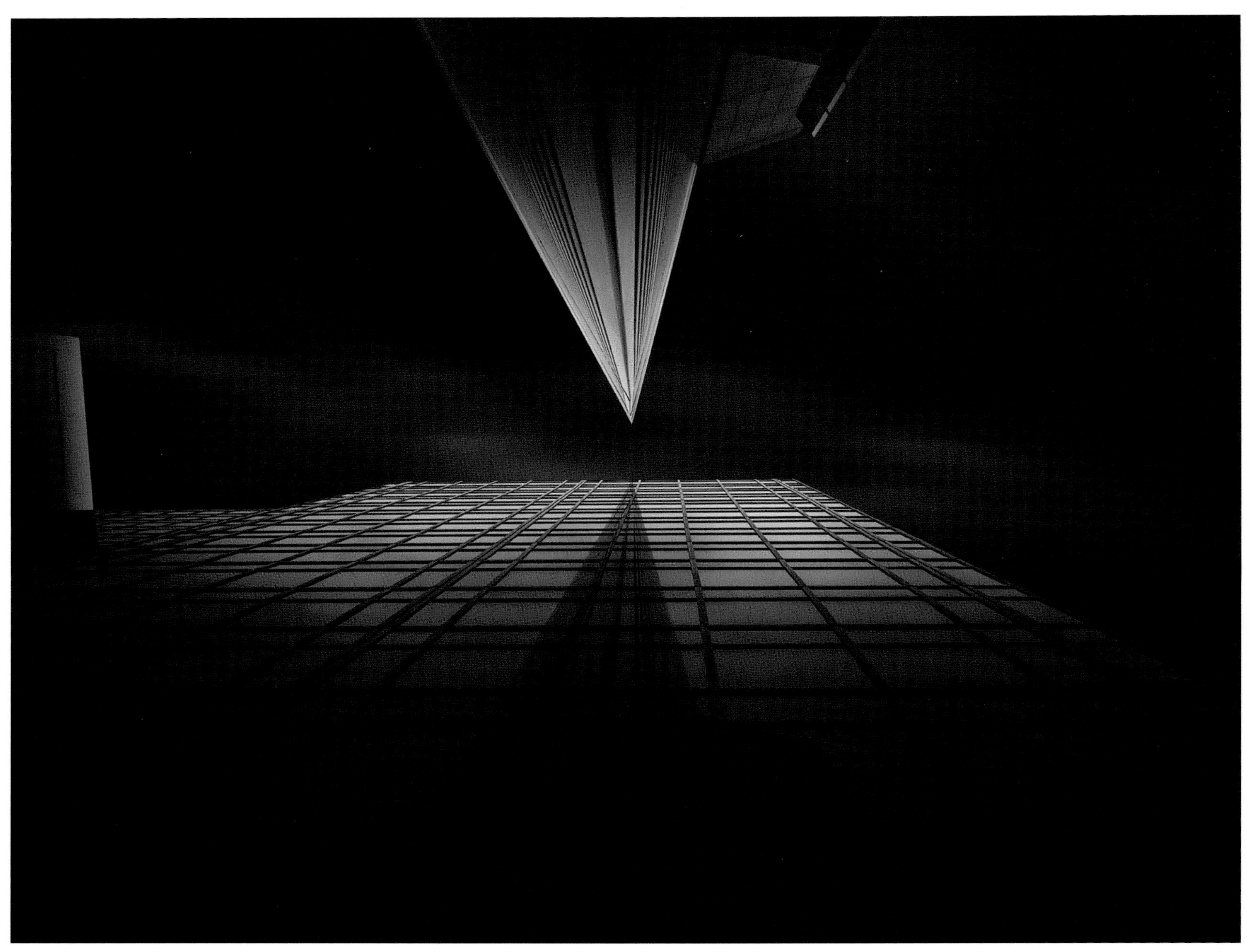

Above: Some extreme ND filters can introduce a color cast. Although this can be fixed in postproduction, it is also a compelling reason to convert images to black and white.
Focal length: 16mm
Aperture: f/16
Shutter speed: 122 sec.
ISO: 100

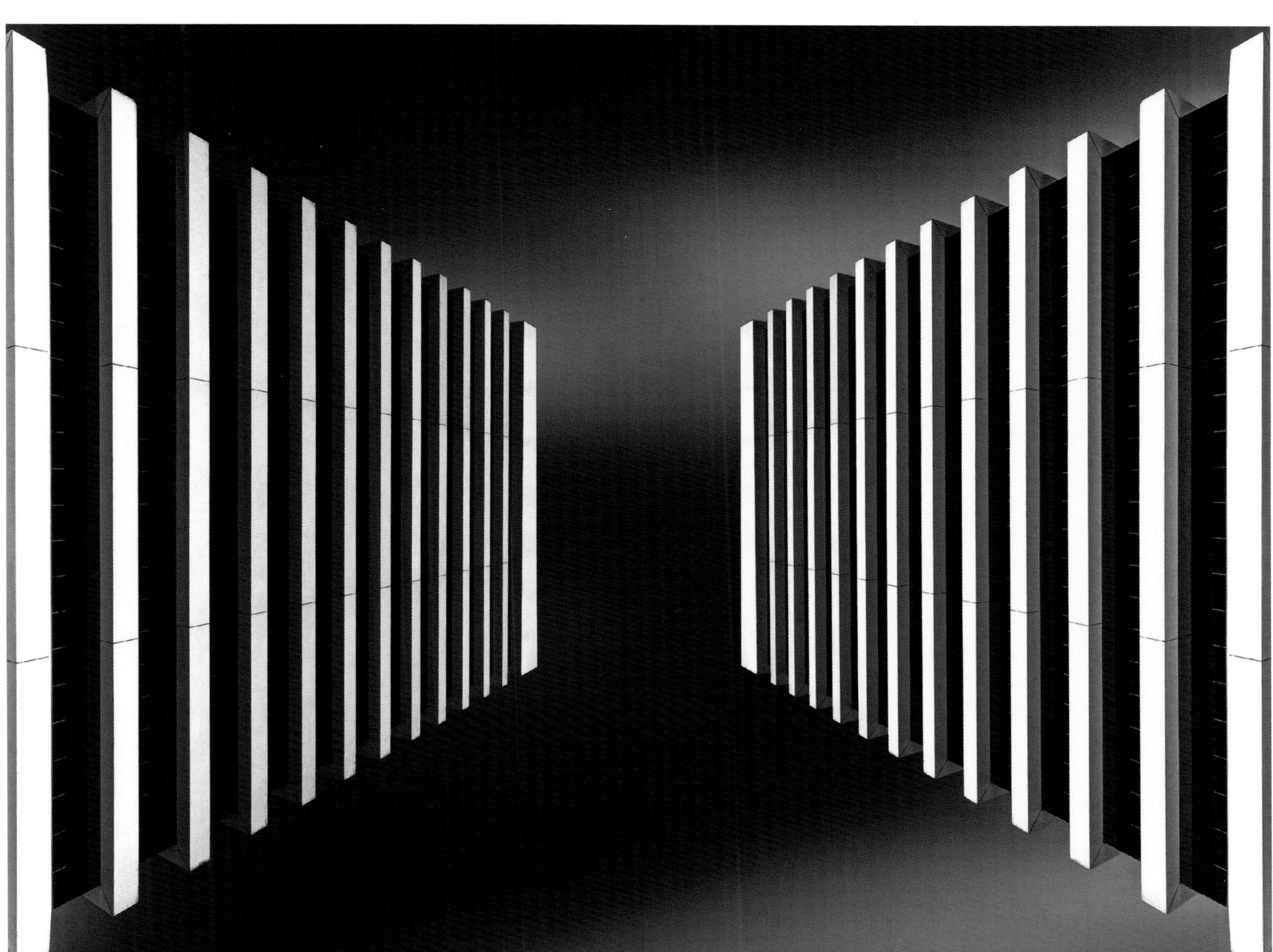

Above: This image required an exposure of just over 1½ minutes to record the movement in the sky as a blur and accentuate the bold architectural design.

Focal length: 24mm

Aperture: f/10

Shutter speed: 92 sec.

ISO: 100

Subject Matter & Composition

Composition is clearly very important in all genres of photography, and is something that has to be considered before any image is captured. However, when you take a long exposure photograph there is a fundamental challenge: you need to try and pre-visualize the result. You will have to predict the movement of elements throughout the scene during the exposure and try to imagine how they might affect the overall image. You also need to think about the elements that will remain stationary in the image, and how they will interact with any moving objects.

Looking through the viewfinder (or at your camera's LCD screen), it is often very easy to concentrate on the focal point in an image and overlook the elements at the edge of the frame. However, it is crucial in long exposure photography to pay extra attention to the edges of the frame before taking the photograph. Look for things that might enter or leave the image while the shutter is open; for example, a tree may be just outside of the viewfinder image, but the wind may blow it partially into frame at times during the exposure, creating a distraction at the edge of your photograph.

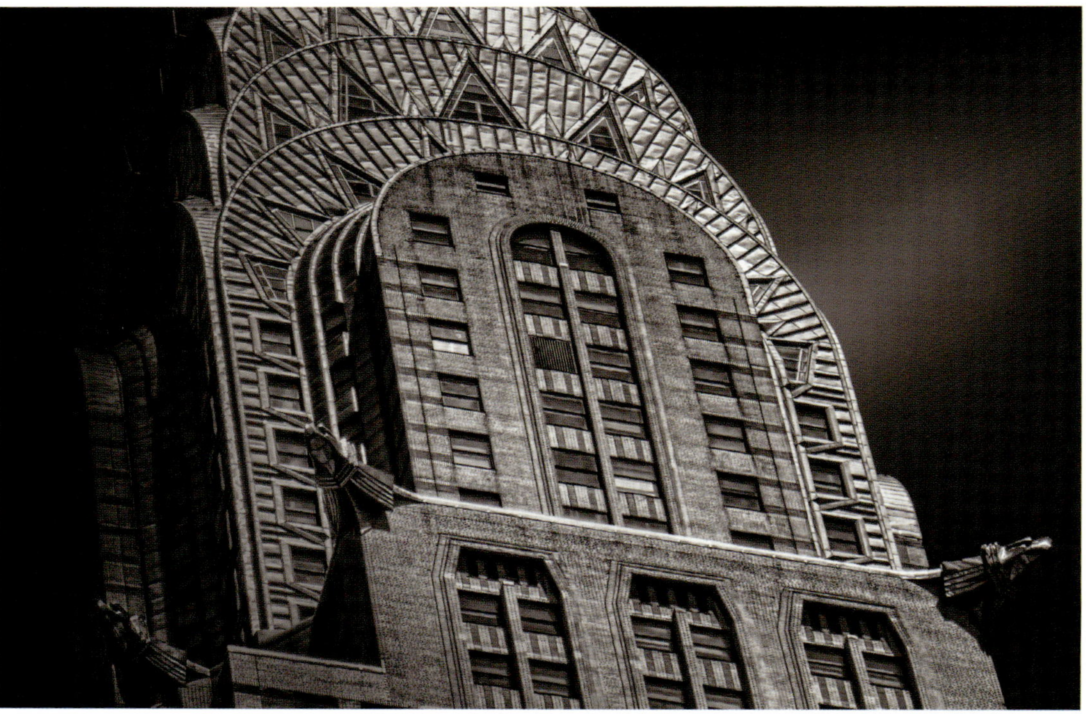

Above right: In this shot, the blurred cloud movement in the sky frames the iconic Chrysler Building in New York City nicely.

Focal length: 125mm

Aperture: f/11

Shutter speed: 78 sec.

ISO: 100

Right: The curve of the shingle beach and water lead the viewer's eye into this image, while the blur of the cloud adds a sense of movement compared with the stillness of the water.

Focal length: 80mm

Aperture: f/16

Shutter speed: 39 sec.

ISO: 100

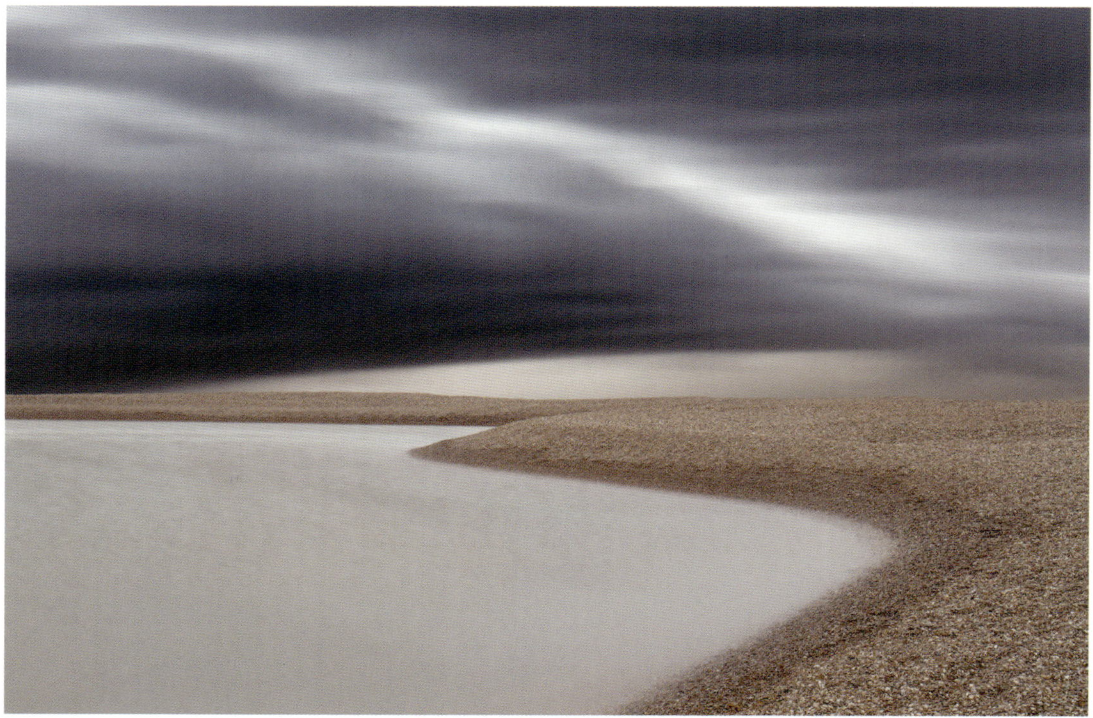

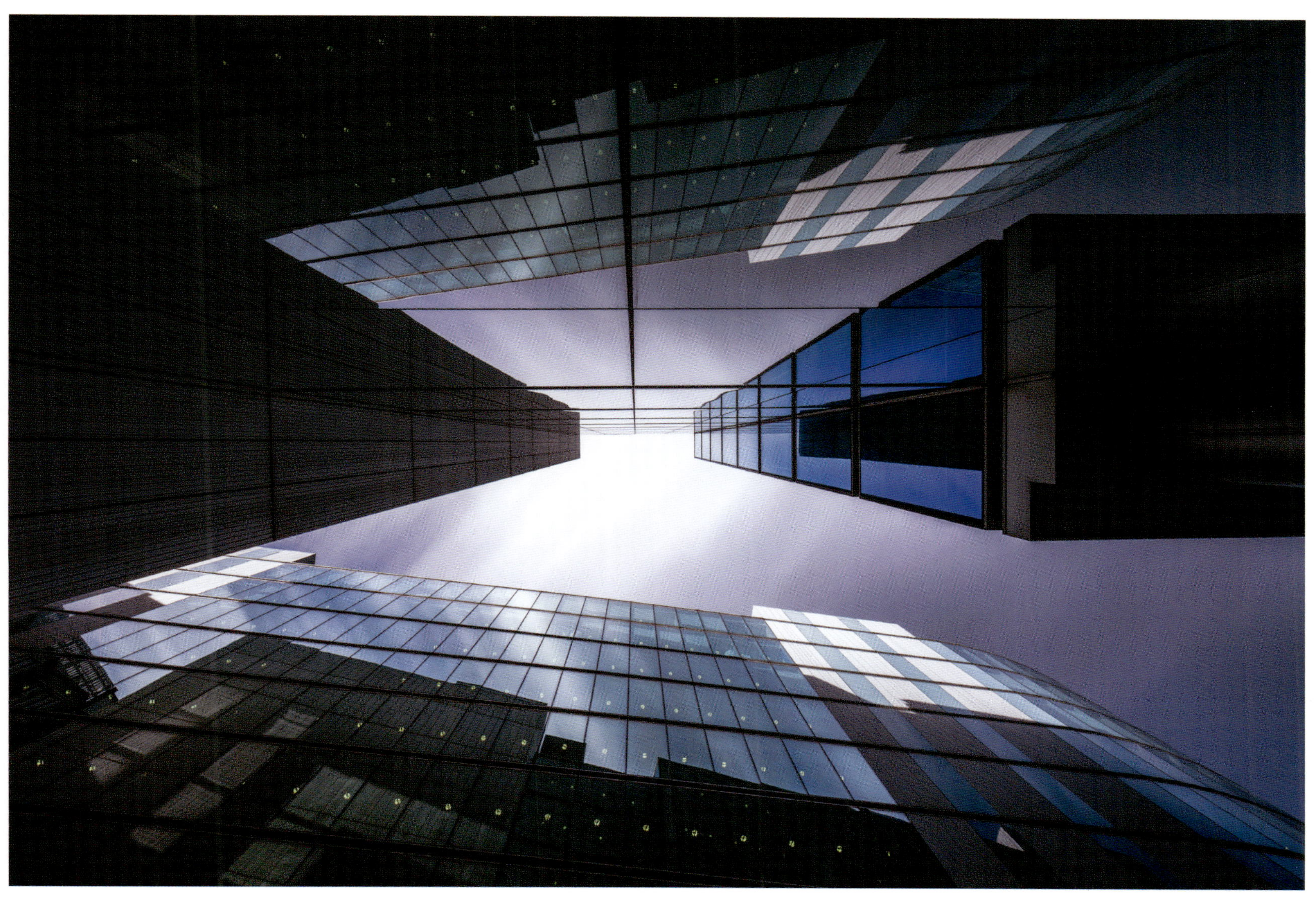

Above: The reflections in this image create a unique, mirrored composition. Using a 10-stop ND filter has also recorded the movement of the clouds in the reflection.

Focal length: 16mm

Aperture: f/18

Shutter speed: 69 sec.

ISO: 100

People Removal

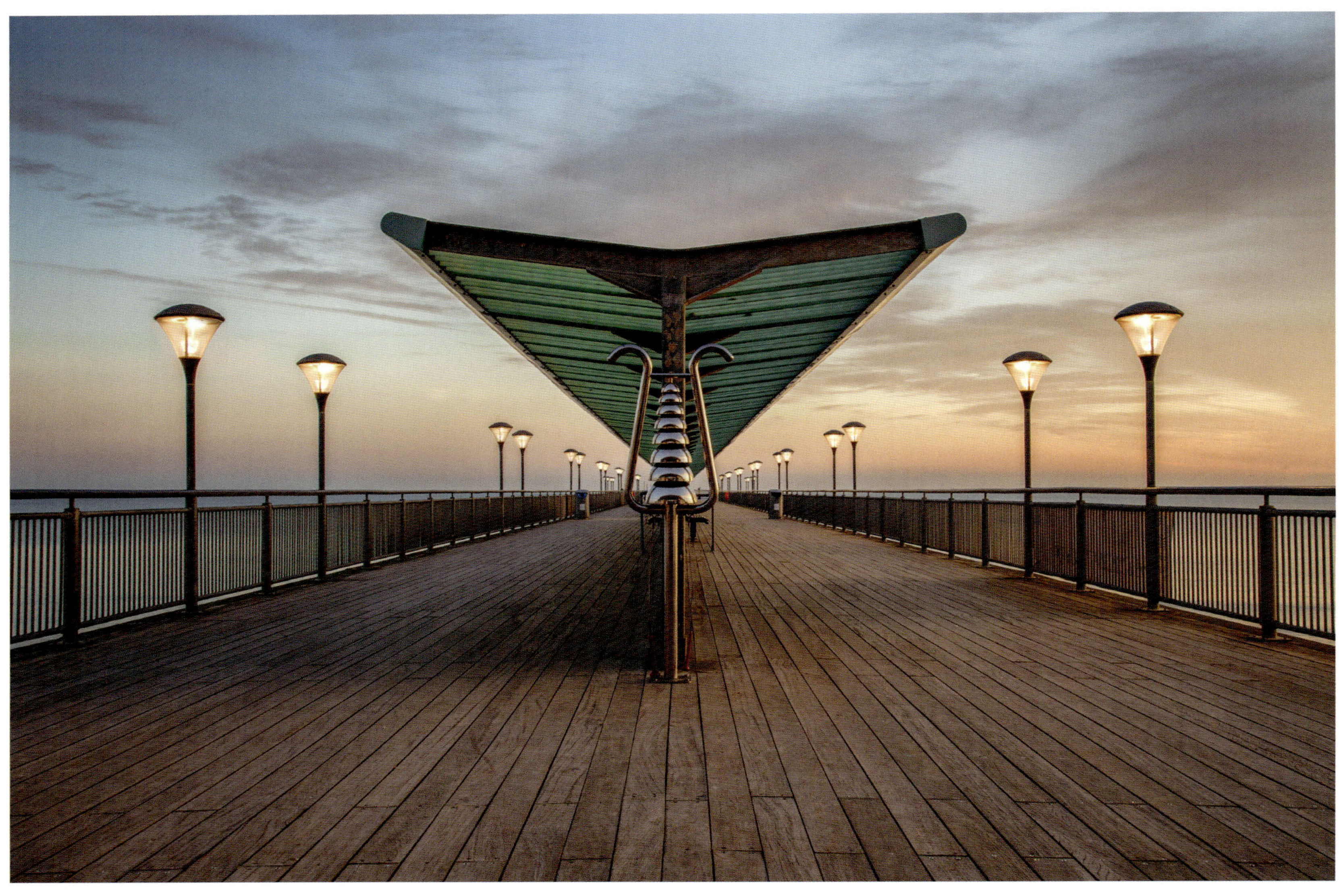

Popular landmarks are often just that: popular. Trying to capture a scene without hordes of people wandering through it can therefore prove very difficult. While visiting sites very early or late in the day may mean fewer tourists around, the light might not be ideal, or the opportunity to time your visit may not be possible.

However, if people are moving through a scene and the camera remains stationary, a long shutter speed will record this movement as a blur.

Extending the exposure time will increase the amount of blur, to the point that the movement will barely be recorded at all; if the subject is moving fast enough (or the exposure is long enough) it will disappear entirely! As the remainder of the scene does not move, your images will only show those fixed features, without including any of the transient elements.

Above: This pier in England was relatively busy with tourists on a warm summer evening. However, the long exposure time created by using an ND filter meant that the movement of the tourists was not captured and the scene appears empty.

Focal length: 35mm

Aperture: f/13

Shutter speed: 122 sec.

ISO: 100

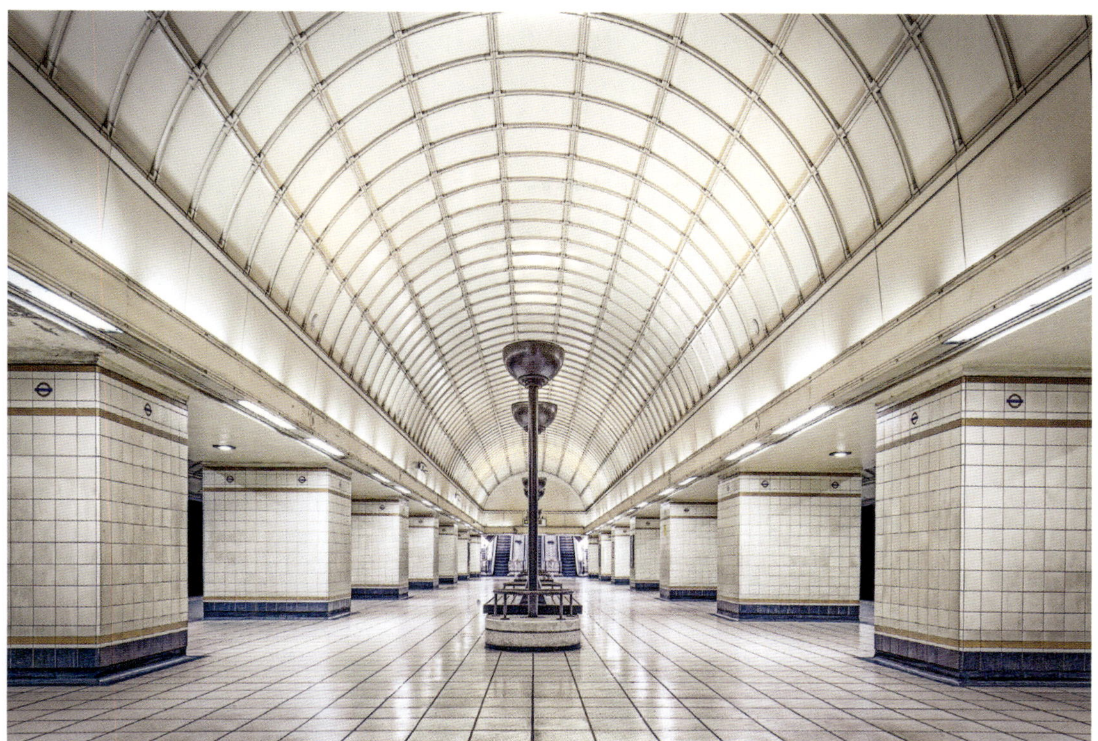

Tips

- This technique works best where the movement is across the frame rather than from front to back.

- If any people or objects remain visible in the final image, try making additional exposures that can be blended in postproduction; eventually they will move and "disappear!"

Ghosting

Although a long exposure can result in people blurring and ultimately not being captured in the frame at all, you can also experiment with "ghosting." This is when the subject remains still for just long enough to be recorded and then moves quickly to another position, mid-exposure. The movement between the different positions will not be recorded, but the subject will appear in multiple places in the same frame as a semi-transparent "ghost."

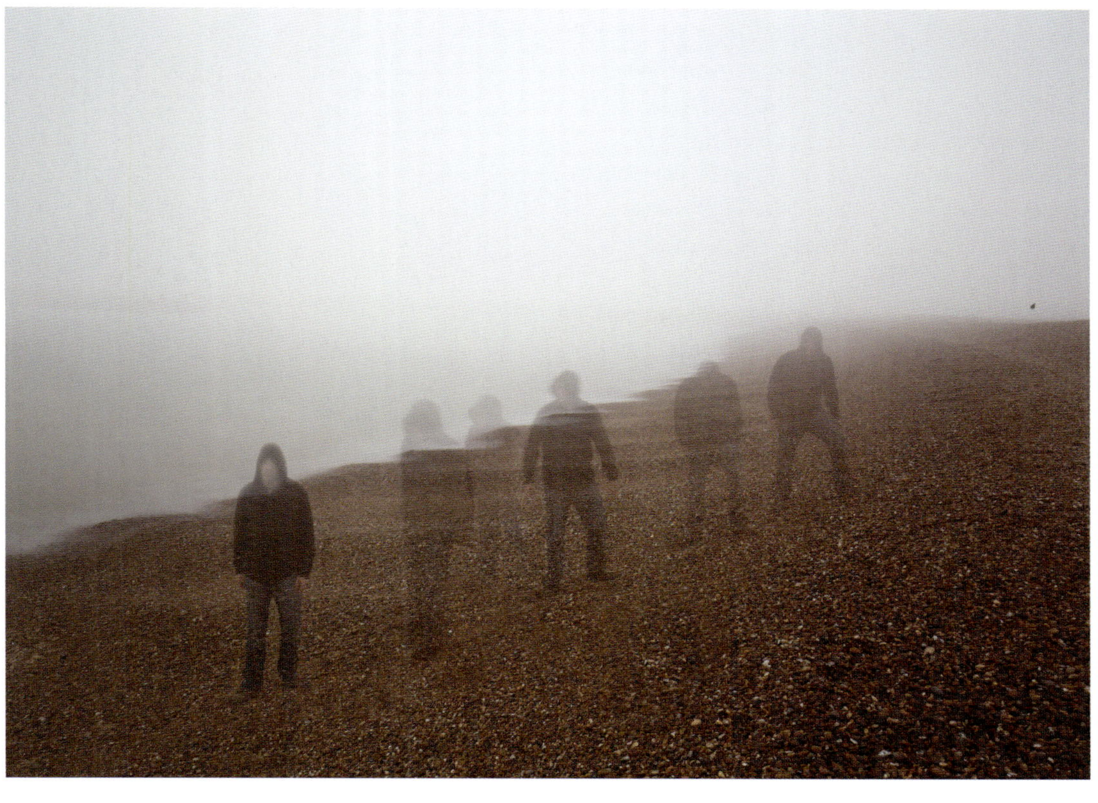

Right: Ghosting is a creative effect that can be used to produce imaginative and unique images.

Focal length: 24mm

Aperture: f/16

Shutter speed: 30 sec.

ISO: 100

Nature in Motion: Waterfalls

Photographs of waterfalls are popular for good reason, as they can add a sense of mysticism and energy to a landscape. Using slower shutter speeds it is possible to blur the movement of water into a silky flow. This emphasizes the power of the fall and adds drama to a scene.

Reducing the details of the water movement also helps create an ethereal effect, so from a creative standpoint it's necessary to think about how blurred you want the water to be. A longer exposure will capture less detail, making the water appear more "silky."

The key to a very smooth effect is to use the slowest shutter speed possible, while maintaining the correct exposure overall for the scene. Using the lowest ISO setting, start by setting a small aperture, such as f/16, and take a test shot. It is easy to overexpose the highlights of the water (or the sky) on a bright day, even when using a small aperture, so remember to check the histogram.

Filters can be key in obtaining great waterfall imagery. When you can't obtain a long enough exposure during the day, it may be necessary to use a Neutral Density (ND) filter to help you extend exposure times. Alternatively (or in addition to an ND filter) a polarizing filter will not only increase the exposure by up to two stops, but can help reduce the glare from wet rocks and the water's surface, and bring out the colors of any surrounding foliage.

Tips

- Watch for slippery wet rocks and keep a small microfiber cloth to hand to ensure your lens and camera stay dry and free from water spray.

- If any foliage is moving during the long exposure, take a second frame at a faster shutter speed to freeze the motion and blend the images during postproduction.

- The speed of the water will affect the exposure time needed to blur it: the slower the water flows, the longer the exposure will need to be.

- Shooting waterfalls on an overcast day will help to minimize any reflections and keep the lighting even.

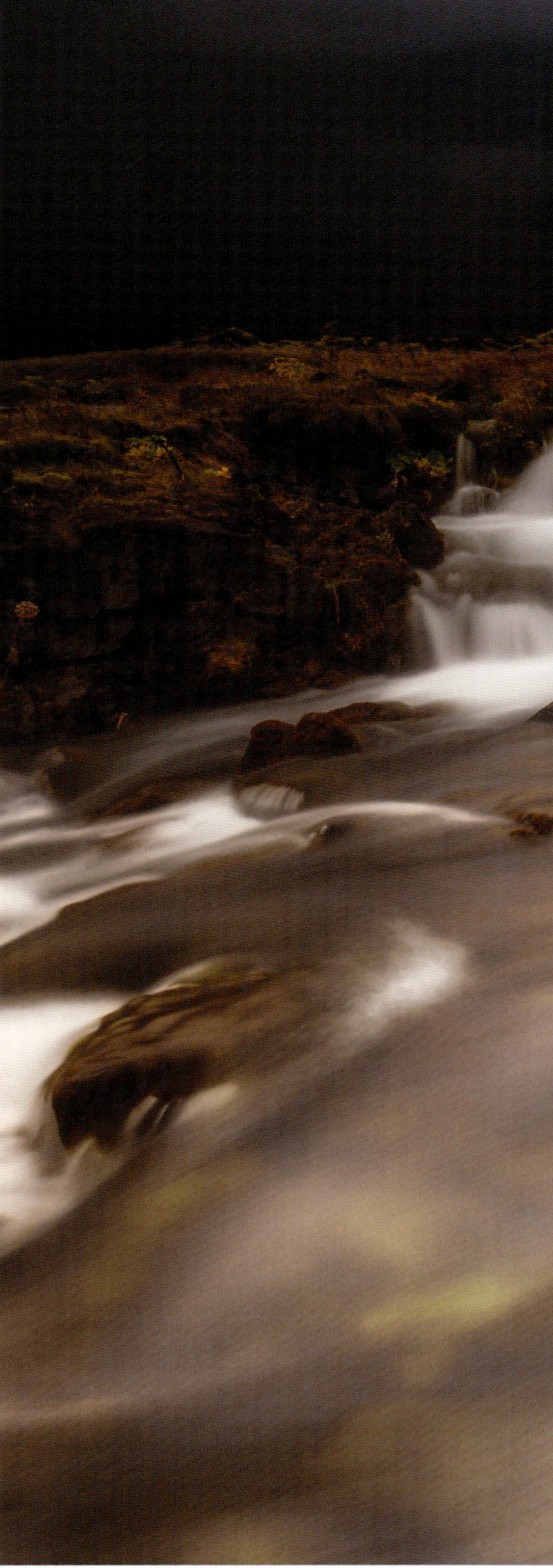

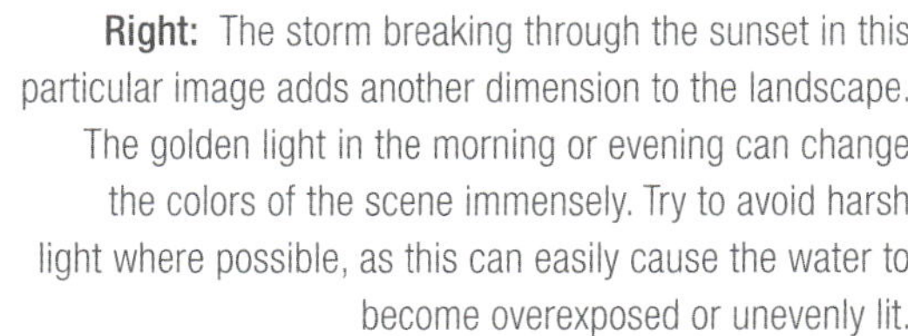

Right: The storm breaking through the sunset in this particular image adds another dimension to the landscape. The golden light in the morning or evening can change the colors of the scene immensely. Try to avoid harsh light where possible, as this can easily cause the water to become overexposed or unevenly lit.

Focal length: 65mm

Aperture: f/11

Shutter speed: 59 sec.

ISO: 100

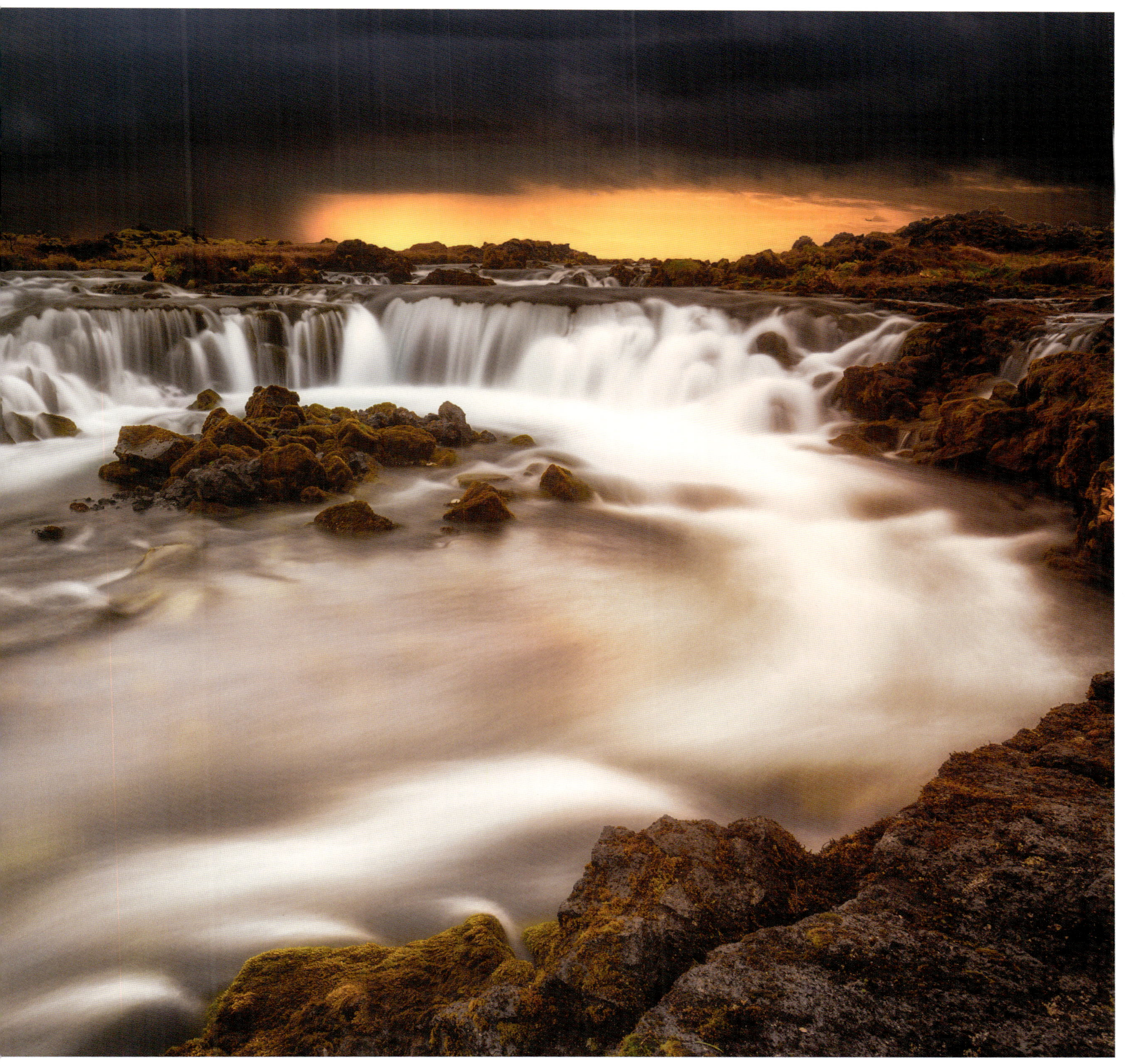

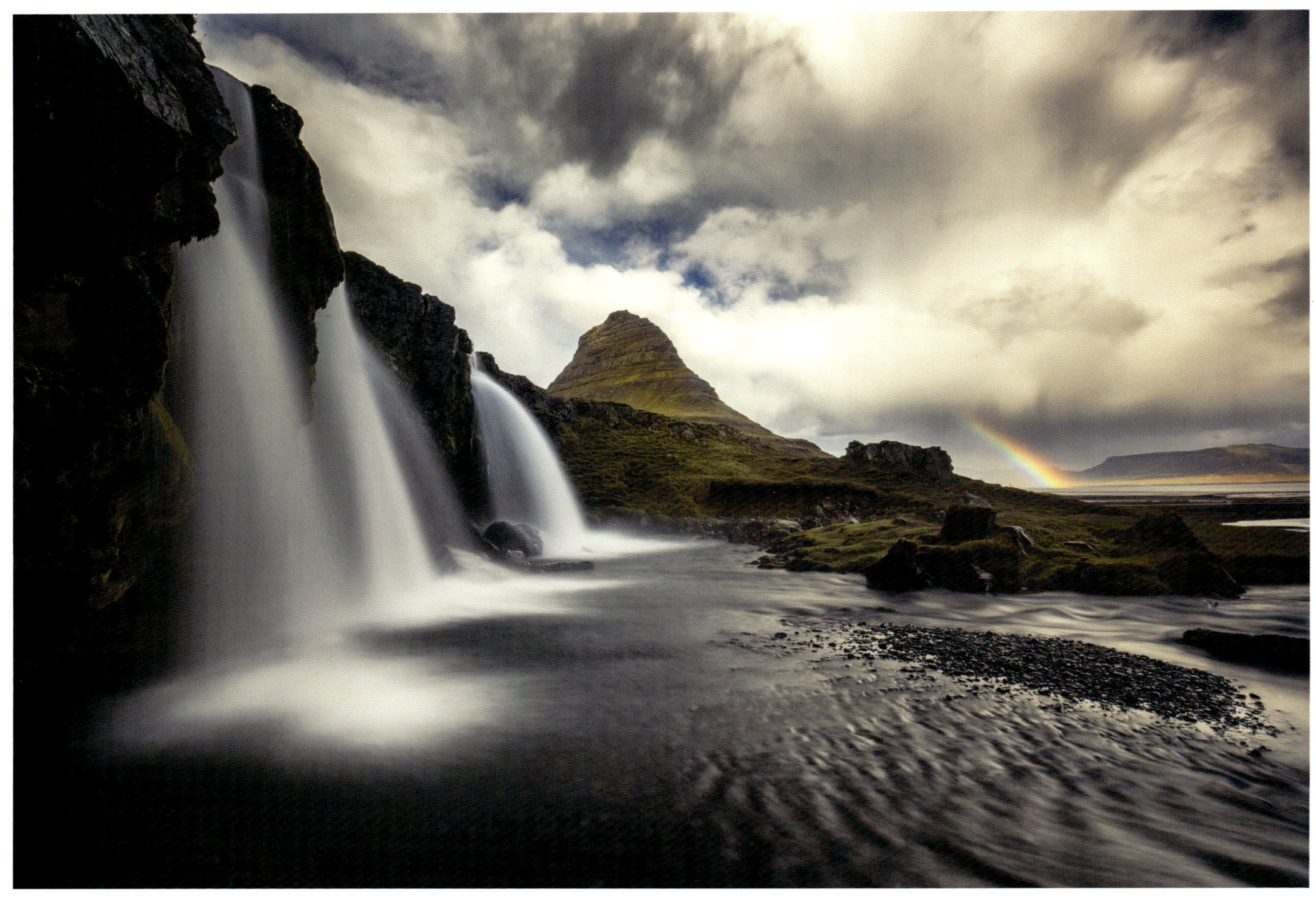

Above: The fast-flowing water at this particular waterfall allowed me to blur the water without using any filters—all I needed was a small aperture setting and low ISO.

Focal length: 16mm

Aperture: f/22

Shutter speed: 1 sec.

ISO: 100

Right: The extreme contrast between a waterfall and its surroundings can often lead to an imposing black-and-white image. Our eyes are drawn to the brightest part of an image, so the blurred water can act as a powerful leading line in a composition.

Focal length: 35mm

Aperture: f/16

Shutter speed: 10 sec.

ISO: 100

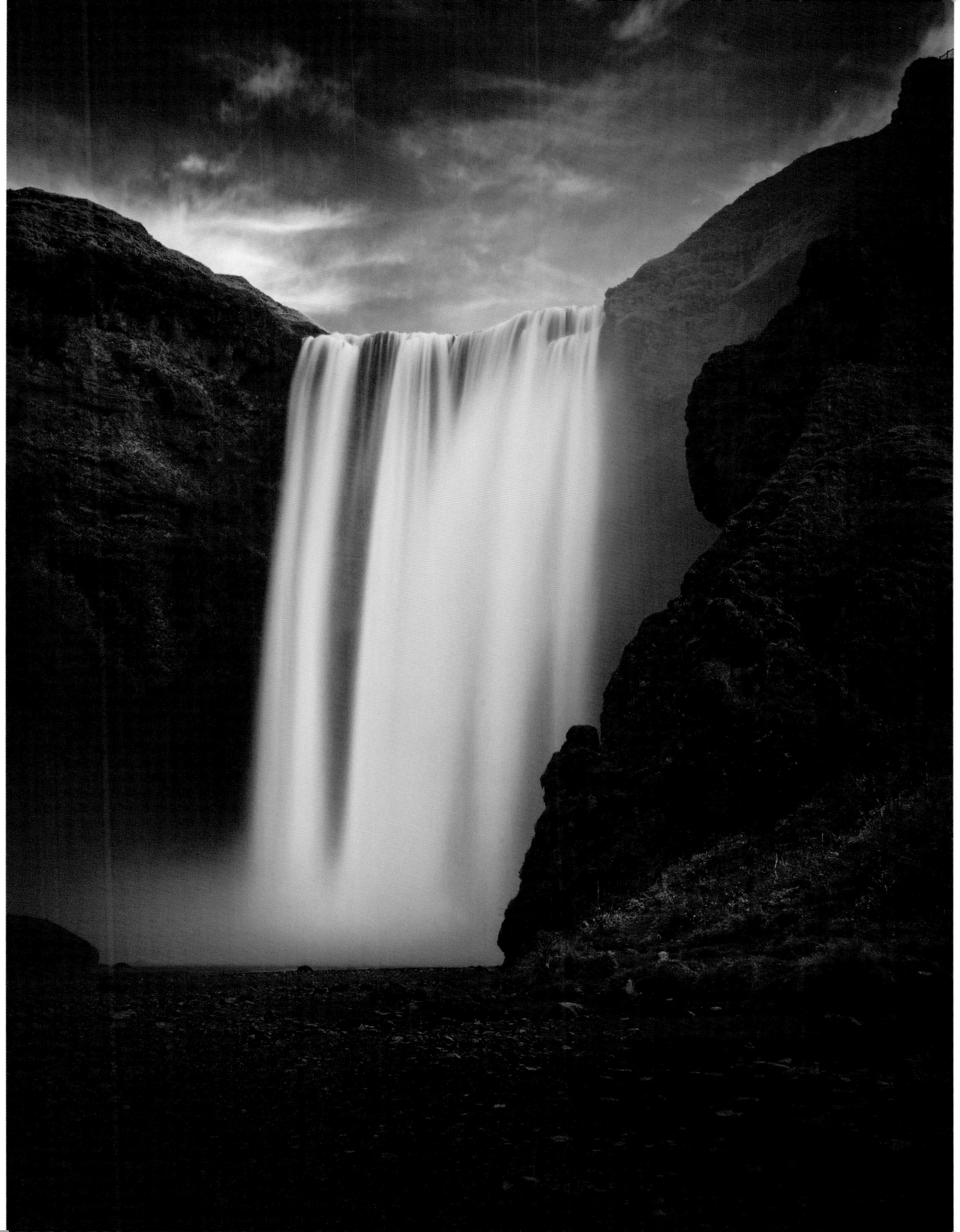

Nature in Motion: Oceans & Rivers

Rivers and oceans cover a large part of the world, making them accessible to a lot of photographers. Depending on the amount of available light and the speed of the tides or waves, the ocean can be recorded in a variety of ways. Without filters, a small aperture and low ISO setting can often result in a shutter speed that's slow enough to capture the movement of the water with a slight blur. However, add an ND filter—especially an extreme ND—and you can transform the ocean into a calm, milky body or a soft ethereal mist.

The flow of a river or stream can be recorded in a similar way: simply choose a shutter speed based on the speed of the flow being captured and the smoothing effect you are after. Look for small rocks to provide focal points, and seek out bends in the river that can work as lead-in lines for your composition.

Tips

- When photographing by the ocean, pay attention to the tide times so there is no risk of you being cut off by a rising tide.

- It is often better to take images on a sandy beach as the tide is receding, as this washes away debris and footprints on the beach, leading to cleaner scenes.

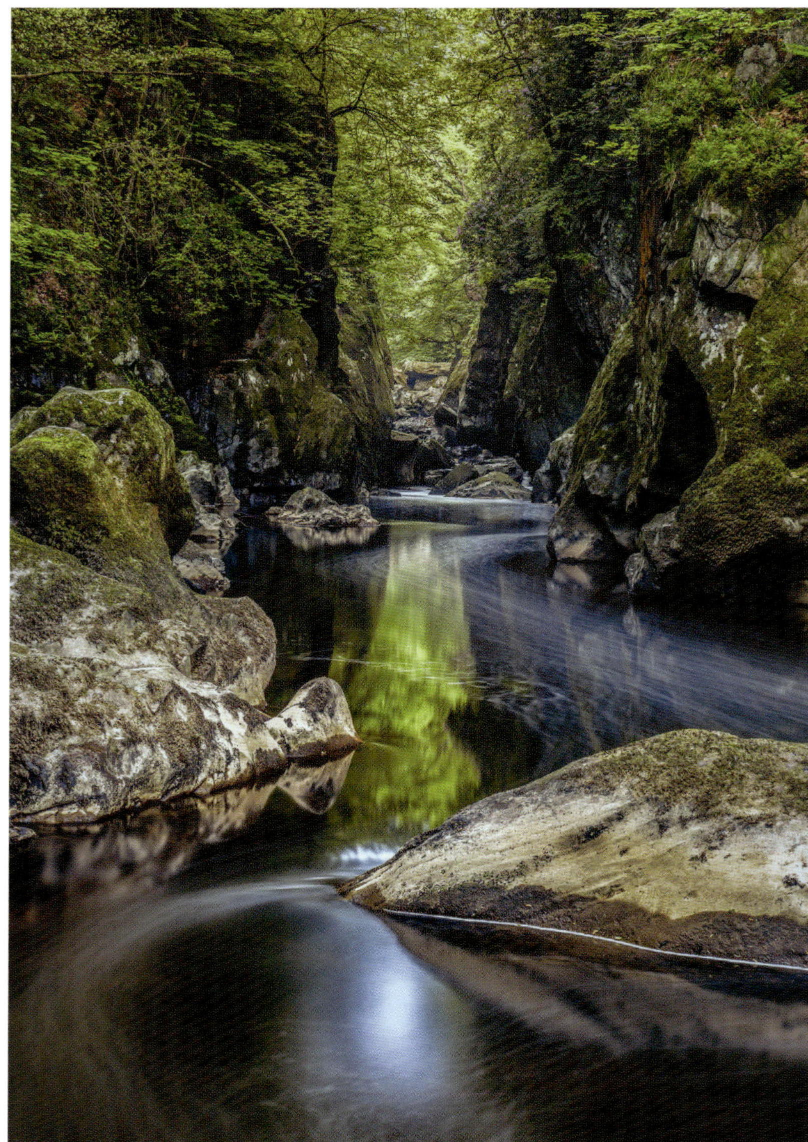

Left: The gradual flow of this meandering river can be seen as the foam on the surface is recorded as a soft blur.

Focal length: 60mm

Aperture: f/14

Shutter speed: 95 sec.

ISO: 100

Right: The derelict West Pier in Brighton, England, creates a unique focal point as the long exposure blurs the movement of the ocean.

Focal length: 32mm

Aperture: f/14

Shutter speed: 11 sec.

ISO: 100

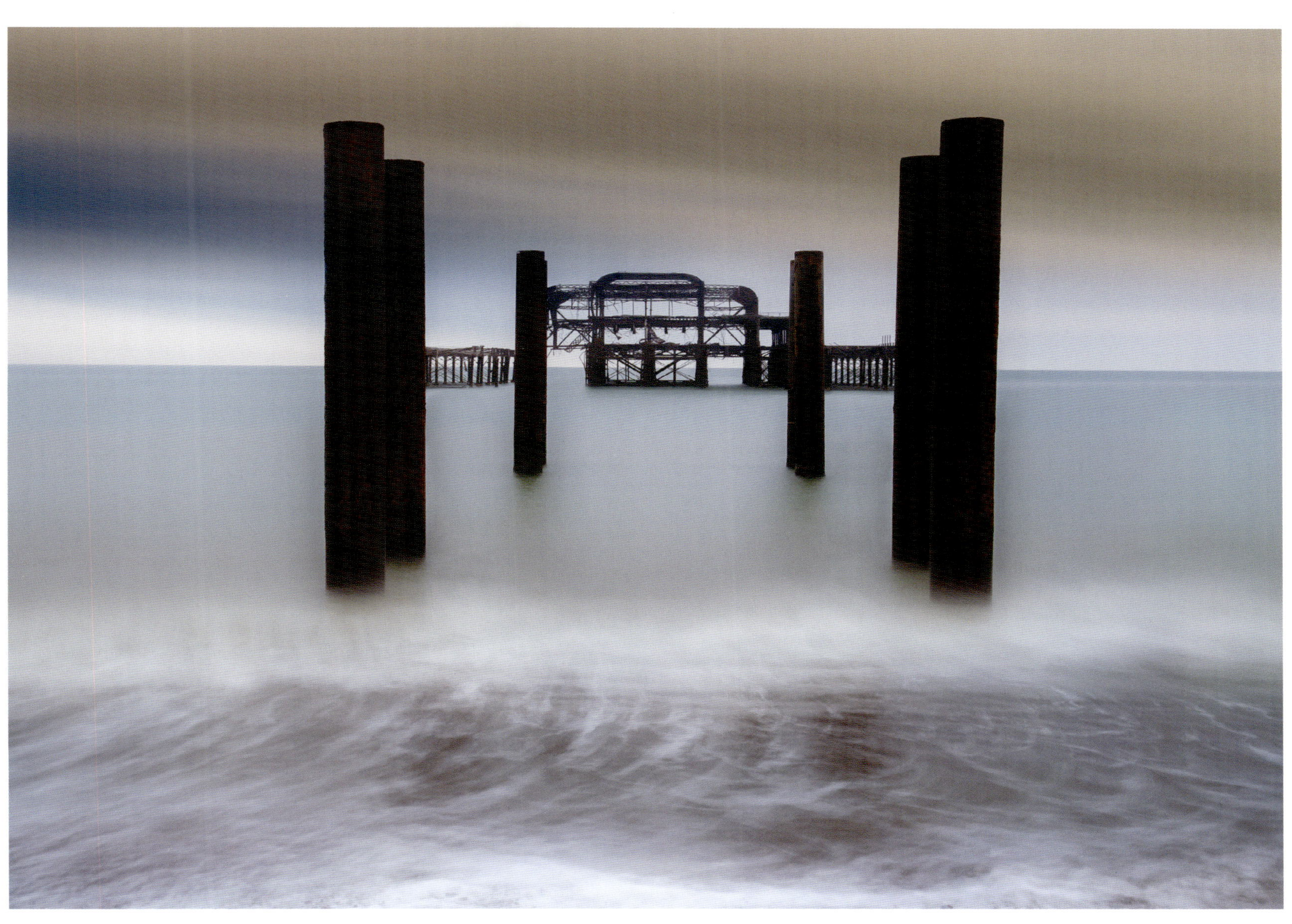

Nature in Motion: Clouds

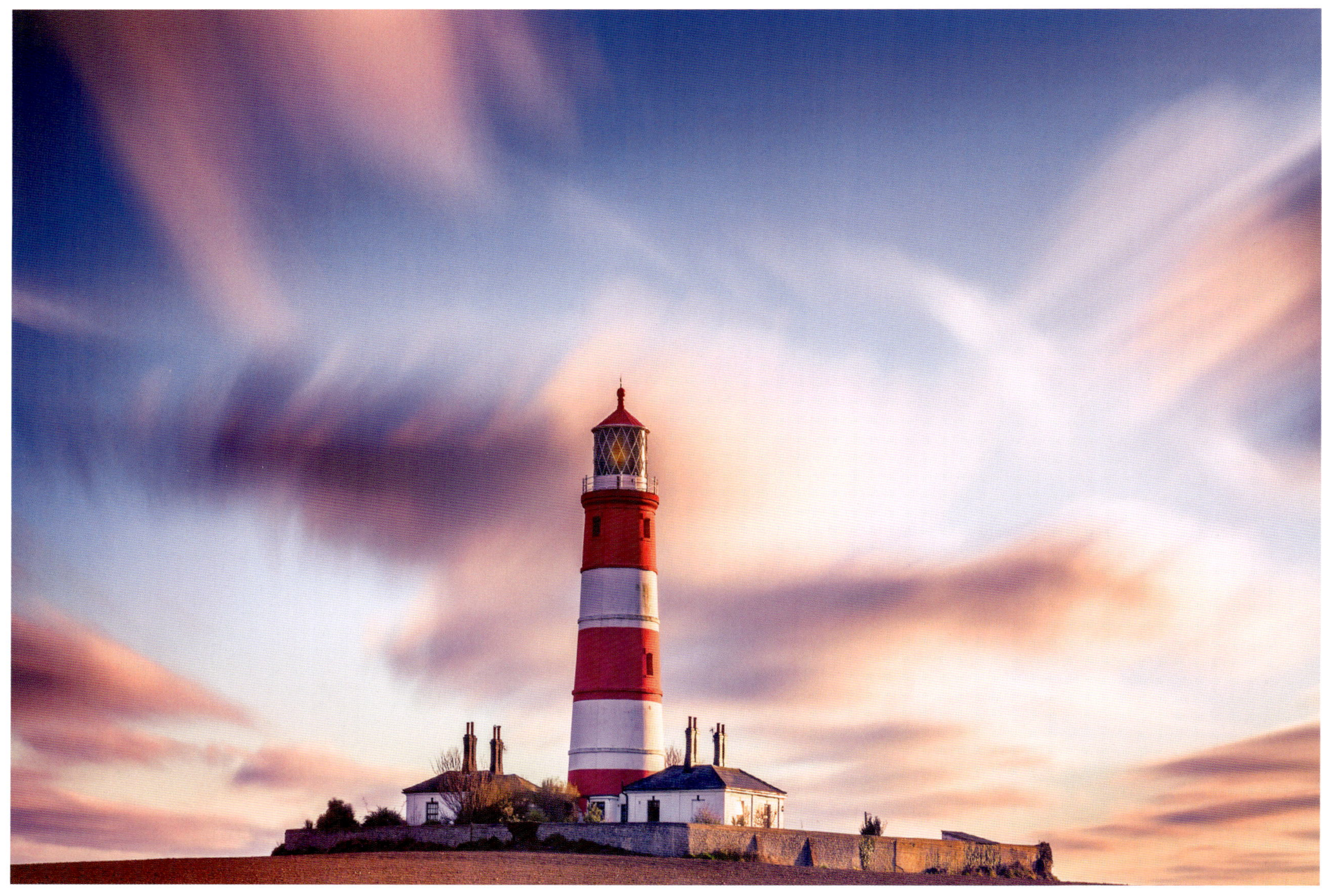

The movement of clouds in the sky can be subtle or strong depending on the wind. Often, clouds are moving so slowly that we can barely notice their movement, but when you use ultra-long shutter speeds, this movement can be captured, adding heightened energy to your images.

There are no correct settings that can be applied universally: the wind speed will determine how much movement is recorded and how much time is required. However, there is usually a delicate balance between too short a time (which will record too little movement) and too long an exposure (which will remove any identifiable or distinct cloud streaks).

Above: The colors of sunset were captured in the clouds as the strong wind blew them in multiple directions.

Focal length: 60mm

Aperture: f/18

Shutter speed: 120 sec.

ISO: 100

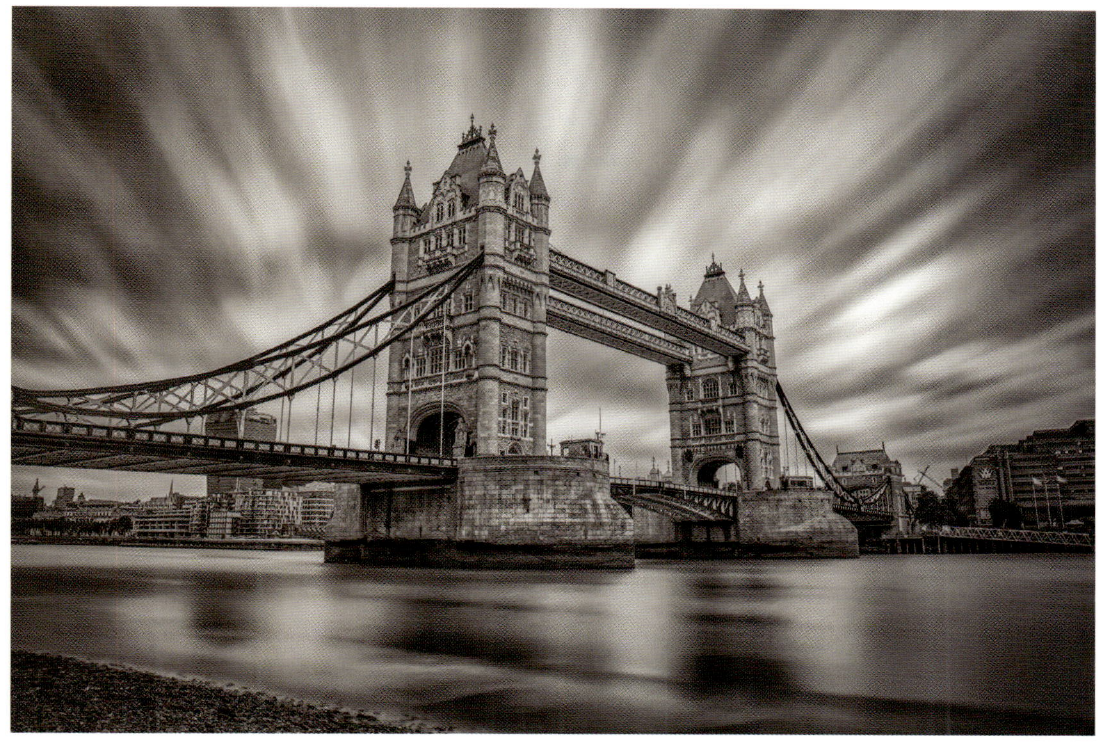

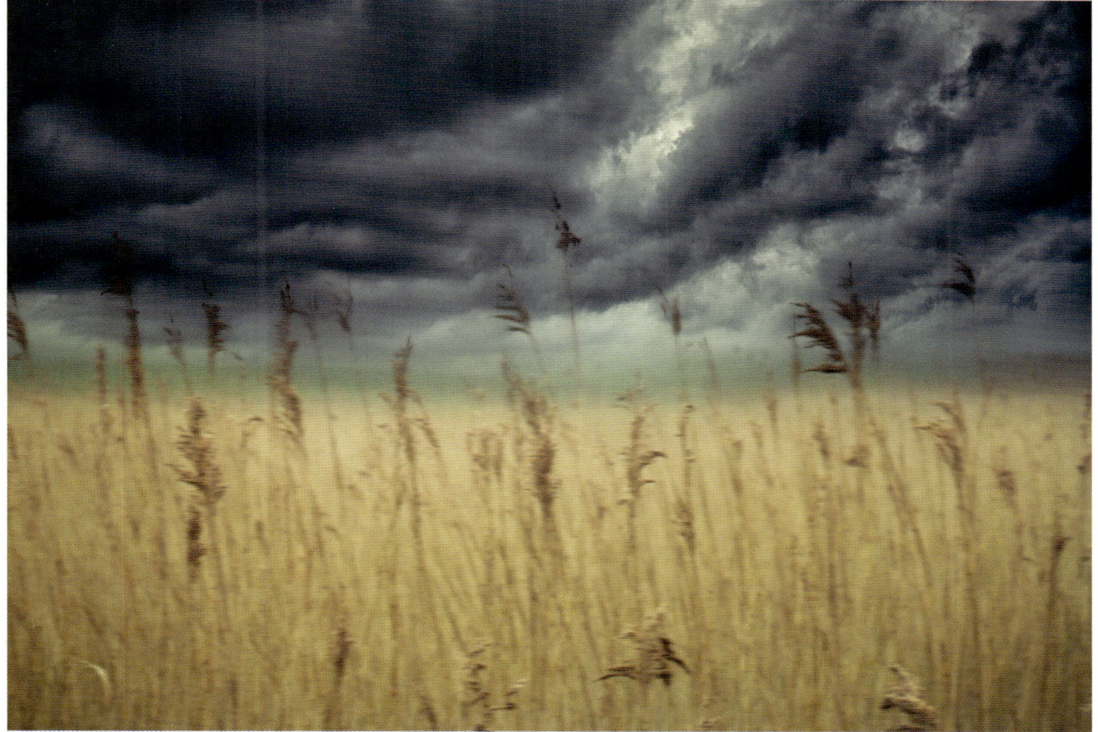

Above left: Clouds moving toward the camera can add a dynamic and compelling look to images, as well as helping to draw the eye to the subject.

Focal length: 24mm

Aperture: f/18

Shutter speed: 140 sec.

ISO: 100

Left: The soft movement of the grasslands and the brooding sky lend this image a mysterious feel.

Focal length: 95mm

Aperture: f/14

Shutter speed: 2 sec.

ISO: 100

Profile: Chris Keeney

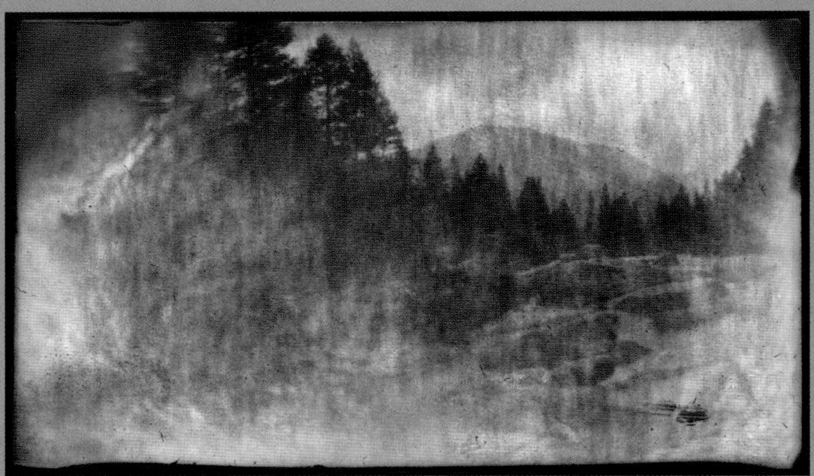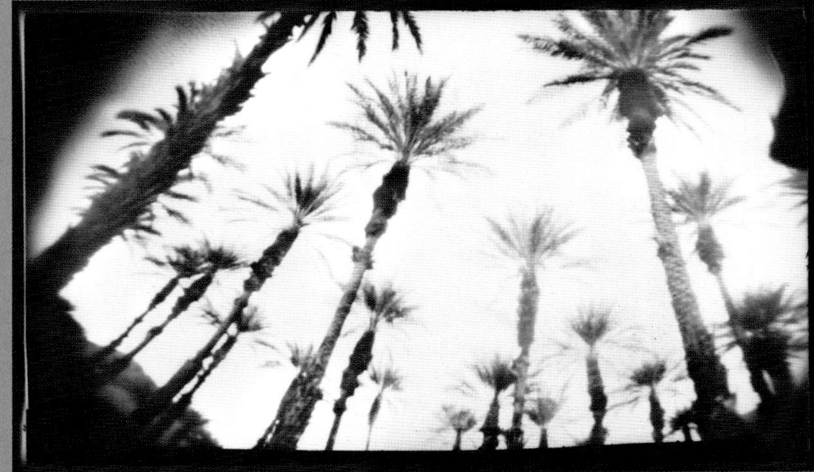

Above & above right:

While camping and hiking in Baja California, Mexico, I stumbled upon an old, rusty chili can. Being the homemade pinhole camera guy that I am, I picked it up and put it in my backpack with an idea in mind. When I got home I discovered that a business-card sized piece of photographic paper fitted perfectly inside the can. My local camera store gave me a used Canon lens cap that was the right size to seal the top and with some black spray paint, a proper size pinhole, and a magnet shutter, the "MexiCanon" was born. Since then I have added a tripod mount that assists in composing the shot and keeps the camera steady while opening and closing the shutter. I love this little camera!

BIOGRAPHY

Based in San Diego, California, Chris Keeney specializes in portrait and event photography. After working as a graphic designer for over 20 years Chris has found a way to blend his interest in graphics with his love of photography. He has also written two photography books, including *Pinhole Cameras: A DIY Guide*.

www.chriskeeney.com

Q) What is your speciality?

A) Professionally, I'm a graphic designer and portrait photographer, but when I travel I like to experiment with lensless photography. I enjoy inventing and making my own cameras and then seeing what kind of images I can create with them. For me, half the fun of pinhole photography is making your own camera.

Q) What drew you to your specialty and why?

A) The idea that someone can transform basic household items into a working camera has always amazed me. Since I was a child I've always liked working with my hands to make things. When I discovered the world of pinhole photography I was excited about all the creative possibilities it had to offer. There is no other photographic medium that allows the photographer to be part of the creative process from start to finish.

Q) What key equipment do you use regularly?

A) Time permitting, I like to use the film and paper negative cameras that I have made myself. However, when time isn't on my side I use my PinHolga and ZeroImage cameras, which are quicker to setup and operate. A fellow pinhole

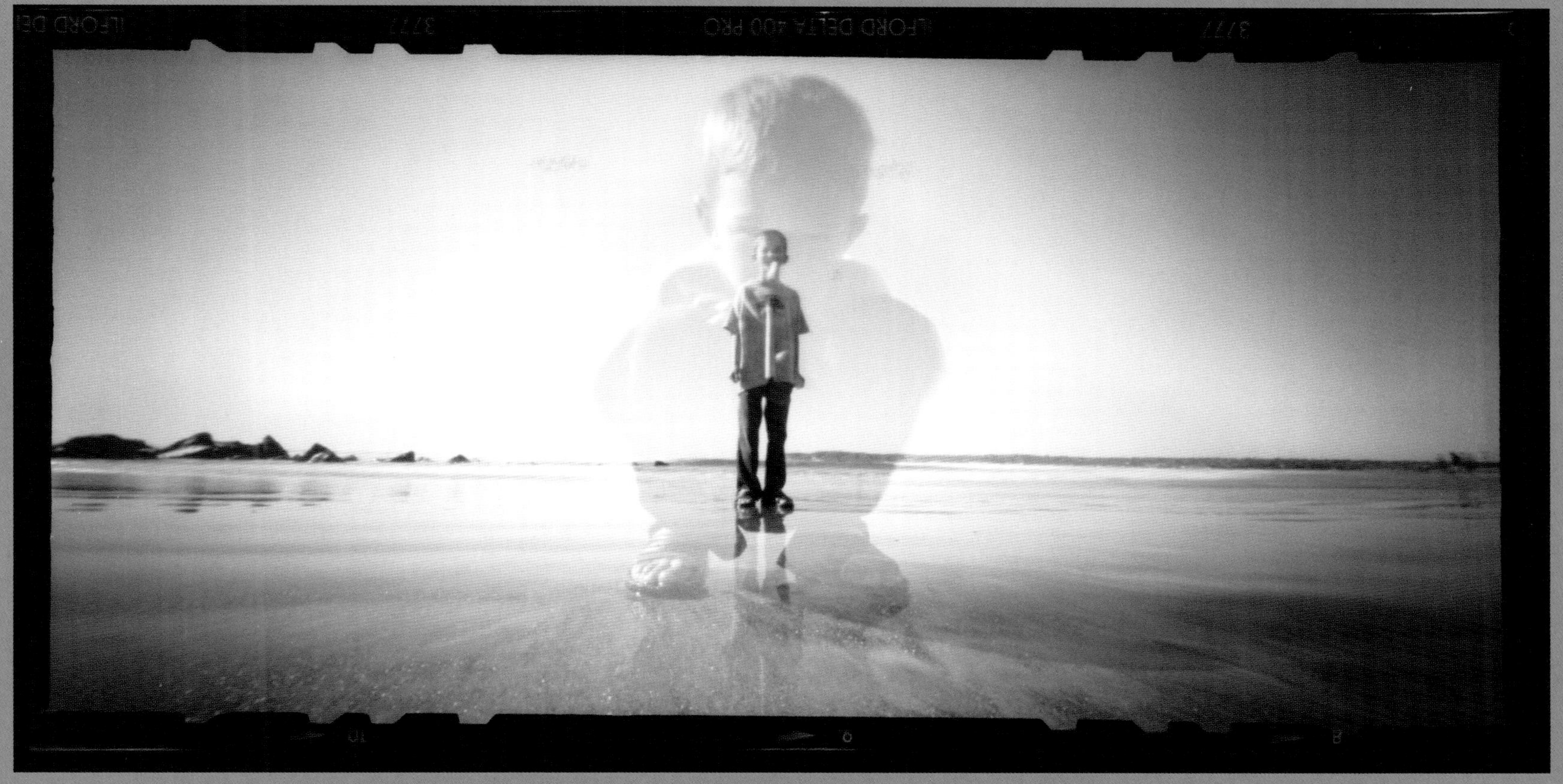

Above:
When time is tight I'll use a commercial pinhole camera rather than a homemade one. This photograph was created with a wooden ZeroImage 6×12cm wide-format pinhole camera on 120 film.

photographer once told me she likens the light captured by pinhole cameras as "slowlight." Since pinhole exposures can be long, a tripod will help a lot to make your photos sharper. If you don't use a tripod, make sure your camera doesn't move during your exposure. I've used rocks and bricks to weigh some of my cameras down to keep them from moving.

Q) How do you visualize and compose your images?
A) Pinhole cameras don't have viewfinders, so you need to "see" and imagine the image in your mind before you set up the shot. Normally I don't go "looking" for photos, instead I let them find me. I'm drawn to fluid subject matter that mixes with things that are stationary. As pinhole photography has an infinite focal plane, I like to find settings that have lots of depth.

Q) How important is postproduction to your imagery?
A) Ninety percent of the photos I create with my pinhole cameras are in black and white. Anyone who has worked with black-and-white photos before will understand the need for contrast. I like to adjust each image to have deep rich blacks, buttery grays, and snappy whites. Some images may require retouching dust as well as cropping out distracting edges or light leaks.

Q) What is your main tip?
A) If you make your own camera… test, test, test to make sure it's light tight and working properly before you take it out on the open road. If you're going to use photographic paper for your negatives, use grade two paper instead of multi-graded papers. Most of all, make it fun or you will become disenchanted by the whole process!

Chapter 8

Intentional Blur

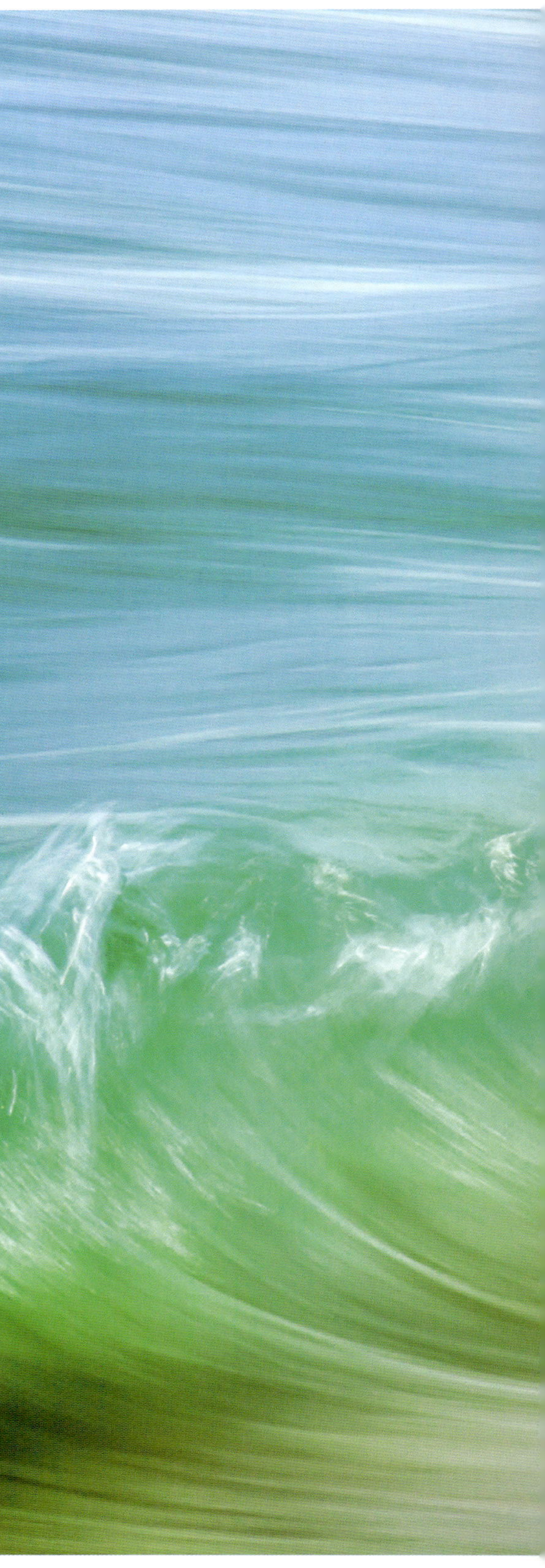

With all of your photographs it is important to decide on the message you want to convey to the viewer. Often, this will mean taking steps to ensure that there is no camera movement and you have focused accurately on the subject; the emphasis in most photographs is generally on clean, sharp imagery showing the scene in fine detail.

However, using longer exposures and controlled movement—either of the camera, the subject through the frame, or both—it is possible to create an alternative style of captivating imagery. These blurred images can invoke an array of feelings and emotions in the audience, and deliver a sense of movement and energy that may otherwise be lacking in a truly static frame.

Right: Creative blur can produce stunning results from subjects that would perhaps not be so captivating if taken with a faster shutter speed.

Focal length: 200mm

Aperture: f/22

Shutter speed: 2.5 sec.

ISO: 100

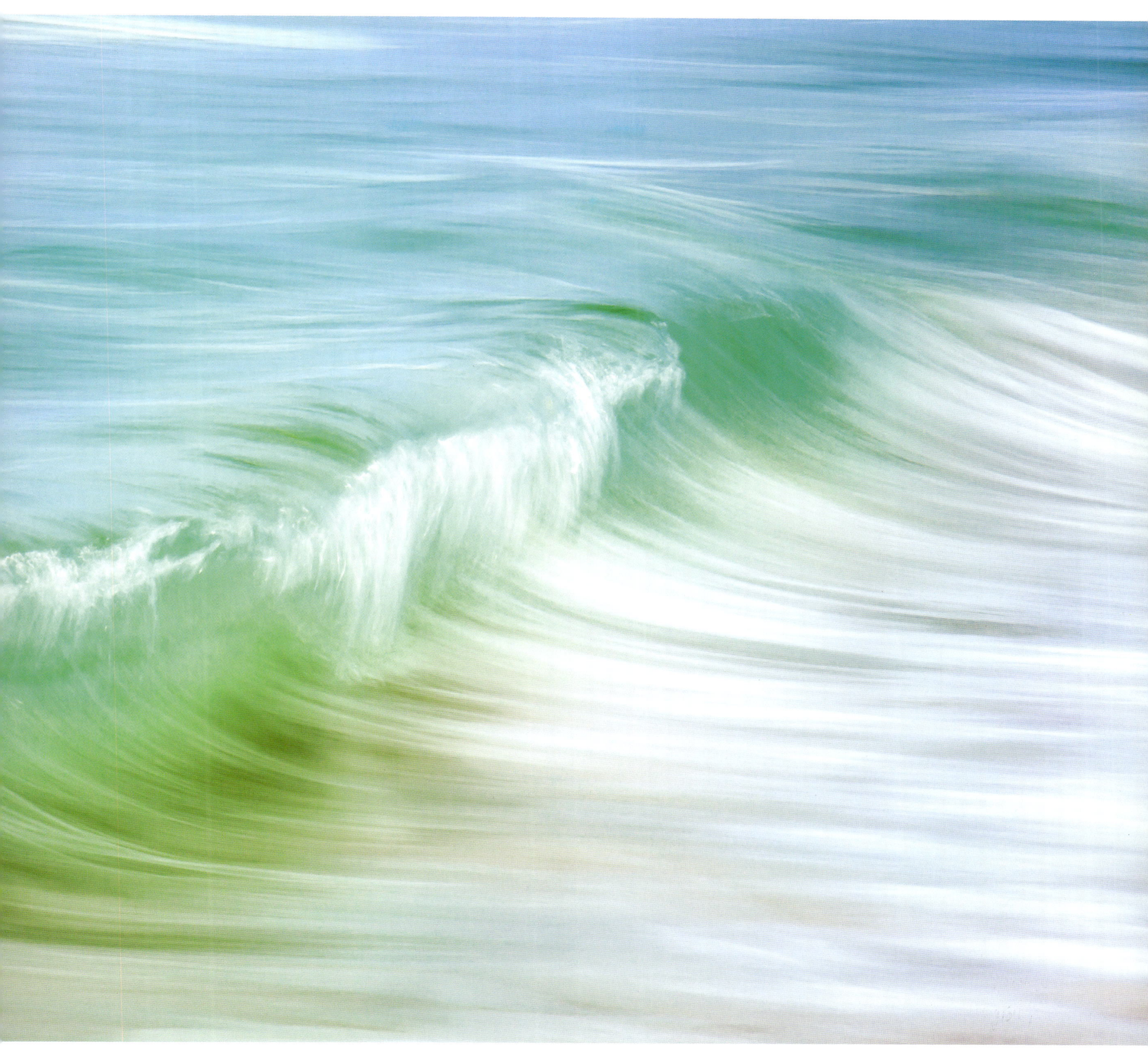

Panning

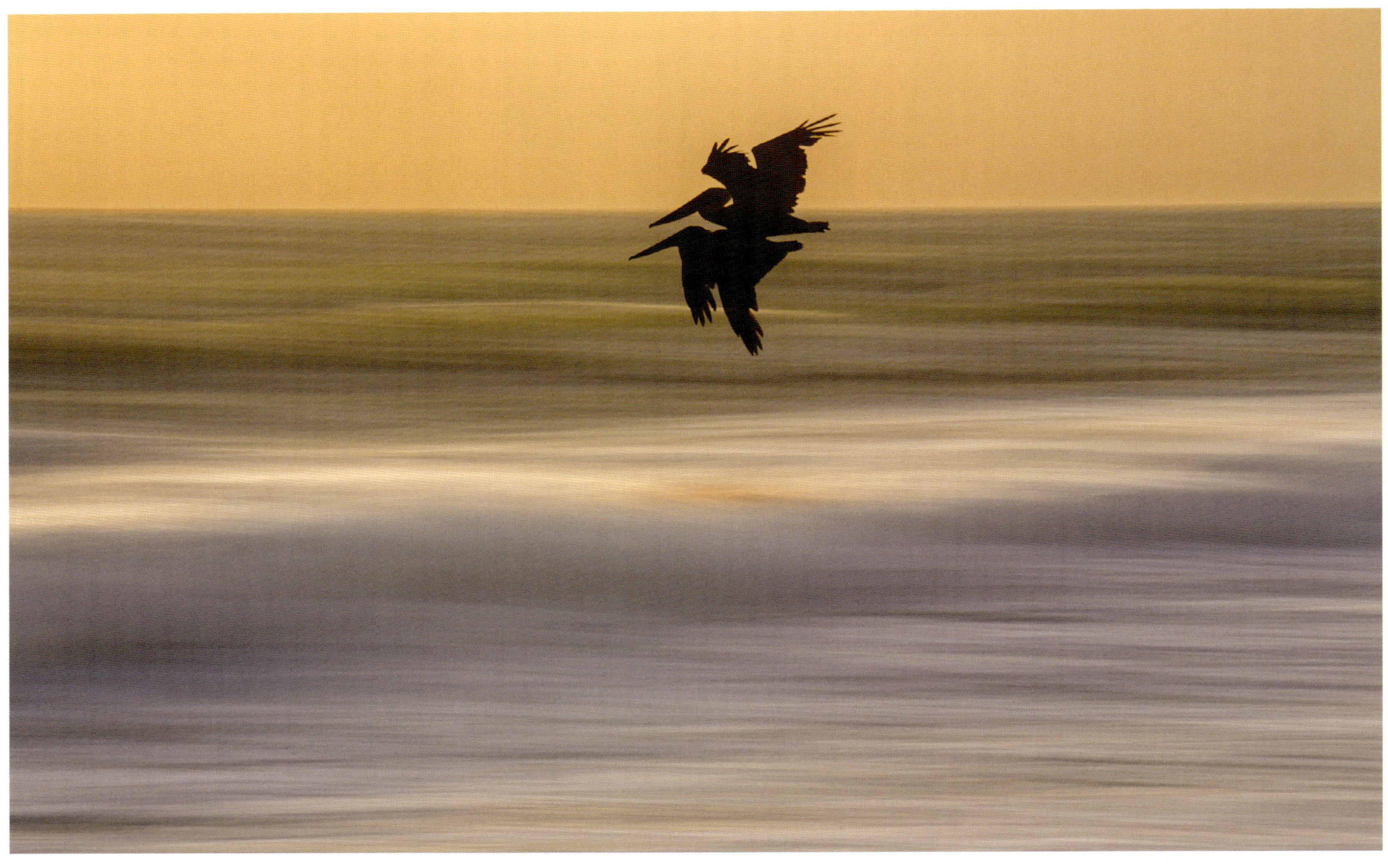

Panning is an effective way of conveying movement in a subject that is in motion. Using a slow shutter speed, the camera is turned to track the subject as it moves through the frame and an exposure is made. The result is the blurring of the background (and foreground) in the image, while the subject remains in (relatively) sharp focus.

The technique takes practice, and there are several skills to master. The first is to balance the shutter speed with the subject speed: the longer the exposure, the more background blur you will have, but there is also a greater chance that your subject will become blurred as well. You also need to keep the camera moving fluidly, so the background blurs smoothly, and you should try to keep the subject in the same place in the frame throughout the exposure.

Look for patterns and colors that will blur together to make an appealing backdrop, and also consider the foreground, as that will blur together with the background. Bear in mind that this technique will not work so well if you have a clear or sparse background, as it will be hard to get a sense of movement.

Above: Tracking these pelicans as they flew over the Atlantic Ocean at sunset creates a wonderful sense of speed. The image was taken with a long lens, which helped to emphasize the blur of the water.

Focal length: 200mm

Aperture: f/16

Shutter speed: 1.3 sec.

ISO: 200

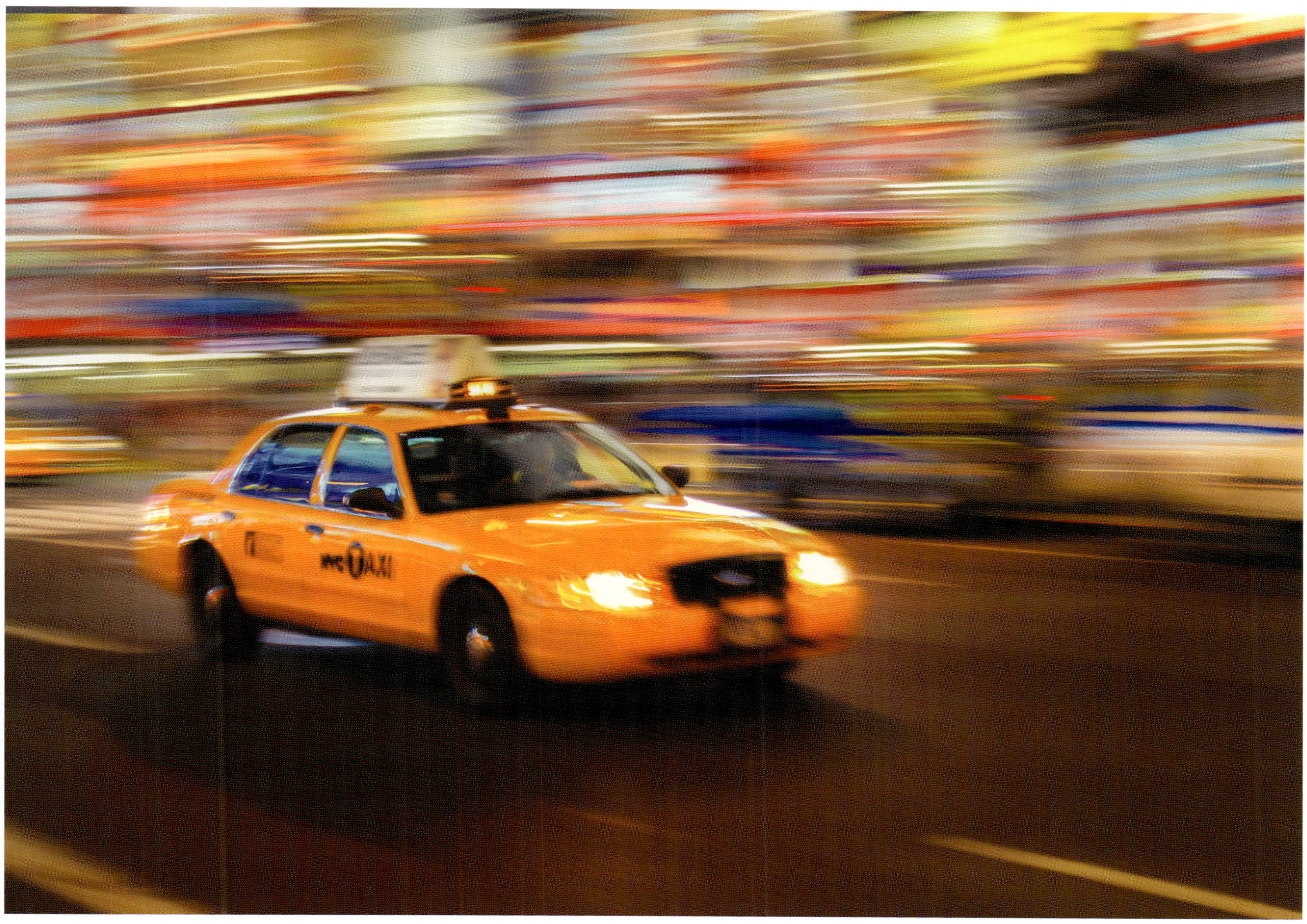

Tips

- Set the camera to its continuous drive mode, so numerous photographs can be taken while the shutter-release button is held down. This increases the choice of getting a nicely balanced image.

- It is important to hold the camera steady, but a tripod may prove too restrictive; handholding the camera is the best option.

- Keep an eye on the histogram and check for overexposed highlights, especially if the sky appears in shot.

- Try experimenting with the direction, flow, and speed of movement to find an appealing result.

Above: The bright city lights provide a striking background as this taxi speeds through the avenues of Manhattan.

Focal length: 36mm

Aperture: f/5.6

Shutter speed: 1 sec.

ISO: 200

Blurring

Although most of the time you will go to great lengths to avoid camera shake and blurred images, there are times when intentional blur can create an exceptional image. There are three scenarios that can all produce very different effects:

The camera remains stationary; the subject moves

This is probably the most commonly used abstract blur and is essentially the opposite of panning. Instead of tracking the subject, the subject is recorded as it moves through the frame; the other parts of the scene remain stationary, helping to "ground" the subject and emphasize the movement.

This technique requires a fine balance, as too much blur can render the subject unrecognizable, while capturing too little movement can just look like a mistake. It is important that the viewer can recognize the subject *and* appreciate that the blur is intentional.

As the camera needs to remain stationary it is a good idea to use a tripod so the static elements remain sharp.

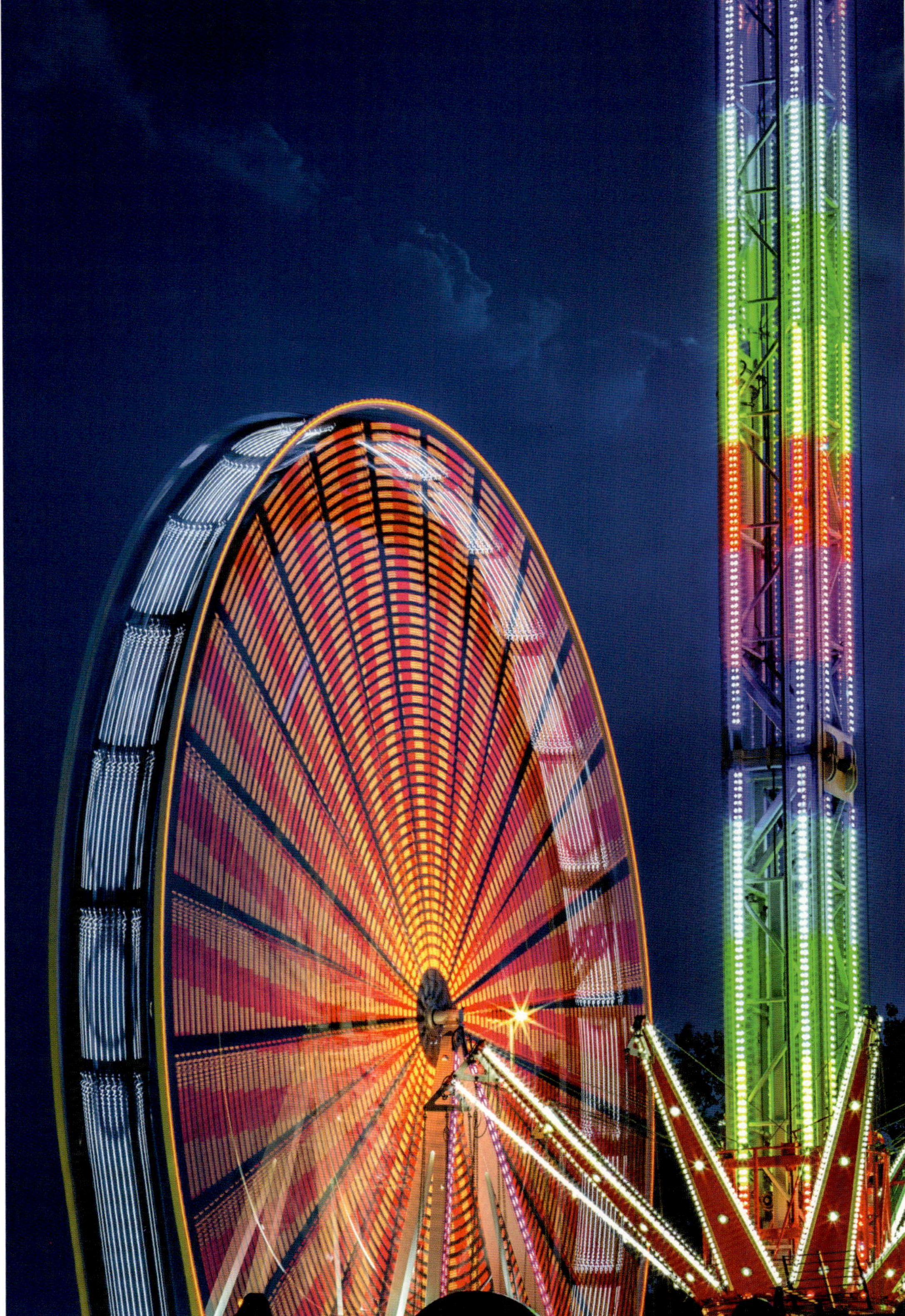

Right: The slow movement and colorful lights of carnival rides makes them popular subjects for creative blur photographs.

Focal length: 121mm

Aperture: f/18

Shutter speed: 2.5 sec.

ISO: 100

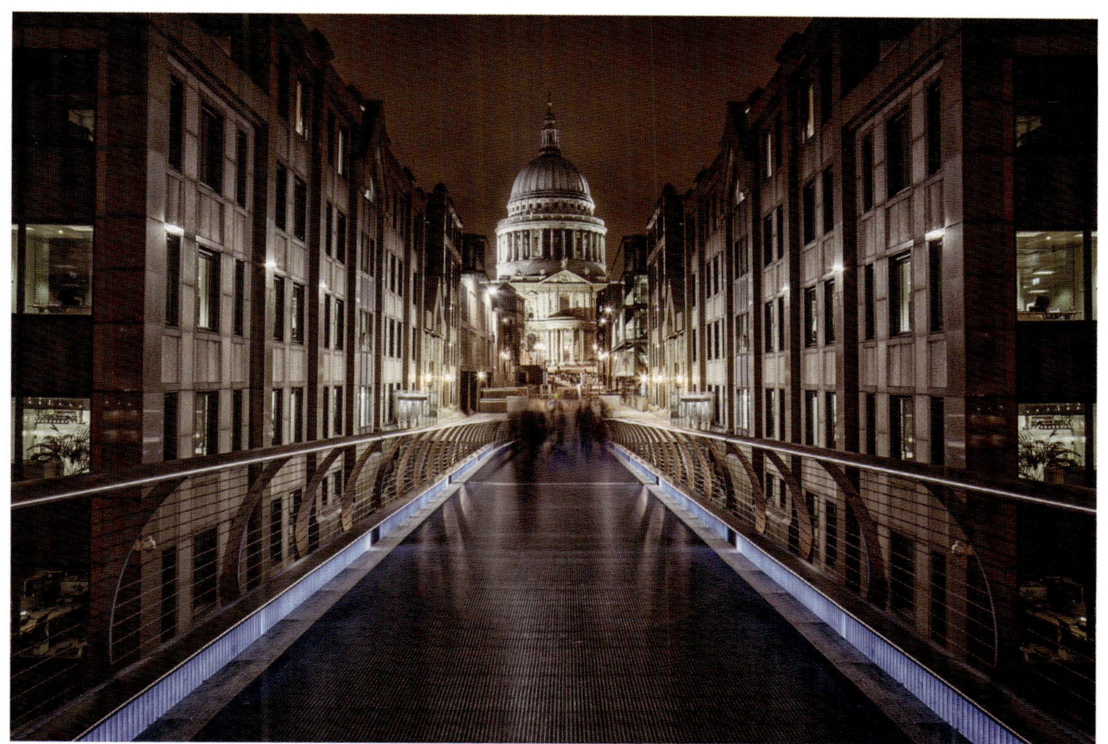

The camera and subject remain stationary; everything else moves

This scenario can produce interesting results when the composition allows. Here, the subject is stationary and is the "grounding element" for the frame. This type of image shows the stationary subject in a fluid environment and can emphasize solitude or stillness surrounded by energy, movement, and life.

Left: Pedestrians moving along this bridge in London at night are blurred by the long exposure, but the rest of the scene is in sharp focus. The contrast creates a sense of heightened energy.

Focal length: 28mm

Aperture: f/16

Shutter speed: 13 sec.

ISO: 200

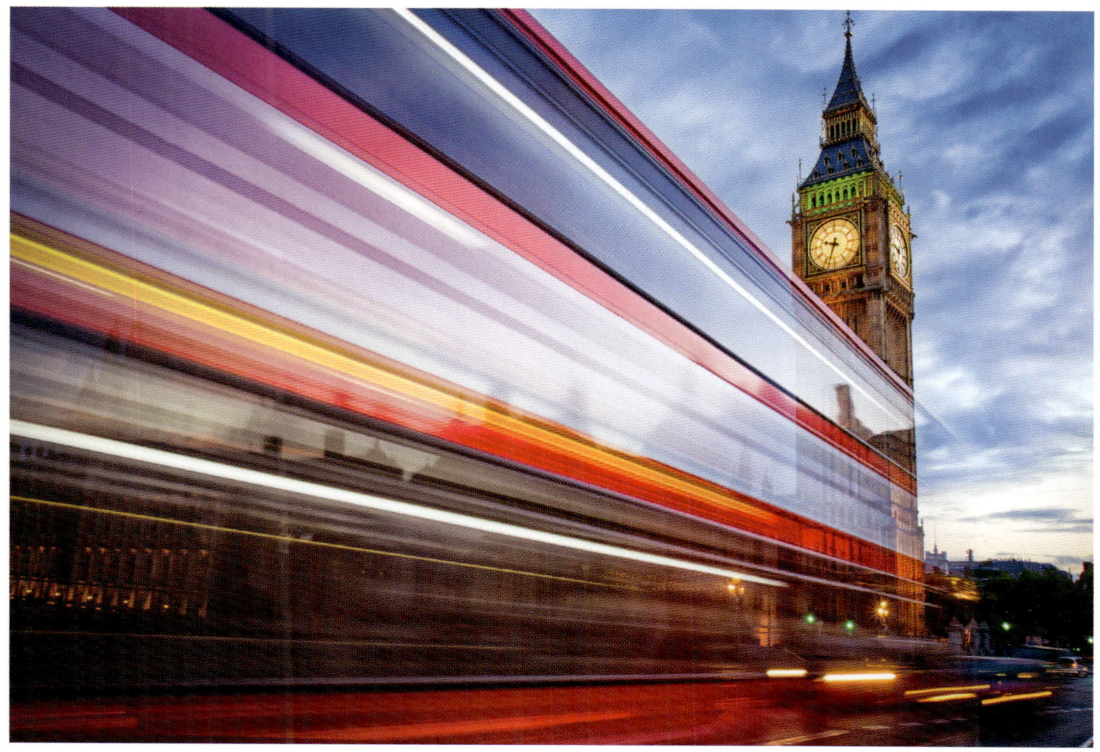

Left: A red London bus appears as a red streak as it passes through this scene, creating a unique, yet identifiable iconic outline.

Focal length: 17mm

Aperture: f/14

Shutter speed: 1 sec.

ISO: 100

The camera moves

When the camera is intentionally moved during an exposure it can create intriguing abstract photographs. Sometimes referred to as "intentional camera movement" or "ICM," the amount of movement, its direction, and its speed will all impact the final image.

Experimentation is required to achieve a desirable effect for each individual composition, but in general, a slow and deliberate camera movement will lead to a subtle and controlled blur, whereas a faster movement can result in a more impressionistic image.

Mounting your camera on a moveable object such as a bike or car can also create some spectacular ICM images, but it is vital that the camera is secured and can be triggered remotely without any risk.

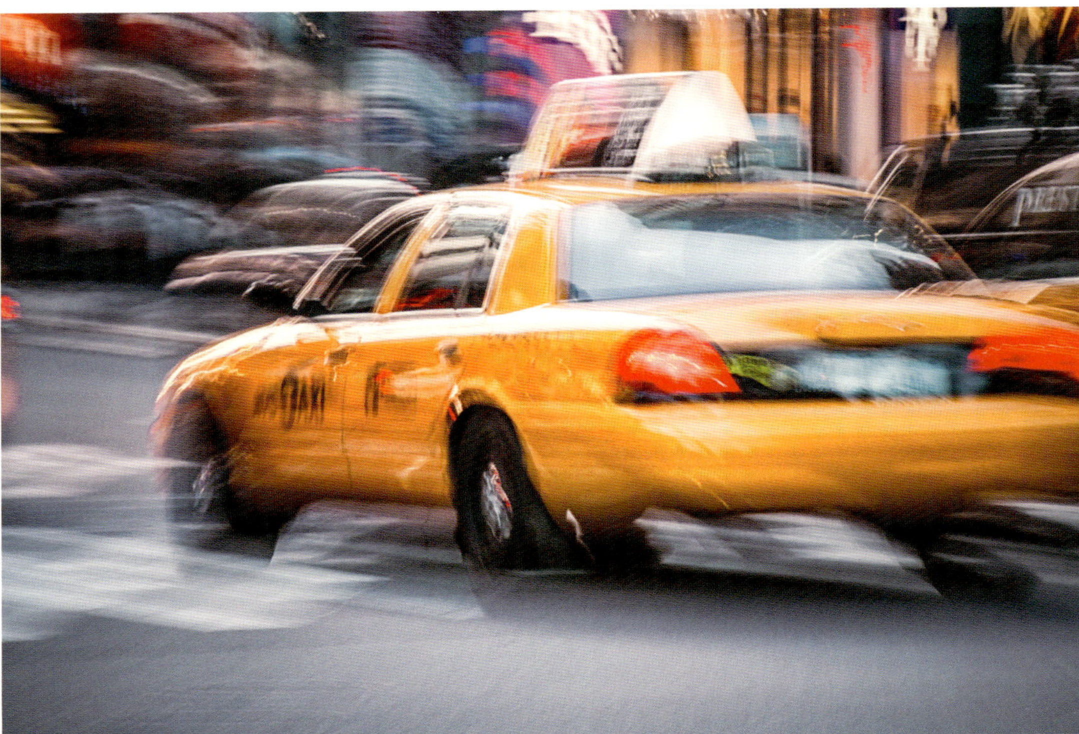

Above right: Deliberately moving the camera during the exposure adds a sense of the energy of New York City to this image, without making the scene unrecognizable.

Focal length: 135mm

Aperture: f/10

Shutter speed: 1.5 sec.

ISO: 200

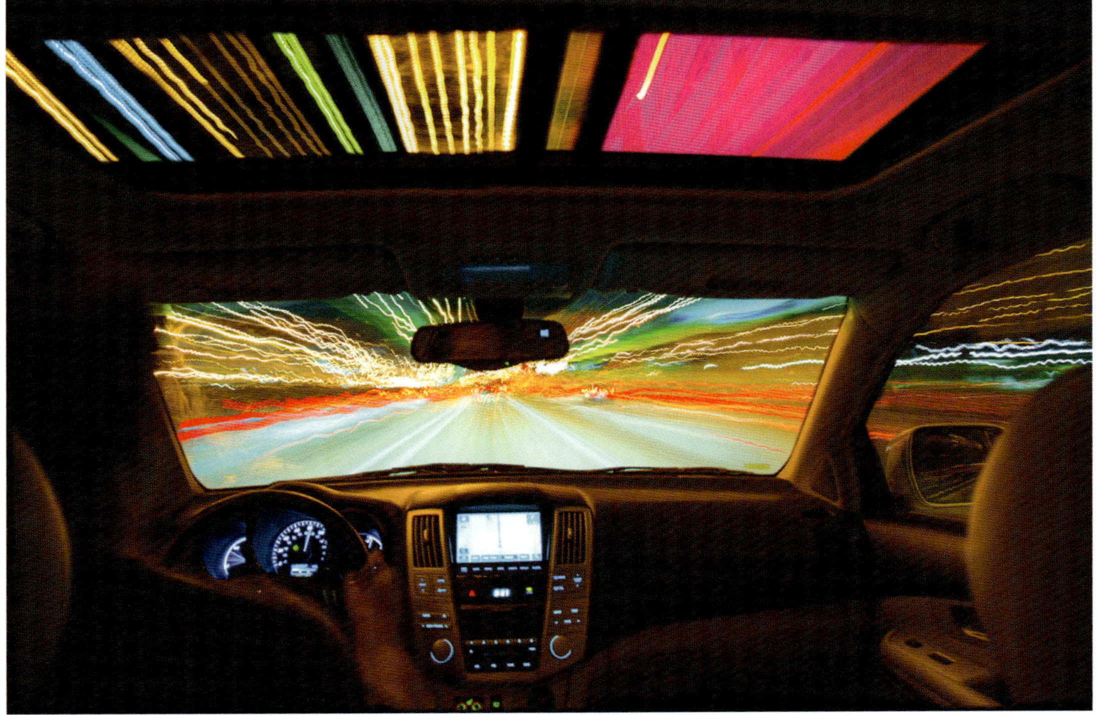

Right: For this shot, the camera was secured on a tripod in the car and the focus was set manually. I also switched the drive mode to continuous and programmed the intervalometer on my remote release to record multiple images as I drove. I then combined some of the light trail images with a "master" shot of the car's interior.

Focal length: 24mm

Aperture: f/7.1

Shutter speed: 13 sec.

ISO: 100

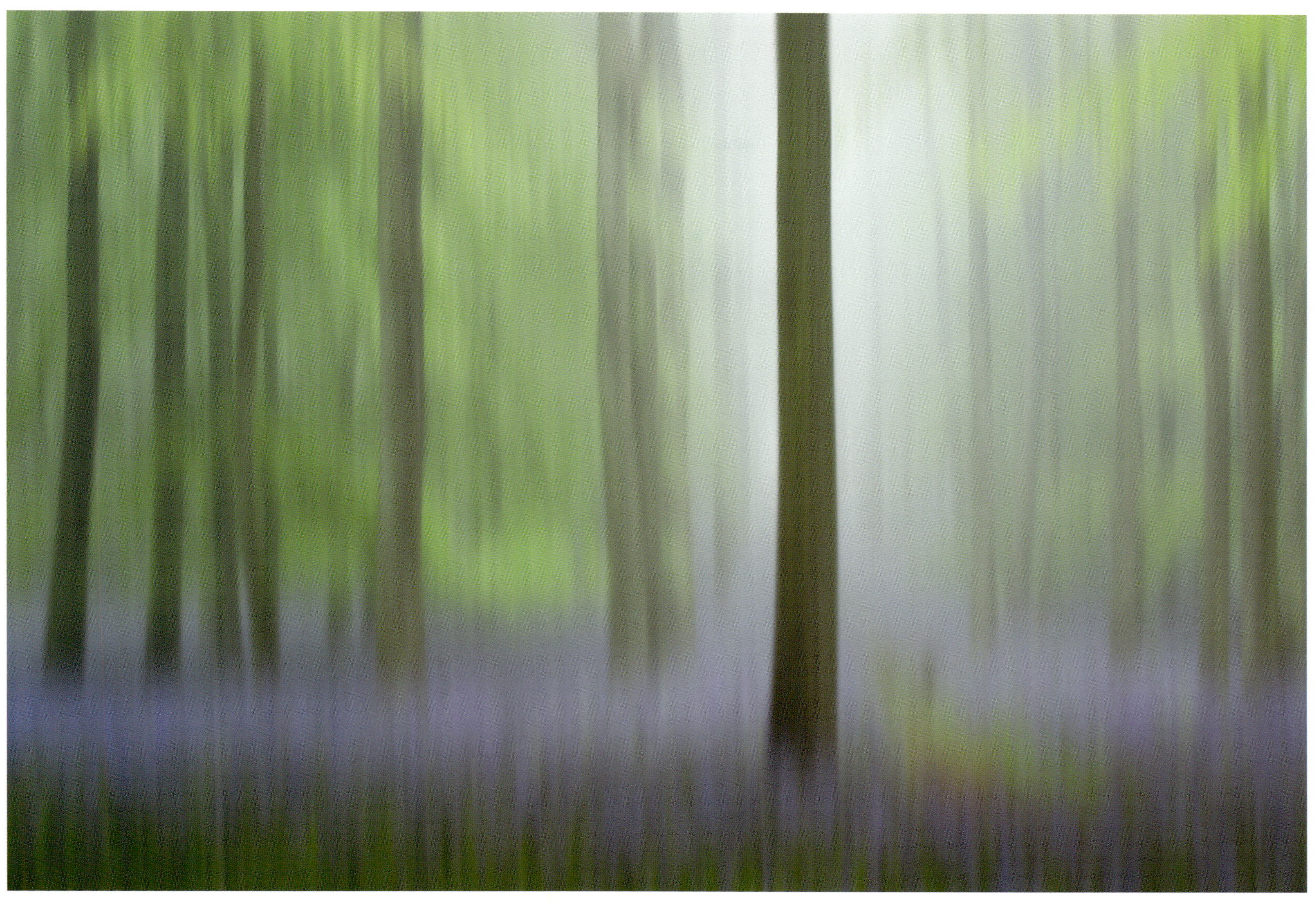

Above: Panning of the camera vertically during a long exposure has transformed this woodland scene into an abstract image. Moving the camera in the same direction as the subject creates a harmonious composition.

Focal length: 75mm

Aperture: f/11

Shutter speed: 4 sec.

ISO: 200

Other Movements

Although you can guess the outcome of some ICM techniques—or at least have an idea of what the result might be—there are other approaches to blur that are slightly less predictable:

Zoom bursts

As the name suggests, this technique requires a zoom lens to create a specific abstract effect that is visually distinctive. With the camera in a fixed position (on a tripod), the shutter is opened and while the exposure is being made the lens' zoom ring is rotated. This zooming motion is captured in the frame, resulting in a "radiating subject" that appears to be increasing or decreasing in size, depending on the direction of the zoom applied.

Altering the speed, duration, or direction of the zoom—or even stuttering the zooming motion—will allow you to produce a wide range of different effects, so experimentation is key.

Below: Creatively rotating the zoom ring while taking this image created a unique effect. It is important that the camera remains locked down on a tripod so this can be done effectively.

Focal length: 173mm

Aperture: f/11

Shutter speed: 1/2 sec.

ISO: 100

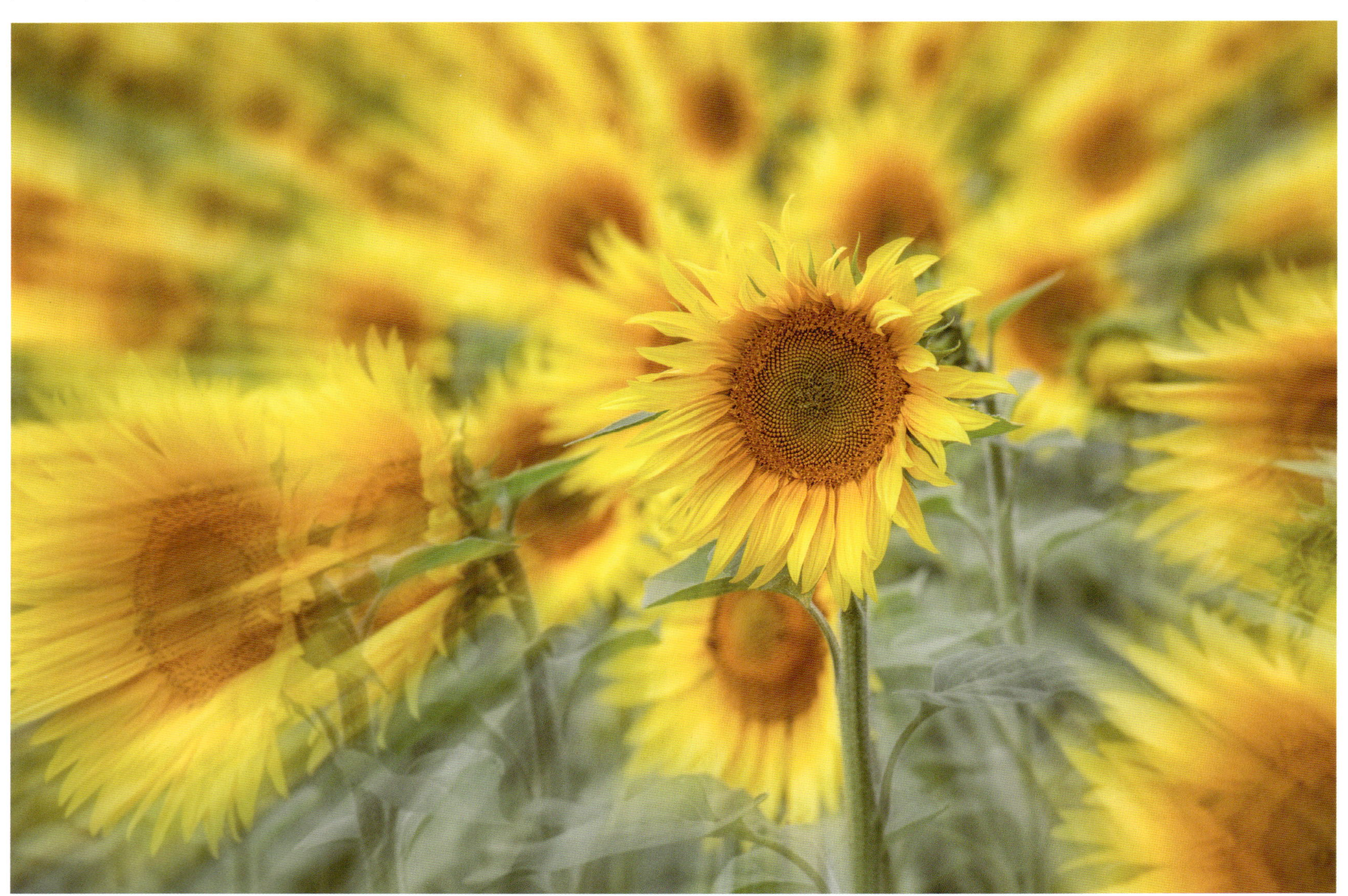

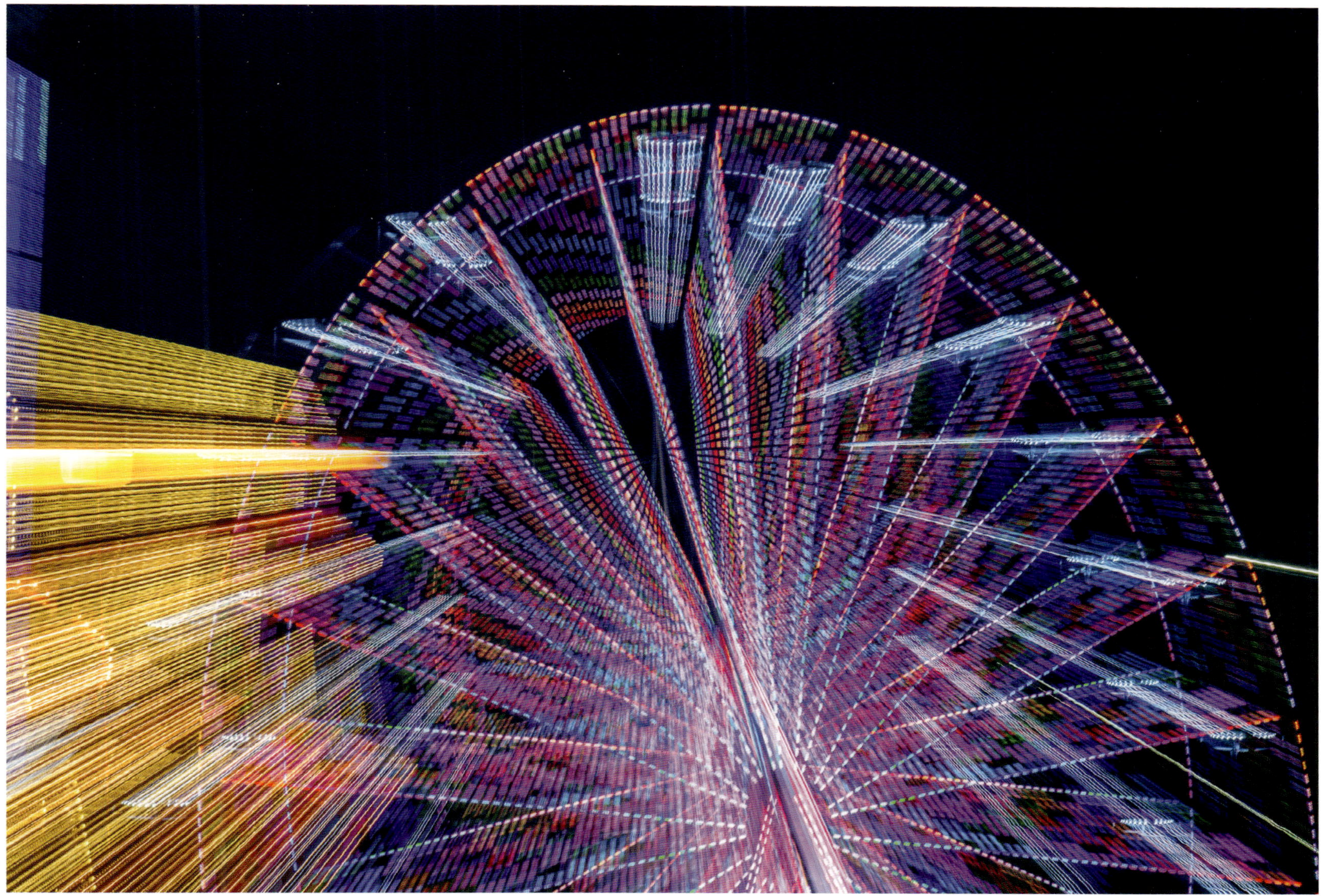

Rotation

Rotating the camera while it is exposing is a relatively straightforward creative effect. Depending on the shutter speed and the speed of the rotation, the scene will be distorted in an abstract way, although too much rotation can easily result in an unrecognizable image that merely confuses the viewer: experiment with the shutter speed and movement to find a balance.

Camera tossing

This technique should not be undertaken lightly! The idea is simple: while the shutter is open, the camera is tossed into the air so that it records the scene as it moves. Ideally, a timer should be used so the shutter opens while the camera is moving. A very long exposure time is unnecessary, so high throws are not required: a shutter speed in the region of 1/4 sec. should prove sufficient. And don't forget to catch your camera!

Above: Colorful lights effectively create abstract images using the zooming technique.

Focal length: 160mm

Aperture: f/22

Shutter speed: 5 sec.

ISO: 100

Profile: Jens Ludwig

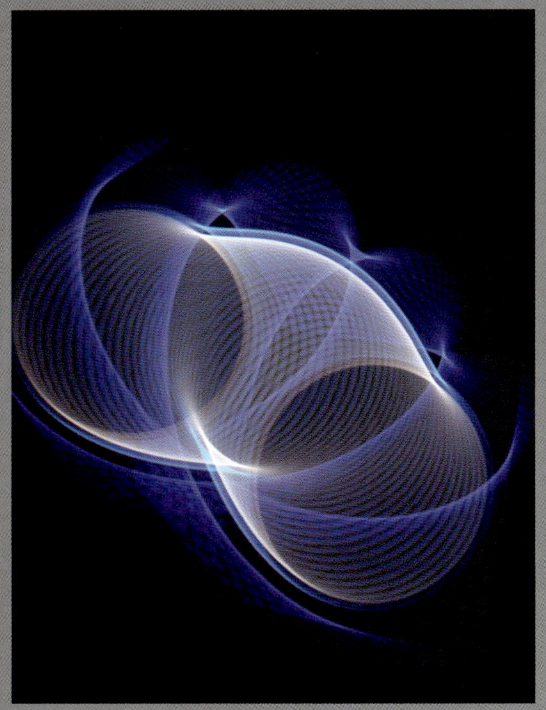

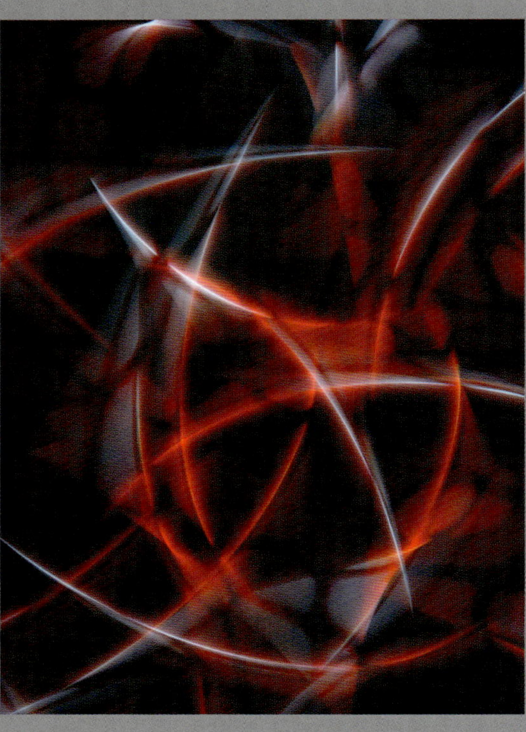

BIOGRAPHY

Jens Ludwig is from Radolfzell on Lake Constance, Germany. His main profession is as a web developer, but he is never without a camera. Although he does a lot of HDR and "straight" photography, his specialism is camera tossing, which he explores through his dedicated website.

Jens' work has featured in numerous publications, both in Germany and overseas, as well as on German television.

www.cameratossing.de

Above far left:

Focal length: 5.8mm

Aperture: f/2.8

Shutter speed: 1/6 sec.

ISO: 400

Above left:

Focal length: 5.8mm

Aperture: f/2.8

Shutter speed: 0.6 sec.

ISO: 400

Left:

Focal length: 5.8mm

Aperture: f/2.8

Shutter speed: 1/6 sec.

ISO: 400

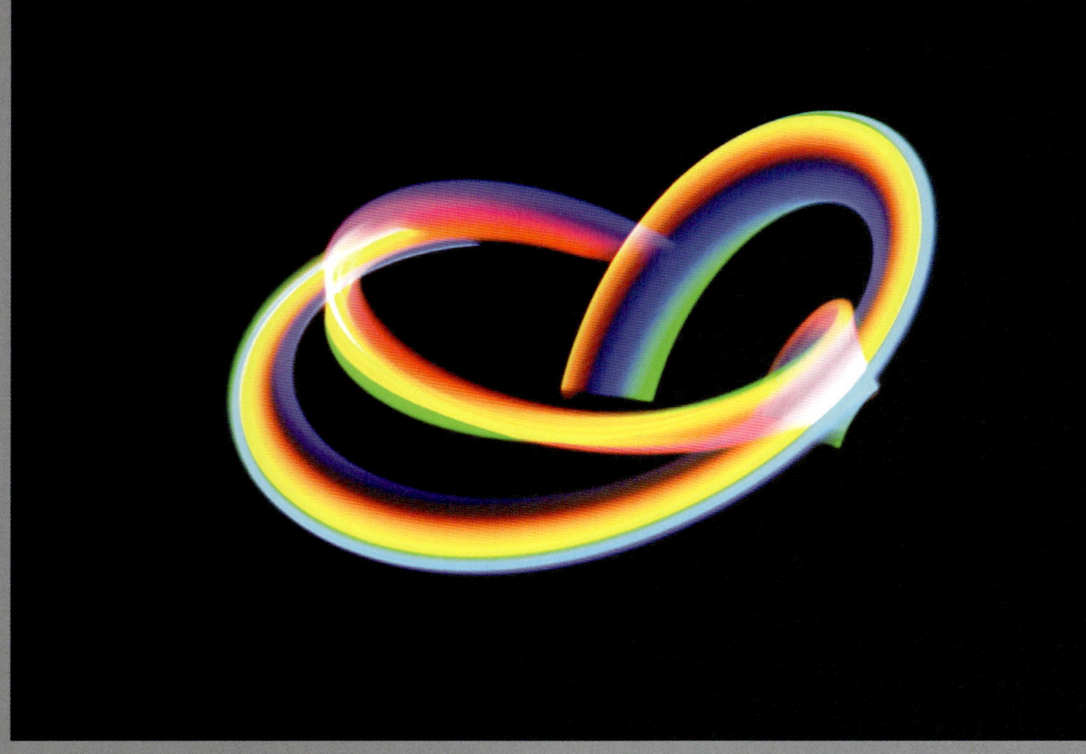

Q) What is your specialty?

A) I specialize in creating unique images by throwing my camera in front of a light source, which can be a simple graphic, such as a few colored circles on a computer screen. The results are fascinating shots of light traces, the appearance of which depends on whether the camera rotates slowly, quickly, or only makes a vertical or horizontal movement; each image is unique. The camera does not necessarily have to be thrown very high—most of the time it can be just a few centimeters. The only requirement is that the camera is free in the air and is not attached by a cord or anything similar.

Q: What drew you to your specialty and why?
A) I started experimenting after watching a report
on TV about the subject. I started with a fairly basic
digital camera and just kept refining my technique.
Simple graphics on a monitor, such as lines,
circles, and squares became my favorite template
for creating the images, but I also like reflections
from CDs—you can achieve a nice rainbow effect
with those.

Q: What key equipment do you use regularly?
A) I use a simple Sony compact digital camera—
no high-end devices. Small compact cameras are
perfect, as they are easy to handle and are not too
heavy. They are also easier to catch than a large
reflex camera!

**Q: How do you visualize and compose
your images?**
A) I usually start by drawing a graphic in an image-
editing program. This might be something simple,
such as a large white circle with a red circle inside,
or sometimes I choose random lines and colors.

Then I try to imagine what kind of outcome it
might give. You can't predict 100% how the image
will look at the end—you just have to see what
happens and try different styles of tossing until
you get the desired result. Over time you figure out
what results you'll get with different types of toss.

**Q) How important is postproduction to
your imagery?**
A) If used, it is only minimal; slightly cleaning
a black background, or cropping or rotating to
position the trail. The motif in itself is created by
the camera during the throw. The only time I might
go further with postproduction is if I want to change
the colors by inverting the image or converting it to
black and white.

Q: What is your top tip?
A) Start with a simple (and not too expensive)
camera and work over a mattress or thick blanket
in case you drop it. As a light source, try different
things, such as strings of small lights, shop
windows, or graphics on a monitor—there are
not really any set limits, but your surroundings
should be dark in order to achieve a good result.

To start with, you can use the self-timer camera
and throw the camera at the right moment,
giving it a slight twist as you toss it. However, my
preferred method is to trigger the shutter exactly
at the moment of release, but this requires some
practice. Otherwise, just try again and again
until you get a nice result. Once you have some
experience, you can start to change the exposure
settings to see what happens.

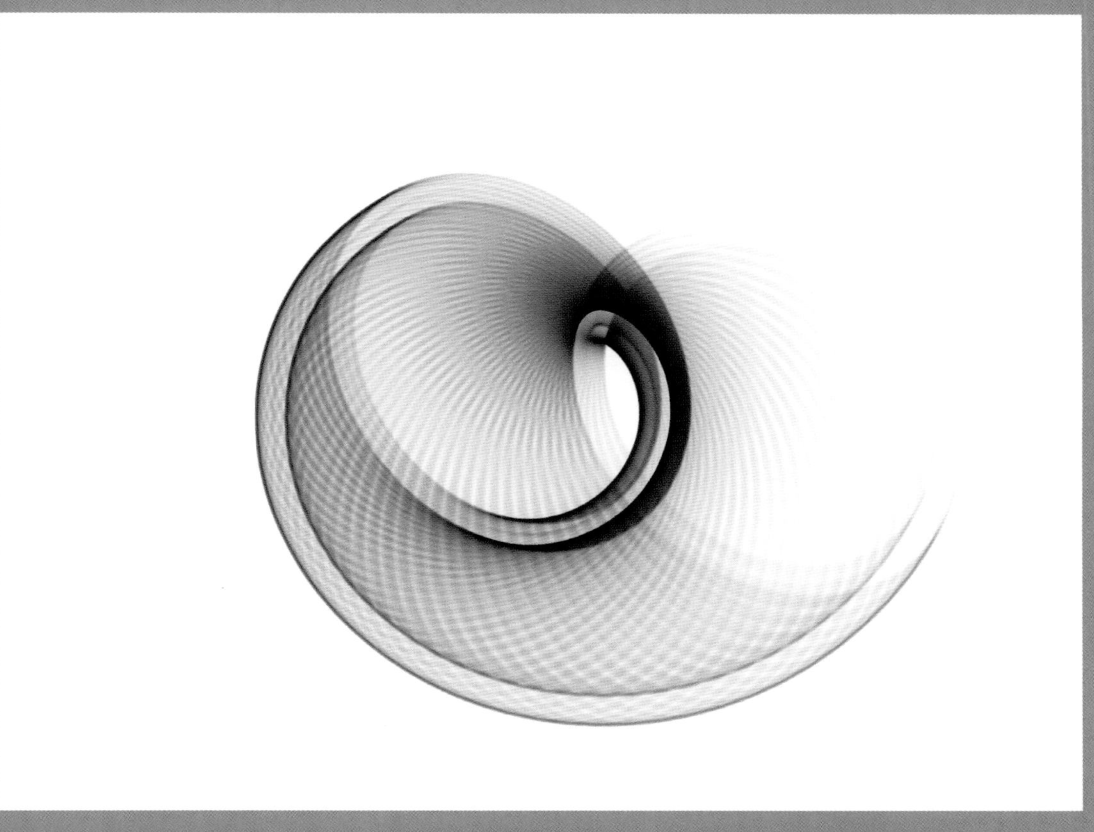

Above:

Focal length: 5.8mm

Aperture: f/2.8

Shutter speed: 1/6 sec.

ISO: 400

Chapter 9
Postproduction

While it is generally a good idea to get your images as perfect as possible in camera, this is not always achievable, so postproduction is an essential stage in the creation of a lot of photographic images.

For some people, postproduction can involve substantial image manipulation, with radical alterations made to colors and elements that were not present in the original shot being added to the frame. For other people, editing might be a minor exercise that sees images cropped or subtle changes made to the contrast or white balance. In either case, postproduction software makes almost anything possible.

Every photographer has their own preferred workflow, so I'm not suggesting that what follows is the "only" possible method. This chapter is merely intended to illustrate the key steps that should be taken by most photographers; it should be viewed as a foundation and guide to developing your own postproduction workflow for your long exposure images.

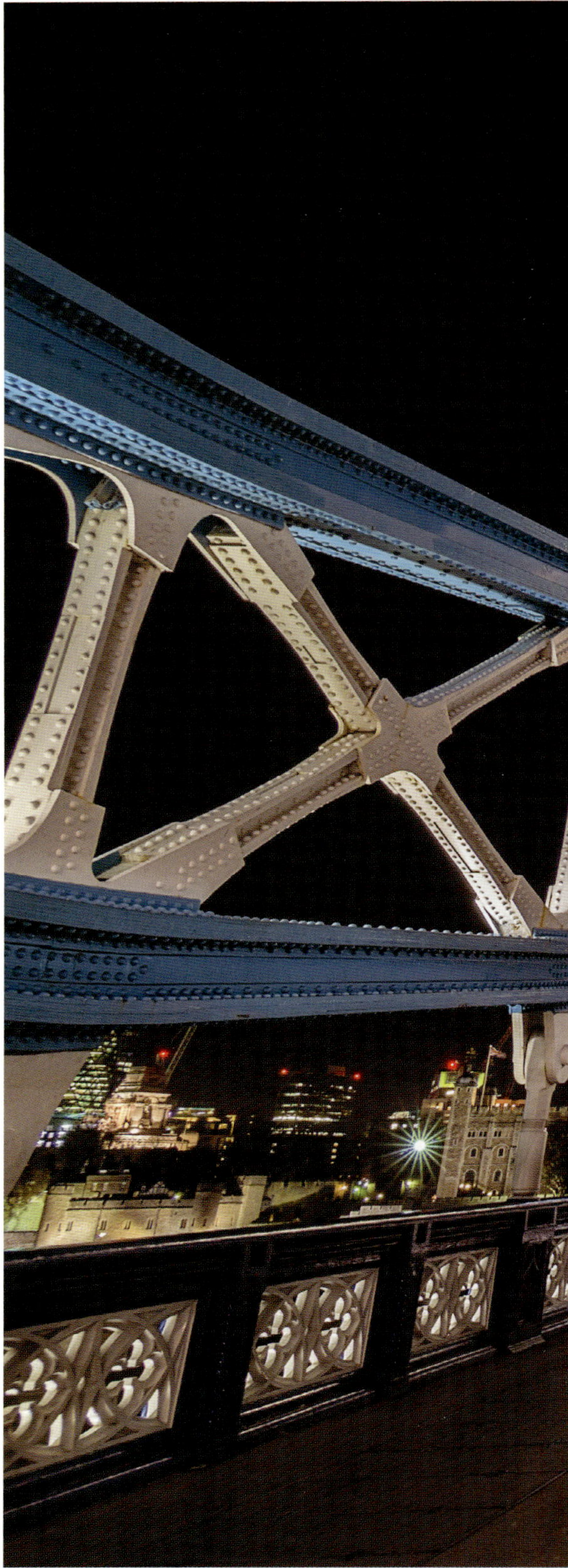

Right: Minor postproduction was carried out on this image to subtly boost the contrast and vibrance of the light trails.

Focal length: 16mm

Aperture: f/11

Shutter speed: 25 sec.

ISO: 200

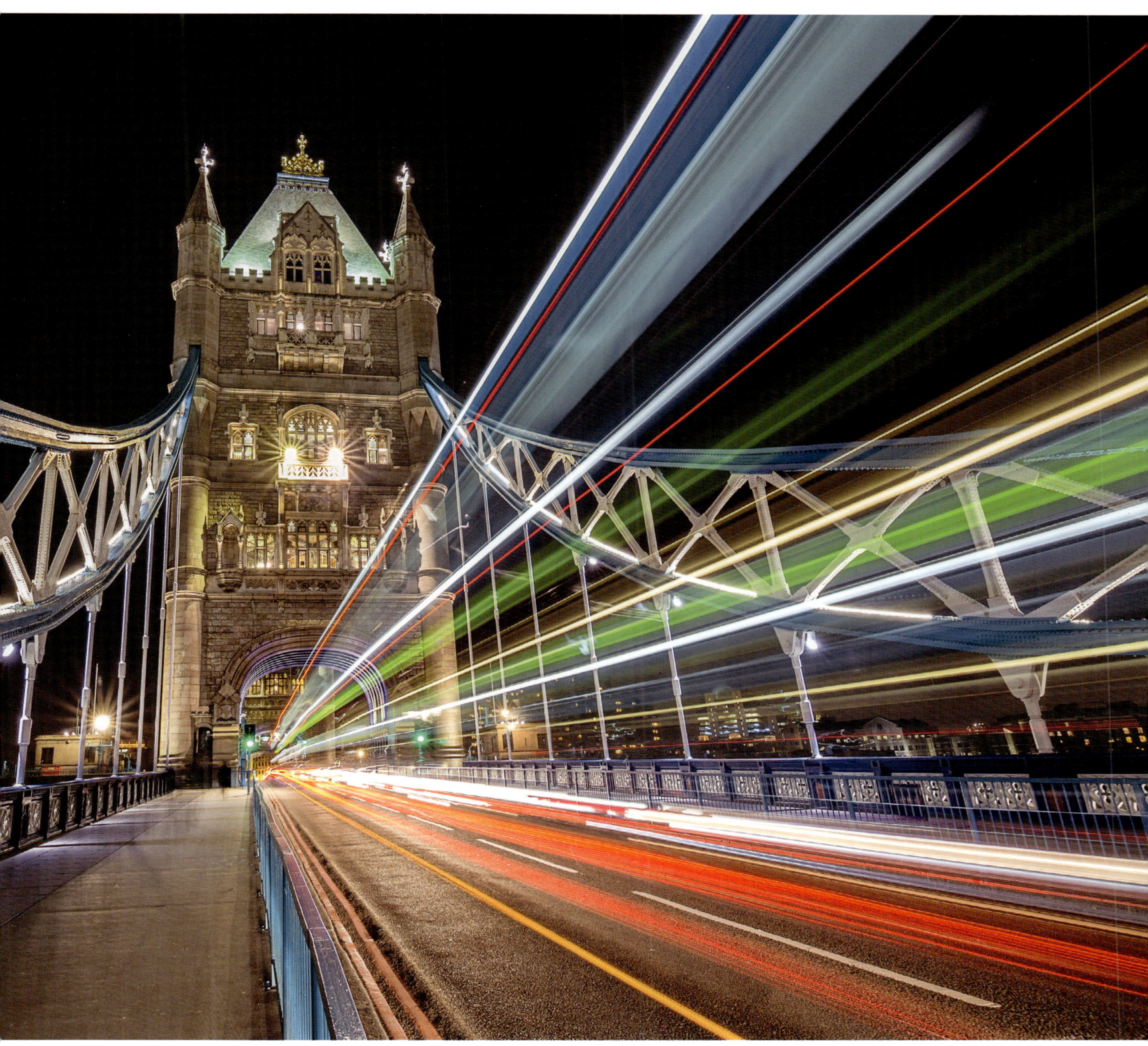

Software

The natural place to start with postproduction is with the software itself. Although there is an array of software available, the forerunners are still products by Adobe.

Adobe Photoshop is the industry standard for "heavy" postproduction work. The array of tools on offer is vast, but so too is the learning curve. There are some important tools in Photoshop that should be understood, though, as their power to transform images is immense. We will explore some of these later in the chapter.

Adobe Lightroom is specifically designed for photographers and combines image cataloging and file organization with postproduction editing controls. Lightroom's main premise is that any editing work does not change the original image file information. Instead, the software records the edit information as a separate small file (a "sidecar file") that is annexed to the original file. This protects the original files and allows further changes or complete resets to be carried out at any stage in the future. This is known as "non-destructive editing."

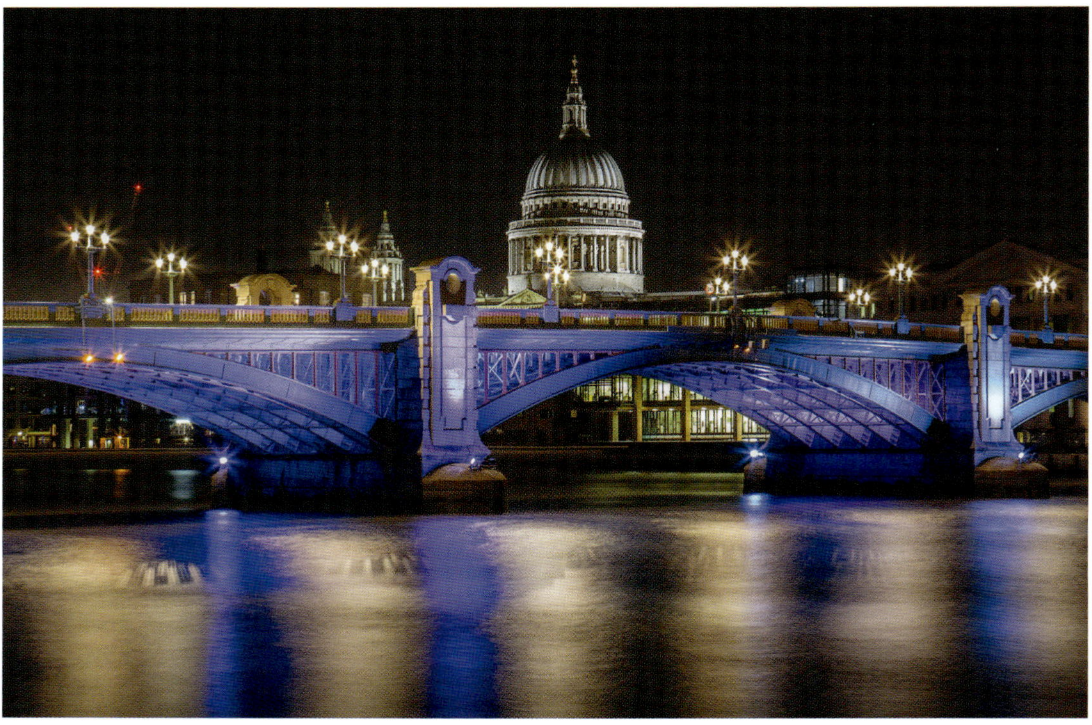

Above: Raw files come straight out of the camera without any adjustments, whereas JPEGs are processed in-camera and compressed to a small file size, leading to a loss of data. Unless you need your pictures immediately it is best to shoot Raw and make amendments in postproduction: this will give you full control over your images.

Focal length: 82mm

Aperture: f/16

Shutter speed: 30 sec.

ISO: 100

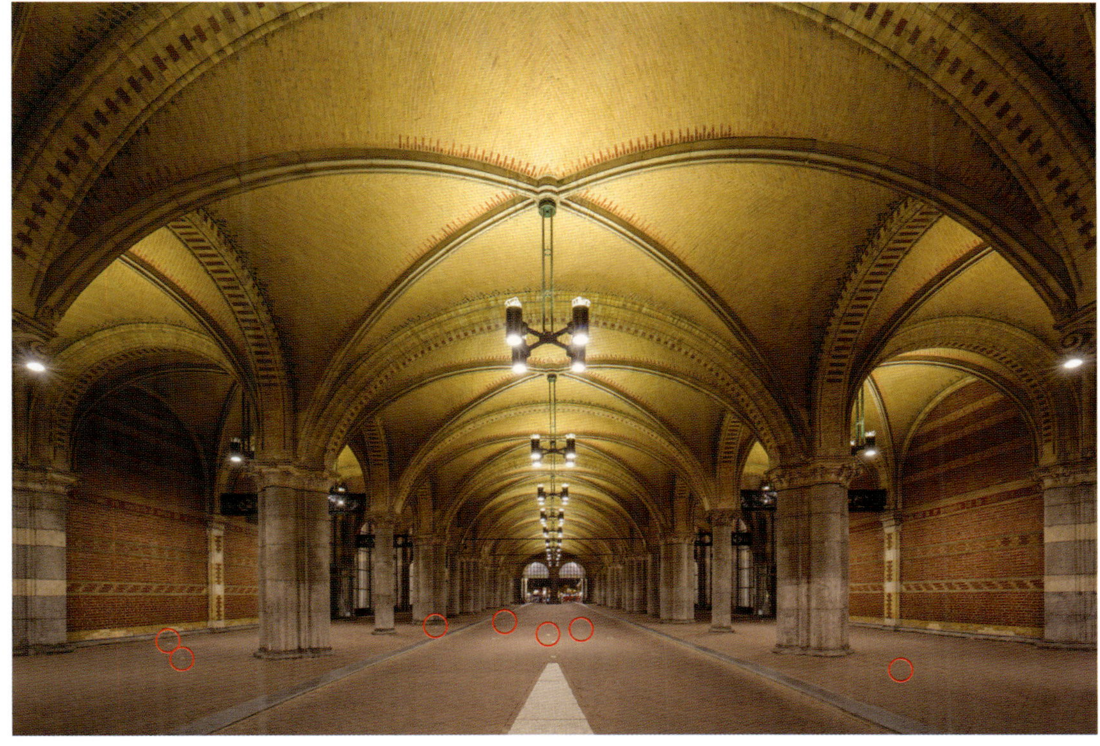

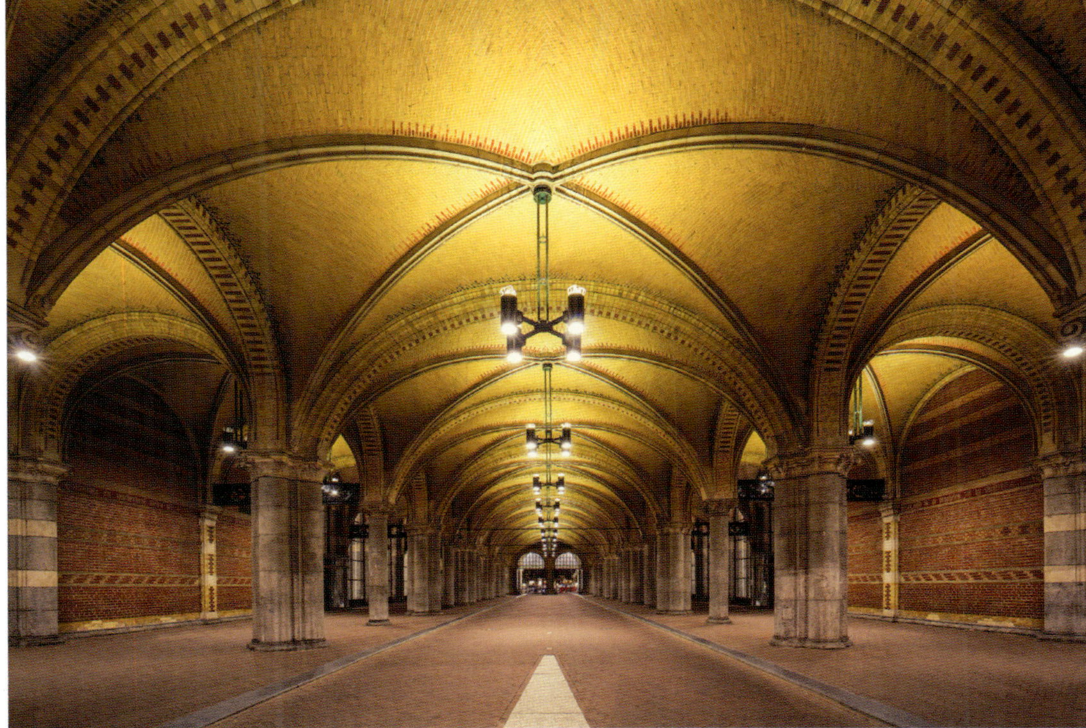

Tips

- Lightroom allows you to edit multiple files in batches, and lets you save groups of adjustments as presets that can be applied to future images. This can be a very time-efficient way of working.

- The software engines that "power" Lightroom and Adobe Camera Raw (Photoshop's Raw-processing module) are the same. Accordingly, the key changes that are done in one will appear in the other.

- It is essential to back up your images before deleting any files from your memory cards. I use two separate external hard drives, so that if one drive fails I will still have my images on the other one.

- It is very useful to add keywords when you upload files to your computer, as this will help you locate them more easily in the future. It does not take long to build up an extensive image library, at which point it can prove difficult to locate specific images.

Above left & left: For this shot I needed to remove distracting litter from the floor (above left). This was more easily done in postproduction than picking it up by hand!

Focal length: 16mm

Aperture: f/14

Shutter speed: 14 sec.

ISO: 200

Essential Edits

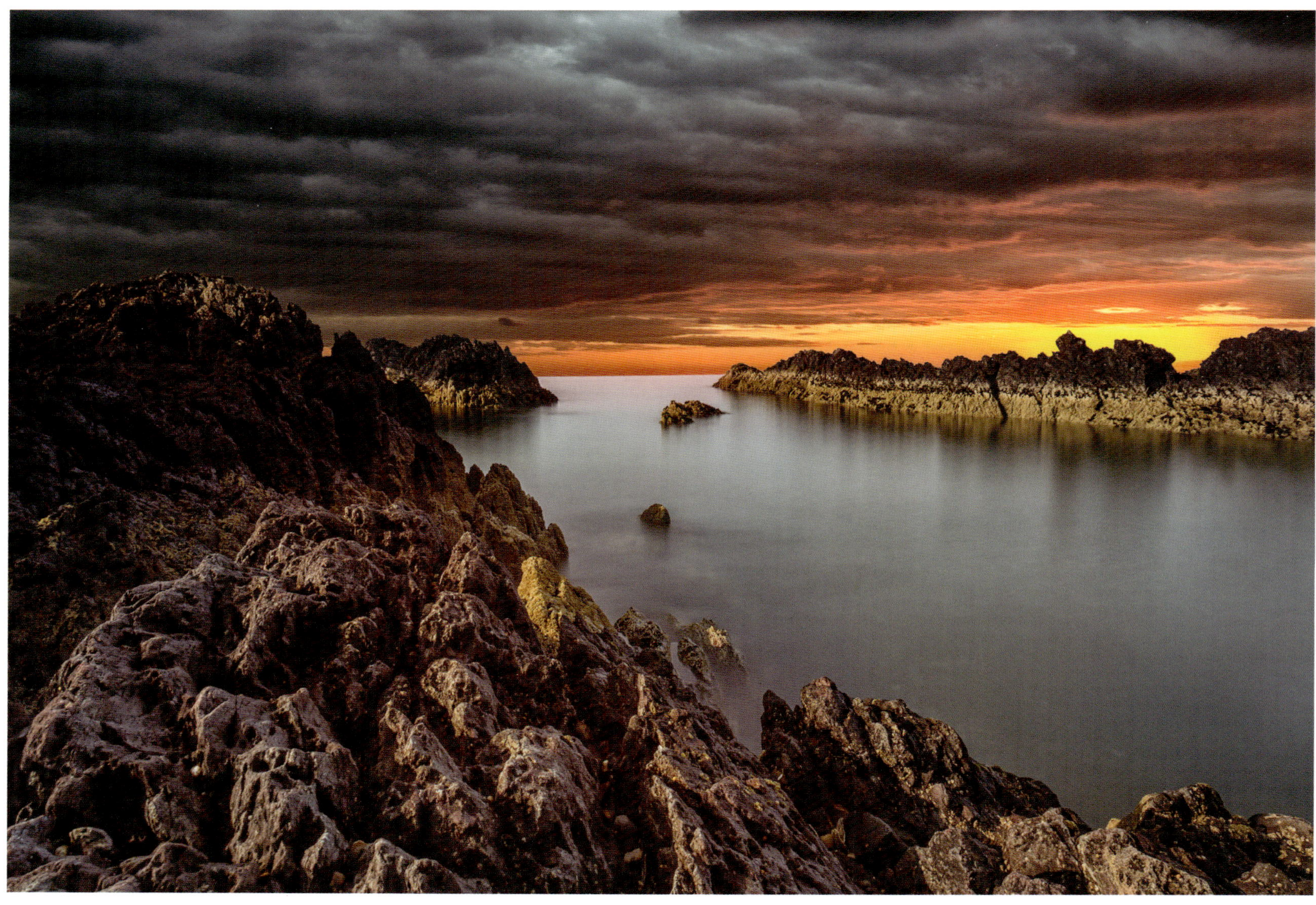

Although everyone will have their own preferences when it comes to image adjustments, there are certain key edits that are useful for many long exposure images, especially those shot in Raw format. While Adobe Lightroom is not the only software option, it's my software of choice here; the same edits can be carried out in most other good image-editing programs.

Above: When shooting sunrise or sunset images, try choosing the Cloudy or Shade white balance presets. These boost warm colors, leading to a more spectacular and saturated look that can suit this type of photograph.

Focal length: 24mm

Aperture: f/16

Shutter speed: 57 sec.

ISO: 100

White Balance

Whether it's because you're shooting at night under multiple artificial light sources, or ND filters have introduced a subtle color cast into your daylight shots, the white balance in long exposure images will often be incorrect.

If the image was taken under a single light source and doesn't look quite right, then simply selecting the appropriate preset from the White Balance menu is all that's usually required.

Alternatively, you can use the manual color sliders to adjust the balance.

Another option is to use Lightroom's "eyedropper" tool and click on something within the image that should be gray. This can be an especially quick and easy way of setting the white balance, although it requires a should-be-neutral target in the image to start with.

Below: The top half of this image has had the white balance set at 4500K, which I think is "right" for the shot. The lower left corner has been set to Daylight (5500K), which is clearly too warm in tone, while the lower right is set to Tungsten (2850K), which is overly cool.

Focal length: 40mm

Aperture: f/16

Shutter speed: 20 sec.

ISO: 100

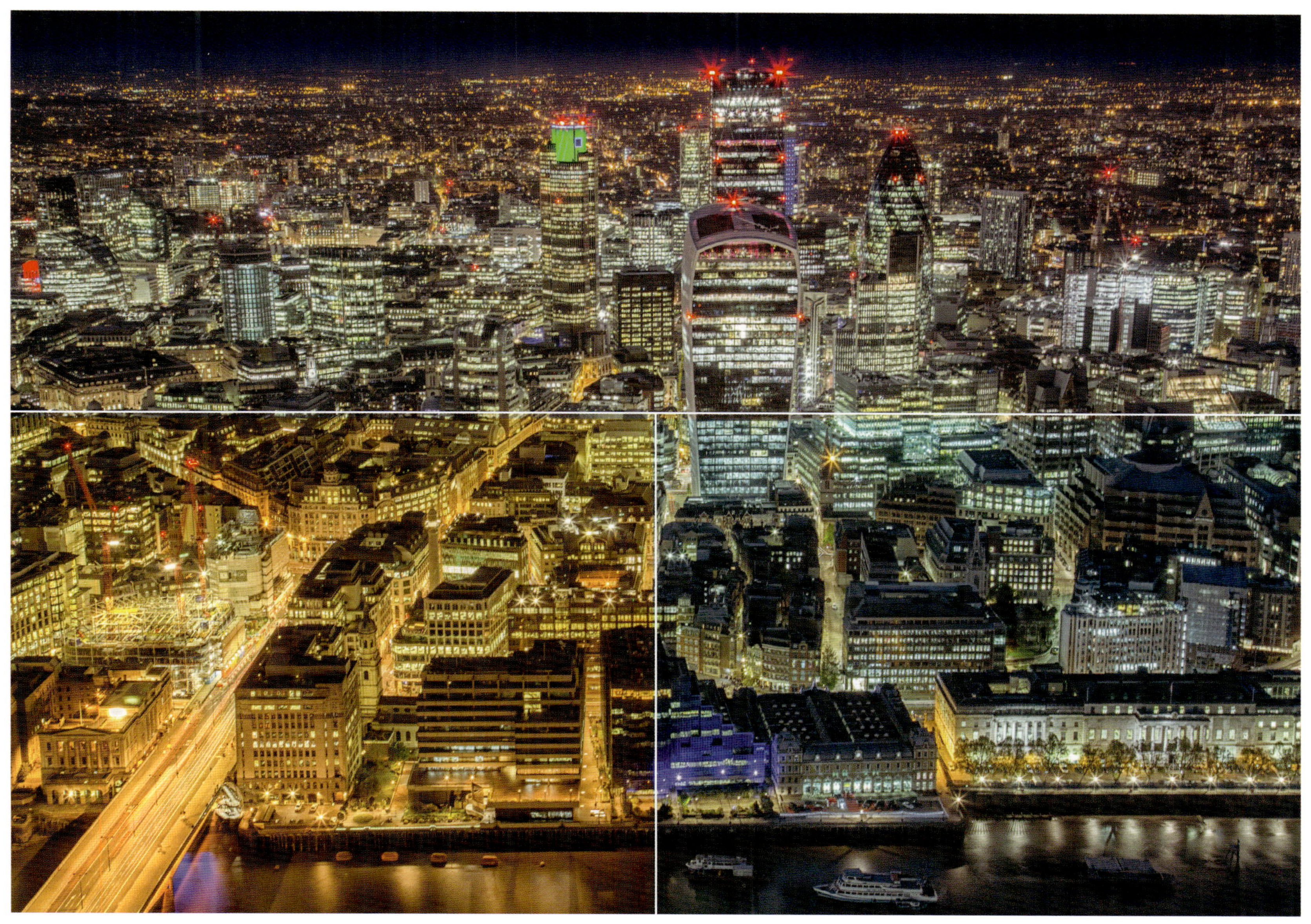

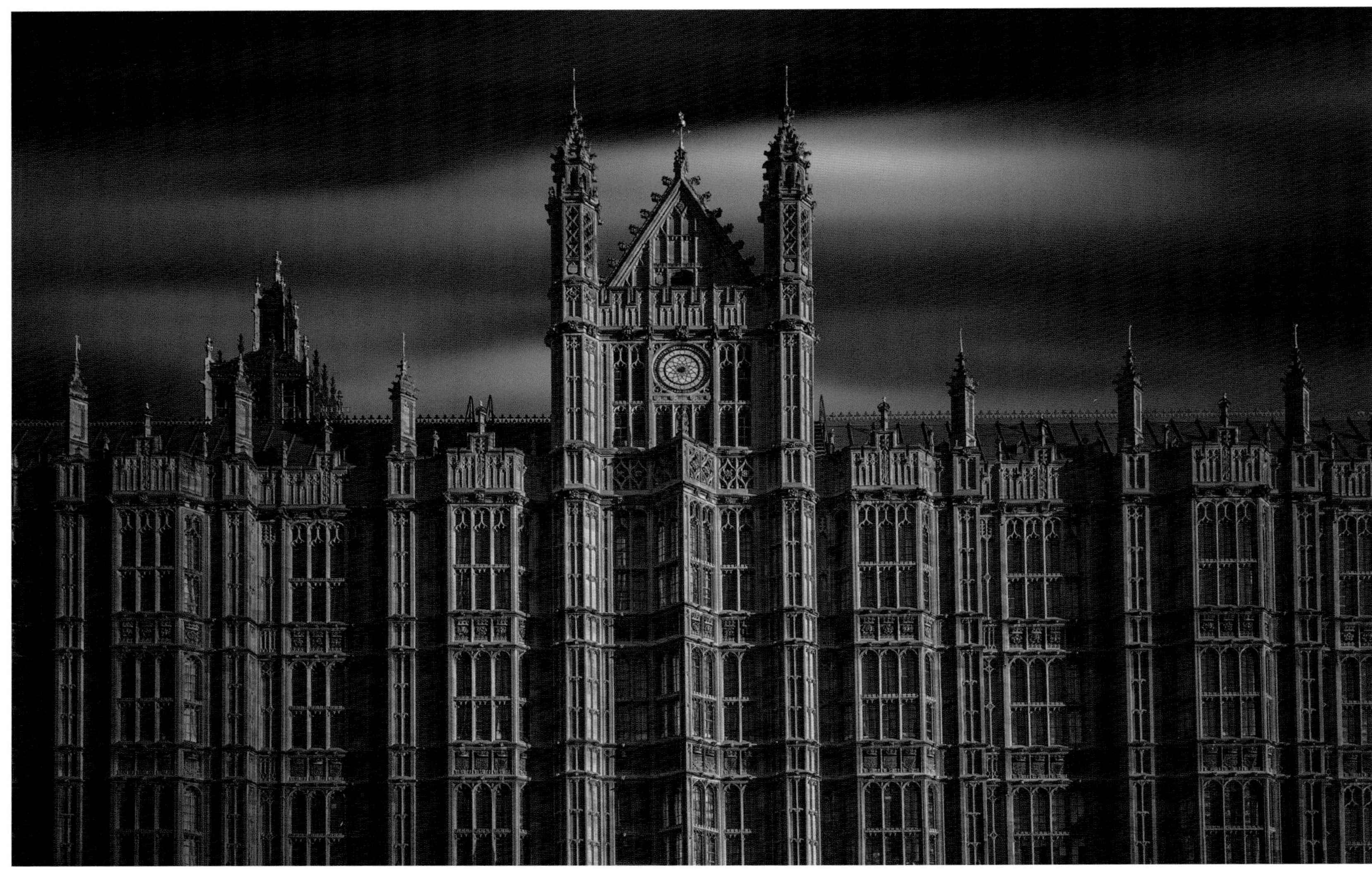

Exposure

Adjusting the exposure slider is not something you will always need to do, but it is quite easy to over- or underexpose an image in the field and not realize it until you are looking at a larger version on screen: a camera's LCD screen does not give an accurate representation of the final image, and the histogram is not only small and hard to read, but is also based on a JPEG thumbnail, rather than the Raw file. In any case, when it comes to postproduction care is needed to avoid setting the Exposure too high and clipping the highlights.

Highlights & Shadows

I find that many of my images benefit from using this pair of sliders. When used carefully, they enable you to recover detail in the tonal extremities and increase the dynamic range of images. Beware of fully opening up the shadows and/or reducing the highlights, though, as this can make an image look unnatural; subtle adjustments will generally create a more realistic effect. These sliders often remove contrast from an image, so it is worth increasing the Contrast slider slightly to compensate.

Above: Raw files record a wider dynamic range than JPEGs, enabling you to reduce the highlights and open the shadows in postproduction to create more balanced images.

Focal length: 28mm

Aperture: f/7.1

Shutter speed: 127 sec.

ISO: 200

Black & White Points

Setting the correct black and white points in an image can help centralize the contrast. Holding down the Option key (Windows) or Alt key (Mac) when moving either of these sliders will show either a black or white mask over the image. As the sliders are moved, a slight color base will appear showing where true white or black appears within the image.

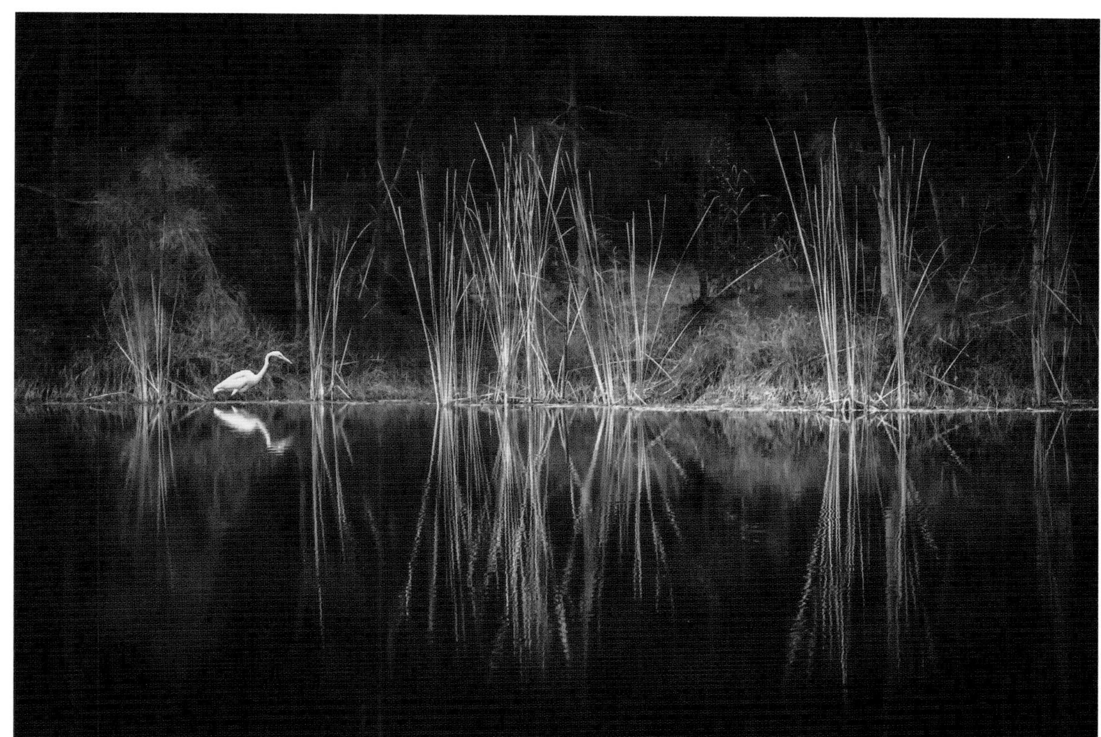

Right: Having the correct black and white points can make or break an image.

Focal length: 65mm

Aperture: f/11

Shutter speed: 2 sec.

ISO: 100

Levels & Curves

These functions allow the tonal range of the image to be amended. The Levels tool has black, mid, and white points that can all be moved to create the desired tonal range.

The Curves adjustment tool allows you to make changes to specific parts of the tonal range using points on an X- and Y-axis.

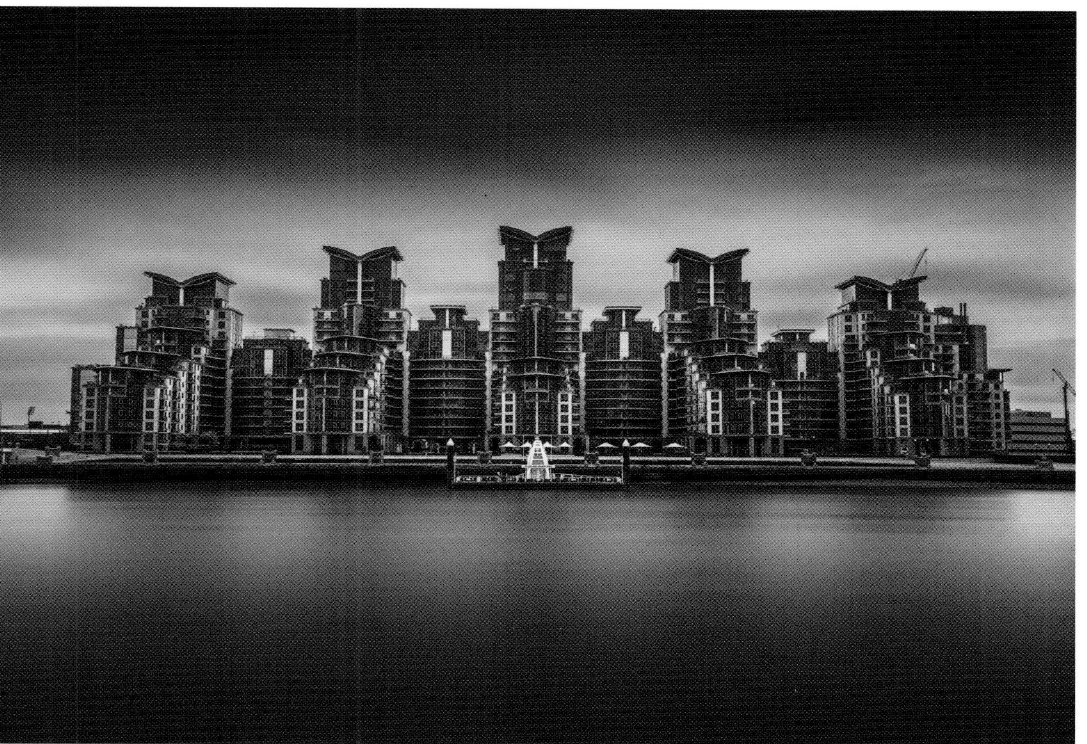

Right: Controlling and fine tuning contrast using Levels and Curves is a key step in almost all postproduction.

Focal length: 35mm

Aperture: f/18

Shutter speed: 47 sec.

ISO: 200

Saturation & Vibrance

At this stage in the editing process you should consider whether you should add extra vibrance or saturation. If further extensive editing is to take place, it is advised not to add these yet.

The Saturation slider is a global adjustment that boosts all of the colors in an image, while the Vibrance slider, when used subtly, only boosts the less saturated colors in the image.

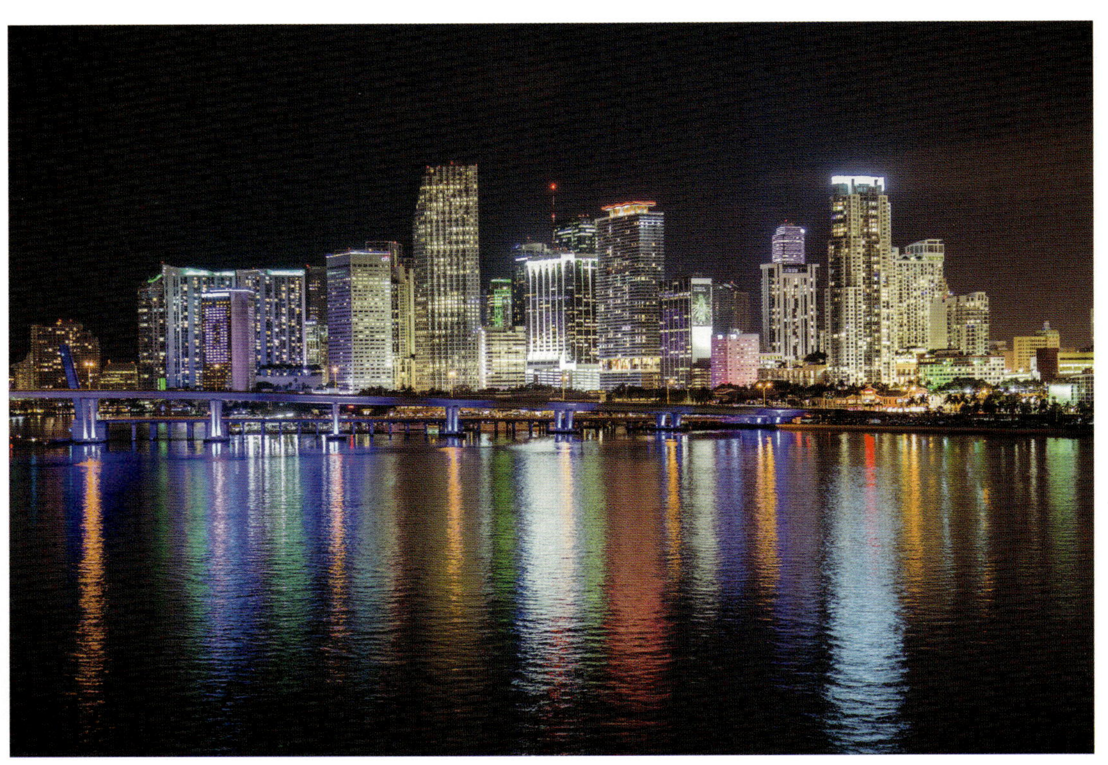

Lens Corrections

The Lens Corrections panel includes some essential edits that should almost always be applied to all images. Remove Chromatic Aberration should be checked for all images and it is also very useful to check Enable Profile Corrections. This utilizes lens profiles within an internal database to compensate for any image distortion or vignetting that occurs with the use of a particular lens.

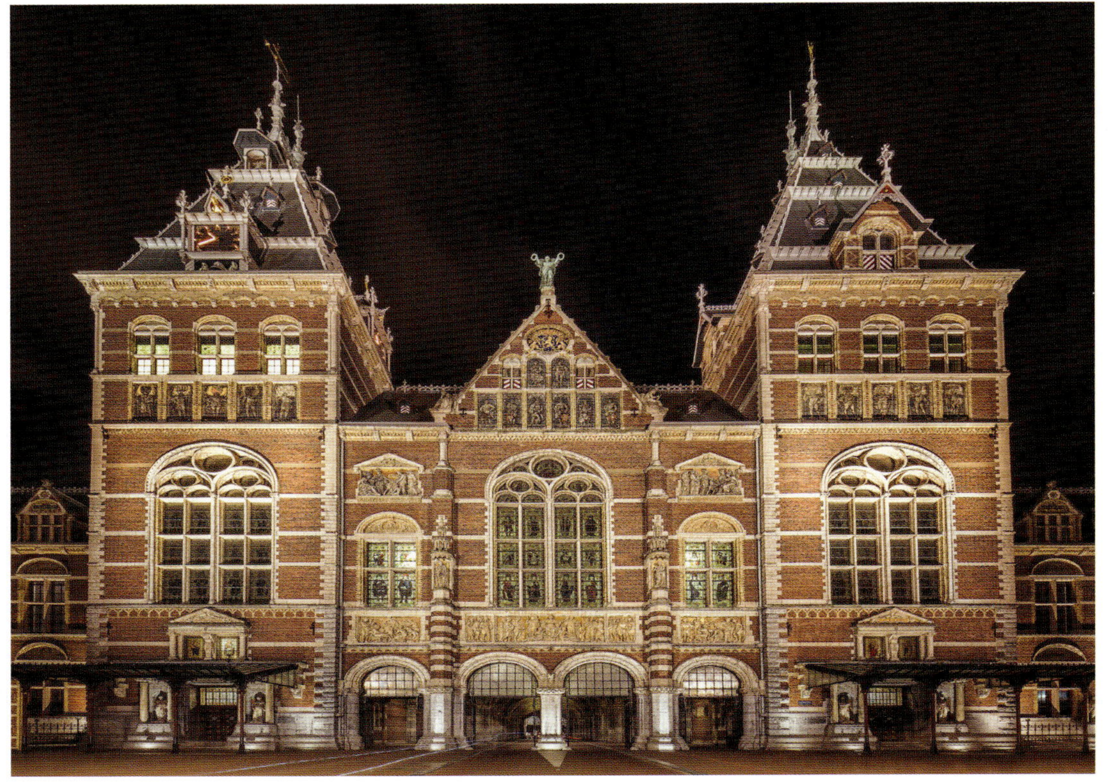

Dust Removal

The combination of small aperture settings
and long exposure times will emphasize the
appearance of any dust on the camera's sensor.
It is recommended to regularly clean the sensor
to minimize this dust, but it is not always possible
or convenient to do this as regularly as needed.
Clicking on the Visualize Spots check box will help
reveal these dust spots so they can be removed
with the clone tool.

Cropping

It is generally best to try and frame your shots
correctly in-camera, but this is not always possible,
especially if you want the image to have a different
ratio to the camera's sensor; panoramic or square,
for example. Lightroom's crop tools are very
powerful and it is worth reiterating that cropping—
like all Lightroom edits—is non-destructive, so your
images can always be "uncropped" in the future.

Vignette

A vignette is a darkening at the corners of an
image, which can be added to help "contain"
the shot. It is entirely optional, but if applied it
is important to ensure that it is subtle: extreme
vignetting can often be detrimental to the image.

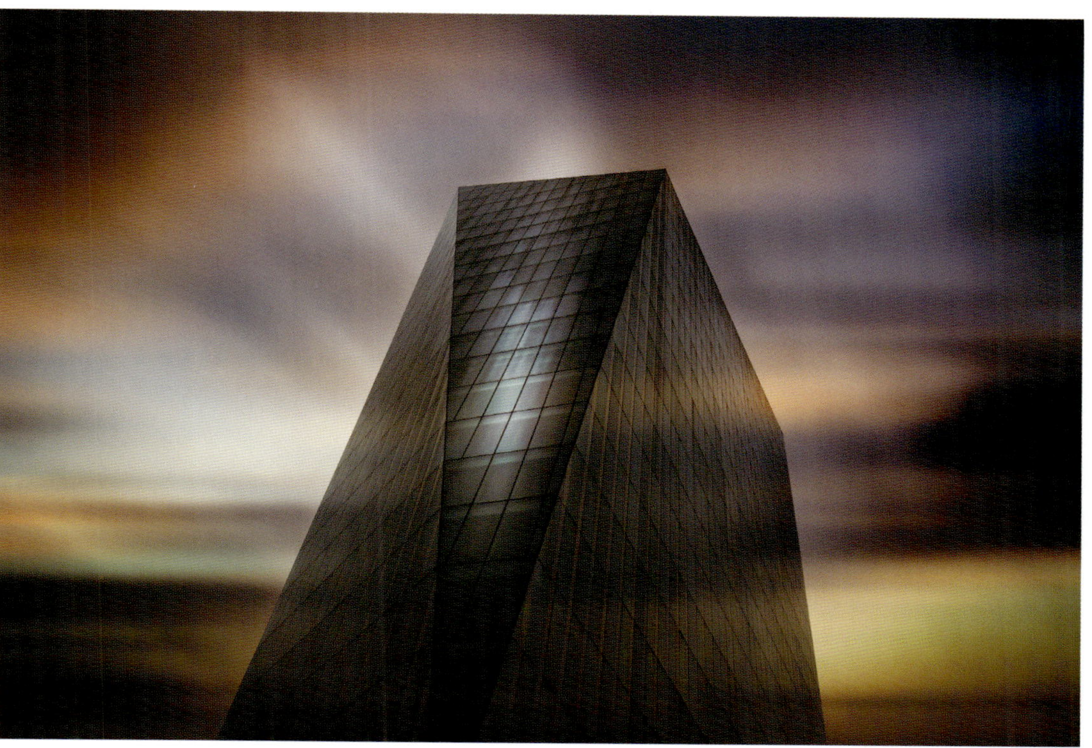

Noise Reduction

As discussed in chapter 2, the very nature of long exposures means that noise can be a significant issue. High ISO settings can also introduce noise, so controlling it can become an important part of your postproduction routine.

Thankfully postproduction software relating to noise reduction has improved substantially over the years. There are many standalone plugins that can assist you when it comes to dealing with noise, although the noise reduction options built into Lightroom and Photoshop also provide a wide variety of solutions.

The primary concern when dealing with noise is that image sharpness will inevitably suffer. The more noise reduction that is applied, the softer the image texture and detail will become. When applying noise reduction it is therefore crucial to do it in a subtle and controlled way, so the image details are not rendered too softly.

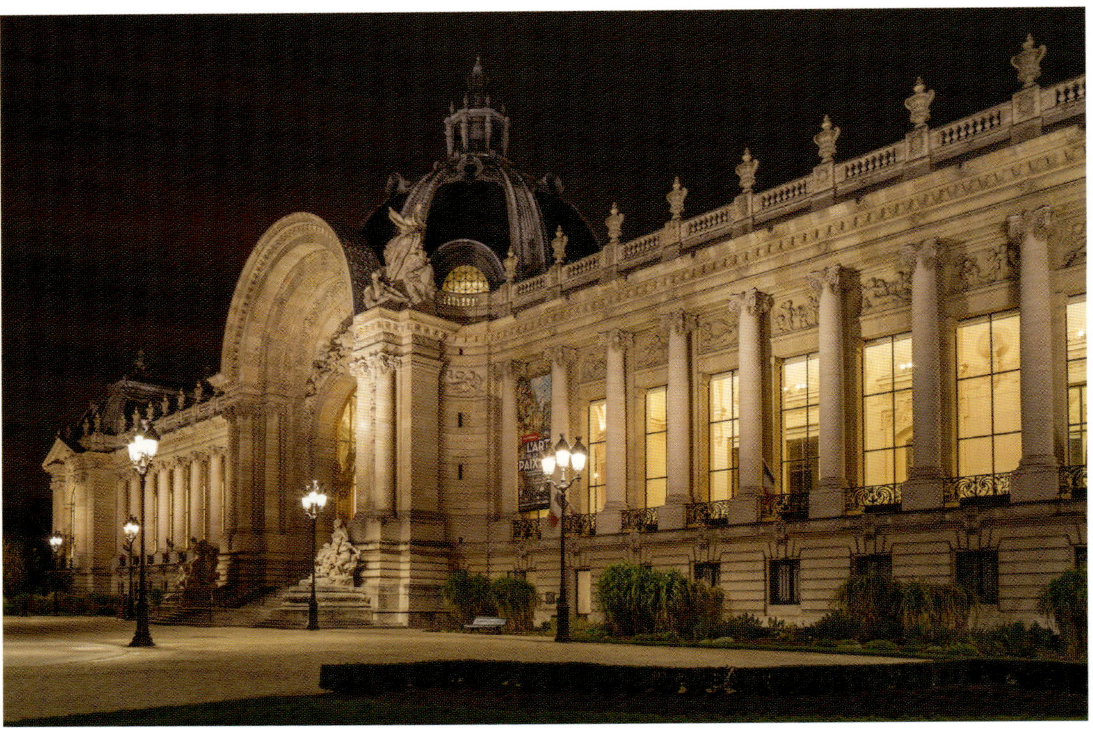

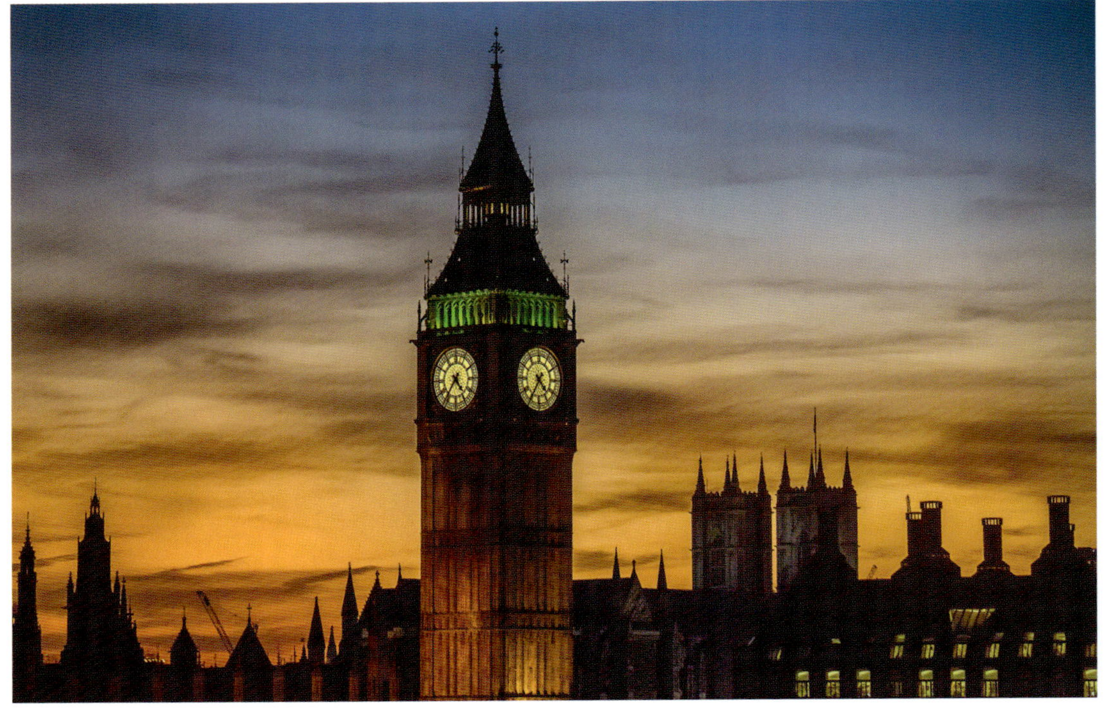

Above right: To ensure that your image retains sharpness in key areas, apply noise reduction selectively to affected areas and not to the image as a whole. In this example, subtle noise reduction was applied to the sky, but not to the building, ensuring that detail and sharpness were retained in this area.

Focal length: 28mm

Aperture: f/16

Shutter speed: 10 sec.

ISO: 100

Right: Noise is most prevalent in the darker areas of an image. Consequently, extra care should be taken to ensure that the correct exposure is made in-camera, so the shadow detail doesn't need to be pushed too far in postproduction: "opening up" the shadows emphasizes noise.

Focal length: 127mm

Aperture: f/4

Shutter speed: 2 sec.

ISO: 400

Sharpening

Sharpening is an important postproduction step for all digital images. It works by increasing the edge contrast around image elements, which gives the appearance of increased sharpness.

Although it's essential to sharpen your images, sharpening should be subtle, as it is easy to overdo it; over-sharpening will quickly reveal itself in the form of extensive "haloing," which creates an unrealistic texture.

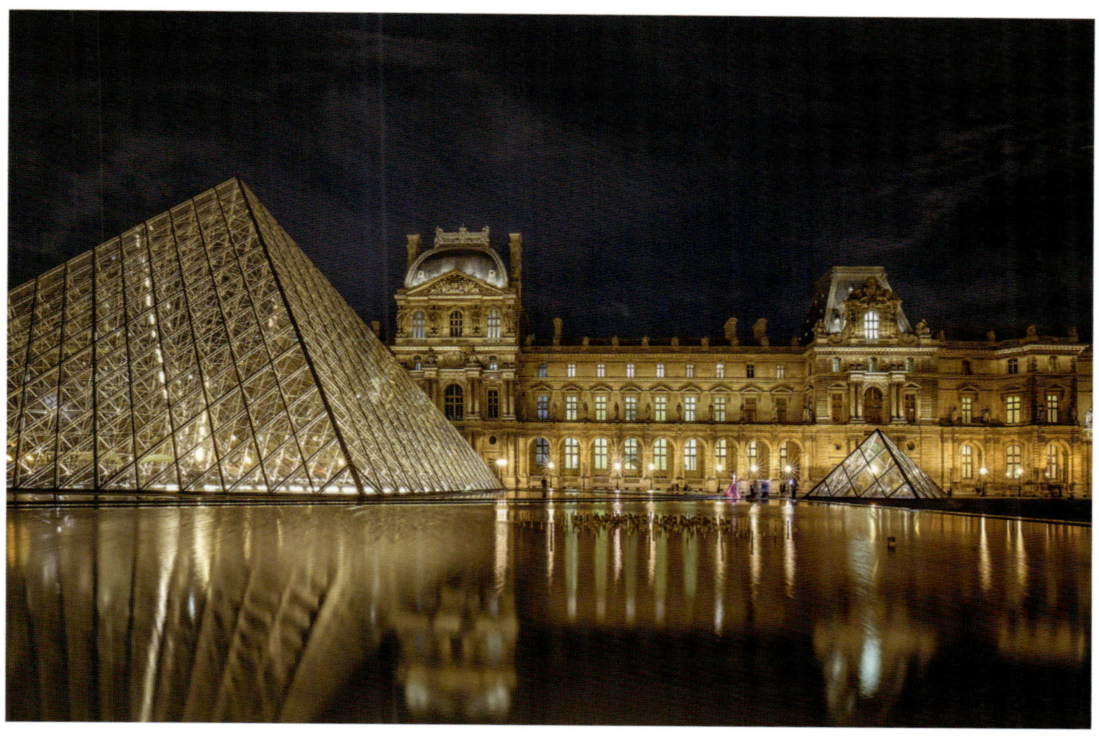

Right: If you use Photoshop (and some other image-editing programs), you can make selections and apply sharpening to the specific areas that require it, rather than the entire image. In Lightroom and Adobe Camera Raw, sharpening is applied globally.

Focal length: 16mm

Aperture: f/16

Shutter speed: 16 sec.

ISO: 200

HOW TO SHARPEN

The basic idea is to add enough sharpening to the final image for it to "pop," without going too far. The changes should be so minimal and understated that the viewer is not even aware that anything has been done. There are multiple sharpening plugins available, but I'm going to continue to focus on Lightroom (and, by extension, Adobe Camera Raw in Photoshop).

The sharpening sliders in Lightroom are paired with the Noise Reduction sliders within the Detail panel. This makes sense, because when noise is removed, there is a natural softening of the detail in an image, which is usually compensated for with the sharpening tools.

Zoom into your image to 100% and move the sliders in very small steps so that gradual and subtle changes are made. The Sharpening slider should not really be moved beyond 20–25, and it is also recommended that you keep the default settings of Radius 1.0 and Detail 25.

When determining the amount of sharpening, it is important to consider where in the image the sharpening will be applied. Holding down the Option key (Windows) or Alt key (Mac) while you move the Masking slider will show—in simple terms—which areas the sharpening will be applied to. The image will be replaced with a temporary mask showing the areas in white where the sharpening will be applied (black areas indicate those that will *not* be affected).

Tips

- By its very nature, sharpening should be the last step in postproduction.

- No amount of sharpening will help correct an out-of-focus image.

- JPEG files can be sharpened in-camera, but unless you need the images immediately it is better to set in-camera sharpening to a low level (or off) and sharpen during postproduction.

- The amount of sharpening needed will depend on the image's intended use: a picture that is going to be enlarged and printed will need a different amount of sharpening to a picture that will be posted on a website.

Image Blending & Layer Masks

As you've seen throughout this book, the broad dynamic range of a scene often makes it very difficult to record it correctly in a single frame. You saw how to bracket a sequence of images on pages 36–37, so here we will look at how you can blend the images together to create a final well-balanced photograph.

The first thing to appreciate is that this cannot be done in Lightroom: it requires layers and layer masks, which are found in Photoshop. The concept of layers is simple: it's like having a photograph on a sheet of acetate or clear film. Each exposure in your bracketed sequence can be opened as a separate layer and stacked in a single file. Only the top layer will be visible to start with, but you can selectively reveal certain parts of the layers below, and hide elements that you don't want in the final image. The opacity of each layer can also be adjusted to control how "see through" each layer is.

Often, the whole of a layer is not required, and you'll only want to use certain parts of it. This is where layer masks come into play. While this may sound complicated, it is a relatively straightforward process: layer masks are what you use to reveal and conceal specific parts of a layer.

Photoshop indicates that a layer is fully transparent when the mask icon beside the layer in the Layers panel is white. Therefore, painting on a black (opaque) layer mask with a white brush will reveal what is underneath it and painting in black on a white (transparent) layer mask will hide those parts of the layer.

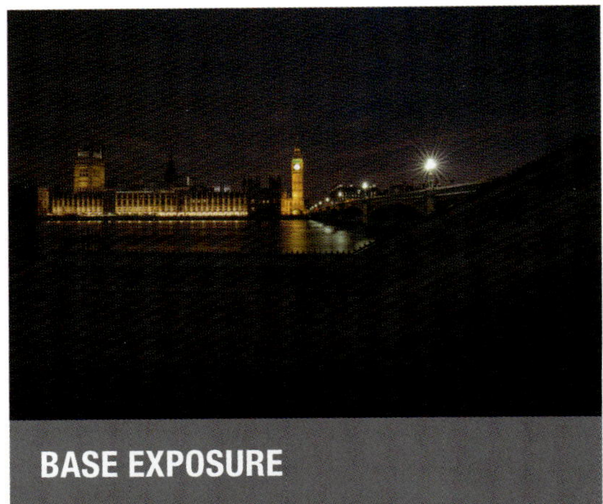

Right: The first exposure in this sequence of three was the "base" version, which provides an "average" overall exposure that favors neither the highlights nor the shadows. In effect, it is exposed for the midtones.

Focal length: 16mm

Aperture: f/16

Shutter speed: 30 sec.

ISO: 100

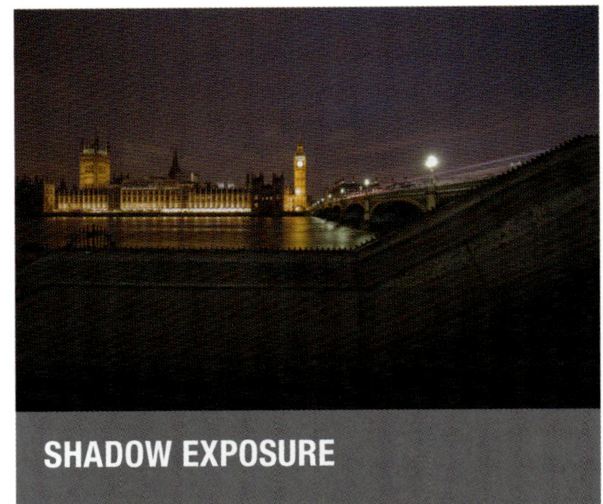

Right: The second exposure in the sequence was overexposed by 1⅓ stops to bring out the shadow detail.

Focal length: 16mm

Aperture: f/16

Shutter speed: 47 sec.

ISO: 100

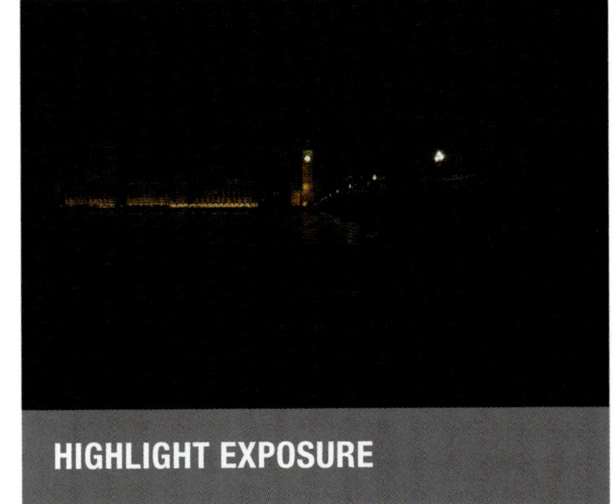

Right: The third exposure in the sequence was underexposed by 1⅓ stops to ensure the highlight detail in the clock face and lights was retained.

Focal length: 16mm

Aperture: f/16

Shutter speed: 8 sec.

ISO: 100

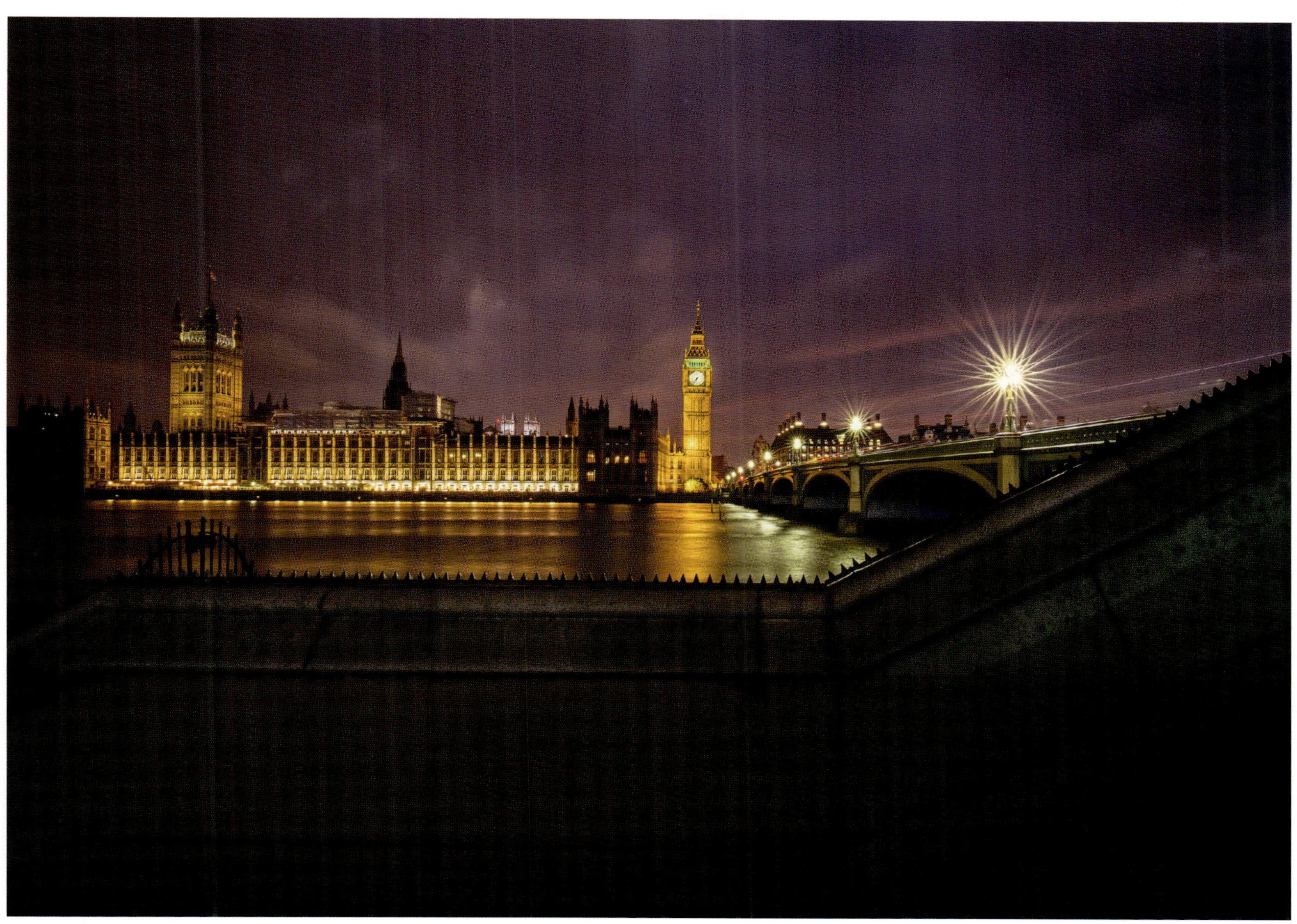

Above: The final image was created by blending the key
elements of the sequence shown opposite, using layer
masks to selectively reveal and conceal parts of the various
layered exposures.

Using Layer Masks

A lot can be written on layer masks, but a simple visual example will begin to demonstrate the power of masking. In the scene shown here, the wide dynamic range between the very bright sky and shaded rocks and foreground made it impossible to obtain a well-balanced exposure in a single image. Instead, I took two shots: one exposed correctly for the sky and one exposed for the rest of the scene.

Opening the two images as layers in Photoshop; you can't use Lightroom for this exercise. The first step is to align them, which simply means highlighting both layers in the layers panel and choosing *Edit > Auto-align Layers* from the top menu. Even if your images were taken using a tripod, there can sometimes be a small amount of movement between the frames, so align your layers first.

The darker image (exposed for the sky) should be at the base of the layer stack, with the other image placed above it. At this stage, only the lighter top layer can be seen.

To hide the overexposed sky and reveal the darker sky from the layer below, a white layer mask needs to be applied to the top layer. To add a layer mask, highlight the relevant layer and click on the layer mask symbol .

A white layer mask is transparent, so the whole of the top layer remains visible, while the layer underneath remains hidden. However, using a brush with black, you can "paint" the white layer mask to reveal what is underneath. In this example I wanted to bring back some detail in the overexposed sky; painting black over the sky area reveals the sky from the darker image below.

If you make a mistake and an area is revealed in error, simply repaint the area with white to conceal it again. Switching between white and black "paint" will also help you fine tune the masks.

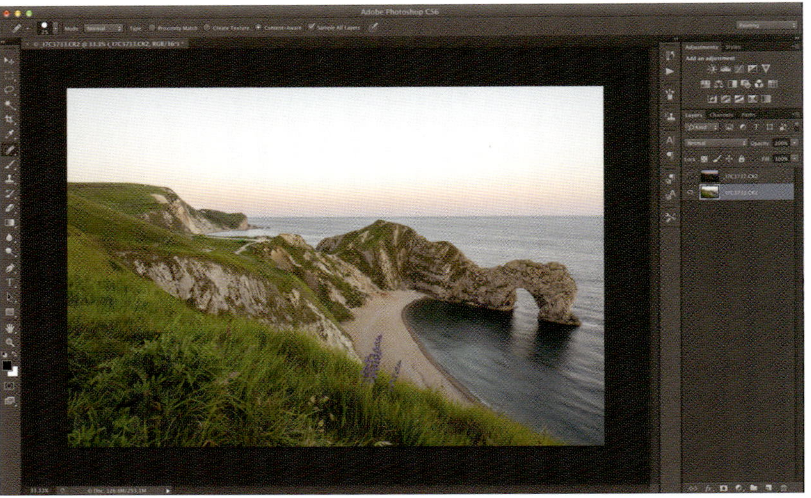

Left: The dynamic range in this scene was very wide, so exposing for the landscape meant the sunset sky "burnt out."

Focal length: 35mm

Aperture: f/18

Shutter speed: 7 sec.

ISO: 200

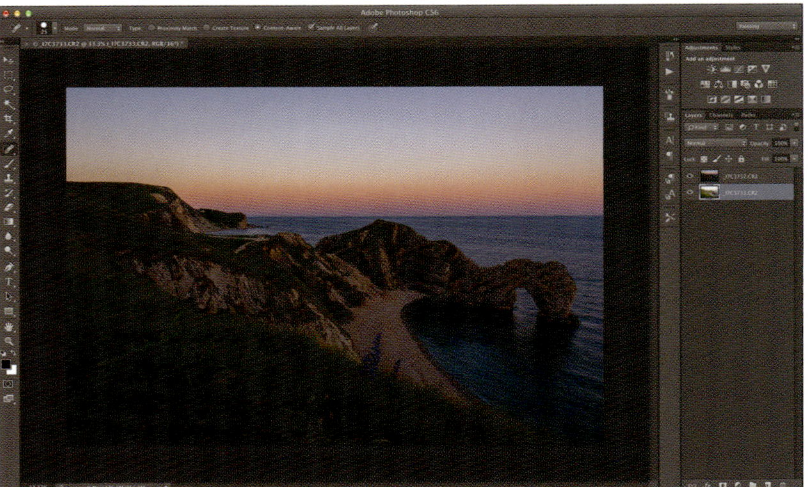

Left: A second exposure was made for the sky and both images were loaded into Photoshop as separate layers for blending.

Focal length: 35mm

Aperture: f/18

Shutter speed: 47 sec.

ISO: 200

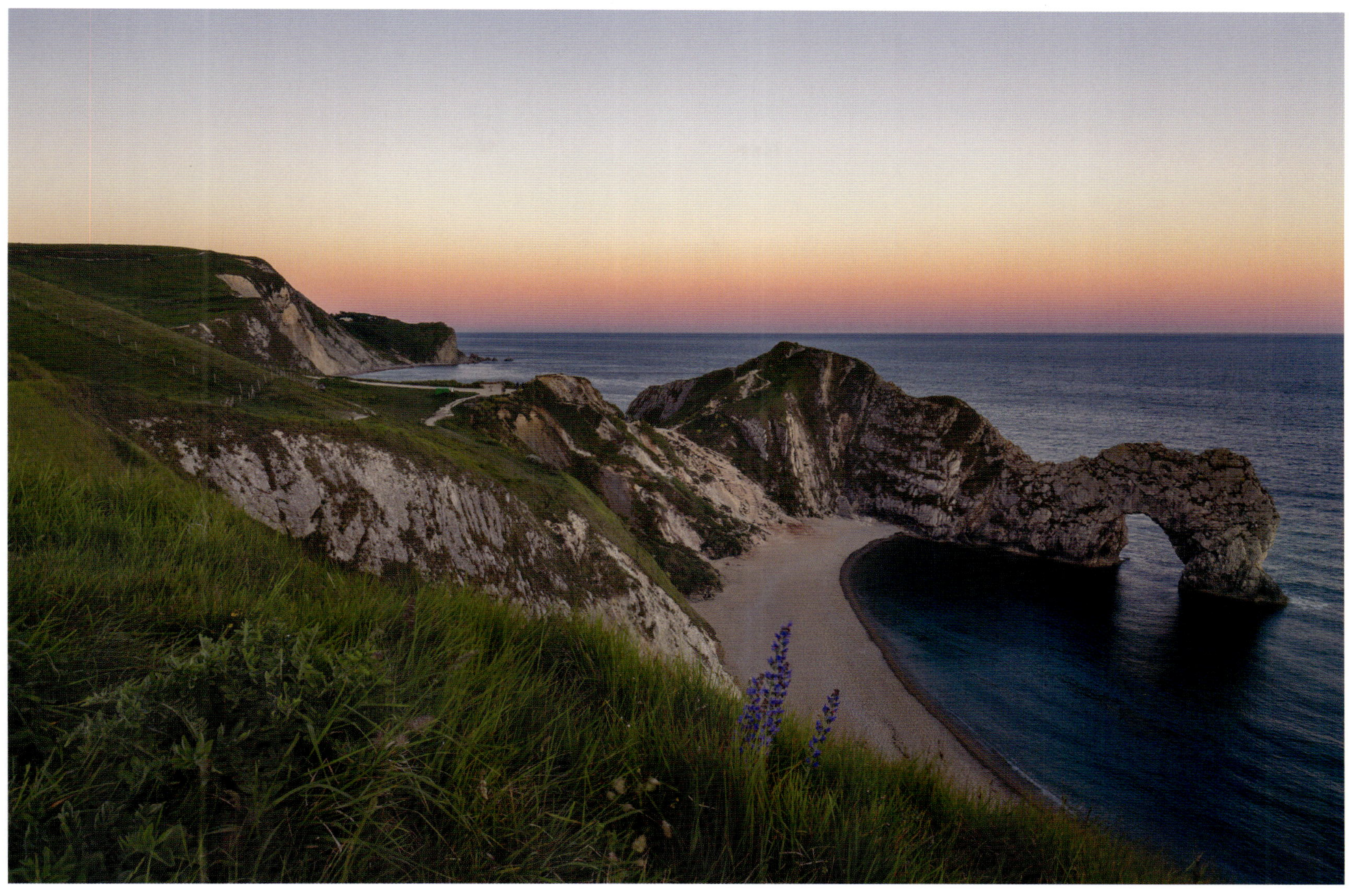

Tips

- Pressing the "D" key will change Photoshop's colors to the default white and black; "X" can then be used as a shortcut to switch between them.

- The key concept to layer masks is to remember that white reveals and black conceals.

- Painting with 100% black or white will hide or reveal the layer with 100% opacity; using 50% gray will reveal or hide the layer by half that amount.

- Use a soft brush with the opacity set in the region of 20% when painting over masks so that changes can be made in a subtle and gradual way. This creates a more natural blend between the layers. The aim is for the viewer to remain unaware that any blending has taken place; this is not to "trick" them into thinking it's a single exposure, but to ensure that the edits aren't distracting.

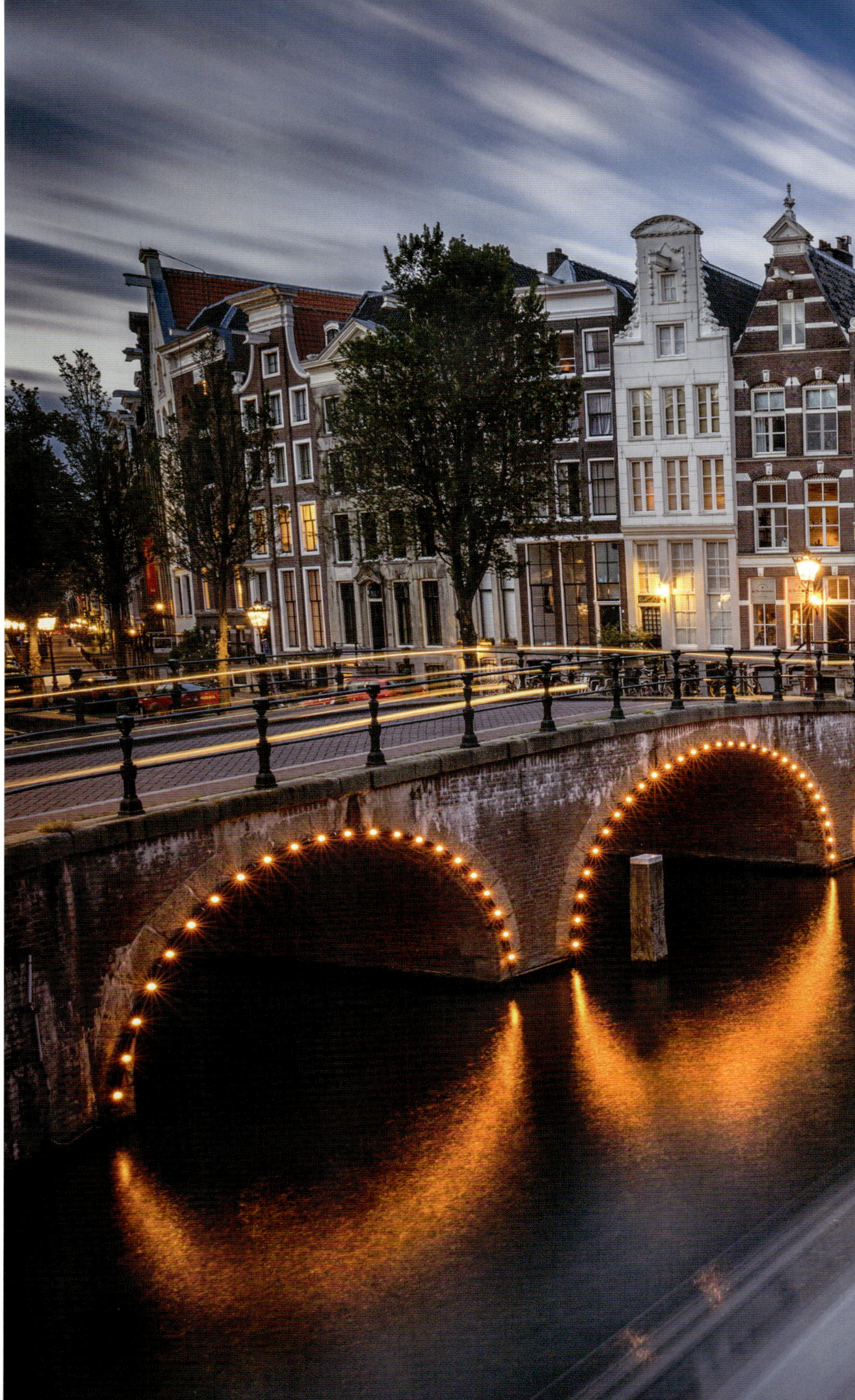

Right: This image brings together an abundance of the long exposure techniques explored in this book: light trails, star spikes, cloud movement, watery reflections, and a mix of natural and artifical light sources all combine to create a compelling photograph.

Focal length: 20mm

Aperture: f/14

Shutter speed: 50 sec.

ISO: 200

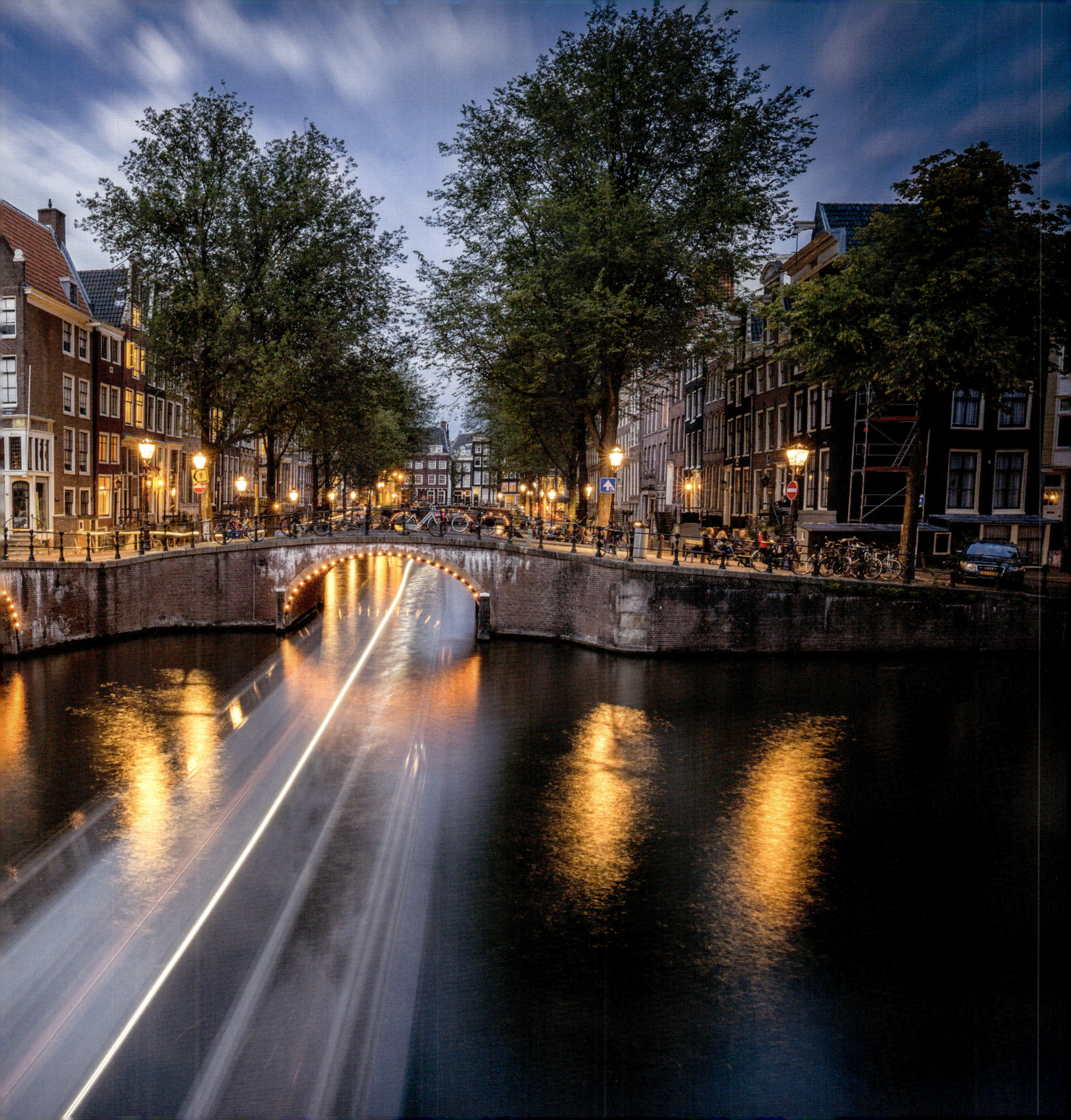

Glossary

Aberration An imperfection in a photograph, usually caused by the optics of a lens.

Angle of view The area of a scene that a lens takes in, measured in degrees.

Aperture The variable opening in a camera lens, measured in f/stops, which regulates the amount of light passing through the lens. The aperture setting is also one of the main factors in determining depth of field.

Aperture Priority A camera mode that allows the photographer to set the aperture, with the camera automatically choosing the appropriate shutter speed for the correct exposure.

Blue hour The period just before sunset through to just after sunset, when the sky turns a deep blue.

Bracketing The process of taking a sequence of images at varying degrees of exposure, (both under- and overexposed). These images can then be combined in postproduction.

Bulb (B) A manual exposure mode that provides complete control over how long the shutter remains open.

Camera shake A leading cause of blurred images; occurs when the camera is accidentally moved or disturbed while making an exposure.

Center-weighted metering An exposure-metering pattern that determines the exposure from the central part of the image frame.

Chromatic aberration A digital color defect that can appear around the edges of high-contrast image elements. Caused when a lens fails to bring all wavelengths of light to focus at the same point.

Color temperature The color of light, measured in degrees Kelvin (K).

Contrast The range between bright and dark areas in a scene or image.

Crop factor The size of the camera's sensor measured in reference to a 35mm piece of film or full-frame digital sensor.

Depth of field (DOF) The area in an image in front of and behind the focus point that appears acceptably sharp. The extent of the depth of field is determined by the aperture setting, focal length, and camera-to-subject distance.

Distortion An optical defect whereby straight lines appear curved in an image.

DSLR (Digital Single Lens Reflex) A camera that uses an internal mirror to reflect the scene from the lens up to the photographer's eye. During the instant that the exposure is made, this mirror flips up out of the way just as the shutter opens, allowing light to reach the image sensor.

Dynamic range The range from light to dark in a scene; also the range that can be recorded by a camera in a single exposure.

Exposure The amount of light allowed to hit the digital sensor, controlled by aperture, shutter speed, and ISO. Also, the act of taking a photograph, as in "making an exposure."

Exposure compensation A manual control that allows you to increase or reduce the camera's recommended exposure.

f/stop The fractional representation of the size of the aperture, based on the focal length of the lens divided by the diameter of the aperture.

Filter A piece of colored or coated glass, or plastic, placed in front of the lens.

Focal length The distance from the optical center of a lens, where the light rays converge to create a sharp image, and the film or sensor.

Full frame A digital camera sensor format the same size as 35mm film frame (36 x 24mm).

Golden hour The hour after sunrise and before sunset when the light is warm and golden.

Ghosting An effect created when a subject remains still for just long enough to be recorded and then moves quickly to another position, mid-exposure, resulting in a ghost-like appearance.

HDR (High Dynamic Range) An image formed by combining a sequence of exposures covering a wider dynamic range than can be captured in a single frame.

Highlights The brightest part of an image.

Histogram A graphical representation of the tones in an image, from pure white to pure black.

Image stacking The process of combining multiple images into a single frame in postproduction.

ISO The numerical values that represent the sensitivity of the camera's sensor to light.

JPEG A file format where data processing of the image (such as sharpening) is performed internally by the camera, which then compresses the file to save data space.

Lens flare An optical artifact caused by non-image-forming light entering the lens.

Live View A viewing mode that allows images to be viewed and framed using the LCD on the back of the camera, rather than the viewfinder.

Megapixel One megapixel equals one million pixels.

Metering The act of measuring the light falling on a scene to determine the exposure required.

Mirrorless Common name given to a camera that doesn't have a reflex mirror (*see* DSLR). The photographer views a live image streamed from the digital sensor to an LCD.

Mirror lock-up The option on some DSLR cameras that enables the mirror to be flipped up and locked in place prior to releasing the shutter. In doing so it minimizes any vibration that may introduce blur into an image.

Multi-zone metering An exposure-metering pattern that divides the frame into zones or segments that are measured individually and then brought together to determine the best overall exposure. Known by various proprietary names, including Evaluative (Canon) and Matrix (Nikon).

Neutral density (ND) filter A filter that limits the amount of light passing through it and into the camera. Commonly used to extend exposure times.

Noise Digital interference that is recorded as a non-image-forming texture.

Overexposure An exposure that is overly bright, often leading to highlight areas being recorded as pure white, with no recoverable image data.

Prime A lens with a fixed focal length.

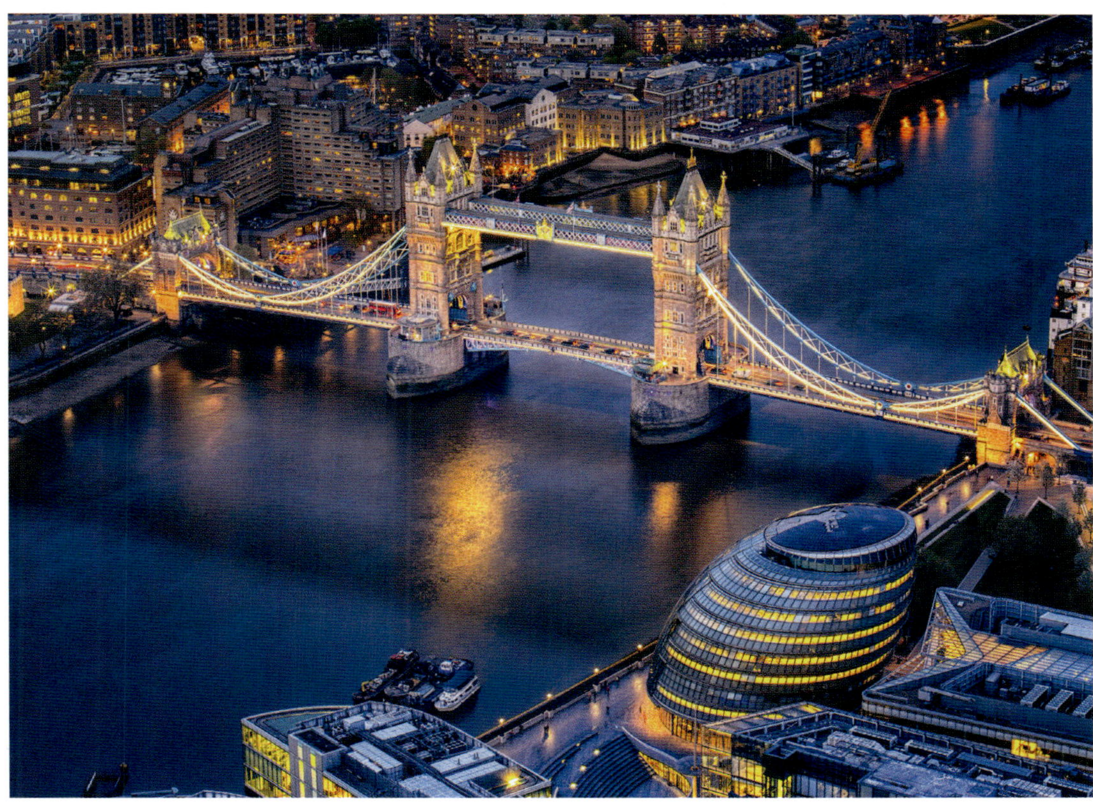

Raw A file type that records the data captured straight from the image sensor, without applying any processing to this information.

Spot metering An exposure-metering pattern that determines the exposure based on a small and precise part of the image.

Stop The unit of measurement used to indicate a halving or doubling of light in an exposure.

Underexposure An exposure that is overly dark, often leading to shadow areas being recorded as pure black, with no recoverable image data.

Vignette The darkening of the corners and edges of an image. Although it can be an optical defect in a lens, or caused by a physical obstruction in front of the lens ("mechanical vignetting"), it is also often applied in postproduction as a creative edit.

White balance An in-camera control that allows a particular color temperature of light to be recorded without a color cast.

Zoom A lens with a variable focal length.

Useful Web Sites

Photographers

Photography & tuition by Antony Zacharias www.antonyz.com

General

Digital Photography Review www.dpreview.com
On Landscape www.onlandscape.co.uk

Photographic Equipment

B+W www.schneideroptics.com
Canon www.canon.com
Format-Hitech www.format-hitech.com
Hoya www.hoyafilter.com
Lee Filters www.leefilters.com
Leica www.leica-camera.com
Lowepro www.lowepro.com
Manfrotto www.manfrotto.com
Nikon www.nikon.com
Olympus www.olympus-global.com
Panasonic www.panasonic.net
Sigma www.sigma-photo.com
Sony www.sony.com
Tamron www.tamron.com
Zeiss www.zeiss.com

Photography Publications

Ammonite Press www.ammonitepress.com
Black & White Photography magazine www.thegmcgroup.com
Outdoor Photography magazine www.thegmcgroup.com

Printing

Epson www.epson.com
Hahnemühle www.hahnemuehle.de
Harman www.harman-inkjet.com
HP www.hp.com
Ilford www.ilford.com
Kodak www.kodak.com
Lexmark www.lexmark.com
Lyson www.lyson.com
Marrutt www.marrutt.com

Software & Actions

Adobe www.apple.com
Apple www.apple.com
Capture One Pro www.phaseone.com
Nik Collection www.google.com/nikcollection
Photopills www.photopills.com

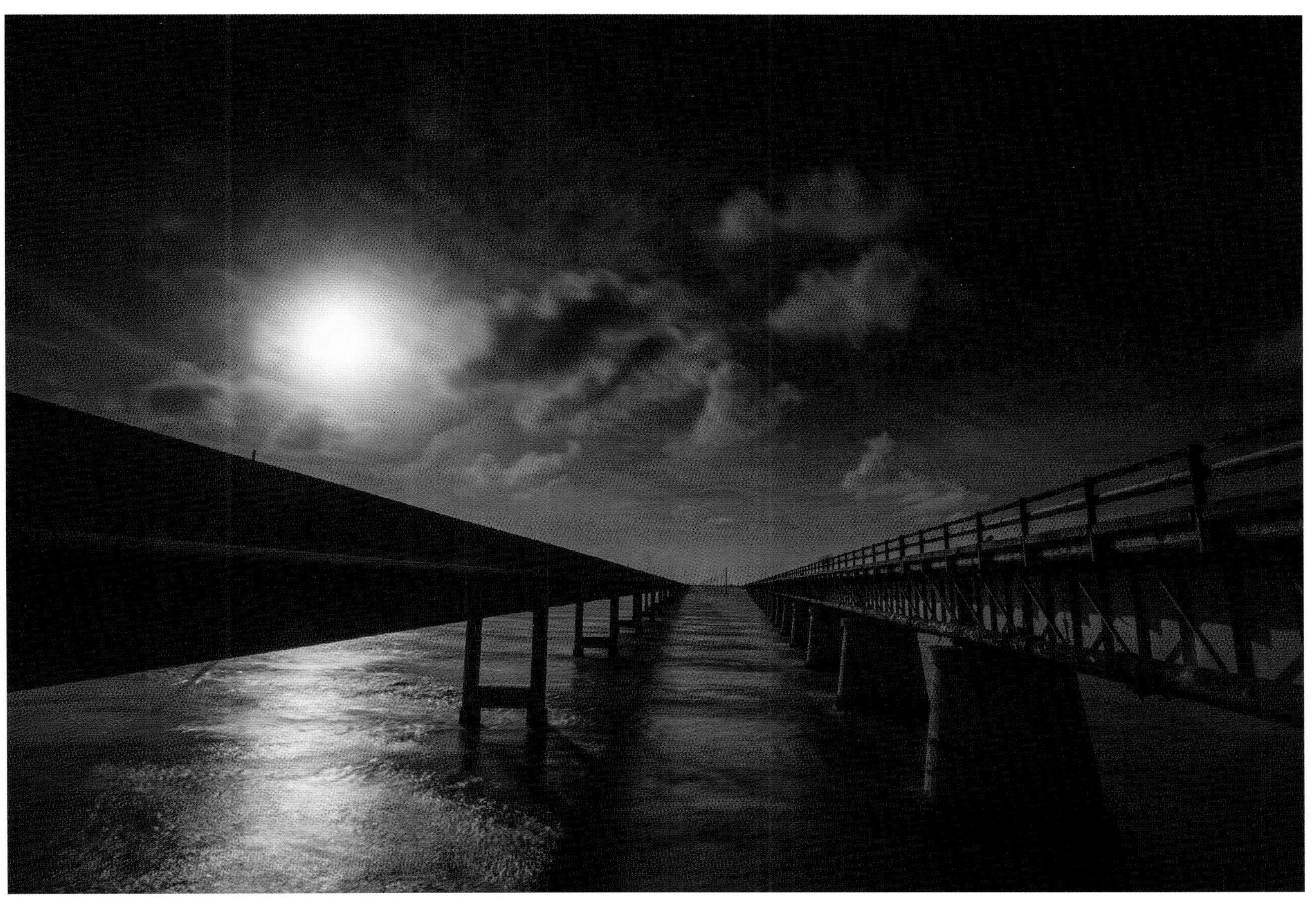

Above: Using the correct aperture is vital in all landscape photography, whether at night or during the day.

Focal length: 16mm

Aperture: f/16

Shutter speed: 290 sec.

ISO: 100

Index

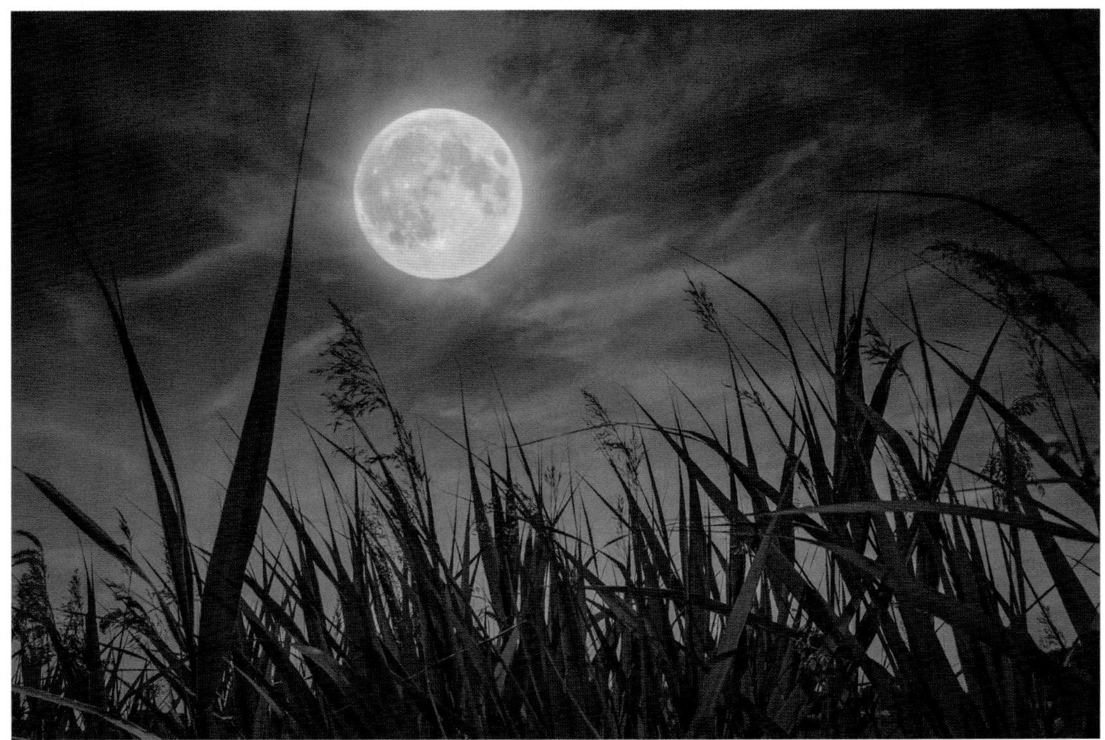

Acknowledgments

It has been both a pleasure and an honor to write this book.

My initial thanks go to Jason Hook and the Ammonite team, for commissioning the book, my parents and Shauneen for their continued support and of course to Theodora, our little star.

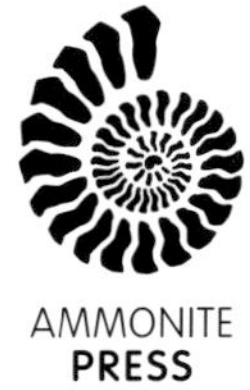

AMMONITE
PRESS

www.ammonitepress.com